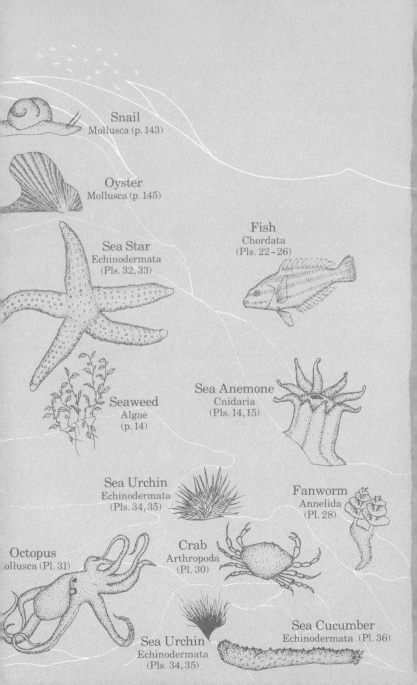

Snail
Mollusca (p. 143)

Oyster
Mollusca (p. 145)

Sea Star
Echinodermata
(Pls. 32, 33)

Fish
Chordata
(Pls. 22–26)

Seaweed
Algae
(p. 14)

Sea Anemone
Cnidaria
(Pls. 14, 15)

Sea Urchin
Echinodermata
(Pls. 34, 35)

Fanworm
Annelida
(Pl. 28)

Octopus
Mollusca (Pl. 31)

Crab
Arthropoda
(Pl. 30)

Sea Urchin
Echinodermata
(Pls. 34, 35)

Sea Cucumber
Echinodermata (Pl. 36)

THE PETERSON FIELD GUIDE SERIES

Edited by Roger Tory Peterson

THE PETERSON FIELD GUIDE SERIES

A Field Guide to
Coral Reefs

Caribbean
and Florida

Eugene H. Kaplan

Drawings by
Susan L. Kaplan

*Sponsored by the National Audubon Society,
the National Wildlife Federation, and
the Roger Tory Peterson Institute*

HOUGHTON MIFFLIN COMPANY · BOSTON

Contributing Authors

Paul Billeter

William G. Bird

Richard D. Bray

Ray Granade

Paul G. Johnson

Robert Kinzie III

Judith C. Lang

Gordon T. Taylor

Malcolm Telford

Vance P. Vicente

Barry A. Vittor

Photography Editor

Seymour Leicher

Copyright © 1982 by Eugene H. Kaplan

For information about permission to reproduce selections
from this book, write to Permissions, Houghton Mifflin
Company, 2 Park Street, Boston, Massachusetts 02108.

Library of Congress Cataloging in Publication Data

Kaplan, Eugene H. (Eugene Herbert), 1932–
A field guide to coral reefs of the Caribbean
and Florida.

(The Peterson field guide series; 27)
Bibliography: p. 271
Includes index.
1. Coral reef fauna — Caribbean area — Identification.
2. Coral reef fauna — Florida — Identification.   3. Coral
reef ecology — Caribbean area.   4. Coral reef ecology —
Florida.   I. Title.   II. Series.
QL125.K36   591.9729   81-13437
ISBN 0-395-31661-8   AACR2
ISBN 0-395-46939-2 (pbk.)

Printed in the United States of America

VB 13 12 11 10 9 8 7 6 5

Contents

Plates

(following p. 140)

Credits

Photographs are by the author except as credited below. Italicized numbers are plate numbers.

Editor's Note

Look beyond the scrubby groves of West Indian hardwoods and the palms; look beyond the dunes, the beach grass, and the broad sandy beaches to the sea. There, under the clear blue water and the white breakers, exists another world, the coral reef, a vastly different world that anyone can explore by simply donning a snorkel, face mask, and flippers.

As in the terrestrial tropics and subtropics there is infinite variety here. On the reefs, birds and butterflies are replaced by fish, some as brightly colored as any of the winged creatures in the Amazon River basin. Others are as dull and well camouflaged as the residents of the jungle floor. Corals, sponges, and anemones excite our curiosity, while shrimps, lobsters, crabs, sea urchins, sea stars, and other bizarre creatures compete for our attention.

This field guide, skillfully assembled by Dr. Eugene H. Kaplan, is arranged by coral reef communities and reef zones as well as by groups of similar creatures that live there. Like most other books in the *Field Guide* series, this guide highlights distinctive features of confusing look-alikes, to help the observer identify species that are similar in appearance. In addition, some plates provide glimpses of the interrelationships (such as cleaning symbioses) between common species you are likely to see on different parts of the reefs.

The author and his associates assure us that this *Field Guide* will help identify at least 90 percent of the forms one is likely to encounter around most of our coral reefs. Serious collecting expeditions are still discovering new species of fishes as well as other marine forms among the coral reefs of Florida and the Caribbean, and new species will probably continue to surface for some time. Although this guide is designed for the specialist as well as the amateur, it cannot possibly encompass all the organisms found on the reefs; see the Field Library for a list of more specialized publications.

This *Field Guide* is primarily for the curious observer, not for the collector. In fact, as Dr. Kaplan explains, divers who are tempted to snap off or pick up a fragile branch of coral can unwittingly disrupt the ecology of the reefs. If one feels the need to collect or possess, what better vehicle than the underwater camera? Whether one uses available light or an artificial source of light, documenting the life of a coral reef on film is a fascinating sport.

The observer with an ecological bent, or the environmentalist's point of view, will find a great deal of food for thought in this guide. Predator-prey relationships, symbiosis, camouflage, survival techniques, food chains, population dynamics, etc., can be observed in infinite variety on the reefs.

The observation of underwater life may be a recreation or a science. It can also satisfy the esthetic sense. The quality of light beneath the surface of the water is ever changing. Forms and colors beyond imagination engage the eye.

The photographic illustrations coordinated by Seymour Leicher and the line drawings by Susan Kaplan support the scholarly and evocative text by Dr. Kaplan and his corps of contributing specialists. It is an impressive cooperative effort in the very best *Field Guide* tradition.

There has been a breakthrough in environmental awareness in recent years. When the first astronaut put his foot on the moon, millions of people suddenly became aware of the uniqueness and isolation of our "small blue planet." Ours is a fragile world, whose seas are suffering from ecological attrition on a global scale.

The problems of survival of whales, porpoises, and seals are easily dramatized and a number of conservation organizations have arisen to publicize their plight. But the smaller organisms of the tidepools and the coral reefs are no less important in an evolutionary and ecological sense, and they are no less vulnerable. To those who know how to look for them, they send out signals when the sea is abused by pollution, exploitation, or some other form of neglect. Inevitably the inquiring snorkeler becomes a monitor of the marine environment.

Do not be an armchair marine biologist, merely thumbing through the plates at home. Take this book with you to Florida and the Caribbean and refer to it before and after you have submerged. It will enrich your submarine experiences and enhance your understanding of the ecology of the oceans.

Roger Tory Peterson

Preface

It is unlikely that you will have the opportunity to climb the highest mountain or trek across the Sahara. But there is one adventure that awaits you, whether you are in your teens or your seventies. You can be transported, at modest cost, to the always balmy, palm-fringed beaches of southern Florida or the Caribbean. You can swim, float, or dive in the clear, warm sea and, peering through your face mask, view a world of riotous color and magnificent beauty. The water seems as transparent as air, the animals exotic and exciting. If you can swim, you can snorkel. After a half-hour lesson, you will be ready to float over a nearby fringing reef.

Many remarkable places await you. On almost any island there will be much to see (Bonaire, for example, is surrounded by close-to-shore reefs). This year you might try Buck Island National Park off St. Croix in the American Virgin Islands; next year, Virgin Gorda in the British Virgins, or one of the Bahamas. If you are a diver, you might try the drift dives off Tobago, the wall off San Salvador, or the blue holes off Andros.

You will see endless multitudes of fishes weaving mysteriously in and out of the crannies of a coral reef. Sooner or later you will ask yourself, "What is that fish doing? Why?"

This book has a dual function. Not only will it enable you to identify many of the organisms you see; it will also tell you about their behavior, natural history, and ecology. The water's transparency and the tameness of the animals on the reef will make you want to know more about the life down there. Nowhere else is it possible to hover motionless over a community of animals and plants, watching them interact, feed, reproduce; or to follow the drama as a predator stalks its prey; or to watch a harmless-looking puffer become a formidable ball of spines as an enemy approaches.

Some mysteries of the reef might go unnoticed unless you are prepared for them. For example, to see a huge, predatory grouper open its mouth wide to allow a cleaning goby to enter is one of the triumphs of fish-watching. What signals does the grouper send out that tell the goby, normally a bite-sized morsel to the larger fish, that it is safe to approach the grouper and pick parasites from its mouth, gills, and flanks? You will learn where to look for the depredations of the fierce Fireworm. And you will find out about the dangers of the reef, so few and easily avoided if you know what they are.

The first thing a traveler packs for a trip to Europe is a guide-book — to the streets of London or Paris, to the British Museum or the Louvre. When you travel to southern Florida or the West Indies, let this book be your guide. Instead of leading you through the maze of streets and markets of a city, it will direct you through the winding channels and grottoes of a reef. It will be a friendly and knowledgeable companion for your voyage into the exciting environment of the coral reef.

So many people have contributed in so many ways that it is impossible to acknowledge all their help. It has been a special pleasure to work with the contributing authors, photographers, and artists, whose dedication to their fields of expertise and willingness to share their knowledge with the layman have been inspiring.

Special thanks go to the trustees of the Bermuda Biological Laboratory and its director, Wolfgang Sterrer, for a Wright Fellowship to study at the laboratory. The Hofstra University Faculty Research Fund made possible long-term study at the Discovery Bay Marine Laboratory, Jamaica, where Jeremy Woodley and Eileen Graham were extremely helpful. Ingvar Kristensen and Hans de Kruyf of the Caribbean Marine Biological Institute, Curaçao, gave useful advice and were most hospitable. Dr. and Mrs. de Kruyf and their sons, Roderick and Baldwin, went beyond the bounds of hospitality; their kindness is gratefully acknowledged. Cap'n Don Stewart helped make my stays on Bonaire as productive as possible.

A book of such diversity, about so rich a biotic community, requires a breadth of knowledge greater than can be retained by one person. A host of experts reviewed the manuscript. Each of the following people gave definitive advice, and some rewrote portions of chapters; their efforts are acknowledged with gratitude: George Dale, Charles Cutress, David Pawson, David Meyer, Kenneth Sebens, Klaus Ruetzler, Eveline du Bois-Reymond Marcus, Ivan Goodbody, Marian Pettibone, Don Kissling, and David Lean.

Two people devoted much time and effort to the task of producing clear, useful photographs. Herb Taylor, as photography consultant, answered innumerable questions and made useful suggestions based on years of experience. Seymour Leicher photographed the hard corals, developed and printed most of the black-and-white photographs, and supervised the production of virtually all of them. The majority of the color photographs were contributed by Dan Harding, whose extraordinary skill combines aesthetics with precision. The artistry of Jo Furman's black-and-white photographs makes it difficult to believe they were taken deep on the reef.

Verena Tunnicliffe and Ray Granade believed in the book long before it became a reality. Their support was constant. Ray contributed a number of photographs and wrote the chapter on dan-

gerous marine animals. Verena, too, contributed photographs and
served as a reader of the manuscript.

Many people on the staff of Houghton Mifflin Company were
involved with this *Field Guide* between its inception and publication. Great warmth, skill, and wisdom were demonstrated by
Morton Baker, Peggy Burlet, Cope Cumpston, Lisa Fisher, Harry
Foster, Maria Kawecki, Richard McAdoo, Austin Olney, Janice
Pecoraro, Stephen Pekich, Barbara Stratton, James Thompson,
and Richard Tonachel. My thanks go to them and the others who
worked so diligently to see the book through the intricate and
difficult tasks of editing and production.

This was a family affair. My wife, Breena, did the layout work
for the plates. Daughter Julie typed the manuscript. Daughter
Susan revealed marvelous drawing skill as the illustrator. All three
exhibited much good will as I alternately dragged them all over
the Caribbean and left them home for long periods as I researched
the waters of the West Indies.

Jess Perlman — friend, poet, philologist, and personal guru —
shared the wisdom of his eighty-seven years. He went over every
word of the manuscript to ensure that everything was comprehensible to the layman. His contribution is reflected throughout.

I would like to dedicate this book to the cheerful, enthusiastic
people who took my courses in tropical marine biology on Mos-
quito Island and elsewhere. Their response to the natural beauty
around them was a source of inspiration.

A Field Guide to
Coral Reefs of
the Caribbean
and Florida

1

About This Book

The ultimate biological experience to those of us accustomed to air-conditioned, glass-enclosed apartments, offices, and classrooms is the sense of total involvement in another world that comes from being among the myriad colors and shapes of the coral reef. The contrast between the dark green of the palm-fringed beach, its white powdery sand, and the aquamarine of the sea overwhelms the senses. The balmy trade winds, heavy with the musky scent of the tropics, stir the imagination and enhance the unreal quality of the scene. The descent into the sea reveals a fantastic world, the coral reef. For some, its infinite diversity and beauty make it an almost mystical experience. The panorama of the coral reef is like the view from a Himalayan mountaintop; they both arouse the same excitement, the same sense of mystery.

This *Field Guide* is designed to lead you through the Turtle Grass beds of the lagoon and across the reef itself. For those of you who are not satisfied with merely looking, it provides information that will enable you to identify with some degree of certainty an immobilized specimen in front of you, and with less assurance fishes and invertebrates glanced at fleetingly as they pass by underwater.

General Organization. Chapters 2 and 3 are overviews of 2 types of reefs — fringing reefs and bank/barrier reefs. Fringing reefs are rather uniform, with few different zones; so Chapter 2 briefly concentrates on the corals that you are likely to see on this kind of reef. Bank/barrier reefs, on the other hand, have complex zonation, which is described in Chapter 3. This chapter also points out the obvious organisms, including corals, that you are likely to see in each zone. In addition, it tells where to look for many of them and what they are doing and gives some details of their natural history and ecology.

Chapters 4 and 7–12 focus more closely on the animals of the lagoon and reef. Each is devoted to a phylum of animals and begins with a general discussion of the phylum — anatomy, behavior, ecology, and so forth. When the phylum is large, the chapter may be subdivided, with discussions of subgroups of the phylum. At the end of the chapter or its subdivisions, species accounts (in the case of fishes, family accounts) give the information needed to differentiate one species from another. In most cases, the accounts are arranged alphabetically by the scientific names of species.

1

Chapters 5, 6, and 13 provide more background information on coral reefs. Chapter 5 explains how coral reefs develop. Chapter 6 discusses their ecology. Chapter 13 turns to more specific interactions between species, symbiotic relationships that ensure the survival of one or both species involved in them.

In Chapter 14, a discussion of venomous and poisonous animals, you will find out how to avoid the few dangerous species, as well as what to do should you be injured or poisoned.

This book is arranged for the reader's convenience in identifying organisms, so taxonomic order is not strictly followed in the organization of the text, plates, and species accounts. Visually similar organisms from different taxonomic categories are sometimes grouped together, and visually dissimilar members of the same category are sometimes separated.

How to Use This Book. Upon your arrival at the water's edge, first determine what kind of reef awaits you offshore. From the beach, look toward the sea. If you see a dark patch off a rocky promontory nearby, it is probably a fringing reef. If you see a surf line offshore, it is likely that the waves are crashing over a bank/barrier reef, separated from the land by a lagoon. Before your first few dives, read the appropriate chapter (Chapter 2 or Chapter 3), and look at the photographs of underwater scenes at the center of the book. This will give you a general idea of what to expect, including the obvious and spectacular inhabitants to look for. Reread the chapter after you return from the reef. Patterns — typical zonation and characteristic species, for example — will eventually become clear.

This book emphasizes a visual approach to identification. When you want to identify an unfamiliar animal, first turn to the front endpaper, which shows typical examples of the different phyla of animals found on coral reefs. To decide what kind of animal you have seen, simply look for the example that most closely resembles your specimen. You then have 2 choices. You can turn to the text where that group of animals is discussed or to the photographic plate(s) that illustrate the group. Plate or page numbers are given with the names on the endpaper. It is usually easiest to turn first to the plates and look for species that resemble your specimen. Facing each plate is a legend page that briefly describes each species illustrated on the plate and gives the page number of the species account. Once you have found a species that looks like your specimen, the next step is to check the species account to make sure the characteristics of your specimen agree with those that serve to identify that species. Different species can closely resemble one another, so never rely on an illustration alone for identification. It is wise to skim through nearby species accounts to make sure that there isn't one that fits your specimen even more closely. Those features that are most helpful in differentiating one species from another are italicized in the species accounts.

Some species are not shown on the photographic plates, but many of these are illustrated by drawings in the text, usually near their accounts. So at times you will have to make the identification on the basis of species accounts alone, or with the aid of a drawing.

As you gain experience, you will become able to recognize some species immediately. To check your identification, look up the species name in the index and then go directly to the page where the species account is given or the plate where the species is shown.

Coverage. This *Field Guide* will enable you to identify the common, easily seen animals from the shallow water of the fringing reef and lagoon down to the deep fore reef of a bank/barrier reef, more than 30 m (100 ft.) below the water's surface. We have checked and rechecked the contents of this book against what we have found on many coral reefs throughout the region and found that it enabled us to identify at least 90% of the organisms we encountered. A map of the area covered by this *Field Guide* is on the back endpaper. The books listed in the field library (p. 271) will be helpful for identifying relatively rare or narrowly distributed organisms.

The whole West Indian faunal province is quite uniform; the warming influence of the Gulf Stream extends from the Florida Keys (and to some extent Bermuda) all the way to Brazil. Bermuda, because it is at the northernmost fringe of the faunal province, has unique assemblages of animals and plants, as well as large gaps. The Bahamas and the Florida Keys, also subtropical, may have somewhat smaller populations and fewer species. Do not take the information on the range of organisms too literally, as many species may be abundant in regions where scientists have not studied or reported them.

Not all animals in a particular habitat are covered. In general, only the commonest species have been included. Several phyla, especially those containing concealed or camouflaged, wormlike animals, are not discussed at all; few of these organisms are noticed by anyone but scientists. In addition, certain phyla, notably Mollusca and Arthropoda, are so diverse that only the large, most noticeable members have been covered. Plants and animals that are found only on or near shores are not treated in this guide.

Names. A common name is provided for most organisms described. Many of these names have been created for this book, as many species had simply never before been given common names. In some cases an animal has a different name on every island — in Papiamento, French, Spanish, and English. We have often used one of the local names or a translation of it.

The scientific name of a species consists of 2 Latin words. The first is the name of the genus to which the organism belongs; the second is its specific name. Genus is capitalized, species is lower-cased, both are italicized — as in *Diadema antillarum* (meaning "diadem, or crown, of the Antilles"). A given combination of generic and specific name is always unique to a single species.

Nomenclature and taxonomy are less stable for invertebrates than for some other life forms. We have tried to use the most up-to-date and widely accepted scientific names.

Scientific names are given in the accounts and in the legends; only occasionally are they used in the text. A scientific name has the advantage of being accepted and recognized worldwide, whereas a common name often varies from one place to another. Don't be put off by Latin names. After you've had a little practice, they will roll off your tongue as if you were an expert. Once someone says, "Don't step on that *Diadema,*" you will never forget its meaning. By the time he had said, "Don't step on that Long-spined Black Urchin," you might already have stepped on it — with unfortunate consequences.

Illustrations. Thirty-seven plates of photographs are at the center of the book, and many drawings appear in the text. A number of the plates are devoted to one class or phylum. Brief descriptive legends face the photographs and provide cross references to the pages where the more detailed species accounts appear.

In many cases a dried specimen and its live counterpart in the water look totally different. For this reason most photographs are of live specimens. As a further aid, corals, sponges, and other organisms that are difficult to identify are shown in situ in a number of photographs of underwater scenes.

Technical Terms. Because this is a book for laymen, technical words have been kept to a minimum. Those that could not be easily avoided are explained in the text and/or in the glossary, beginning on p. 263.

Collecting. Animals such as corals grow slowly, and a souvenir wrenched from the bottom will leave a lasting scar on the reef and modify its ecology. In addition, the exquisite colors that are so profuse on the reef fade soon after the animals have been removed; by the time you get your trophies home, they will look like shadows of their former selves and will smell bad, too. So please avoid the temptation to collect. Content yourself with watching or photographing instead. To identify an organism it usually is not necessary to collect the specimen. You can simply examine it carefully and remember its distinguishing characteristics. Or you can tie a 15 cm (6 in.) square piece of Plexiglas to your waist and attach a grease pencil (both are available in scuba shops) so that you can make notes underwater.

Measurements. In a few years the metric system will most likely have superseded the outmoded U.S. system; this book may help you make the transition. All measurements are given in metric units, and their U.S. equivalents appear parenthetically. A metric-U.S. rule is on the next page and the back cover.

Field Equipment. Snorkel, face mask, and fins are standard equipment for field work in southern Florida and Caribbean waters. Purchase a simple snorkel without pleats, balls in a cage, or other additional features. Try on several face masks; one may be more comfortable than the others. If you wear glasses, most scuba shops can supply you with a mask that has the faceplate ground to your prescription. Do not buy a mask with a purge valve; it will leak after a while. For simple snorkeling, full-foot fins are better than the "rocket" type. Make sure they fit, but be sure to allow room for thick gym socks, which will prevent chafing. Rocket-type fins must be worn with booties and are advised only for scuba divers and serious snorkelers.

If possible, bring along a weight belt with about 5 kg (11 lbs.) of weights. Adjust the amount of weight until you are slightly negatively buoyant. This makes it easier to dive down and allows you to remain near the bottom for a few seconds longer when you are snorkeling.

Ordinary cotton gardening gloves will protect your hands until you learn enough about the area to avoid contact with dangerous organisms. Bring a hat or cap and a small medicine kit containing such items as a topical anesthetic, Band-Aids, a good sunscreen, an antiseptic, and meat tenderizer (see Chapter 14).

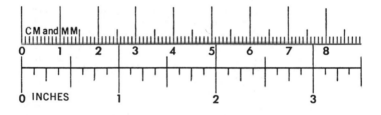

2

The Fringing Reef

Fringing reefs grow on the hard surfaces of rocky shores. This kind of reef may extend outward into deep water, but only if the necessary hard surface for the settlement of larval coral animals is available. The fringing reef consists of a variety of corals scattered over the rocks beyond the lowest tide mark. The corals, which cannot survive exposure to air, become more abundant as the water deepens. Then, at depths of 3–6 m (10–20 ft), the reef often shelves abruptly into sand. Patch reefs (isolated boulders of coral) extend outward laterally, becoming increasingly sparse as one moves farther from the main reef.

The fringing reef is characterized by a diversity of coral types, with little zonation and little predominance of one species over another in terms of the number of coral heads. In mass, however, the basic reef-builder, Boulder Coral, is predominant. It forms boulders, sometimes 2 m (6 ft.) high and often with irregular shapes. The tops of these boulders may show depressions in which detritus has accumulated, killing the polyps and leaving a white scar. The tan or green boulders are covered by equidistant, starlike cups with septa extending from each cup like rays of light.

Other boulder-forming corals found in abundance on rocky fringing reefs, especially those with some exposure to the open sea, are 2 starlet corals: Round Starlet Coral and Shallow-water Starlet Coral. These usually form large round boulders, but they sometimes look like hemispheres only a few centimeters in diameter. They can encrust rocks on more exposed areas. The regularly spaced cups look like black dots on a grayish or brownish white background. The 2 species differ primarily in the degree of slope of the cup walls and in the number of septa. These differences are not apparent underwater.

Brain corals may encrust rocks or may form small boulders, to 1 m (3¼ ft.) in diameter. They are predominantly species of *Diploria*. Depressed Brain Coral has wide "hills," each with a depression, and narrow "valleys." The depression distinguishes this coral from Common Brain Coral and Sharp-hilled Brain Coral. Sharp-hilled Brain Coral has narrow hills and wide valleys. In the daytime you can often see the bright green polyps that have receded into these valleys. Common Brain Coral is more or less intermediate between the other 2 species.

Common inhabitants of the fringing reef are the fire or false

6

Fig. 1 A scene from a fringing reef. Boulder Coral is in the foreground, Flat-topped Fire Coral in the background. Note also the small clump of Orange Coral below the Long-spined Black Urchin at the left.

corals of the genus *Millepora*. They are tan or golden-brown, with flat, platelike vertical growths topped with white. The upper edges of Flat-topped Fire Coral are squared off; those of Crenelated Fire Coral are extended into whitish bumps. Encrusting Fire Coral is, as its name implies, an encrusting species, seldom growing more than 2–3 cm ($\frac{3}{4}$–$1\frac{1}{4}$ in.) from the surface of the rock it covers. It looks like a wrinkled, purplish tan excrescence on the rock.

All species of *Millepora* may be recognized by their smooth appearance. They lack the well-defined cups of the true, stony (scleractinian) corals. They can inflict painful welts if brushed against. Curiously, handling them with fingers and palms does not usually result in an unpleasant reaction, because the skin of the hand is calloused and thick enough that the poisonous nematocysts of polyps hidden in pinholes in the coral skeleton cannot penetrate it.

Scattered among the other corals, sometimes forming small zones occupied exclusively by a single species, are Elkhorn and Staghorn Corals. Elkhorn Coral forms flat, horizontal, golden branches with distinct tubular cups projecting from all surfaces. It can survive in shallow water, sometimes actually projecting from the water's surface. If you find yourself in an area occupied almost exclusively by Elkhorn Coral, be careful not to become too enthusiastic about penetrating into the thicket of flat Elkhorns lest you find yourself in a cul-de-sac, forced to swim over the top of the coral to get back to deep water. This often results in a scratched belly, and such wounds heal slowly in the tropics.

Staghorn Coral looks like bumpy deer antlers, the bumps being the tubular cups characteristic of *Acropora*. This species can form scattered thickets among the other corals, but it is much in demand by tourists; so the reef you are studying may have been denuded of Staghorn Coral by souvenir hunters.

Less common than the other corals mentioned is Large Grooved Brain Coral, which has wider hills and valleys than the *Diploria* species. It is brownish and appears to have a thin line dividing the septa that compose each hill.

Common corals found in shallow water are members of the genus *Porites,* the finger corals. Thick Finger Coral looks like clumps of tan or grayish fingers projecting from the bottom. It is one of the few species of hard corals that are sometimes found with polyps extended in the daytime; this gives the colony a fuzzy, whitish aura. The tips of the fingers are usually swollen just before tapering to a blunt point. The thickest of the finger corals, this species has fingers about 1.5 cm ($\frac{3}{4}$ in.) in diameter. Thin Finger

Fig. 2
Sea fan

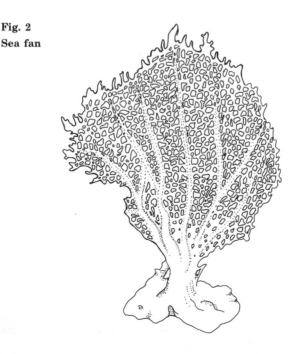

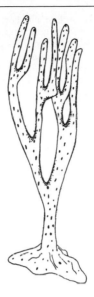

Fig. 3
Deadman's Fingers

Coral has more delicate fingers, each less than 1 cm (½ in.) thick, which lack the swollen tips of Thick Finger Coral. There is a beautiful purple variant. In some areas whole flats are covered with Thin Finger Coral in shades of bright yellow, cream, or tan. Yellow Porous Coral is an encrusting form commonly found on rocks. It is bright sulfur-yellow and has abortive-looking bumps, as if the fingers were trying to push out.

Living on the fringing reef are a great many organisms that obtain sustenance, protection, or support directly or indirectly from the corals. Projecting from crevices of Boulder Coral are the tan, sometimes pink-tipped tentacles of the Giant Caribbean Anemone. These tentacles may be 12.5 cm (5 in.) long. Sometimes if the anemone has not found a suitable hiding place, it will sit in the open, resplendent with orange body and whorl of long tentacles. At such a time it is possible to pry up its pedal disk carefully with a knife and remove the animal to an aquarium. It will kill and eat minnows placed in the tank and will move around, slowly and ponderously, on its basal disk.

The soft corals are well represented on the fringing reef. The most magnificently colored of these are the sea fans, *Gorgonia*, which are purplish, green, or yellow. Deadman's Fingers, another soft coral, forms brown, fuzzy, flexible colonies in clumps 30 cm

(1 ft.) or more high. The polyps of soft corals are often extended in the daytime, hence the thick fuzzy appearance of the colonies. Run your fingers down the stalk, and the polyps will retract, leaving a thin, purple-gray, slimy columnar structure.

Most of the organisms found in the rear zone of the bank/barrier reef also inhabit the fringing reef. They are discussed in the next chapter (see pp. 11–54).

3

The Bank / Barrier Reef and Lagoon

Look seaward from the window of your room or from a high spot near the beach. Can you see a clear-cut line of surf a kilometer or so from the shore? Often the sea between the shore and this surf line looks light aquamarine, and beyond the line the water rapidly changes to a deep royal blue.

The line of surf denotes the bank/barrier reef, a rich area of coral growth separated from the land by a shallow lagoon floored with white sand. The light passes through the transparent water and reflects from the sand, hence the aquamarine color. Beyond the reef the sea is too deep for light to reflect from the sand, and much light is absorbed in the depths; the result is a dark blue color. The bank/barrier reef is even more beautiful than the fringing reef, for it has forests of Elkhorn Coral with 3 m (10 ft.) branches and submerged canyons richly populated with fishes and soft corals.

The lagoon begins near shore and may gradually deepen to 6 m (20 ft.) or more before becoming shallow again close to the reef itself. The reef can be thought of as 2 major areas, the reef crest and the fore reef, each comprising a number of zones. Morphology and zonation vary from one reef to another, but Fig. 4 shows the profile of a generalized bank/barrier reef. Each zone, as well as the lagoon, has characteristic features and populations of organisms. The groupings of coral in each zone are particularly distinctive. Though some species, notably Boulder Coral, are dominant in several widely separated areas of the reef, they may look quite different in each. Other corals, such as Elkhorn Coral, are confined to a narrower range of environments. A coral reef and its lagoon are like forest and field, with peaceful grazers and ferocious predators. Each animal has its niche, and no 2 niches are exactly alike.

Typically the reef crest is composed of a rear zone, a reef flat (also called the rubble zone or *Zoanthus* zone), a *palmata* (or breaker) zone, a barren (or lower *palmata*) zone, and either a mixed zone or a buttress zone. The rear zone begins where the bottom of the lagoon begins to slope upward and continues to the point where the reef flattens, just a few centimeters from the water's surface. The depth of the water on this reef flat averages only 50 cm (20 in.). On some old or shallow reefs the reef flat extends outward for 400 m (¼ mi.) or more. Seaward of this zone, the reef drops off, rather steeply at first, then somewhat more gradually. The *palmata* zone, or breaker zone, is the area where the ocean's

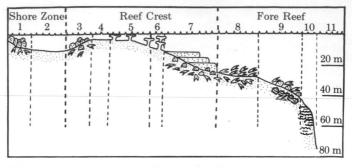

Fig. 4 Zonation of a composite Jamaican bank/barrier reef — cross section; coral colonies and vertical dimensions exaggerated.

1 = inshore zone
2 = lagoon
3 = rear zone
4 = reef flat (rubble zone or *Zoanthus* zone)
5 = *palmata* zone (breaker zone)
6 = barren zone (lower *palmata* zone)
7 = mixed zone or buttress zone
8 = fore-reef terrace
9 = fore-reef escarpment
10 = fore-reef slope
11 = deep fore reef

Legend

ᗉ = live Elkhorn Coral

⊰ = dead Elkhorn Coral rubble

ⓐ = Boulder Coral (shallow water)

≋ = lettuce corals, *Agaricia* species

⌀ = live Staghorn Coral

⊽ = dead Staghorn Coral rubble

⌂ = Boulder Coral (deep water)

waves crash full force on the reef. It extends from the surface to a depth of about 5 m (17 ft.). The lower, less steep portion is known as the barren zone, or lower *palmata* zone. Beyond the barren zone, the reef continues to slope downward, usually in a mixed zone, which may stretch as far as 40 m (130 ft.). Some reefs, however, have a buttress zone — with huge coral masses jutting out into depths of 20 m (67 ft.) or more — instead of a mixed zone. The water may be as shallow as 6–8 m (20–27 ft.) where the mixed zone or buttress zone begins.

A terrace, an escarpment, a slope, and a vertical cliff are the zones of the fore reef. The gentle slope of the mixed zone continues in the fore-reef terrace, a relatively wide — 30–100 m (100–330 ft.) — plain that begins at a depth of about 10 m (33 ft.). On some reefs, at a depth of 15–25 m (50–83 ft.) or so, the terrace abruptly meets the fore-reef escarpment. The slope of an escarpment may be relatively gentle or as sharp as 45°. Below the escarpment the fore-reef slope angles downward less sharply, at 20–40°, between depths of about 55 m (185 ft.) and 60 m (197 ft.). It is usually about 40–60 m (130–197 ft.) wide. Beyond, the reef abruptly drops off as a vertical cliff, the deep fore reef, plunging deeper than the diver can go.

The zonation described above is characteristic of many well-formed bank/barrier reefs found off the coasts of Caribbean islands, usually facing the prevailing trade winds. But no reef is typical. Morphology and zonation vary from reef to reef. Virtually every coral reef has some geomorphological or hydrological factor that makes it unique. The conditions around a given reef determine its zonation and what organisms live in each zone. (See pp. 52–54 for a discussion of some variations.)

The rear zone of the reef crest is often ideal for snorkeling and underwater photography. It can be reached by swimming or by a quick trip in a small boat across the lagoon. Although the water in the rear zone is usually shallow enough that you will be able to stand and rest after swimming across the lagoon, you should have a guide or go by boat the first time out. Reef morphology is extremely variable, and the rear zone may not be as safe or as well developed as described above.

More northern areas, such as the Florida Keys and Bermuda, tend to have isolated patches or marginal reefs rather than bank/barrier reefs. They are, however, often quite far from the shore, sometimes requiring nearly an hour's ride. Patch reefs ("boilers") may be relatively near shore. Ask about them at the local dive shop.

Although the extensive shallows of the Florida Keys and Bahamas are not true lagoons, some of the organisms inhabiting them are mentioned in the following discussion of the lagoon. Some organisms found in more than one area are discussed only under one heading. Sponges, for example, may be found in lagoons and Turtle Grass beds but are treated later in the chapter under "The Reef Crest."

The Lagoon and Turtle Grass Bed

A number of large and interesting animals inhabit the lagoon. Even sandy spots — large, bare patches of uncovered, sterile-looking sand — may be surprisingly productive if you know where to search. To find the Sea Pussy or Cake Urchin, for example, look for small hillocks of sand with larger particles on their summits. Wave your hand over the mound to set up a strong current that will wash away the sand. When the sediment settles, you will see a bristly, brown, oval animal about 13 cm (5 in.) long. You can pick it up for close inspection without danger, for its spines are small and relatively blunt.

Many plants find calm waters and a soft bottom a suitable environment. However, the stiff-jointed *Halodule* grasses of the intertidal zone cannot compete with other grasses and are replaced in knee-deep water by thick-bladed Turtle Grass or thin, rounded blades of Manatee Grass.

Manatee Grass is sometimes found in pure stands but most often is mixed with Turtle Grass. It can dominate in brackish water. In bays that have freshwater runoff or receive the outflow of streams, dense beds of Manatee Grass cover the bottom. In water deeper than 10 m (33 ft.) it sometimes forms deep meadows.

Turtle Grass grows wherever there is protection from wind-driven current and surf. It is abundant in tranquil lagoons that are protected by coral reefs. Its broad leaves — to 1 cm ($\frac{1}{2}$ in.) wide — reduce the velocity of the slowly flowing currents to almost nothing, and even the tiniest particles in the water, no longer buoyed up by the water's movement, drop to the bottom. In this way Turtle Grass beds act as huge filters, removing particles from the water and depositing them as a fine sediment. At least 113 species of algae are known to grow on Turtle Grass leaves, and numerous encrusting animals (including sponges, hydrozoan polyps, flatworms, and tunicates) spend their lives on the gently undulating blades.

Turtle Grass is the dominant seed-bearing plant of the shallows. Though capable of spreading by means of rhizomes to cover acres, Turtle Grass has not forsaken sexual reproduction and can produce flowers. The pale white flowers, produced in spring and summer by only 1–5% of the plants, are less than 2.5 cm (1 in.) in diameter. To find them, you must swim with your nose almost touching the leaves. Push the leaves aside, and look for the flowers near the base of the plants. What look like petals are reproductive structures (stamens or stigmas).

The algae growing among the grasses are exotic and beautiful. Two fan-shaped species project from the bottom on stalks. *Udotea flabellum,* one of the hard fan algae, has a thin, wrinkled, light green fan, is highly calcified, and moves stiffly. *Avrainvillea nigricans,* a soft fan alga, may be heart-shaped, with a relatively thick, flat, spongy blade.

Several distinct species of Merman's shaving brushes are common. *Penicillus pyriformis* has a conical, flat-topped head. *P. capitatus* has a rounded head and looks like a brand-new shaving brush. *P. dumetosus* has a thick upward-tapering stalk; its head is the broadest of the 3 species and somewhat rounded.

The most important alga in Turtle Grass beds, as well as on the reef, is *Halimeda. H. opuntia* forms mats of dark green, 6 mm ($\frac{1}{4}$ in.), calcified disks, each 3-lobed and 3-ribbed. The mats may cover several square meters of the bottom, excluding even Turtle Grass. Fanworms find refuge here, and the many spaces between disks are havens for small crustaceans, worms, and sea slugs. *H. incrassata* grows vertically on short stalks, each plant separated from the others by sand. It is composed of flat disks, ar-

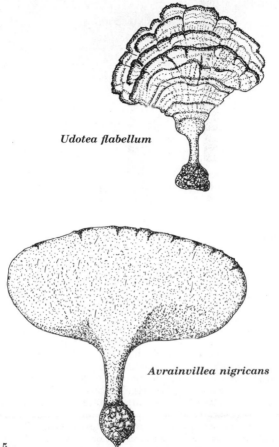

Udotea flabellum

Avrainvillea nigricans

Fig. 5

ranged in branches growing in one plane, and may be 20 cm (8 in.) high. *H. monile,* which also reaches 20 cm (8 in.), has elongate, rounded, beadlike segments.

The many *Caulerpa* species produce flat, horizontal rhizomes from which vertical stems extend, bearing a wonderful variety of "leaves." *C. racemosa* looks like clusters of miniature grapes, each grape no larger than 3 mm (⅛ in.) in diameter. *C. sertularioides* looks like an Indian headdress of feathers.

Fig. 6
Penicillus dumetosus

In Florida, the Bahamas, and the northern Caribbean *Rhipocephalus phoenix* is often mixed in among the other calcareous green algae. The short stalk of this distinctive alga is topped by a columnar mass of small, vertical, scalelike plates.

Turtle Grass beds, the "meadows of the sea," support innumerable browsers that eat the grass itself or the detritus produced when it dies. Some even eat the rich sand for its organic particles. Apparently, few predators disturb the tranquility here. Occasional flashes of light reflected from the flank of a Great Barracuda signal the death of a member of the clouds of Reef Silversides, Dwarf Herrings, or Dusky Anchovies. Halfbeaks — usually the Ballyhoo and the Redfin Needlefish — patrol the area in small schools. Though they generally do not grow much longer than 30 cm (1 ft.), at night they look quite fierce in a flashlight beam. Their prey, schools of Hardhead Silversides, are so densely packed that they form almost solid masses of silver.

Some fishes extract food from the sand by taking in a mouthful and straining out small, bottom-dwelling animals. The sand is released through the gill openings after each mouthful has been strained. The commonest sand-eaters are the mojarras, which swim in small schools and have silvery bodies, protruding lips, and indistinct bars or blotches on their flanks. The Yellowfin Mojarra, the largest common species, reaches 38 cm (15 in.) long and is wide-bodied, with a deeply forked tail.

Sergeant Majors and other damselfishes, wrasses such as the Slippery Dick or Puddingwife, and juvenile French Grunts congregate around small outcroppings of finger corals and Staghorn Coral. Goatfishes, using the pair of barbels on their chins to stir up the bottom, feed on small organisms buried in the sand.

If you are lucky, you will see Palometas swimming in schools. They are vertically flattened, broad, and silvery, with long, black, backward-pointing dorsal and ventral fins. Young Permits may also be swimming in the area. This fish, even broader than the Palometa, looks like an almost-round, silvery disk, usually less than 10 cm (4 in) long

One of the most interesting fishes here is the Southern Stingray. Flattened and slate-gray or brown, it lies hidden under a thin coat of sand, with just its eyes and spiracles (gill openings) visible. If you disturb it, it will undulate the edges of its body in graceful rippling movements and glide away from you. If you step on its tail, it may embed its long poisonous spine in your leg (see p. 256). But this rarely happens, as the fish will retreat at the first sign of a human's presence.

The most dramatic bottom-dwelling organisms of Turtle Grass beds are the Reticulated or Cushion Sea Star and the Donkey Dung Sea Cucumber. The anterior (oral) end of this cucumber has many short tentacles that end in brushlike extensions. The tentacles are withdrawn if the animal is disturbed.

Two other large cucumbers live in Turtle Grass beds: the Three rowed Sea Cucumber and the Five-toothed Sea Cucumber. The latter is known for the peculiar location of its 5 large, white, square teeth: they are in its anus. To differentiate these 3 species of cucumbers, hold them gently just beneath the water's surface and examine the flattened soles. The podia of the Donkey Dung are dark brown and scattered over the rose or white sole; those of the Three-rowed are brown and in 3 distinct rows; and those of the Five-toothed are light-colored and scattered.

The Three-rowed Cucumber is the only large species in Bermuda. The Donkey Dung dominates Turtle Grass beds throughout the Caribbean and Florida. (The Florida Sea Cucumber is slightly smaller and similar to the Donkey Dung; in Florida it is the commonest species, but in Jamaica and on other islands it occurs only in muddy areas near mangroves.) The Five-toothed Cucumber is particularly abundant in the Bahamas and Jamaica, though never as common as the Donkey Dung. It sometimes offers a special surprise to the viewer. If you place a Five-toothed Cucumber in a bucket of water and frequently change the water, you can keep the Cucumber alive overnight. The next morning you might be one of the lucky few to see an iridescent Pearlfish, which lives inside the cucumber; it escapes every night to feed and returns every morning, worming its way inside the cucumber, past the teeth, through the anus (see Fig. 62, p. 196).

Other echinoderms that you are likely to see are the Sea Egg, the Variable or Green Sea Urchin, and the Long-spined Black Urchin.

Fig. 7 A scene from a Turtle Grass bed. At the front left of the Donkey Dung Sea Cucumber is a Club Urchin. The tuft of tentacles behind the urchin is a Ringed Anemone. To the left of this anemone a cluster of Green Colonial Anemones is growing on sand.

The Long-spined Black Urchin may be completely absent from a Turtle Grass bed if no coral is nearby. It seems to require coral reefs to hide in during the day.

The Variable or Green Sea Urchin is slightly smaller than the Sea Egg. The Sea Egg has a black and white appearance overall; the Variable or Green Urchin looks greenish or pure white. These urchins may be so abundant as to cover the bottom.

Turn over a live Sea Egg, and look at the 5 white teeth at the center of the oral area. They are attached to a complex structure of white, bonelike struts shaped like an old-fashioned 5-sided lantern. The structure is called Aristotle's lantern. The muscles that move the teeth are attached to and pull against this structure, giving the teeth considerable strength to grind up organic detritus.

The Long-spined Black Urchin, a truly fear-inspiring species, is king of the Turtle Grass bed. Though its test is smaller, it appears to be larger than the other 2 urchins because of its very long spines — sometimes longer than 30 cm (1 ft.). The spines are hollow, needle-sharp, and barbed. They can be rotated and will point at you if you hover close to the urchin underwater. Should your hand be impaled on a spine, the pain would be like that of a hornet's sting. The mucus on the spines contains a mild poison, and the tips of the spines may break off in the wound (see p. 255). But they are absorbed after a few days, and the pain usually disappears after half an hour or so.

Long-spined Black Urchins are usually found in groups of 10–20 or more at a depth below 2 m (6½ ft.) in daytime (see Fig. 9). It is clear that they are not randomly distributed. One possible expla-

Fig. 8

Long-spined Black Urchin

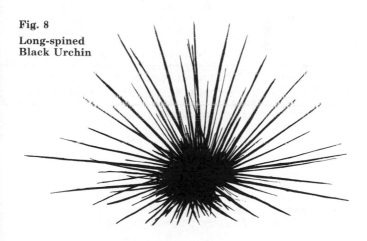

Fig. 9 A group of Long-spined Black Urchins. Note the characteristic triangular pattern.

nation of their "schooling" behavior relates to their search for shelter. As daylight approaches, an urchin, after a night's grazing, may begin to move toward a shadow, which represents the shelter of a crevice in the reef. But as the urchin draws near, the shadow may turn out to be another Long-spined Black Urchin, whose formidable spines provide precious little shelter. So the urchins spend the rest of the day jockeying for position around one another, seeking shelter where there are only spines. Other urchins, in their daily migration back to the reef, are drawn to the scene by the black shadows and join the group; soon there is a herd of urchins in a sandy area. All this maneuvering without real eyes!

Marble-sized balls of Shallow-water Starlet Coral may be lying free in Turtle Grass beds, and platelike crusts of this species may be found on rocks near shore. Ivory Bush Coral and Common Rose Coral live, unattached, on the lagoon bottom.

Small, creamy-white, branching colonies of Ivory Bush Coral project from or lie on the sand. This coral is similar to Staghorn Coral, but its cups project less, it is creamier and less translucent, and its branches are much thinner. In addition, it is much more common in lagoons and Turtle Grass beds, especially in Bermuda.

Common Rose Coral forms a small, flat, 5 cm (2 in.) long oval with an undulating, deep tan to brown rim. On the bottom of each colony is the remnant of a white calcareous stalk, which was once attached to the substratum but broke off when the coral matured.

Living unattached on the bottom is dangerous, since waves can overturn these small colonies, threatening the polyps with suffocation in the sand. But they have evolved an amazing defense mechanism. The polyps absorb a great deal of water and then forcefully eject it through their mouths in unison, undermining the bottom and tilting the colony over. Extending their bodies and pushing on the substratum, the polyps cause the whole mass to rock back and forth and eventually turn upright.

Crenolated Fire Coral may occur in Turtle Grass beds in water less than waist deep because it can attach itself to any hard object on the bottom. Learn to recognize this coral. To brush against it means instant pain and a red welt (see p. 253). The coral resembles a flattened sand castle, with crenelations and battlements bleached white. If you suspect that a coral near you is this species or another *Millepora,* examine it closely with your mask on. If it is one of these fire corals, it will appear to have no cups, and its surface will be smooth.

Young colonies of Brown Encrusting Soft Coral may grow on rocks or rubble in the lagoon. They look like small, purple, encrusting masses, sometimes with brown fuzz when their polyps are extended.

A number of mollusks occur in Turtle Grass beds and the shallow water of the lagoon. Among them are snails, pen shells, clams, sea slugs, octopods, and squids.

The Queen Conch is the most spectacular. This huge snail with a flaring, bright pink lip is uncommon on the more populated islands

Fig. 10

Queen Conch

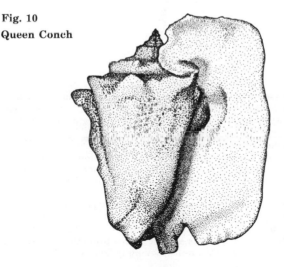

because it is eaten by natives and collected by tourists, and in the Bahamas its shell is exported for cutting into cameos. It is still relatively abundant in such places as the British Virgin Islands and the shallow waters off Cozumel, Mexico. When you pick up a Queen Conch for closer observation, you might be startled to find a tenant in its shell — the harmless, fist-sized Red Hermit, the largest hermit crab of the West Indies. The crab will withdraw into the shell when handled.

The cannibalistic Tulip Snail, which glides over the sand in search of other snails, has reddish flesh and a smooth, graceful shell circled by intermittent brown lines.

Fig. 11

Tulip Snail

The Stiff Pen Shell and the Amber Pen Shell, which look like large — 15 cm (6 in.) — arrowheads half-buried in the sand, frequent Turtle Grass beds. The shells are quite delicate, so be careful not to step on them.

Buried beneath the surface, among the intertwined roots of Turtle Grass, are many clams, the largest and commonest of which is the Tiger Lucine. Nearly 7.5 cm (3 in.) across when fully grown, it has radiating ribs on the outside of its round, white shell and sometimes a pink or lavender border on the inside.

As you snorkel in shallow water about 1 m (3¼ ft.) deep, look for patches of tan, filmy, forked *Dictyota* algae. Here and among Turtle Grass blades you will find sea slugs. The almost shell-less, snail-like Ragged Sea Hare is a most difficult quarry because the forked, filmy, leaflike projections extending from its back are the same color and consistency as *Dictyota*. The bed may be full of plump, 20 cm (8 in.) specimens, but you must search for them closely. Look for what appears to be a tuft of uncharacteristically pulsating *Dictyota*. Picking up a Ragged Sea Hare can be a satisfying experience, as it may weigh over 0.5 kg (1 lb.). The Spotted Sea Hare is even larger and more common. It is olive-drab and has black ringlike spots.

While you are looking for sea hares, you may come across a crevice in the lagoon floor that at first glance appears unoccupied. Look again, and notice whether large seashells or pieces of crab carapace are strewn in front of the opening. If so, the hole is surely the den of an octopus, which is less than fastidious about its surroundings and leaves its leftovers on its doorstep. Octopods are nocturnal hunters, so it is likely that the den will be occupied. Peer inside. You will see an eyeball glaring balefully out at you. If you reach into the den to try to remove the octopus, your attempt will probably fail. Its strong arms and suckers will enwrap and adhere to all the surfaces of the chamber. You may tear off several of the animal's arms before you get discouraged, so please don't try.

You will probably also see some purplish Atlantic Oval or Reef Squids as you snorkel in the lagoon. These wonderful animals will hover near you, unafraid, peering at you like tourists.

Numerous crustaceans, including many species that occur in the rear zone (see p. 36), inhabit the lagoon. They can be difficult to find because they change color and camouflage themselves so easily.

In sandy areas you may see shamefaced or box crabs. When one is disturbed, it covers its face with its large, armored front legs, and its general squareness is enhanced — the source of both common names. These crabs will bury themselves rapidly in the sand if discovered but can be safely picked up because they do not use their claws aggressively. If you see such a crab with a ridge of 6 or 7 teeth on its front legs that looks like a cockscomb, it is the Yellow Shamefaced or Box Crab, also called the Cockscomb Crab. A

Fig. 12   Spotted Sea Hare

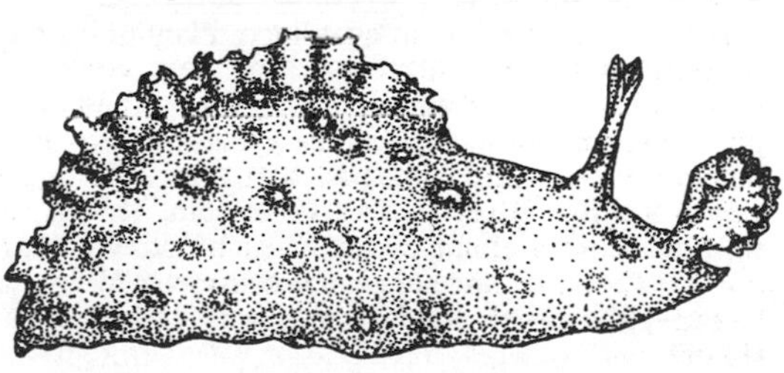

flamelike pattern on the dorsal surface proclaims the specimen a Flaming Shamefaced or Box Crab.

Several large anemones dominate the lagoon, as well as the back reef, and a number of smaller species live on and around Turtle Grass. The most magnificent is the Giant Caribbean Anemone. The Ringed Anemone, more subdued in color, is also more reclusive. Usually a thick mass of its tentacles is seen projecting from a hole, its body invisible deep within the recesses of the coral or rock haven. The Knobby Stinging Anemone, similar but larger, can burrow into the sand.

Some areas of sand in the lagoon may be covered with green ruglike mats. These are colonies of the Green Colonial Anemone. Another large, matlike anemone is the Sun Anemone, whose disk is covered by stubby, light green tentacles. (Some algae also form mats; see p. 14.)

Occasionally the lagoon will seem to be filled with many large bluish jellyfish pulsating their diaphanous disklike bodies as they slowly swim along, at the mercy of the windblown currents. These are harmless Moon Jellies.

The presence of a large number of jellyfish is called a bloom. A bloom, not to be confused with a migration, is an occasional, sometimes periodic, massive increase in the population of an organism, owing to the production and maturing of eggs deposited in the area. When conditions are right, the ocean appears to be crowded with an organism that only a few days before seemed absent. Jellyfish, comb jellies, and other planktonic animals and plants are particularly prone to such a burst of reproduction.

Another bloblike animal that can suddenly appear in numbers is the Portuguese Man-of-war. A small fish, the Man-of-war Fish, lives at the base of the tentacles of this siphonophore. If you see more than a few exquisite, blue-tinged, balloonlike floats as you walk along the beach in the morning, don't go into the water. The stinging cells (nematocysts) on the Portuguese Man-of-war's almost invisible tentacles are particularly toxic and, when they penetrate the skin, produce a painful burning sensation. A swimmer enmeshed in the mass of tentacles will come out of the water bearing red welts like lash marks, each a lesion caused by the stinging cells of one tentacle.

If the salinity is low in a protected lagoon or bay with a muddy bottom (such as a mangrove-edged bay), you will probably see at least 5 or 6 Upside-down Jellyfish in any field of view, each gently pulsating on the bottom. This species swims in typical jellyfish fashion, with undulating bell and mouth facing downward. But watch it when it settles to the bottom. It will turn over, mouth upward, raise a cloud of sediment by slowly undulating its bell, and eat the small animals in the sediment. When light is adequate, it can get enough food from plant cells (zooxanthellae) in its tissues.

This most unusual jellyfish is named after the mythological Cassiopeia, who proclaimed her beauty to be greater than that of the Nereids (sea nymphs). As punishment for her vanity her beloved daughter, Andromeda, was chained to a rock to become the prey of a sea monster. Andromeda was eventually saved by Perseus, but the Nereids had their revenge in the end. When Cassiopeia died, the gods elevated her to become one of the constellations. The Nereids arranged for the constellation to be placed so high in the northern sky that for half the year it would be upside down — a most ignominious position for a queen. Her predicament has been memorialized in the name of the beautiful Upside-down Jellyfish, *Cassiopeia xamachana*.

Egg-shaped, walnut-sized, jellylike blobs that are so transparent as to be almost invisible are comb jellies. They move by beating their 8 rows of cilia (see p. 69), and they, too, are often seen in huge numbers.

The Reef Crest

You will know you're approaching the reef crest when the bottom of the lagoon begins to rise rapidly toward the water's surface. The first scattered coral heads appear — often dead mounds of Boulder Coral, the main frame-builder or reef-producer. Algae grow thickly on the hard, unyielding surface of the dead coral head, softening its silhouette; and the big boulder stabilizes the sand around it, thus allowing an oasis of algae to be established.

The number of coral heads increases gradually. Some are alive. If you look above the surface, you will see a zone of Elkhorn Coral and a boiling surf surprisingly nearby.

The rear zone is a region of varied coral populations, sometimes rich and diverse, sometimes sparse. Common shallow-water species predominate, especially boulder-forming (massive) ones, such as Boulder Coral, Common Brain Coral, Round Starlet Coral, and Yellow Porous Coral. Elkhorn Coral, Staghorn Coral, and Thick Finger Coral, all of which are branching species, are less common.

On the reef flat, or rubble zone, the coral population is less diverse than in the rear zone. A few living stands of Elkhorn Coral survive in a sometimes extensive area of coral debris. Most of this rubble is chunks of Elkhorn Coral that has been broken by storms in the *palmata* zone and washed back. The only corals that live in this relatively barren zone are fire corals and sea fans. The calcareous *Goniolithon* and *Halimeda* algae are abundant. They grow in the sand and on the crumbling coral skeletons, filling spaces and crevices.

On some reefs the rubble is covered with a thick, green, rubbery mat of the Green Colonial Anemone or with small, tan, leathery mats of the Encrusting Colonial Anemone. Some chunks are cov-

ered with carpets of the disk-shaped Sun Anemone. Occasionally the Green Colonial Anemone (*Zoanthus sociatus*) is so common that the zone may truly be called the *Zoanthus* zone.

Many organisms that bore, especially the Red Rock Urchin and sponges of the genus *Cliona,* constantly work toward reducing the rubble to smaller riddled pieces. These sponges are, in fact, a major destructive force. They can hasten the erosion of reefs and shores by making labyrinthine channels in, and thereby weakening, large pieces of coral, which storm waves or heavy surges then break from the reef.

An interesting encrusting protozoan is the foraminiferan *Homotrema rubrum.* This one-celled animal forms tiny, hard, bright red patches at coral bases and on seashells and rubble. In fact, you will find these red patches on almost every hard object you retrieve from the sea.

Swimming near the rubble zone of the reef crest, you will be aware of the *palmata* zone, or breaker zone, an area of breaking waves and a forest of gigantic trees of Elkhorn Coral, with an understory of encrusting algae and the ubiquitous fire corals. This zone can be dangerous for swimmers, as the coral often grows to the surface and surging currents can make it difficult to maneuver. The Elkhorn Coral, with its relatively stout, brittle branches, takes the full force of the waves. It thrives in this turbulent environment. Notice that the coral's secondary branches stream backward, directly opposite the prevailing wind-driven currents, just like a windswept pine tree on a cliff overlooking the sea. So harsh is this habitat that no other coral species can compete, and Elkhorn Coral (*Acropora palmata*), almost alone, makes up the upper reef crest, or *palmata* zone.

The topography of the reef crest helps assure the dominance of Elkhorn Coral. The reef flat is washed and scoured clean by turbulent seas. The slope at its front, the *palmata* zone, carries sediment downward and away. Elkhorn Coral, lacking an effective cilia-mucus cleaning system, thrives in the sediment-free water. It grows so fast that it shades out most other corals. Only fire corals seem to be able to find a foothold in some turbulent areas.

The destruction of Elkhorn Coral by storms, when huge waves tear off branches and overturn whole colonies, leads to a gradual enlargement of the rubble zone. Live Elkhorn Coral grows for-

Fig. 13 (opposite) A scene from the back reef. The large coral in the foreground is Large Grooved Brain Coral; note the overhangs along its edges, which are frequent haunts of squirrelfishes. Growing out of one of the crevices is a colony of Flower Coral. Immediately behind the brain coral, in the center, is a boulder-shaped head of Round Starlet Coral, with heads of Large-cupped Boulder Coral on both sides and a Red Finger Sponge (the vertical rod) at the right.

ward, limited only by its requirement for shallow, turbulent water. Thus the whole reef slowly extends seaward, leaving extensive flats of calcareous sand where the rubble zone once was.

As the reef crest continues to descend into the barren, or lower *palmata,* zone, Elkhorn Coral is still dominant. Here it grows in low, spreading, fan-shaped colonies. In depressions, where water moves more slowly, massive corals begin to appear. Common Brain Coral, Large Grooved Brain Coral, Staghorn Coral, and the boulder, finger, fire, and lettuce corals are common. Patches of these corals are separated from one another by regions of coral rubble and fine sand where coral growth is reduced — hence the name barren zone. The barrenness may be caused partly by the Long-spined Black Urchin, which can be particularly abundant. This urchin will devour almost any encrusting organism that might grow here.

Seaward of the barren zone a few mounds may appear, followed by huge masses of coral. This buttress zone, the most impressive part of the reef, consists almost entirely of gigantic coral masses, or buttresses, separated by sand-floored canyons. House-sized boulders, created largely by colonies of Boulder Coral, are covered with a variety of other corals. The walls of these boulders, virtually always in partial shade, are often covered with distinctive, leaflike plates of Tan Lettuce-leaf Coral. Corals that are moundlike in shallow water — Yellow Porous Coral, for example — form shinglelike plates along the walls. A few spectacular spires of Pillar Coral reach toward the surface, and large colonies of brain corals are abundant. Corals that are relatively rare in shallower water, such as Large Cactus Coral and Large Flower Coral, are common in this, the richest zone of the reef. Some corals grow laterally from the top of one of these masses to the top of another, forming a bridge between close-set buttresses and transforming the narrow canyon between them into a tunnel.

Sand, coral chunks, and remains of other once-living organisms descend from above and carve grooves and valleys in the buttress zone. This never-ending rain of debris prevents coral from filling in the spaces that have been eroded. Many fishes are here, and beautiful tube-dwelling worms with multicolored fans extend from the walls of these canyons, making swimming through them a truly thrilling experience. Soft corals, especially tall sea feathers, are common. The sandy canyon floors, extending seaward like fingers between the coral masses, are the only relatively impoverished areas.

Buttress zones are spectacular but relatively uncommon. Often the outer zone of the reef crest is a densely populated region abounding with Staghorn Coral and several species of massive corals — the mixed zone.

The dense coral masses are dissected by a few narrow channels. Their coarse sandy bottoms are rippled at right angles to the prevailing waves. When branches of Staghorn Coral break off during storms (a common occurrence) and fall onto the sand, some survive, despite scouring by moving sediments. Such actively growing colonies can cover a small sand channel. Here the colonies characteristically have greatly thickened, horizontal branches that are oriented toward the shore.

Colonies of Boulder and Staghorn Corals suddenly become abundant. Boulder Coral forms either immense, rounded mounds — to 3 m (10 ft.) — with skirted, platelike edges, or high knobby colonies. Equally variable are its colors: shades of yellow-and green-brown, dark brown, and gray. A number of other corals, including fire corals, Large Grooved Brain Coral, and Round Starlet Coral, are also common. Pillar Coral, though not particularly abundant anywhere, is more profuse in the mixed zone and some areas of the fore-reef terrace than in other regions.

Halimeda grows between the lobes of Boulder Coral. The bases of the lobes provide a substratum from which many other algae and smaller hard and soft corals grow — for example, plates of Tan Lettuce-leaf Coral and Sunray Lettuce-leaf Coral, which are especially common; clumps of finger corals, which are often a meter or more wide; Deadman's Fingers; Sea Rods; sea fans; and sea feathers. Juvenile Short Coral Snails may also be found on the Boulder Coral. Though they feed on coral polyps, removing coral tissue and some of the zooxanthellae, they rarely kill their host coral.

A few colonies of Elkhorn Coral, having settled on dead areas on the sides of the Boulder Coral, spread their branches above the Boulder Coral. The Elkhorn Coral can shade the Boulder Coral to such an extent that the amount of light reaching the Boulder Coral's zooxanthellae is insufficient to support photosynthesis. In addition, the Elkhorn Coral restricts the flow of water to the Boulder Coral's tissues and thereby diminishes its supply of plankton. In these ways, the Elkhorn Coral threatens the live portions of the Boulder Coral with starvation and death. If the Boulder Coral dies, the Elkhorn Coral can completely overgrow its skeleton. But the Boulder Coral can fight back. It will destroy any Elkhorn Coral tissue within reach of its mesenterial filaments (see p. 111).

The abundant thickets of Staghorn Coral usually consist of several colonies with many intermingled branches. Look carefully for signs of separate colonies: differences in branch thickness or orientation, tissue color, and spacing of side branches. Because many branches grow so closely together, they often collide. When the branches are from the same colony, their tissues and skeletons fuse perfectly. This fusion may help keep the colony on the bottom during storms. When branches of different colonies come together, irregular tissue and skeletal deposits often form at the region of contact, resembling bad weld jobs. (Occasionally one branch grows around another.) Because such an area snaps easily, the pseudo-fusion is probably a less effective stabilizer than the true fusion

within a colony. Staghorn Coral is particularly delicate, so be careful not to touch it with your fins. If you snap off its brittle
branches, you will have damaged it needlessly.

The base of most Staghorn branches is dead and is often covered
with a miniforest of small filamentous algae. Dead branches may
be covered with crustose red algae, the tiny Pale Anemone, or
small colonies of lettuce corals. Many branches have been hol-
lowed out by the *Cliona* boring sponges. Branch tips that are
white, sometimes for a distance of 2 cm ($^3/_4$ in.), are a sure sign of
predation by the Fireworm.

Adult Short Coral Snails, often with their shells covered by
crusts or filaments of algae, live on Staghorn branches. Unlike the
juveniles on Boulder Coral, the adults eat live tissue, creating conspicuous scars that may be several millimeters wide.

The Threespot Damselfish encourages the growth of algal
"lawns" — masses of *Ceramium* and other filamentous algae — in
a couple of ways. The fish often stakes out a patch of Staghorn
Coral, which may include an area where algae have settled on the
skeleton exposed by the Short Coral Snail; it fearlessly protects its
territory by attacking herbivorous fishes (as well as by nipping
invading divers) and thus prevents them from eating large
amounts of the algae. In addition, the Threespot Damselfish itself
nibbles on live coral, producing areas suitable for algal growth.

Organisms of the Reef Crest

Hard Corals. In the rear zone Boulder Coral often forms lobed
colonies with white patches. The patches are dead areas where
polyps have been killed as detritus settled from the water, pitting
the coral. Sea urchins and snails occupying these patches further
grind them down. So some heads of Boulder Coral may even look
multilobed, in contrast with the often perfectly hemispherical
heads of brain and starlet corals.

Several species of brain corals — for example, Depressed, Common, Sharp-hilled, Large Grooved, and Tan Brain Corals — occur
in the rear zone. Practice will be necessary before you can distinguish one species from another in the field. (See pp. 83 and 84 for
the features of the septa and of the hills and valleys that are characteristic of each species.)

Round Starlet Coral, another important reef-producer, is easier
to identify. When this species is growing next to the more irregular
boulders of Boulder Coral, the differences between them are evident. The cups of Round Starlet Coral are deeply depressed and
look like well-defined dots. Those of Boulder Coral are superficial
and not dotlike.

Thick Finger Coral appears in gray-white clumps, often a meter
or more across, each thick "finger" often covered with extended,

fuzzlike polyps. Small patches of Staghorn Coral lie on the bottom. These bumpy, white colonies look like horns discarded by a herd of stags at the end of rutting season. Unfortunately, these unattached colonies tempt unsuspecting divers to remove them as broken or dying coral. As a result, Staghorn Coral has been removed from some reefs, substantially altering their ecology.

All 3 species of fire corals are common in the rear zone. Crenelated Fire Coral is often the most dominant. (See p. 21 for a warning about these corals.)

Cactus Coral, often growing out of the sand, and Tan Lettuce-leaf Coral may be abundant in shaded areas. Cactus Coral is so called because, when dried, its large-toothed septa make it look bristly.

A conspicuous coral, sometimes abundant and sometimes completely absent, is Large-cupped Boulder Coral. It is the only boulder-forming species with large, 8 mm ($\frac{3}{8}$ in.) (sometimes blister-like) cups. You may find the elegant Stokes' Starlet Coral along the outer edge of the rear zone, often growing in sand. And close to or even projecting from the sand, at the base of a large boulder, may be small clumps of the beautiful Flower Coral, whose branches arise from a stalk.

Perhaps the most dramatic coral to search for is Pillar Coral. A colony of 4 or 5 columns may grow out of the sand or project from between other corals. Each column is about 7.5 cm (3 in.) in diameter and in the rear zone usually no higher than 1 m ($3\frac{1}{4}$ ft.). When the polyps are extended, the coral looks like a nightmarish, fuzzy castle.

Soft Corals. The beautiful soft corals are conspicuous in the rear zone, growing from any stationary surface — hard coral, rubble, or rock. Their flexible, undulating, vertical elements contrast with the unyielding massiveness of the boulders of hard coral.

The most exotic and impressive are the sea fans. The green, yellow, or purple fanlike colonies may be more than a meter in diameter, and they move back and forth with every surge of the sea, like a woman slowly fanning herself. The 2 species are difficult to distinguish in the field. From a few centimeters away, look closely for tiny dots covering the flexible, but hard, latticelike skeleton. These holes are the cups, through which project the living polyps that entrap small planktonic organisms swimming or floating nearby. The fan corals are efficient predators, spreading their netlike forms across the current. In turn, they are preyed upon by one of the most beautiful snails, the Flamingo Tongue. The Flamingo Tongue browses exclusively on the polyps of soft corals, inserting its proboscis into the cups and rasping away the living tissue with its radula (filelike tongue).

The thin, fleshy mantle of the Flamingo Tongue is so attractive that it is worth swimming from one sea fan to another until you find one. All mollusks have a mantle, a mass of tissue that secretes

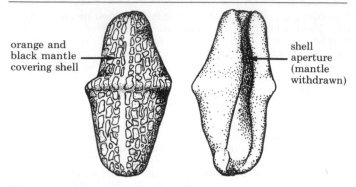

orange and
black mantle
covering shell

shell
aperture
(mantle
withdrawn)

Fig. 14   **Flamingo Tongue**

the shell. In most mollusks it is normally hidden inside the shell. But the Flamingo Tongue flamboyantly displays its mantle, which is covered with orange and black, leopardlike spots. Why does this snail flaunt itself so improvidently? Perhaps because it can withdraw its mantle into its thick shell and regenerate parts that have been torn or eaten. Or perhaps the color is a major factor in sex recognition (as is the bright red of the cardinal), the obvious purpose being to ensure reproduction and continuation of the species.

The other soft corals look rather treelike. Those with the fewest branches — an isolated stalk or group of vertical elements — are Deadman's Fingers and *Plexaurella grisea,* one of the sea rods. The polyps of sea rods make the colonies look like groups of brown, fuzzy columns as high as 1 m (3¼ ft.). If the polyps are not extended or if you run your finger down one of the columns, causing the polyps to retract, a purple, lumpy skeleton will be visible. To distinguish these 2 soft corals in the field, cut off a small section of one of the "fingers." If it is Deadman's Fingers, you will see white, calcareous spicules; if it is the sea rod, the core will be brown, plasticlike gorgonin, the supporting material of all common soft corals except Deadman's Fingers. In addition, on the back reef the sea rod is much more abundant than Deadman's Fingers.

Eunicea mammosa, a knobby candelabrum, has many bumpy, finger-thick branches coming from a central stalk. It rarely grows higher than 45 cm (1½ ft.). Tournefort's Knobby Candelabrum has fewer branches, all in one plane, and looks much like a yellow-brown, rough-sided candelabrum.

Perhaps the commonest branched soft coral of the rear zone is Common Bushy Soft Coral, but differentiating it from other *Plexaura* species is difficult in the field. These corals differ from knobby candelabra in having elongate depressed slits (rather than bumpy cups) and much longer branches that divide into sub-branches.

Sea feathers form large, drooping colonies, like clusters of giant feathers, and sometimes grow as tall as a man. Slimy and Smooth Sea Feathers are best distinguished by feel.

The sea blades look like purple or yellow clumps of tall, broad grass. Each branch is like a blade of grass and has a barely discernible central rib.

Extensive areas of rubble or rock may be covered with flat crusts, which are colonies of Brown Encrusting Soft Coral. Small, purple, encrusting masses, with slitlike cups, growing on a rock or piece of rubble are probably young colonies of this species.

Anemones. In crevices between coral heads or on rocks or dead coral you may find tan or green mats of colonial anemones of the genera *Palythoa* and *Zoanthus*.

Fig. 15

Smooth Sea Feather

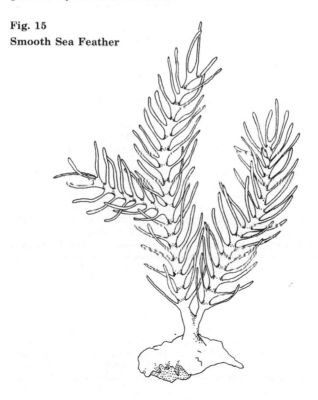

When extended, *Palythoa* species look very much like crowded, fringed mushrooms. When closed, they form a leathery mat with slits or oval holes less than 1 cm ($\frac{1}{2}$ in.) in diameter, sometimes covering as much as several square meters of a hard surface.

The Green Colonial Anemone can colonize the sand in the rubble zone, as well as in the lagoon. When expanded, the oral disks of the polyps are so crowded that they press against one another, forming a latticework of living tissue. If the reef you are examining has no well-developed rubble zone, look for this anemone between coral heads.

You may see a disk that looks like a circular rug or a tan or green sunburst, often as wide as your hand. This is the Sun Anemone. Frequently groups of these anemones partially cover rocks and dead corals.

The Stinging Anemone is highly camouflaged and may be indiscernible among the algae covering rocks and dead coral heads of the back reef. It can deliver a sharp sting, so be careful. However, even the thinnest of gloves are adequate protection against its stinging cells. Occasionally crowded colonies of tiny, long-tentacled Pale Anemones can be found in crevices on the back reef. And look under ledges and on cave walls for the Maroon Anemone.

Sponges. Live sponges look dramatically different from dried ones used as bath sponges. They are fleshier-looking, but not all of them feel spongy. Some are cheeselike, others are shiny and smooth. They may be massive (a thick, solid-looking mound or cake shape), encrusting (flat and sheetlike), fingerlike (closed vertical columns), chimneylike (open-ended cylindrical columns), or vaselike (a tapered vase or cup shape). Branching and bushlike sponges are common in the lagoon and rear zone; some species extend across the reef.

A number of organisms live in, on, and around sponges (see pp. 125 and 246). As you look at sponges, don't pass up the opportunity to search for some of their inhabitants and neighbors as well.

The Red Finger Sponge has thick, irregular, 30 cm (1 ft.) high branches, with occasional large oscules. Though it is usually brick-red, algae on its surface may color it pink or strawberry. Close relatives are the Green Finger Sponge and the Blue-green Finger Sponge. The Green Finger Sponge is often a small, yellow-green mound, but it may produce as many as 6 cylindrical branches to 4 cm ($1\frac{1}{2}$ in.) in diameter. The Blue-green Finger Sponge has thinner branches — to 2 cm ($\frac{3}{4}$ in.) wide — that are no higher than 5 cm (2 in.); they are green, with shades of blue, brown, or gray.

The Black Bush Sponge grows to a height of 25 cm (10 in.). It may have as many as 50 branches, each 1–3 cm ($\frac{1}{2}$–$1\frac{1}{4}$ in.) in diameter. When squeezed, this sponge exudes purplish slime. Look for ropy colonies of orange *Parazoanthus swiftii,* a colonial anemone, which often cover this green-tinged, blackish sponge.

The Lavender Tube Sponge can have 6 or more warty, purplish gray tubes, each open at the top and about 4 cm (1½ in.) across.

The fleshy Yellow Tube Sponge has a reticulated pattern of ridges or lumps on its surface. It may form one or several tubes, and a membranous shelf may be seen at the large opening of each tube. Sometimes many thin, lumpy, fingerlike extensions project around the opening.

You may find many small, symmetrical, red and green spheres with crowded, round bumps or lobes and a central oscule in each lobe. These are sponges of the genus *Tethya*. One species, the Orange Egg Sponge, looks like an orange golf ball.

The Smooth Lump Sponge forms an amorphous 5 cm (2 in.) gray, brown, or cream mass with irregular lumps. No oscules are visible, but the oscular areas are often darker than their surroundings.

Colorful crusts are produced by many sponges. The Black Chimney Sponge forms crusts. It has chimneys — less than 1 cm (½ in.) wide and 3–7.5 cm (1¼–3 in.) high — that project from sand in Turtle Grass beds. Purple, black, or green crusts are often species of *Adocia*. A few thin, raised, 1 cm (½ in.) high tubes rise from a nearly smooth surface. One of the commonest shallow-water sponges looks like a mass of mottled brown liver. Smooth, shining sheets of this Chicken Liver Sponge overgrow extensive areas — 30 cm (1 ft.) or more — of sand, dead coral, rocks, or almost anything else.

In the rear zone the largest sponges are the loggerheads. The Loggerhead Sponge looks like a smooth, rounded, slate-gray cake that has been cut off at the top. The Common Loggerhead Sponge looks like a barrel, somewhat narrower at the base than at the top. Sometimes this sponge lives in water so shallow that its top is exposed.

The grayish stinking sponges are covered with pointed warts. The Pillow Stinking Sponge may be a stubby cylinder or pillow shape, with a rim of black holes. The Stinking Vase Sponge forms a sharp-rimmed vase 30 cm (1 ft.) or more across. The Variable Stinking Sponge is usually a rounded mass, sometimes with short, cylindrical branches and large, dark oscules. Its olive-drab warts are smaller than those of the other species.

Beware of brushing against the 2 irritating sponges (see pp. 131 and 132). The rough, brown, encrusting or lumpy Touch-me-not Sponge is common at depths of 10–15 m (33–50 ft.) on coral reefs, but it can be found under ledges in shallow water. More easily identifiable is the encrusting, bright red or orange Fire Sponge. It forms low amorphous mounds or sheets, especially on walls of rock or coral.

The Red Boring Sponge may be mistaken for the Fire Sponge, but its red crust is invariably covered with tiny, white, buttonlike colonial anemones.

Worms. Look closely at a head of boulder or brain coral for penny-sized, glowing spots of red, maroon, or yellow. These are worms whose tubes are so deeply embedded in the coral that only the expanded colorful branchiae are visible. You will see round, feathery fans (fanworms) or 2 miniature red pine trees (Christmas tree worms) protruding from the coral. Move a finger slowly toward the feathery branchiae. When it is about 1 cm ($\frac{1}{2}$ in.) away, the worms will sense your presence and instantly disappear! They withdraw so rapidly into their tubes that the old magician's cry "Now you see it, now you don't" is applicable.

The fanworms belong to the genera *Sabella* and *Sabellastarte,* the Christmas tree worms to *Pomatostegus* and *Spirobranchus. Sabella* has 1 whorl of tentacles; *Sabellastarte* 2, one inside the other. *Pomatostegus* usually has red tentacles in the form of a U-shaped tree; *Spirobranchus* has 2 diagonally projecting "Christmas trees," each with 4 whorls, decreasing in diameter toward the apex.

The Fireworm is a nighttime feeder that may be seen moving across sandy areas or curled up in a coral space. One wonders how this brightly colored worm can survive as it meanders conspicuously over the bottom. This, however, is the case of the worm turned. One of the most effective predators of the back reef and lagoon, the worm attacks anything slow enough to be caught. It does so by everting (turning inside out and extending) its tubelike pharynx, which secretes enzymes to digest the prey. When the worm is attacked, its formidable setae (the white tufts of barbed spicules) penetrate the antagonist's skin and work their way in, like the quills of a porcupine. When broken, they release a painful toxic jelly. Be careful not to touch this worm (see p. 256).

Crustaceans. As in the lagoon, crustaceans are abundant but hard to find in the rear zone.

Look in clumps of finger coral. Or shake a clump of Thin Finger Coral into a water-filled container. Among the plethora of goodies in the spaces between the fingers will be several crabs, including the Green Reef Crab, the Spotted Decorator Crab, and the Sponge Spider Crab. The Spotted Decorator Crab gets its name from its habit of planting all sorts of algae, sponges, and other sessile organisms on its brown, triangular body. Should it find itself with an insufficient food supply, it simply feeds off the garden growing on its back! This crab has a forked rostrum, resembling straight horns projecting anteriorly from its head. Its color varies (brown is predominant); its chelipeds are grayish white, with small, round, purplish spots. The Sponge Spider Crab, another decorator crab, also has a forked rostrum but the horns are curved. In addition, it has 3 spines projecting from the posterior of its carapace. A less common decorator crab is the Lesser Sponge Crab, which is usually covered by a tan sponge.

If you see an arrow-shaped crab with spidery legs walking over the surface of coral on the back reef, it is the unmistakable Arrow Crab.

Some crabs are found more easily by looking for evidence of their presence than for the crabs themselves. Such is the case with the Elkhorn Coral or Gall Crab, which is common on Elkhorn Coral and to a lesser extent on Staghorn Coral. The immature female takes up a position on the coral, remains there as the coral grows around her, and finally becomes imprisoned in the gall (see p. 249). Look for the characteristic galls — nickel-sized, light-colored bumps with central holes — usually at the forks between the coral branches or along their edges.

If you see a brown and white, whiplike structure, apparently with a life of its own, projecting from a hole, it is probably a long antenna of a Spiny Lobster. Follow the antenna back into the crevices. You will see 2 black eyes on stalks, with curved ridges arching above them. Most of these lobsters are little longer than 30 cm (1 ft.), and the average length is constantly decreasing as the lobster is exploited as a food resource.

The Spiny Lobster is protected on many Caribbean Islands and Florida because it has been sadly decimated by the demands of hotels and restaurants. Keep this in mind if you are thinking of the delights of a lobster meal. In addition, even though this lobster has no claws, its antennae have sharp spines. If you grasp the lobster, it will lay its antennae back on your hand. The spines will rasp your skin, and in an attempt to swim away the lobster will jerk madly in your hand. Eventually it will simply break the antenna off, leaving you with less than a meal.

Perhaps the most magnificent shrimp in the rear zone is the Banded Coral or Barber Pole Shrimp. It hides in coral crevices, but you might see this cleaning shrimp on the tip of a coral head, ready to offer its services to passing fishes. If you are lucky enough to see a cleaning station in operation, you will have had the ultimate underwater experience (see p. 246).

Other colorful cleaning shrimps to look for are the Red-backed Cleaning Shrimp or Scarlet Lady and the Peppermint or Veined Shrimp.

It is difficult to get a look at the Red Snapping Shrimp because it is so well hidden beneath the tentacles of the Ringed Anemone, the only place it is found. However, if you gently poke the anemone, the shrimp may come out in response to your challenge. It has round, white spots on its abdomen and long, red and white antennae.

While you are searching for the Red Snapping Shrimp on a Ringed Anemone, keep an eye open for tiny Pederson's Cleaning Shrimp and Spotted Cleaning Shrimp. These tiny, transparent shrimps commonly live among the tentacles of the Giant Caribbean Anemone and other large anemones. They must be searched for carefully but are very common.

Some shrimps are more easily found by listening for them. In the snapping shrimps of the genera *Alpheus* and *Synalpheus* one claw is greatly enlarged and modified with a pistonlike structure. When the piston is rapidly pushed into a socket, it creates a strong shock wave that travels through the water, making a pop or click. Occasionally thousands of these shrimps congregate, producing a veritable cacophony of pops and clicks. The small Short-clawed Sponge Shrimp and the similar *Synalpheus minus* are abundant inside sponges and in coral crevices, which are also habitats of the larger Banded Snapping Shrimp.

Mantis shrimps live in sand burrows or coral crevices. They assume a stance like that of a Praying Mantis, the second thoracic appendages clasped close to the thorax in an attitude of prayer. Don't try to pick one up. It will lash out with these large appendages and rip open your thumb with the razor-sharp finger of its claw. Mantis shrimps are not true shrimps, because they have abdominal gills and usually a rather arched thorax, which makes them appear to be partially reared back with head erect as they stand on the bottom. Their eyes are large, black, and stalked. The commonest species on coral flats and in the rear zone is the Common Rock Mantis Shrimp, which may be 5.5 cm ($2\frac{1}{4}$ in.) long.

Fishes. Take time to float above the reef, motionless, watching the fishes. Some 400 species live there. Their bright colors and multiplicity of shapes present an endless panorama. Large fishes may be spectacular, but don't overlook the delicate beauty of some of the tiny species.

As beautiful as the fishes are to look at, the true reward comes from observing their behavior. When you follow a particular fish and become aware of its personality and habits, not only will your appreciation of fishes be enhanced; you will also gain some insight into the web of interdependent behavior patterns that maintain the total reef ecosystem.

At first it might be difficult to focus on one fish long enough to figure out what it's up to, because another fish will catch your attention and distract you. Don't be discouraged. Eventually you will be able to concentrate on one at a time, and some fascinating behavior patterns will become obvious. Spend a little time learning to differentiate 15–20 common species. Looking for the fishes mentioned below (only some of the common species) will enable you to begin to separate individual species from the welter of shapes and colors that may overwhelm your visual sense. (The family descriptions, each including a representative species, on pp. 217–241 and Pls. 22–26 will be helpful, too.) Be sure to read about fish behavior in Chapter 12. Then seek out one species at a time and keep observing it as it goes through its routine.

Look for a sandy bottom between coral heads. A fish might be poking around, raising small clouds of sand with a pair of barbels on its chin. It is probably a Spotted Goatfish or a Yellow Goatfish.

The Yellowfin Mojarra, common in the lagoon, may be seen near sandy areas of the rear zone. It actually eats the sand, straining out small animals and releasing the cleaned sand through its gills.

A funny-faced fish with comical movements, the Spotted Trunkfish, is the clown of the reef. It busily lashes its pectoral fins back and forth until they are blurs of movement, but it hardly seems to progress at all. Its black-and-white-spotted or mosaic-lined body stands out sharply against the muted pastels of its background. If you follow one for a while, it will swim to the bottom to feed. As it blows a stream of water at the sand, excavating a hole to expose small crabs or shrimps, you might see a Slippery Dick or another small wrasse shoulder the trunkfish aside and dart in to capture the newly exposed prize.

Other browsers will appear to be feeding on the coral. Some eat the coral itself; others eat only the algae growing on the coral; yet others eat both.

The large, colorful parrotfishes are virtually the only regular browsers on coral, eating the polyps and skeletons and scraping algae from dead surfaces. The hundreds of teeth in their jaws are so strong that they are capable of rasping large chunks of coral from a colony. Move close to a parrotfish so that you can watch and listen to it feed. You will hear an unmistakable rasping noise as it scrapes off pieces of coral. The polyps are digested, and the rocklike skeleton, now ground into small particles, passes out of the anus in a white cloud. This grinding process is one of the major ways in which coral is converted to sand.

One usually pictures parrotfishes in large, placidly grazing schools. The schools, however, ordinarily comprise young males and mature females. Supermales, on the other hand, are territorial,

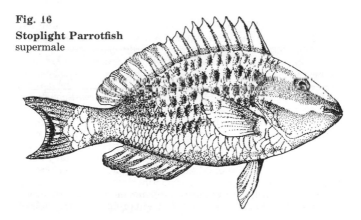

Fig. 16

Stoplight Parrotfish
supermale

and you will often see a supermale Queen Parrotfish, aglow with green, blue, and orange, driving another male away from its territory. It was probably once a functional female (see p. 215).

Keep an eye open for the major herbivore of the reef, the Doctorfish, so named because of the "lancet" (scalpel-like spine) in a white streak on either side just before its tail. The Blue Tang, a frequent companion of the Doctorfish, usually moves in small schools of fewer than a dozen. But if you are lucky, you will see a wonderful sight — a school of 30–40, swimming so closely together that they look like an iridescent blue cloud. Should these fishes enter the territory of a damselfish as they feed on algae growing on dead coral or in crevices, they will be attacked by the damselfish. Since almost every coral head is the territory of a damselfish, these pugnacious fishes make an important ecological contribution. By driving away the grazers (fishes, such as surgeonfishes and tangs, which descend on an area and pick it clean of algae), the damselfishes help create little oases of green on their territories. Look for meter-wide damselfish "gardens."

If you see an exotic-looking fish that is wide and flat and has an elongate snout, it is probably a butterflyfish. Its long snout enables it to remove small organisms from crevices in the coral. Butterflyfishes are almost always found in pairs. The Foureye and Banded Butterflyfishes are the commonest of the several species on the reef.

The Foureye Butterflyfish is aptly named, for it has 2 false eyespots near its tail, one on either side. This type of camouflage confuses predators. Most attacking fishes swallow their prey headfirst, since the barbs on its fins are pointed backward. Forcing down a resisting fish tailfirst is a scratchy affair. The big, black false eyespots may, however, so confuse a predator that it engulfs the tail end of the Foureye. Finding itself with a mouthful of spine, the predator often lets go.

Nevertheless, at times a fish does successfully attack another fish tailfirst. I once saw this happen. A school of Brown Chromis that I had been admiring was momentarily dislocated. A space appeared in the center as the fish frantically swam outward, and then the school closed ranks. Underneath, returning to the bottom, was a 13 cm (5 in.) Inshore Lizardfish with a 7.5 cm (3 in.) Brown Chromis struggling in its jaws. The lizardfish swallowed the chromis tailfirst. This seems less surprising when you take a close look at the Inshore Lizardfish. It appears to be mostly mouth, its huge jaws sloping upward from under the eye in a perpetual pugnacious grin. This lizardfish sits motionless on the bottom, camouflaged to look like a pebbly, sandy surface. Though normally sluggish, it launches itself rocketlike from the bottom when prey is near and rarely misses. It catches its victim by surprise, since many small fishes are oriented toward midwater or surface predators.

As you scuba dive, look upward. You will probably see schools of

Brown Chromis or Blue Chromis, both of which abound on the reef. These lovely, small fishes tend to swim in loosely packed schools at several levels.

If you see one or several large fishes in an unusual position, such as hanging in the water head down, or aslant, with mouth gaping, you have probably happened upon a cleaning station (see p. 246). Juvenile Blueheads are common cleaners. Ordinarily dull yellow with pink and black accents, these juveniles become bright yellow when they are picking off parasites from the skin and mouth of the other fish. While acting as cleaners, they are invulnerable to the predators that would normally devour them. Cleaning is not a full-time occupation; even juvenile Blueheads eat small crustaceans and mollusks.

Often invisible to neophyte fish-watchers, the Trumpetfish suspends itself head down in a clump of soft coral, its long, thin body resembling the coral stalks. Only its constantly searching eyes reveal its predatory nature. Small fishes, attuned to a world of horizontally oriented enemies, swim past this apparently unthreatening vertical element. Suddenly the Trumpetfish darts forward, creates a strong current in its elongate mouth, and sucks its prey into its small but efficient jaws. The prey fish rapidly disappears, and the Trumpetfish resumes its post, almost invisible once again. Or it moves on, horizontally, sometimes tenaciously flattening itself against the flank of a passing grouper or another relatively large fish. Eventually the Trumpetfish frees itself and within a few moments is swaying in perfect unison with the stalks in another clump of soft coral.

A new dimension opens when you swim into coral crevices or peer under overhanging branches of Elkhorn Coral or into coral caves. If you are tempted to position yourself more accurately by grasping the coral, be careful to avoid harmful organisms. Watch out for the Fire Sponge, which often covers crevice walls; the Long-spined Black Urchin, which hides in holes in the daytime; and fire corals, among which a number of animals seek protection (see pp. 131, 190, and 85).

One more warning: Before sticking your hand into a crevice, look into it carefully. A dreaded moray eel may be hiding there. If you see a pair of well-toothed jaws, back off. Though morays do not normally attack humans, they will when prodded or provoked in their lair. The most dangerous species is the Green Moray, which is gray but covered with poisonous, yellow-green mucus. It can reach 1.8 m (6 ft.). The Spotted Moray, the commonest and least secretive, sinuously winds its way among coral heads, coming briefly out in the open in the daytime.

The most abundant fishes in the semidark under coral ledges and in recesses are squirrelfishes. These beautiful, large-eyed fishes have deeply forked tails. Longjaw, Longspine, Dusky, and Reef Squirrelfishes have rather distinct, red and white longitudinal stripes. At night squirrelfishes come out to forage for small crustaceans, their large, black eyes providing considerable visual acuity in the dark. The Blackbar Soldierfish, with the wonderful name Wow 'i boyo in Papiamento, is crimson and has a vertical black bar just behind the gill. A bright red school may be packed into a shallow recess under a coral head.

Other shy inhabitants that hide under coral outcroppings are the groupers, some of which reach 2 m (6½ ft.) and hundreds of kilograms. They can rapidly change color to blend with their environment. The least difficult to find are the Red Hind and the Nassau Grouper. The former has many small red spots all over its body; the latter is striped. Large Nassau Groupers often become so adjusted to humans that they will come out of hiding for a handout of bread at diving resorts.

Important reef predators, groupers eat many species of fishes smaller than themselves and thus help to regulate fish populations. However, they have been decimated by spearfishing on many reefs in unprotected waters, and the ecology of those reefs has thereby been upset. Ironically it is the groupers' habit of hiding in crevices that often proves their undoing. When approached by a spearfisherman, instead of fleeing, a grouper retreats, pressing itself against the wall of its lair, and thus becomes vulnerable to the spear.

In some grouper species the fish change sex. They begin as females and become males at sexual maturity. Groupers must produce large numbers of eggs because they provide no care for their young. In fact, the eggs and larvae float away as part of the plankton, and very young groupers have never been found near the reef.

Among the most beautiful reef fishes is the Fairy Basslet, called by some the Royal Gramma. This tiny, purple and yellow fish orients itself toward the lightest surface. If in a cave with a light-colored sandy floor, for example, it will swim upside down, its dorsal surface facing the sand.

Gobies and blennies are often visible on coral heads "standing" on their outstretched pectoral fins. Some have a blunt head with an almost human face. Their diminutive size and bulldoglike facial expression make them look cute, but don't be misled. They can be as vicious as barracudas. Blennies and gobies differ in that blennies usually have 1 dorsal fin and gobies have 2 separate dorsal fins.

The Redlip Blenny is common, especially in the southern Caribbean (Tobago and Bonaire, for example). Large for a blenny, it is black, but its red lips and pectoral and dorsal fins stand out like flames. Approach to within a meter as one perches on a coral head. If you go closer, it will scuttle over the coral to hide on the side away from you.

Neon and Sharknose Gobies are worth searching for: should you find 1 or 2 perched on a coral head, you may see a cleaning station in action (see p. 246). If a diver lines up for a turn at this barber-

shop, he may have his fingers cleaned by an unobservant or
unfastidious goby. These slender, tiny fishes are usually black,
with a light-colored stripe from snout to tail.

As you quietly swim over the reef, marveling at the beauty of the
fishes below you, something may suddenly become visible in the
corner of your eye. When you turn your head to look at it, you will
find yourself confronted by a large barracuda, its teeth clearly visible as it hovers just 2 m (6½ ft.) away. Don't panic, even if the fish
swims around you in gradually decreasing circles. All predators are
confined to a particular prey size, and you are too large to trigger
the barracuda's feeding patterns. Remember, too, that virtually no
one has ever been intentionally bitten by a barracuda. (If it mis-
takes your camera or shiny belt buckle for a prey fish, that's something else again.)

Grunts are attractive schooling fishes that can grind together
teeth located deep inside their throat. They amplify the sound
with a drumlike swim bladder to produce a plaintive groaning
noise — hence their name. Though the sound can be heard underwater, it is most commonly heard after the fishes have been caught
and are writhing on the bottom of a boat. Look for densely packed
schools of young French Grunts among Staghorn Coral antlers. If
you see a school — perhaps a hundred or more — milling around a
small coral patch, move closer and watch them huddle together.
They will seem to be posing for what could be a spectacular photo-
graph.

The magnificently colored Queen Triggerfish is a fish-watcher's
prize. It can be as long as 50 cm (20 in.), with an orange-yellow
underside, iridescent blue bands from snout to eye, and a broad,
blue band near the tail. To eat a Long-spined Black Urchin, a
triggerfish grasps one of the urchin's spines, flips the urchin over,
and thereby exposes the relatively defenseless oral surface.

Angelfishes swim majestically, often aslant, as if to show you all
the beauty of their shining flanks. The French Angelfish and the
Queen Angelfish are relatively common, as is the Rock Beauty,
which is particularly abundant in the southern Caribbean. Young
French Angelfish are black, with wide, yellow, vertical bands;
when very young, they are cleaners. The Queen Angelfish has a
dark blotch, its "crown," above its eyes. The Rock Beauty's bright
yellow front and tail contrast with the deep black of the rear half
of its body.

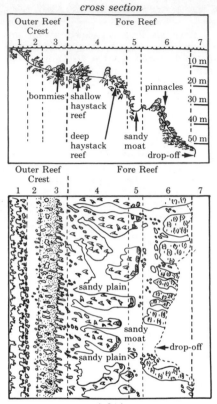

cross section

aerial view

1 = *palmata* zone (breaker zone)
2 = barren zone (lower *palmata* zone)
3 = mixed zone
4 = fore-reef terrace
5 = fore-reef escarpment
6 = fore-reef slope
7 = deep fore reef

Legend

𝖸 = live Elkhorn Coral

◁ = dead Elkhorn Coral rubble

⌂ = Boulder Coral (shallow water)

≋ = lettuce corals, *Agaricia* species

⬗ = live Staghorn Coral

⤸ = dead Staghorn Coral rubble

⌂ = Boulder Coral (deep water)

Fig. 17 Zonation of a composite Jamaican outer reef crest and fore reef — coral colonies and vertical dimensions exaggerated.

The Fore Reef

Judith C. Lang

The fore reef begins at the seaward edge of the buttress or mixed zone, at a depth of about 10 m (33 ft.). Thickets of Staghorn Coral alternate with sandy patches and channels on the fore-reef terrace. Huge, flat-topped mounds (haystack reefs), composed largely of Staghorn colonies, extend seaward, perpendicular to the shore, in a series of broad, rather parallel lobes. In some areas the channels coalesce and widen into sandy plains in the midregion of the terrace, separating some of the mounds into shallower and deeper sections. Shoreward the lobes are no higher than 1 m ($3\frac{1}{4}$ ft.), but near the seaward edge of the terrace they may be 5 m (17 ft.) or taller. A few calcareous green algae, mostly species of *Halimeda, Penicillus,* and *Udotea,* grow in the sand.

Fig. 18

Halimeda simulans

The Staghorn Coral grows in colonies on the tops and sides of the mounds, resembling the colonies in the mixed zone. Near the outer edge of the terrace its branches are shorter and more slender, and the colonies are smaller. They are separated by large areas of dead coral branches, by live colonies of the tiny yellow Branching Coral, and by scattered boulders of massive corals.

Even at these depths Staghorn colonies are moved by storms. Thus their dead bases can be successfully colonized only by sessile organisms that can survive occasional shifting, such as *Briareum* and *Erythropodium* soft corals, some other hard corals, and small algae.

Fig. 19 An outer fore-reef terrace at 16 m (54 ft.). Staghorn Coral predominates here. Small heads of Boulder Coral and various soft corals are also visible. A sandy plain is in the background.

Most of the massive corals on the fore-reef terrace form scattered outcrops on the reef lobes and sandy areas and are sometimes clumped along the flanks of the lobes. These corals are much smaller and usually less conspicuous than in shallower water. The diversity of species is much greater around the coral boulders than around the nearby colonies of Staghorn Coral. Growing on the boulder sides are platelike colonies of Yellow Porous Coral, lettuce corals, Large Cactus Coral, and *Mycetophyllia ferox* (another cactus coral). Many gorgonian soft corals (especially *Plexaura, Eunicea, Gorgonia, Muriceopsis, Pseudopterogorgia, Pseudoplexaura,* and *Plexaurella*), sponges, and fleshy algae requiring firm attachment sites also settle on these patches.

The fore-reef escarpment is a relatively gentle slope beyond the terrace. Lobes of coral continue downward, ending on a sandy plain or moat. The channels between coral masses become everwider areas of shifting sand, composed mostly of the remains of skeletons secreted by organisms growing on the terrace and escarpment. Sediment and bits of coral are stirred up by deep waves and the burrowing activities of animals, especially sea biscuits. The sediment slowly moves down the slope, often forming large cones at the bases of the channels.

Coral communities resemble those of the terrace, but massive corals, especially boulder and star corals, are more conspicuous. Staghorn Coral is still abundant but becomes increasingly smaller and sparser as the water gets deeper; it is of little importance below 20 m (67 ft.). In fact, at the escarpment base most of the Staghorn seen is simply dead rubble that has fallen from the terrace.

Calcareous algae grow on the sand at the escarpment base, as well as on the sides and bases of the hard corals. Gorgonians and sponges also grow on the hard corals of the escarpment.

Sometimes the terrace terminates with a sill (which prevents most sediment from descending any farther). In this case the escarpment will be a nearly vertical cliff or a relatively steep slope. In the dim blue world below the escarpment little light is available for photosynthesis by zooxanthellae but platelike lettuce corals and other deepwater species manage to survive.

On the fore roof slope, which angles downward less sharply than the escarpment, large areas of sand are often mixed with very evident coral outcrops — sometimes small patches, sometimes large, 10 m (33 ft.) high pinnacles. The pinnacles may be separated from the escarpment by a narrow sandy moat, itself partially filled with small outcrops of coral.

The coral communities on the outcrops and pinnacles are different from those of the terrace. Boulder Coral is the predominant frame-builder on the upper fore-reef slope, at times covering nearly half the surface. Here, though, it forms large, flattened, overlapping plates, not rounded colonies. When viewed from the side, they look shingled, like a Chinese pagoda roof. To maintain space between colonies the coral polyps extrude their mesenterial filaments, which digest many coral tissues within range (see p. 111). Encrusting organisms densely cover the undersurfaces of the shin-

Fig. 20 A fore-reef slope at 30 m (100 ft.). This pinnacle reef is composed primarily of Boulder Coral in its flattened, shinglelike deepwater form. A Black Durgon (a triggerfish) is swimming over Common Bushy Soft Coral.

gles. Sponges are among the commonest, including a few members of Class Sclerospongia (see p. 126). One study found over 300 species of attached animals inhabiting the lower surfaces of corals and other cryptic reef environments in Jamaica.

A few massive corals and platelike lettuce corals — Lamarck's, Fragile, and Sunray Lettuce-leaf Corals and *Agaricia undata,* for example — are also here, as are a few individual large round cups of *Scolymia,* the only genus of solitary coral in the Atlantic Ocean. Small fields of leafy *Agaricia* lettuce corals cover the bottom. Colorful *Mycetophyllia aliciae, M. reesii,* Large Flower Coral, and Flower Coral add beauty. In addition, a number of gorgonians grow from dead coral skeletons.

Lower on the fore-reef slope, below 45 m (150 ft.) or so, Boulder Coral diminishes. Flat, platelike lettuce corals become dominant, along with conical and columnar colonies of Large-cupped Boulder Coral. Because so little light penetrates this deep, the soft corals are species that lack algal symbionts; *Ellisella* and *Diodogorgia* are abundant.

Numerous corals on the pinnacles have been killed or colonized by numerous sessile plants and animals. Green calcareous algae — particularly *Halimeda tuna, H. gracilis, H. goreauii,* and *H. copiosa* (a uniquely deepwater plant with large, round, dime-sized segments) — are especially common colonizers. A number of sponges overgrow or bore into dead coral skeletons. Others grow on or burrow into live corals, sometimes killing them. The Orange Sponge, however, is a defender of Boulder Coral. It harmlessly encrusts the coral's lower surface and prevents boring sponges from invading the skeleton below.

Many corals, their bases riddled and weakened by boring sponges, can be pushed over by deep waves or careless divers. Platelike forms are particularly vulnerable, because they have only a small base by which to attach to the substratum. If a coral is dislodged, it may roll or slide down the slope and over the drop-off below. Most deepwater lettuce corals, however, have a thin, light, flattened skeleton, and the fall is often broken by other corals or irregularities in the reef surface. Encrusting sponges may even support such a plate and keep it on the reef long after its base has disappeared.

At 60 m (197 ft.) or so the slope contour drops off suddenly. **Caution:** It is dangerous to dive this deep. Most observations have been made from the windows of small submersibles.

Even on this vertical cliff, the deep fore reef, a few corals are visible, but they cannot build reefs. Colonies of lettuce corals are very flat and shinglelike. Large-cupped Boulder Coral forms a few flattened, encrusting heads. Deepwater *Halimeda* species can be common in the upper regions. Numerous sponges, sclerosponges, whip-shaped gorgonians, and black corals (antipatharians) also live here.

Organisms of the Fore Reef

It can be fascinating to follow a particular coral species and watch its shape change with depth. Boulder Coral, for example, forms hemispherical mounds near the surface; as the water gets deeper, the coral becomes increasingly flatter until, in water below 24 m (80 ft.), it is flat and shinglelike. As you descend, you will also see evidence of the brittle, weakened nature of corals growing beyond their optimal habitat; coral colonies so damaged by boring sponges that they have been pushed over.

Soft corals are the first indicators of deepening water. At first you may feel a sense of unfamiliarity as you look around. Then you will begin to notice that the soft corals, though no less abundant, are somewhat different from those in the shallows. For example, the featherlike Slimy and Smooth Sea Feathers may predominate in a veritable forest of sea feathers at 7–10 m (23–33 ft.); below 33 m (110 ft.), however, these species disappear, and similar, usually smaller species appear, especially the Deepwater Sea Feather. A particularly delicate soft coral below 30 m (100 ft.) is Deepwater Lace Coral.

A number of species of hard corals that are uncommon or absent in shallow water also become abundant in deep water. Solitary Large-cupped Fungus Coral and *Scolymia cubensis* produce large pie-shaped cups. Their colonial relative, Large Flower Coral, is also a deepwater inhabitant. Lettuce corals can be more than 30 cm (1 ft.) across and on many reefs are so plentiful as to form a zone around 50 m (165 ft.). When you dive, look for the distinctive cup patterns of these corals (see Pls. 10 and 11).

Black corals (antipatharians — see p. 87), with many shapes, are also found in deep water. One of the shallowest species resembles a thick wire. Others are branched or netlike and hard to distinguish from soft corals.

In water deeper than 30 m (100 ft.) pale fleshy projections extending from the sandy bottom may be sea pens, *Pennatulacea*. Look closely. All the polyps will be clustered at the top of the colonies; none will be along the sides.

Below 30 m (100 ft.) you may see Upside-down Jellyfish lying on bare expanses of sand, gently pulsating their upward-facing, zooxanthellae-filled undersides.

Unusual anemones, with a ring of tentacles around the edge of the oral disk and another around the mouth, may sometimes be found in the sand. They produce a tube (made of stinging cells, mucus, and sand grains), which makes them look somewhat like giant fanworms (sabellids), especially when the long tentacles are streaming in the current. Although these anemones — members of Order Ceriantharia — are usually nocturnal in shallow water, on the deeper slopes they may be extended during the day. (To identify species, see p. 77.)

Sponges become more and more common beyond the buttress zone or mixed zone, sometimes dominating the underwater seascape. Most scuba resorts will have "sponge gardens" listed as one of their dives. Look for the Tub Sponge and Pipes-of-Pan Sponge.

The Touch-me-not Sponge is one of the largest sponges on the terrace (see p. 253 for a warning about this species). It apparently spreads by killing corals and then growing around and over their skeletons. On the escarpment the easily identified Iridescent Tube Sponge may be growing on hard corals.

At least 100 species of lumpy, encrusting, tubular, and ropy sponges abound on the fore-reef slope. Among the more important genera are *Aplysina, Ircinia, Agelas, Mycale, Spheciospongia,* and *Cliona. Ectyoplasia* and *Plakortis* grow over coral skeletons, perhaps after killing their tissues. You will probably see *Cliona langae,* the Red Boring Sponge, and the Yellow Boring Sponge burrowing into and overgrowing live or dead corals that are not protected by the harmless crust of the Orange Sponge.

In water deeper than 20 m (67 ft.), look in caves or shaded crevices for limy orange nodular masses — usually 10–20 cm (4–8 in.) in diameter but sometimes as large as 60 cm (2 ft.). A thin layer of tissue will cover a solid calcareous skeleton. Note the radiating lines in a starlike configuration of the oscules. You have discovered *Ceratoporella nicholsoni,* one of the few Caribbean sclerosponges so far described (see p. 127), and are among the handful of divers in the world who have recognized it.

Scars of the Fireworm are seldom seen on the fore reef, but the Short Coral Snail is common on the terrace. You may also see the Caribbean Coral Snail, with its distinctive purple aperture, the Chocolate-lined Top Snail, and possibly the Lettuce Sea Slug. The Caribbean Coral Snail has not been observed feeding on living coral, but the Chocolate-lined Top Snail is a known coral-grazer, apparently with a preference for lettuce corals, such as Tan Lettuce-leaf Coral. Tiny, circular lesions are evidence of its predation. The Lettuce Sea Slug may be sitting on corals on the fore-reef lobes, presumably sunning the chloroplasts in its digestive tract.

The Long-spined Black Urchin is common on the fore-reef terrace. Feather stars (crinoids) begin to appear in numbers at about 9 m (30 ft.). Orange, plumelike arms of the Orange Sea Lily protrude from crevices. To see the beautiful Black-and-white Sea Lily, the largest and least shy crinoid, is a treat. To see it standing fully exposed on a coral head is truly memorable. The only large sea cucumber you are likely to see below 10 m (33 ft.) is the impressively active Furry Sea Cucumber.

On the fore-reef terrace a large school of small, gray Mottlefin Parrotfish will sometimes swim into your view. This fish feeds on benthic algae and (perhaps) small crustaceans; it occasionally bites off pieces of live corals. You may see a school in search of food invade the territory of a Threespot Damselfish (which is

Short Coral Snail

Chocolate-lined Top Snail

Fig. 21   Lettuce Sea Slug

common here as well as in other zones) and, owing to its vastly greater numbers, temporarily displace the damselfish. When the parrotfish depart, the algae torn loose from the substratum will slowly settle to the bottom in a green cloud. Notice that filamentous algae and the leafy brown alga *Lobophora variegata* are abundant only within damselfish territories at the outer terrace.

If a somber but curious-looking fish appears on the terrace and follows you, it is probably a Mahogany Snapper. While you are there, look overhead. Schools of iridescent Blue Chromis may be swimming by at several levels, like clouds in the sky, feeding on passing zooplankton.

In water deeper than 30 m (100 ft.) you may be lucky enough to find an acre-sized colony of Garden Eels. Each eel, attached to the bottom by a hardened, fleshy, pointed tail, will be extended vertically, facing the prevailing current. Watch the garden of eels as they all undulate to snap plankton from the water. Move closer. The nearest ones will descend into their burrows; those farther away will withdraw only partially. A perfect gradation — completely hidden, partially descended, and fully extended eels — will be visible.

A beautiful but shy deepwater fish, the Blackcap Basslet, can sometimes be seen under Boulder Coral shingles on the fore-reef slope.

Groupers appear to be more abundant in deep water. Look in caves for the Nassau Grouper, which can reach a length of 1.2 m (4 ft.). The prize, however, is the Jewfish, a veritable monster that has been reported to weigh as much as 317 kg (700 lbs.). Don't be afraid if you suddenly come upon one under a ledge. This fish is shy and has very elegant taste — it prefers Spiny Lobsters.

Variations on the Theme

On islands that slope sharply to great depths, such as Curaçao and Bonaire, the reef zones are correspondingly narrow. On these islands fringing reefs (see Chapter 2), often with well-developed *palmata* zones, merge with an extensive mixed zone that descends at a sharp angle to the sandy sea floor some 30 m (100 ft.) below the surface. Massive boulder-forming corals are dominant; Staghorn is relatively uncommon. Conversely, on some reefs the fore-reef terrace is very wide. Enormous sand plains, sometimes covered with arborescent gorgonians and soft sponges, may replace the thickets of Staghorn Coral that are so common in Jamaica.

Off Grand Cayman the fore reef is divided into an inner, shallow terrace and an outer, deep terrace. The 2 terraces are separated by a small escarpment or slope. In some areas large buttress reefs form at the seaward edge of the lower terrace.

On some windward reefs in the western Caribbean, where the seas are normally rougher than in Jamaica, the fire corals form a zone *seaward* of the Elkhorn on the reef crest and, with crustose red algae, take the full force of the breaking waves. In even more turbulent areas (parts of Panama, Mexico, St. Croix, and some eastern Caribbean islands) crustose red algae build small ridges in the region of breaking water. Elkhorn Coral is apparently successful only in the breaker or surf zones in areas of moderate wave strength.

The continental reefs, Florida, and the Bahama Islands present other variations. Most Caribbean islands were forged by smoke and flame in volcanic eruptions. As the sea rose and fell, the volcanoes acquired a mantle of coral rock. But the steep sides of the volcanic cones dictated that their reefs plunge rather rapidly into deep water.

Coral growth is different along the continental land mass and the Bahamas. Coral grows on wide, shallow platforms, often quite far from shore. The Florida Straits carry the warm waters of the Gulf Stream only a few kilometers off the Florida coast, and many of the Bahama Islands are bathed in Gulf Stream waters. The higher temperatures stimulate some surprisingly vigorous coral development.

South Florida originated as vast coral reefs that flourished about 110,000 years ago during the last major interglacial period. When glaciers subsequently formed, the sea receded and exposed the coral. The main reef became the western keys (from Big Pine Key to Key West) and the eastern part of the Florida mainland, including Miami. The eastern keys — including the islands from Fowey Rocks off Miami, past Key Largo, to the seaward edges of the keys around Big Pine Key — were formed from outlying patch reefs and longshore reefs.

Though modern fringing reefs are virtually absent off the coast of Florida, patch reefs — more or less isolated coral communities — are found 570–800 m ($\frac{1}{3}$-$\frac{1}{2}$ mi.) and more offshore along a terrace or ridge. They are probably the remains of ancient coral reefs. The 2–3 m ($6\frac{1}{2}$-10 ft.) high ridge is composed of a broad platform of gorgonians and colonies of hard corals at depths of about 7–9 m (23–30 ft.). The corals are often small and encrusting, with a few species predominating. Ivory Bush Coral, Stokes' Starlet Coral, and Large-cupped Boulder Coral are often the commonest. Sharp-hilled Brain Coral forms large, flat, bumpy patches rather than hemispherical heads. Gorgonians are abundant. Branching forms such as Tan Bushy Soft Coral, the spiny candelabrum *Muricea muricata,* its relative *Eunicea calyculata* (which is also spiny), and sea feathers are the commonest.

The patch reefs shelve to a wide, sandy plain that extends seaward for several hundred meters and to a depth of 18 m (60 ft.) or so. At this point a sheer rocky ledge plunges down 3–4 m (10–13 ft.). This is the reef crest — the uppermost portion of a well-developed reef similar to the deepwater regions of Caribbean reefs. A sloping platform ends with a rugged, hilly region at least 20 m (67 ft.) deep. This area is covered with rocky knolls, some of which are 8 m (27 ft.) high, and ends at a sill. The knolls are separated by grooves filled with rubble and sand.

Beyond the sill the reef slopes sharply, forming the outer reef slope. Hillocks become progressively smaller until, at 30–40 m (100–130 ft.), the rubble-covered fore reef slopes gently downward. All of these deepwater zones are covered with sponges and soft and hard corals wherever a sediment-free surface protrudes. Populations are similar to those found at corresponding depths in the Caribbean.

Small sandy islets, the outlying Florida Keys, have developed on drowned patch reefs. Those a few kilometers offshore in the wash of the Gulf Stream provide a suitable substratum for coral growth. You can dive on such reefs at John Pennekamp Park, Key Largo. Other well-developed reefs, all at least 5–11 km (3–7 mi.) offshore, are Looe Key off Big Pine Key, Alligator Reef, Sombrero Reef, and American Shoal. Thirteen particularly well-developed reefs form an arc beginning at Looe Key and extending toward Key West. They have well-developed *palmata* zones, buttresses of boulder corals, and many of the same faunal assemblages as classic Caribbean reefs, often in shallow water.

The Bahama Islands originated as a shallow coral-covered plateau surrounded by deep trenches. The approximately 700 islands, together called the Great Bahama Bank, are the tops of elevated areas of the plateau. The third largest barrier reef in the world lies off Andros. It is a 110 km (70 mi.) long aggregation of patch reefs strung together several kilometers offshore. Many of the islands have extensive patch reefs, some with complex zonation.

4

Jellyfish, Comb Jellies, Sea Anemones, and Corals

The members of Phylum Cnidaria and Phylum Ctenophora exhibit great diversity. Some appear to be simply blobs of jelly. Others cover rocks with bouquets of flowerlike shapes and bright colors. Still others form the boulders and calcified forests constituting coral reefs. Both cnidarians and ctenophores are radially symmetrical and are often lumped together as the Radiata. We will discuss the cnidarians first, and the ctenophores later in the chapter.

Phylum Cnidaria was formerly called Coelenterata, after the large coelenteron or body cavity, hereafter referred to as the gastrovascular cavity. This dominant feature is a hollow chamber composing much of the volume of the animal. It has the dual function of digestion and distribution of food. The most unusual characteristics of the phylum, however, are the nettlelike stinging nematocysts — poison dartlike microscopic hairs used to capture prey. The stem of the Greek word for nettle is *cnid-*, hence the phylum name, Cnidaria.

The classification of this phylum cannot be based on appearances alone, for the sex life or life history of these organisms is so unique and strange that it must also be considered. The coral polyp and the anemone are rubbery, more or less permanently attached animals with mouths and circlets of tentacles facing upward. Yet Phylum Cnidaria also includes what are commonly called jellyfish. What do the attached forms have to do with the diaphanous jellyfish slowly pulsating through the seas, with its mouth and tentacles facing *down* rather than up? The answer is complicated, for in many cases the so-called jellyfish is really the alter ego of the attached polyp.

The life cycle of the cnidarians has 2 phases — the asexual, sessile (attached to the bottom) polyp and the sexual, free-swimming medusa (what most people know as the jellyfish). Fig. 22 compares the anatomy of the 2 phases. Note that both have an oral and an aboral end. In the medusa the mouth (oral end) faces down; in the polyp it faces up. Both have a large gastrovascular cavity. The mouth is located on a projecting area of the oral disk called the manubrium. This is not pronounced on the polyp but is enlarged in the medusa. Both have masses of reproductive tissue projecting into the gastrovascular cavity; in the medusa, looked at from above (the aboral surface), they sometimes form the outline of

Fig. 22

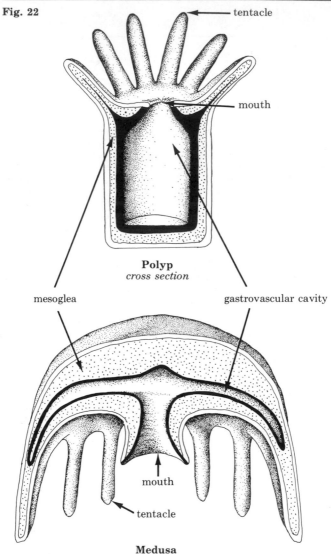

tentacle

mouth

Polyp
cross section

mesoglea

gastrovascular cavity

mouth

tentacle

Medusa
cross section

leaves of a 4-leaf clover. Both medusa and polyp have a whorl of nematocyst-laden tentacles surrounding the mouth. A major difference between the two is the presence of a largely acellular mass of jellylike mesoglea between the epidermis and gastrodermis in the medusa.

The medusa has extensions of the gastrovascular cavity called radial and ring canals. These have, at symmetrical points around the circumference of the bell, statocysts or balancing organs, which permit the jellyfish to maintain its equilibrium, oral end down, as it swims in the currents of the sea. Note that both polyps and medusae are circular or radially symmetrical.

Metagenesis. The polyp can reproduce only asexually. It produces offspring by budding — either by projecting miniatures from the body of the adult or by throwing off miniature medusae from special polyps in a colony, whose total function is to bud-off medusae. Since these polyps are interconnected with the others, the common gastrovascular cavity provides food for these specialized polyps, which lack tentacles.

After being released from the polyp, the medusa pursues a free-living life as part of the plankton of the sea. When it has grown to maturity, it produces either sperms or eggs. The sperms are released into the water and eventually enter the mouth of female medusae (often drawn in by ciliary currents) and fertilize the eggs. Usually the eggs are brooded by the medusa until the ciliated larval planula is able to swim out of the mouth. It pursues a free-living existence for a few hours or days, settles on a suitable hard substratum, and becomes a polyp.

Of what advantage is this alternation of generations or metagenesis to the cnidarians? Why pursue such a complex life cycle? The answer lies in a key concept in the theory of evolution. All species have one goal: survival. Any aspect of the life of an organism that helps maintain the existence of the species is desirable. By reproducing asexually, the polyp is able to populate an area without the services of a mate. If even one planula lands on a massive rock, its progeny can cover that rock within a short time, each resultant polyp budding-off several duplicates of itself. But therein lies the rub, for although asexual reproduction allows massive production of offspring, *each is identical to the others* because all have a common genetic heritage from the original planula. Variety is the stuff of evolution; if all members of a species are identical, any change in the environment that threatens one threatens all. If the concentration of particulate matter in the water increases, those corals with relatively weak cilia-mucus systems will die. But if in any population of coral polyps a few have an unusually effective cilia-mucus system, they will be able to remove the excess sediment and survive, passing on their genes for sediment-removal apparatus to their offspring. If the threat is constant, soon there will be no more of the original poorly ciliated ancestral variant. A new species, with enhanced sediment-removal characteristics, will appear. Sexual reproduction increases the chances for variety since the genetic makeup of one parent is mixed with that of the other, producing new combinations.

The cnidarians, then, have the best of both worlds, asexual polyps and sexual medusae. However (and there always is a "however" when dealing with living things), some kinds of cnidarians have done away with one of the phases of the life cycle. For various reasons some species have reduced the polypoid stage, and others have, for all intents and purposes, eliminated the medusa — but not its function. For while the asexual budding phase is desirable, it is not absolutely necessary. Not so for the capacity to reproduce sexually. Variety is so important that, although the medusa may be reduced to an insignificant mass of tissue, a bump on the gastrodermis of a polyp, its function is not lost. Although there may be no sign of the medusa at all, the reproductive tissue and the sexuality it represents are present in virtually all cnidarians.

Taxonomy. Cnidarians are divided into 3 classes; a major difference among them is the extent to which 1 of the 2 phases of the life cycle is reduced:

1. Class Hydrozoa — Polyp phase dominant; medusoid stage often reduced or absent. Medusae, if present, often short-lived, with a velum, or shelf, on the underside of the umbrella. Often form fuzzlike colonies of polyps on rocks. Includes **fire corals, hydroids, and siphonophores.**

2. Class Scyphozoa — Medusoid phase dominant; rarely form sessile (attached) polyps. Large, beautiful medusae are almost invariably scyphozoans. Polyps may be reduced to bumps on medusa tentacles or may be absent. Medusae lack velum. All marine. Includes **jellyfish.**

3. Class Anthozoa — Never a medusoid stage; often form large or elaborate polyps, or colonies of polyps. Includes **sea anemones, soft corals, and true (stony) corals.**

Class Anthozoa has 2 major subclasses:

1. Subclass Alcyonaria — Colonial polyps producing spicules of calcium carbonate. Body gelatinous or otherwise flexible, sometimes supported by a flexible, plasticlike rod of gorgonin, a protein similar in consistency to fingernails. Polyps often in cups. Polyps have 8 pinnate (feathery) tentacles and 8 septa. **Soft corals.**

2. Subclass Zoantharia — Either no skeleton and a fleshy body, or a hard skeleton; never a flexible skeleton. Polyps never have 8 tentacles and septa; usually have multiples of 6. Colonial or solitary polyps. **Sea anemones and true (stony) corals.**

One order of Class Hydrozoa and several orders of Class Anthozoa are important on the coral reef:

1. Order Milleporina (Class Hydrozoa) — Form hard skeletons similar in appearance to those of true (stony) corals but lacking cups. Two kinds of polyps, feeding gastrozooids and sensory, protective dactylozooids. Polyps project from pinholelike openings, often in a pattern as shown in Fig. 23. Nematocysts have a virulent toxin that causes painful, weltlike wounds on human skin. **Fire corals.**

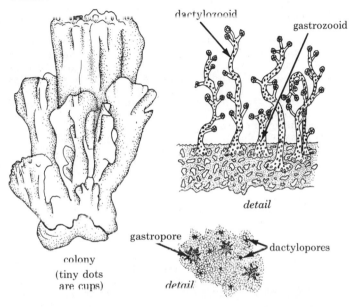

dactylozooid

gastrozooid

detail

colony
(tiny dots
are cups)

gastropore

dactylopores

detail

Fig. 23

Flat-topped Fire Coral

Redrawn, by permission of McGraw-Hill, from Libbie Hyman, *The Invertebrates: Protozoa through Ctenophora;* copyright © 1940 by McGraw-Hill.

2. Order Gorgonacea (Subclass Alcyonaria, Class Anthozoa) — Form fans, whips, and featherlike colonies that undulate with the currents. Consist of a thin, flexible calcareous covering of intermeshed spicules over a central rod of gorgonin. Polyps extend at right angles to the axis, on all sides of the stalk. **Sea fans, sea whips, and most other Caribbean soft corals.**

3. Order Pennatulacea (Subclass Alcyonaria, Class Anthozoa) — One large polyp with tiny polyps protruding from the side or top, but never on all sides of the stalk. Lack the axial rod of gorgonin, and are soft and fleshy. **Sea pansies and sea pens.**

4. Order Actiniaria (Subclass Zoantharia, Class Anthozoa) — Solitary (never form colonies); no skeleton. Fleshy body often covered with circlets of large tentacles; often large and brightly colored. Some burrow beneath the substratum, but most are sessile. **True anemones.**

5. Order Scleractinia (Subclass Zoantharia, Class Anthozoa) — Form hard calcareous skeleton with cups containing partitions (septa). Colonial, forming large masses and reefs, or solitary with 1 or few cups. Polyps never have 8 tentacles or septa. **True (stony) corals.**

6. Order Zoanthidia (Subclass Zoantharia, Class Anthozoa) — No skeleton. Form mats on rocks or rubble. Look like flat encrustations with evenly spaced openings or like green masses dominating the rubble zone behind the crest of coral reefs. Relatively few species, but can be abundant. **Colonial anemones.**

7. Orders Coralliomorpharia and Ceriantharia (Subclass Zoantharia, Class Anthozoa) — See pp. 72 and 73. **False corals and tube-dwelling anemones.**

Anatomy of a Polyp. The tentacles form a circlet around the oral disk, or peristome, in the center of which is the mouth. The pharynx is an extension of the epidermis into the body, forming a throatlike structure. It projects into the generalized body space or gastrovascular cavity which is lined with gastrodermis. The gastrodermis has several important types of cells — notably gland cells for secreting digestive enzymes and cells filled with 1-celled plants or algae. These chlorophyll-bearing plant cells (dinoflagellates) are collectively called zooxanthellae (see pp. 106–108).

The gastrodermis is folded into curtainlike projections that divide the body of the polyp internally into wedgelike segments. These projections are called mesenteries. They are always in pairs. Those that extend from top to bottom and reach inside the body as far as the pharynx are called complete mesenteries; those that do not reach the pharynx are incomplete mesenteries (see Fig. 24). In corals, between pairs of mesenteries are thin, calcium carbonate walls, the septa. The septa provide support for the coral.

The living mesentery, projecting into the gastrovascular cavity, ends in threadlike mesenterial filaments that are composed almost exclusively of gland cells. Food often sticks to these filaments and is thus exposed to the full flow of the digestive enzymes secreted by the gland cells. Digestion is rapid. The speed of the digestive process of the polyp is often demonstrated by placing a minnow in an aquarium with a Ringed Anemone (anemones are large polyps). As soon as the fish comes into contact with the tentacles, it is paralyzed and carried to the mouth. The degree of adhesion is great, and it is difficult to pull the fish from the grasp of the tentacles. Both penetrant and glutinant nematocysts (see p. 63) cause this adhesion.

After a few minutes the only visible sign of the fish is its tail

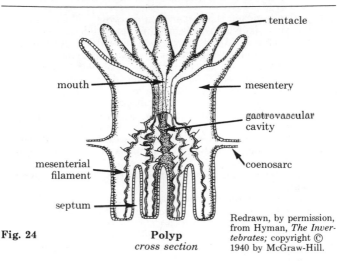

tentacle

mouth

mesentery

gastrovascular
cavity

mesenterial
filament

coenosarc

septum

Fig. 24   **Polyp**
cross section

Redrawn, by permission,
from Hyman, *The Inver-
tebrates;* copyright ©
1940 by McGraw-Hill.

protruding from the mouth of the anemone. By holding the tail to
prevent the fish from being completely swallowed or by attaching
a thread to the tail, it is possible to remove the fish and examine it
every half-hour or so. After only an hour, extensive digestion will
be visible.

Some corals feed in the same manner as anemones: they brush
the food-laden tentacles across the mouth. Others, corals with
short tentacles, use cilia-mucus systems. Small organisms and organic particles become entrapped in the mucus covering the tentacles and oral disk. They are then moved toward the mouth by
ciliary action, tracts of cilia beating toward the mouth.
Mesenterial filaments often protrude from the mouth and grasp
the food as it is carried toward the mouth by the cilia. In species
with long tentacles much of the ciliary movement is away from the
mouth toward the tips of the tentacles or down the body toward
the base of the polyp (aboral end). These corals are somewhat
more resistant to inundation with fine sand resulting from storms
or from runoff from nearby land masses, since the cilia-mucus system has as its primary function the cleansing of the body. It has
been shown that Hawaiian reef corals can survive for several hours
under 10 cm (4 in.) of sand, so short-term inundation is tolerated.
Generally, however, corals die when subjected to surprisingly
small concentrations of particulate matter if the inundation is
continuous.

Digestion begins in the gastrovascular cavity and continues intracellularly as individual cells pick up the partially digested food. Amebocytes (ameboid cells) carry food through the gastrodermis, through a thin, almost acellular inner region to the epidermal cells. The gastrovascular cavity takes the place of both digestive and circulatory systems since food is broken down and then transported in this space. The gastrovascular cavities of colonial coral polyps are interconnected; thus food obtained by one polyp can be transported throughout its own body and to other polyps.

Excretion of nitrogenous wastes (the remains of protein digestion) occurs on a cellular level; there are no excretory tissues per se. Solid wastes, such as indigestible remains of prey, are released through the mouth.

There are no respiratory structures; oxygen diffuses through the body wall.

The neural apparatus consists of a delicate nerve net composed of nerve cells (neurons). It is located around the oral disk and the mouth and extends to the tentacles. Conductivity is different from that of higher organisms since the impulse can move in both directions rather than in only one direction as in humans. Response to a stimulus is general; so whole tentacles or several tentacles might respond to a localized touch stimulus. Touching a polyp causes it and the surrounding polyps to withdraw, an indication that some neuronal connection exists between polyps.

Since cnidarians have no organs, sexual tissues consisting of sperm or egg mother cells are aggregated on the mesenteries projecting into the gastrovascular cavity. Sperms are usually shed into the gastrovascular cavity and released through the mouth. They eventually enter another polyp through the mouth and fertilize the eggs, which are brooded on the mesenteries. The larvae, called planulae, are ciliated, multicelled ovals, like hairy microscopic footballs, which swim out of the mouth to pursue a free-living existence as part of the plankton for a few hours or days. If a suitable substratum is found (that is, hard, unyielding, and not susceptible to sedimentation), the planula settles and becomes a polyp. Four, then 6 pairs of complete septa appear. Six or 12 tentacles then arise simultaneously. Very soon after settlement the polyp begins to produce its hard skeleton. After a short period of growth the new polyp will bud-off other polyps, which grow in a pattern typical of the species, producing antlerlike branching colonies, brainlike boulders, or various other shapes.

The Nematocyst. The tentacles of all cnidarians contain knobby areas that comprise groups of specialized cells called cnidoblasts (see Fig. 25). Each cell has a trigger, the cnidocil, which is usually activated by physical contact but sometimes by chemical stimuli (such as minute quantities of animal juices in the water), causing the cell to burst open and extrude its contents. Inside each cnidoblast is a coiled thread, a nematocyst, which explodes out of the cell. Only those nematocysts located in the stimulated area are discharged. The mechanism for release is probably intensified water pressure in the cell, brought about by a sudden increase in the permeability of the cell membrane. Water rushes in and the pressure increases until the operculum pops open and the nematocyst is forced out, turning inside out as a sock does when pulled off one's foot. Thus the barb or coiled thread that is inside the nematocyst as it lies in the cnidoblast becomes the tip and comes into contact with the prey.

There are at least 17 kinds of nematocysts. They are generally grouped into 3 functional categories (see Fig. 26): (1) volvents have a whiplike end that wraps around spines of prey; (2) glutinants have a sticky secretion that sticks to the prey; (3) penetrants have barbs at their tips and penetrate the prey, often injecting a toxin causing paralysis. A cnidarian may not have all of these types, but penetrants are especially common. It is remarkable that all this complex apparatus is contained inside one cell, the cnidoblast. To get the proper perspective, note the nucleus in the cell.

Cnidoblasts, containing their nematocysts, often are formed far from where they are used. They migrate, usually by ameboid movement, to the tentacles or oral disk where they lie in groups,

Fig. 25

Cnidoblast
cross section

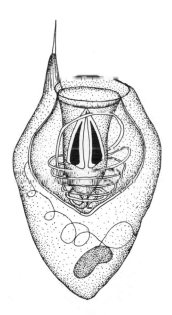

Fig. 26
Nematocysts

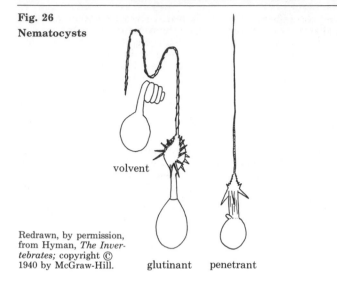

volvent

Redrawn, by permission,
from Hyman, *The Inver-
tebrates;* copyright ©
1940 by McGraw-Hill.

glutinant   penetrant

visible as knobby growths in the epidermis. When discharged, the
cnidoblasts die and are cast off. It has recently been found that
nematocysts contain a whole family of toxins; the exact composition of the poison may vary from species to species. Experiments
on small animals with extracts of these poisons reveal that they
can cause anesthesia, paralysis, itching, skin irritation, severe digestive disturbance, and congestion of the respiratory tract ending
in death. The toxins produced by corals are usually either harmless
to man or cannot normally be introduced into the body because
human skin is too thick. An exception to this is the toxin produced
by the fire corals of the genus *Millepora,* which can cause a painful
localized welt when one brushes against the coral. This welt disappears rapidly, usually after 1–2 hours, unless the victim is particularly sensitive to it. The reaction is probably a localized anaphy-
lactic (immune) response to the introduction of the proteins
constituting the toxin.

Jellyfish and Hydroids

Jellyfish. These are usually members of Class Scyphozoa. They
are rarely encountered in isolation. When conditions are right, the
millions of unseen juveniles in the water grow rapidly, and suddenly there is a bloom. The plankton is enriched by the jellyfish,

and the water is filled with pulsating, virtually transparent blobs of "jelly."

In the succession of generations, the jellyfish is the alternating form of the polyp. It is called a medusa, after a lady famous in Greek mythology for her coiffure of snakes. And the analogy is apt, for the nematocyst-bearing tentacles of the medusa are like a nest of vipers to plankton and small fish.

The medusa is wrapped in the same 2 layers of cells as other cnidarians: an outer skin (epidermis) and an inner skin (gastrodermis). The same gastrovascular cavity is responsible for digestion and circulation, with a series of canals from this central cavity to make food distribution easier. Between its 2 skins, the medusa is filled with an acellular jelly, the mesoglea.

A major structural difference between medusa and polyp is that the manubrium (mouth) of the medusa faces down. The body, or umbrella, is capable of pulsating, and the jellyfish moves by alternately expanding and contracting, forcing water out from beneath its umbrella in weak but effective jets. Medusae are perhaps the largest members of the plankton, for although they can swim, their feeble progress is no match for windborne currents and they are at the mercy of the sea. That is why, when offshore winds blow, millions accumulate in harbors on windward shores, until it seems that one could walk across the water by stepping on their dying bodies.

Only a few species of true medusae are frequently encountered in the waters off Florida and the West Indies.

Siphonophores. Animals of Class Hydrozoa, Order Siphonophora, are colonies of polyps that produce floating bells. Although they resemble true (scyphozoan) jellyfish and are closely related, the siphonophorans produce the major part of the body, the float, through the efforts of many polyps, whose lives are spent attached to the float's underside. The float has no gastrovascular cavity or system of canals; its function is exclusively to maintain the animal at or near the water's surface. Some forms actually produce a medusa-shaped float that pulsates, permitting the colony to swim.

Hydroids. Many rocks and dead heads of coral are covered with a fuzzy coating of juvenile sponges, tunicates, algae, and colonies of minute polyps of Class Hydrozoa. For the most part the polyps cannot be differentiated from the confusing mass of animals and plants crowded together on the hard surface. A few large species of hydroids (hydrozoan polyps) are recognizable. They form colonies as high as 5 cm (2 in.), some resembling white feathers, others tiny candelabra. The commonest species are members of 3 families: Sertulariidae, Plumulariidae, and Aglaopheniidae. Several species will deliver a shocklike sting if touched. Beware of the feathery colony of *Lytocarpus philippinus*. Some of the candelabrum-like hydroids will sting, too; so it is best not to touch any hydrozoan colony unless you are wearing gloves.

Common Species

Jellyfish

MOON JELLY *Aurelia aurita*   Pl. 16

Among the most beautiful and most benign jellyfish. Body bluish, transparent, to 25 cm (10 in.) across. Distinguish by the only easily identifiable structures inside its body — *the 4-leaf-clover pattern of its reproductive tissues.* It's a pleasure to float along with one, watching its body pulsate. Tentacles short, virtually invisible. Nematocysts harmless — unless you pick up a Moon Jelly in the water, in which case you will feel an unpleasant prickly sensation on your arms and chest; irritation disappears moments after you put the medusa down.

SEA WASPS   Pl. 16

Carybdea, Chiropsalmus, and related genera

Members of Order Cubomedusae are small jellyfish with *4 squared-off sides and 4 tentacles or groups of tentacles.* Body higher than wide. Can deliver a painful sting. In fact, one of the most dangerous marine animals is a thimble-sized cubomedusan of the Pacific, *Chironex fleckeri.* Those in the Caribbean are less virulent but compound the distress they cause by traveling in schools; so a person is usually stung by many jellyfish at the same time (see p. 253). Fortunately most spend the day in deep water, rising to the surface after dark. Swim rapidly, to 6 m (20 ft.) per minute. Attracted to light and to swarms of plankton drawn to light; sometimes seen near well-lit piers. Wearing a wet suit for night diving will protect you. Uncommon in shallow water except in summer, when they may appear near swimming beaches.

5 common species, most in the genus *Carybdea* (Pl. 16). All *Carybdea* species have transparent whitish bells, usually higher than wide, with 4 distinctive flaps (pedalia) under the bell, 1 at each corner of the cuboidal body. A tentacle, to 30 cm (1 ft.) long, dangles from each pedalium and is armed with venomous nematocysts that are triggered by contact with small fishes, worms, or pelagic mollusks. Once the prey animal begins to leak amino acids from its wounds, a new nematocyst barrage is triggered, and the tentacle shortens until it can place the prey in the mouth. The tentacle is so sticky that a large fish will tear it off in its struggles. *Chiropsalmus* is a genus similar to *Carybdea* but these species have *several tentacles, rather than 1, dangling from each pedalium.* In both genera, bell about 2.5 cm (1 in.) across.

UPSIDE-DOWN JELLYFISH *Cassiopeia xamachana*   Pl. 16

Perhaps the most spectacular common medusa. Mouth surrounded by frilly extensions (oral arms); these branch into thousands of lacy extensions (lappets), which look like edges of many petticoats and contain thousands of yellow-brown zooxanthellae.

Swims in the normal position (mouth down) *but flops over when it settles,* exposing underside to the sun (see p. 24). In areas with a preponderance of soft sediment, hundreds may cover the bottom. Harmless or stings mildly. Brown or olive and white. To 30 cm (1 ft.) across.

SEA NETTLE *Chrysaora quinquecirrha* **Pl. 16**
Aptly named for its bothersome sting. Common throughout Florida and West Indies. Blooms have been known to make bathing impossible, closing beaches as far north as Chesapeake Bay. May be milky white, but usually colorless with white spots scattered like stars in the sky; sometimes reddish markings radiate outward from center, like spokes in a wheel. To 10 cm (4 in.) across. Usually 24 tentacles, but as many as 40 in larger specimens. *4 simple oral arms extend from mouth for several body lengths.*

JELLYBALL or CANNONBALL JELLYFISH **Fig. 27**
Stomolophus meleagris
Large, firm, brownish hemisphere to 25 cm (10 in.) across. Bell milky bluish or yellowish, edged with a brown band. Forked lappets around mouth but no trailing tentacles. Does not sting. 16 slitlike mouths on knifelike projections on upper part of manubrium. Tiny, constantly moving tentacles drive food toward these mouths, but most food taken in by central mouth.

Fig. 27

Jellyball or Cannonball Jellyfish

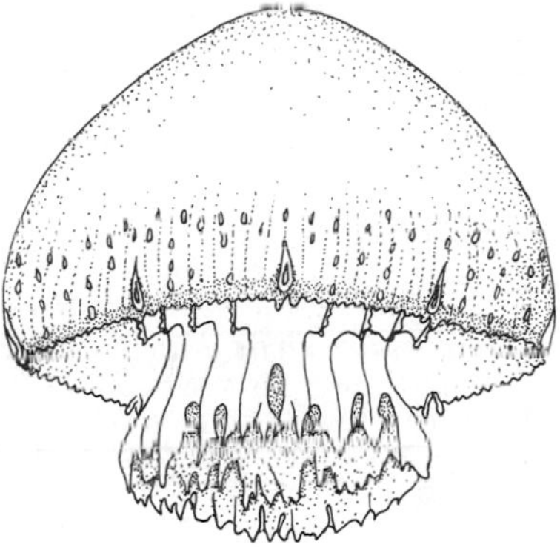

Siphonophores

PORTUGUESE MAN-OF-WAR *Physalia physalia* **Pl. 30**
Iridescent blue floats, particularly common in Florida Keys, where huge numbers may wash ashore. Float (pneumatophore) bladderlike, filled with air rich in carbon monoxide, produced by a gas

gland at its base. A complex colony of polyps suspended from pneumatophore; major types: feeding polyps (gastrozooids), each with a single branched tentacle, and short buttonlike reproductive polyps (gonozooids). Nematocysts on feeding and fishing polyps particularly virulent. Fishing tentacles to 10 m (33 ft.) long, suspended beneath the float windward. Pelagic fish such as mackerel and silversides brush against tentacles, becoming paralyzed in seconds; tentacles then shorten until within reach of the feeding polyps. Gastrovascular cavities of all polyps interconnected, allowing food to be distributed throughout colony.

Bathers coming into contact with the fishing tentacles are attacked by hundreds of nematocysts, each delivering enough toxin to cause intense pain and redness. The combined effect is like that of a whiplash. Children may be seriously injured; adults may experience discomfort for days. First aid consists of administration of a topical pain killer and antihistamines (see p. 254).

The small, banded Man-of-war Fish lives at the base of the tentacles, eating the leftovers from the colony's daily catch. It must be quite agile, for it is not immune to the venom of the jellyfish's nematocysts. If dipped up in a net with its host and inadvertently pressed against a tentacle, it will be killed.

BLUE BUTTON *Porpita porpita* **Pl. 16**
Small — about 2.5 cm (1 in.) across — shaped like an ordinary jellyfish, but has a *black margin and dark radiating lines on its float*. Similar to By-the-wind Sailor in that it has a horny chambered pneumatophore, a central feeding polyp dangling from the bottom of the float, and tentacle-like fishing polyps hanging from the margin. If you find a Blue Button in the water, look closely for the tiny pelagic sea slug, Blue Glaucus, *Glaucus atlanticus,* which feeds on it.

BY-THE-WIND SAILOR *Velella velella* **Pl. 16**
Flat disk-shaped float with a gelatinous triangular sail permanently set to steer the colony out to sea when blown by the prevailing winds, the easterly trade winds. An amazing reaffirmation of the efficacy of the evolutionary process is the fact that the sails of specimens in the southern hemisphere are set at an angle opposite that of their northern brethren so as to take advantage of the trade winds of that hemisphere. Purplish, about 7.5 cm (3 in.) across, with an internal, horny, chambered pneumatophore. Similar to Blue Button (above).

Comb Jellies

If you often swim in salt water, at one time or another you must have run across almost colorless blobs of jelly — members of Phylum Ctenophora, the comb jellies or sea walnuts. These oval blobs are especially visible at night, when the touch of an oar will cause them to luminesce. A comb jelly looks like an old-fashioned incandescent bulb, with the feebly glowing filament having 8 loops. The oval body is marked by 8 radiating lines of invisible cilia. When examined closely in the water, the 8 rows of cilia shimmer with iridescence. The cilia are arranged in comblike masses, each comb running across the row, as if a hundred combs were laid, one in front of another, around the edge of a football from tip to tip.

Comb jellies spend their lives swimming slowly through the open sea. At one end is a huge mouth that gapes wide, swallowing plankton. A gastrovascular cavity with 8 radiating meridional canals distributes the food. Most of the body is filled with the same kind of jelly (mesoglea) as in the true jellyfish. Comb jellies lack nematocysts. They sometimes have sticky cells (colloblasts) that entrap plankton. These cells are often found on a pair of tentacles, characteristic of 1 of the 2 classes of ctenophores, Tentaculata. Members of the other class, Nuda, have no tentacles. In Class Tentaculata the tentacles stretch out alongside the animal and trap plankton. Occasionally a tentacle is wiped across the mouth, which removes the food and consumes it.

Both sexes are found in the same animal. Fertilization is external; sperms and eggs are expelled through the mouth and meet outside the body.

Common Species

BEROE'S COMB JELLIES *Beroe* species
No tentacles or oral lobes. Dull milky or brownish (more opaque than *Mnemiopsis*), sometimes with red tints. To 20 cm (8 in.).

VENUS' GIRDLE *Cestum veneris*
A *flat transparent ribbon,* often 1 m (3¼ ft.) long, that inhabits open water. Swims with graceful undulations. Rows of cilia on *edges* of body. In sunlight, resplendent with iridescent colors; at night, brilliantly luminescent. Because it is elongate and flattened like a flatworm, this species has become the subject of controversies about whether it represents a transition between the 2-layered lower animals (the jellyfish) and the more complex, 3-layered higher animals.

SEA WALNUTS or LOBATE COMB JELLIES   Fig. 28
Mnemiopsis species
Transparent. Tentacles so small as to be practically invisible. Body somewhat flattened, with *2 large oral lobes* extending beyond the huge mouth. Tiny tentacles incorporated into 4 ciliated flaps (auricles) surrounding the mouth. A common species is *M. macradyi* (Fig. 28). To 10 cm (4 in.).

Fig. 28

A comb jelly,
*Mnemiopsis
macradyi*

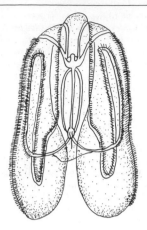

Sea Anemones

Compared with corals, sea anemones — members of Class
Anthozoa — may be thought of as giant polyps, some more than
30 cm (1 ft.) across. They often look like a mass of tentacles projecting from a crevice, swaying to and fro with the currents. Occasionally one of the tentacles will contract suddenly when some
microscopic organism touches it; but most of the time the tentacles sway gently like a long-petaled flower. The analogy to a flower
ends with appearance. Anemones are predators capable of paralyzing and engulfing animals as large as minnows and sea urchins.
One common species, the Stinging Anemone, has such powerful
nematocysts that its sting may feel like an electric shock to an
unwary swimmer.

The body of an anemone is a thick column. At its upper end is a
ring of tentacles, which may be a simple fringe of tiny, toothlike
projections, a flat mass of equal-sized, wartlike or fingerlike bumps,
or long, graceful, hollow, pointed tubes. The tentacles surround a
flat area, at the center of which is the mouth, a narrow slit. At one
or both ends of the slit is a ciliated groove, the siphonoglyph. The
groove is usually open, its cilia beating a constant stream of water
into the gastrovascular cavity to bring oxygen to the tissues inside,
which would otherwise die in the stagnant inner recesses of the
saclike body.

The whole upper surface of the anemone, on which the tentacles
and mouth are found, is called the oral disk. At the other end is the
pedal disk, the often rough-surfaced bottom of the anemone used

for attachment. It is capable of maintaining a strong adhesion to a hard surface. Scraping an anemone off a rock is difficult, even with a knife. Although anemones are considered sessile (attached) animals, they are capable of considerable movement. They can shuffle along on their pedal disks and will often move about in an aquarium. In fact, some will change position restlessly until they find a suitable area, usually a rough surface.

Anemones can eat organisms of various sizes, from microscopic plankton to small fishes. Some are primarily suspension feeders. Zooplankton are captured either by the sticky mucus-covered surface of the tentacles or by the nematocysts. The prey is passed along the oral surface of the anemone by cilia until it reaches the mouth. Although anemones have no brain as such, they do have a network of nerve cells adequate for coordinating the capture of prey and feeding. When food is placed on the tentacles, the mouth opens. The Sun Anemone has a broad, flat disk covered with short, stubby tentacles. When an unsuspecting animal, even a sea urchin, passes near the disk, it folds over the prey like a trap, tentacles bombarding the animal with nematocysts. Soon the mouth gapes wide and the prey is swallowed.

Internally, the body of an anemone is separated into compartments by curtainlike mesenteries. Each mesentery is edged with threadlike mesenterial filaments that hang free into the gastrovascular cavity and are covered with nematocysts. The latter kill and hold prey organisms while nearby cells secrete enzymes for digestion. Food molecules are distributed by ameboid cells, and wastes are egested through the mouth. There is no anus. The mesenterial filaments can be projected through the mouth or through holes (cinclides) in the sides of the body column.

Symbiotic Relationships. The combination of shelter and protection provided by the circlet of tentacles has made the anemone a favored host for a number of permanent guests.

Both the Giant Caribbean Anemone and the Ringed Anemone are hosts to Pederson's Cleaning Shrimp and the Spotted Cleaning Shrimp. These tiny, transparent shrimp have a way of waiting at the tip of a tentacle, as if expecting a fish to happen by. They will clean the anemone of debris and the fish of external parasites, and, if you present your finger to a waiting shrimp, it may do the same for you. If you poke a Ringed Anemone, you will probably provoke a Red Snapping Shrimp, hidden beneath its tentacles, to defend it.

A fascinating relationship exists between the large Star-eyed Hermit Crab and the Tricolor Anemone. The crab approaches the anemone and taps gently at the edge of its base. At first the anemone contracts, withdrawing its tentacles. After a short while the anemone relaxes, its tentacles expand, and it loosens its grip on the substratum. The crab then picks up the anemone in its claws and places it near its shell. Even rough treatment by the crab does not seem to bother the anemone now, and it uses its tentacles and pedal disk to get a firm grip on the shell. After about 3 minutes the transfer is complete. The anemone is now a permanent resident on the shell of the crab. It provides protection for the crab with its formidable nematocysts, and it receives considerable mobility as the crab bounces along the bottom searching for food. If a large Tulip or Apple Snail shell is presented to the anemone, it may be provoked to settle on the surface of the shell (the Tulip Snail is much favored), but I have never seen a Tricolor Anemone on a live snail (see p. 245).

Parazoanthus is a small button- or mushroom-shaped colonial anemone that lives on sponges. Although hundreds may cover the outer surface of the sponge, the anemones do not feed on their host but use the sponge as a surface on which to settle, thereby avoiding the desperate competition for attachment areas on the crowded reef. *Parazoanthus* may be a space parasite, robbing its host of surface area and impairing its filtering ability to some degree, or, as some think, it may actually benefit its host.

Parazoanthus is always of a color that contrasts with that of its host sponge. One would think that the anemones would have evolved camouflage to protect them from predators that, though repelled by the spicules and noxious secretions of the sponge, would pick off the bite-sized anemones. Recent studies have shown that the reverse is true. *Parazoanthus* has poison in its tissues. A small dose injected into each of 9 mullets killed all 9 in an average time of 23 minutes. So what appears to be a simple parasitic relationship has evolved into a form of mutualism: the sponge provides the substratum on which the anemone lives; the anemone provides protection for the sponge. Angelfishes and filefishes, the major sponge predators, have learned to avoid the anemones, and sponges with *Parazoanthus* on their outer surfaces are safe from predation. In fact, on many reefs the only sponges surviving are those covered with anemones. In this unusual case the parasite actually protects its host. This phenomenon is not unknown in other phyla. It is to the benefit of the parasite to keep its host as healthy as possible, for when the host dies, the parasite is doomed.

Common Species

Four orders of sea anemones are encountered in Caribbean–southern Florida waters:

1. **True anemones** (Order Actiniaria) may be solitary or may occur in groups of unattached individuals. Usually with thick columns; often with long, tapering tentacles.

2. **False corals** (Order Coralliomorpharia) may be solitary or colonial. Oral disk covered with buttonlike or wartlike tentacles or

with clumps of short hairlike tentacles. One or several mouths may project upward on short conical papillae from oral disk.

3. **Colonial anemones** (Order Zoanthidia) usually form mats of interconnecting polyps. Oral disks crowded together, each fringed with a ring of tiny tentacles. Species living on sponges are separated, distributed in rows, or scattered on the surface of the sponges but connected by rootlike stolons.

4. **Tube-dwelling anemones** (Order Ceriantharia) have elongate, wormlike bodies that secrete tubes made of nematocysts, with sand grains glued together with mucus. The common Caribbean species are nocturnal and have a fringe of long, streaming tentacles and a circlet of short tentacles around the mouth.

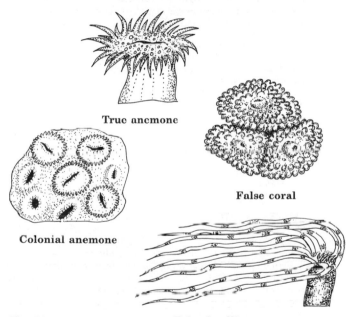

True anemone

False coral

Colonial anemone

Fig. 29   Tube-dwelling anemone

True Anemones

MAROON ANEMONE *Actinia bermudensis*   **Pl. 15**
Short tapering red tentacles in several rings around oral disk. Whole animal *maroon*. Column smooth, with circle of bright blue warts at margin. In caves and under rocks. *Similar species:* Red Warty Anemone (p. 74) is also red.

PALE ANEMONE *Aiptasia tagetes*   **Pl. 14**
Small — about 2.5 cm (1 in.) tall — brownish or whitish, and
translucent. Column thin, long. Tentacles of 2 sizes: a few long,
easily visible tentacles and many small ones visible on close exami-
nation. Disk usually 1 cm (½ in.) wide, with almost 100 tentacles in
narrow rings around edges. Usually in crowded colonies of unconnected individuals on rocks or mangrove roots.

SARGASSUM ANEMONE *Anemone sargassiensis*
Tentacles of various sizes; length of longest equal to radius of oral
disk. Reddish brown, with dull white radial lines from mouth to
base of tentacles. To 4 cm (1½ in.) across oral disk; column to 2 cm
(¾ in.) high. Soft, flabby, lightly attached. Adults under overhangs, in caves, among boulders and jetties. Young less than 1 cm
(½ in.), often on floating sargassum.

ROCK ANEMONE *Anthopleura krebsi*   **Pl. 14**
Length of tentacles equal to radius of oral disk. Tentacles greenish
yellow to dull rust-red. Column dull greenish yellow, with conspicuous *rows of rust-red warts*. To 3 cm (1¼ in.) across oral disk;
column height a little less. Intertidal, among rocks and in crevices
on exposed rocky coasts.

RINGED ANEMONE *Bartholomea annulata*   **Pl. 15**
Large. Tentacles abundant, very long — to 12.5 cm (5 in.) — thin,
quite transparent, but covered with continuous *spiral band of
white batteries of nematocysts;* project from crevice in thick mass.
Column often hidden in crevice. *Similar species:* Knobby Stinging
Anemone, *Heteractis lucida,* has white *dotlike* (not bandlike)
nematocyst batteries covering its tentacles.

RED WARTY ANEMONE *Bunodosoma granuliferum*   **Pl. 14**
About 96 short, tapering, *olive-green tentacles* splotched with
white and arranged in several rings. A fringe of leafy or bubblelike
vesicles on collar, underneath tentacles. Column covered with
warts in vertical rows. Mouth area projects from oral disk and is
usually red or scarlet. Color varies, most often brick-red. Usually
closed in daytime, looking like a red lump on rocks or coral —
about 3 cm (1¼ in.) in diameter. Stings mildly. To 8 cm (3¼ in.)
across disk when expanded. *Similar species:* Maroon Anemone
(p. 73), also red. *Related species: B. cavernata* lacks stripes on
column, white flecks on tentacles; common on mangrove roots in
brackish water in Florida.

TRICOLOR ANEMONE *Calliactis tricolor*   **Pl. 15**
On hermit crabs. A thick fringe of relatively thin tentacles gives
disk a furry look. Tentacle color varies, often white or tan. Column
usually plum or yellow-brown, with several rows of small dark
spots just above base. Usually less than 5 cm (2 in.) across disk.

GIANT CARIBBEAN ANEMONE   Pls. 15, 18, 30
Condylactis gigantea
Large and colorful. Tentacles to 15 cm (6 in.) or longer, thick, tapering, tan, usually *tipped with pink, purple, or green bulb;* faint, light, radial striations. Column thick, sometimes green, often bright orange or coral; in Florida and Bahamas often tinged with purple. Common on coral reefs and in rocky shallows.

STINGING ANEMONE *Lebrunia danae*   Pl. 15
Oral disk edged with *long tapering tentacles* (expanded at night) and shorter, highly *branched, inflatable false tentacles* (expanded during day), which are actually extensions of margin. Brown and white. *Stings.* May form network as large as 30 cm (1 ft.) of false tentacles with rest of animal hidden.

COLLARED SAND ANEMONE   Pl. 14
Phyllactis flosculifera
About 20 long tentacles (length about equal to diameter of oral disk), not always visible except at night. Column elongate, with sticky warts near base; column buried in sand. At margin of disk is a collar of many bubblelike vesicles. Disk greenish brown, dull pale violet, or ocher; to 8 cm (3¼ in.) across, usually smaller. Scattered around Red Mangrove roots or rocks from intertidal and subtidal zones to shallow depths. Very common sand-dweller.

BEADED ANEMONE *Phymanthus crucifer*   Pl. 15
About 200 *short tapering tentacles* in several rings around edge of oral disk. Most of disk covered with warts and lines radiating from mouth. Color variable, usually olive or brown and white, sometimes with red overtones. Column usually buried in sand; when disturbed, anemone withdraws beneath surface of substratum. To 15 cm (6 in.) across disk.

SUN ANEMONE *Stoichactis helianthus*   Pl. 15
Short — usually about 1 cm (½ in.) long — stubby tentacles cover oral disk, giving a *ruglike* appearance. Disk pale green, round, to 15 cm (6 in.) across. Often in groups, covering a rock. *Similar species:* Duerden's Sun Anemone, *Homostichanthus duerdeni,* has more tentacles, which are more crowded. Long column buried in sand of Turtle Grass beds; *solitary* rather than in groups.

False Corals
UMBRELLA FALSE CORAL   Fig. 30, p. 76
Paradiscoma neglecta
Oral disk flat, olive-green or brown. *Thick, stubby, irregular tentacles* of varying sizes project outward from disk edge. May have radiating white streaks on disk surface. To 8 cm (3¼ in.) across disk.

Fig. 30
Umbrella
False
Coral

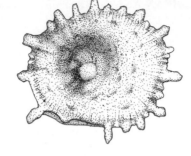

ST. THOMAS FALSE CORAL   **Pl. 14**
Rhodactis sanctithomae
Disk covered with clumps of *tiny leaflike or hairlike branched tentacles*. Tentacles at edge of disk tiny, unbranched. When expanded, oral disk may have pale blue lines radiating from central mouth to margin. Olive-green with blue overtones or purple-pink. Column edge may form low collar around disk. To 10 cm (4 in.) across disk, usually smaller.

FLORIDA FALSE CORAL *Ricordia florida*   **Pl. 14**
Tentacles *wartlike, iridescent green or orange,* scattered over disk surface. 1 or several larger wartlike projections (mouths), usually near center of disk. Crowd together on rocks to form mat, often encrusting young Lister's Tree Oysters. Individuals to 2.5 cm (1 in.) across disk.

Colonial Anemones

ENCRUSTING COLONIAL ANEMONE   **Pl. 14**
Palythoa caribaeorum
Forms a flat *leathery tan or white mat* on rocks or dead coral. Individuals usually 1 cm ($\frac{1}{2}$ in.) or less across disk. Colony often less than 1 m ($3\frac{1}{4}$ ft.) in diameter, forms an irregular patch on rocks. Many individuals in colony may be closed, so fringe of tiny tentacles not always visible. *Related species:* (1) *P. variabilis* forms brown leathery polyps connected at bases by tubelike stolons; not usually crowded into mats. To 3 cm ($1\frac{1}{4}$ in.) across disk. Sometimes among Green Colonial Anemones, often buried to disk in sand. (2) *P. grandiflora* is larger — to 4 cm ($1\frac{1}{2}$ in.) across disk, to 6 cm ($2\frac{1}{2}$ in.) tall. Oral disk brown; tentacles lighter than disk.

SYMBIOTIC COLONIAL ANEMONES   **Pl. 19**
Parazoanthus species
Live on sponges. Small — to 6 mm ($\frac{1}{4}$ in.) in diameter and height.

Contrastingly colored mushroomlike polyps scattered over surface of sponge. (1) *P. swiftii* is common, bright *orange or yellow,* with 26 tiny tentacles; to 2.5 mm (1/12 in.) across disk. (2) *P. parasiticus* (Pl. 19) is *tan or brownish,* with a white column and 28 brown tentacles; to 1.5 mm (1/16 in.) across disk; scattered over surface of many sponges, especially Red Boring, Common Loggerhead, and Tube Sponges. (3) *P. puertoricense* is *maroon or burgundy;* common on Pipes-of-Pan Sponge in deep water.

GREEN COLONIAL ANEMONE Pl. 14; Fig. 31
Zoanthus sociatus
Forms a *green mosaiclike mat* on bottom, coral rubble, or in crevices between coral heads. Individuals about 2.5 cm (1 in.) tall, fleshy. Oral disk green, about 9 mm (3/8 in.) in diameter, surrounded by 2 adjacent rings of about 30 short stubby tentacles. *Related species: Z. solanderi* is similar but slightly larger.

Fig. 31

Green Colonial Anemone

Tube-dwelling Anemones

BANDED TUBE-DWELLING ANEMONE Pl. 15
Arachnanthus nocturnus
In shallow or deep water brown tube projects from rubble or sand-covered rubble. *Marginal tentacles predominantly brown-and-white banded* when contracted; banding less visible when tentacles expanded. Inner tentacles short, incurved. Outer tentacles of several sizes, tend to stream in direction of current; fewer than 100 tentacles in outer ring. Nocturnal. Usually 1–2 cm (1/2–3/4 in.) across disk.

AMERICAN TUBE-DWELLING ANEMONE
Ceriantheopsis americanus
Lives in smooth tube made of nematocysts, sometimes covered with sand grains or mud. Tube projects from sandy bottom. 2 rings of tentacles: *outer ring of over 100 (100–125) equal-sized tentacles,* usually brown but may be maroon or purple; inner ring of short tentacles around mouth. Body elongate, wormlike, to 20 cm (8 in.) long. Usually nocturnal. Often in intertidal or shallow subtidal zone.

Corals

Imagine a landscape of white rock pockmarked with thousands of holes. At night, out of each hole extends a hand with 6 or more fingers, writhing and snapping at anything that passes by. To complete this bizarre scene, visualize the hands covered with hairs. To touch these hairs could mean instant death, for some are poisonous. Now imagine a generous dollop of mucus covering everything. Each hand is connected to the others by a thin layer of tissue extending over the surface of the rock, so the whole is a mat of living tissue.

This science-fiction description is close to the reality faced by minute planktonic organisms floating helplessly toward a coral reef in warm tropical seas. The hands referred to are the coral animals or polyps, each with 6 or more tentacles armed with cells capable of shooting out threads tipped with poison or sticky mucus, or whiplike ends that can entrap and wrap around anything with spines or projections. No other animal group uses these unique weapons; few other animals can remove tiny organisms from the water with such efficiency. Virtually nothing can be found in the water of the lagoon after it has swept across the coral reef; almost all the plankton has been removed by the carnivorous polyps. Yet, as efficient as the colony of coral animals is, its huge biomass cannot be sustained by what it can trap in the water sweeping over the reef. The great enigma of the tropics is the way in which the coral colony survives in seas whose meager crop of plankton cannot possibly meet its nutritional needs.

What Is Coral? The coral animal, or polyp, has a columnar form. The lower end is attached to a hard floor of its own making; the upper end is free to extend into the water column. It consists of a circlet of tentacles surrounding an oral disk containing a slitlike mouth. The animal has only 2 major layers to its body: an outer skin, the epidermis, and an inner layer, the gastrodermis. (A third layer, consisting primarily of fibers and an acellular jelly, the mesoglea, is rudimentary.) The epidermis and gastrodermis can perform virtually all the functions necessary to sustain life. Together, they compose the coenosarc, or living tissue, of the polyp. The coenosarc extends from the body of each polyp to its neighbors. Thus the whole colony, often consisting of thousands of individuals, is connected in one mass of living polyps — each capable of independent existence. Yet the internal space in the body of each polyp, the gastrovascular cavity, is connected to that of the others. Food that passes through the mouth enters the gastrovascular cavity and is rapidly digested. It can then travel by diffusion or be carried by ameboid cells (amebocytes) throughout the communal body to any of the polyps.

The tentacles are retractile, with muscle fibers running through them and along the length of the body. Relaxation of these fibers allows the body and tentacles to extend to their maximum length, in many cases one to several millimeters. Each polyp sweeps the water in a tight circle, the circumference of which abuts that of its neighbor, making an almost impenetrable network of tentacles. Water currents, usually wind-blown, carry plankton toward the reef. These minute animals and plants are as a rule relatively helpless, being able to swim only feebly against the currents. As they brush by the tentacles of the polyps, they trigger the explosion of specialized cells in the epidermis that extrude long, hollow, microscopic hairs called nematocysts, which unravel in a burst, penetrating or sticking to the planktonic organism and capturing it. The tentacle then retracts rapidly, wiping the organisms it has captured across the mouth, which takes in the prey, passing it down the muscular pharynx (throat) into the gastrovascular cavity where it is digested.

There are 2 kinds of corals, hard and soft, depending on the type of skeleton they secrete. The polyps of hard corals deposit around themselves a solid skeleton of calcium carbonate, most familiar to us as chalk. The epidermis of the hard coral secretes walls of calcium carbonate, so the animal is in a cup or corallite, into which it withdraws in the daytime. Thus most swimmers see only the skeleton of the coral. Only at night, in the bright beams of an underwater light, will the observer see the coral as a mound of fuzz — the polyps extended and sweeping the water. Thin partitions of calcium carbonate are secreted inside the body. They correspond with thin layers of tissue dividing the body into pie-shaped wedges and are called mesenteries. Each mesentery surrounds its own stony partition, a septum; so when the polyp dies it leaves behind a distinctive pattern of radiating walls inside the cup.

The soft corals have microscopic needlelike spicules of calcium carbonate embedded in a soft matrix rather than a solid mass. They are often supported by a horny substance, gorgonin, to form colonies with the shape of a flexible plume or fan. These are the exquisite sea whips and sea fans that undulate with the currents, their color and action rivaling that of the reef fishes. The polyps of the soft corals can also be retracted into their cups, but they are often extended during the daytime, giving the coral the appearance of thick, brown, green, or purple fingers protruding from rocks or reefs. Run your fingers down one of these plumes. It will shrink, the polyps retracting to leave just a network of thin, flexible rods, usually about the thickness of a pencil.

Coral polyps range in size from less than 1 mm ($\frac{1}{16}$ in.) to 25 cm (10 in.). There are 2 easily recognized types, corresponding to the natural division between the hard and soft corals. The polyp of a soft coral always has 8 tentacles and 8 septa. The term *octocoral* is applied to this group. The 8 tentacles are always pinnate — that is, they have small lateral projections, giving the tentacles a feathery appearance.

The hard corals have 6 or more tentacles, but never 8, and, though the tentacles can have various shapes, they are never pinnate. Under a microscope the tentacles of live polyps appear to be covered with fine hairs. These cilia, moving in the semiliquid mucous medium that covers the polyps, keep detritus from smothering the organism. Corals are, however, susceptible to sedimentation. If the water in which they live contains even relatively small quantities of suspended sediment, this will overwhelm the cilia-mucus system, and the corals will die. The degree of sensitivity to sedimentation is demonstrated by the remaining corals in the coastal waters of the United States. Fewer and fewer living corals are found in John Pennekamp Park in the Florida Keys because of the sediment released from construction in areas more than 65 km (40 mi.) away.

HARD CORALS

The polyp of a hard coral continually secretes a skeleton around itself. Thus its cup grows in both length and diameter. Because the bottom of the cup is renewed frequently, the polyp is continually pushed up and remains on the surface of the mass as it enlarges.

The skeleton of the colony as a whole is termed the corallum; thus the whole boulder or branched colony is the corallum. The cup in which an individual polyp grows is the corallite. The bottom of the corallite beneath the polyp is the basal plate. When horizontal plates are produced across the bottom to raise the polyps, they are called dissepiments if they are small and tabulae if they extend across the whole bottom. The hard wall of the corallite surrounding the polyp is the theca. If there are small extensions of the septa at the bottom of the corallite, these are called pali. If the septa extend above the top of the corallite onto the surface of the corallum, they are called exsert (protruding) septa. The septa sometimes fuse with a central supporting rod called the columella. When the polyp is dead, what remains is a distinctive pattern of radiating septa, both complete and incomplete, and the central, rodlike columella. These structures are used to differentiate the corals from one another, since the number and shape of the septa differ from species to species.

The living tissue, or coenosarc, of the polyp extends out of its corallite and across the top of the corallum to join with neighboring polyps. Thus the whole surface of a piece of coral is covered by a continuous mat of living tissue. It is invisible to the naked eye because it is transparent; it feels slimy because it is covered by mucus. The term *coenosarc* is also appropriate for the mat of tissues between the polyps, because it is essentially a continuation of the polyp and has both epidermis and gastrodermis (see Fig. 32). The identical nature of polyp and interpolyp tissue mass is demon-

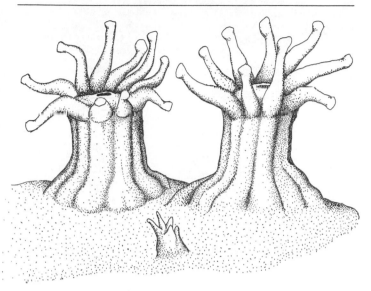

Fig. 32 3 Coral polyps attached by a common coenosarc

strated by those species that bud-off to produce daughter polyps — first a mouth appears, then a tentacular ring, anywhere on the mass of tissue between the polyps. Mesenteries form soon after, and the new polyp is complete.

The polyps may be widely spaced, each occupying its own complete corallite, or the corallites may have common walls. If the corallites are so close together that they join one another to form sinuous valleys, the result is a meandrine (meandroid) or brain coral. In this case the polyps are incomplete, consisting of a common fringe of tentacles and many mouths and pharynges (see Fig. 33).

At first sight one is overwhelmed by the gorgeous coloration and great variety of organisms around the coral reef. After many viewings and a surprisingly long time one's awe subsides somewhat and various features begin to become apparent. With study, even the exotic coral reef assumes the proportions of a typical ecosystem. There are the eaters and the eaten, the camouflaged and the obvious, the plants and the animals. Eventually it is possible to discern repetitions in types of corals and to distinguish zones where one or several species predominate. Even on clearly zoned reefs a few hours of study will enable one to recognize the dominant organisms.

Fig. 33

**A group of
incomplete polyps —
characteristic of
brain corals**

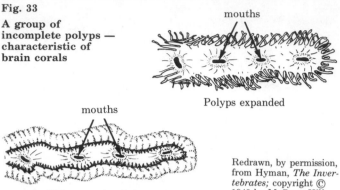

mouths

Polyps expanded

mouths

Polyps contracted

Redrawn, by permission,
from Hyman, *The Inver-
tebrates;* copyright ©
1940 by McGraw-Hill.

Common Species

STAGHORN CORAL *Acropora cervicornis*   **Pl. 7**
Colonies cylindrical, branched. *Cups protruding, tubular.* Not in
Bermuda or Brazil.

ELKHORN CORAL *Acropora palmata*   **Pl. 7**
Colonies flattened, branching, resembling *moose* (not American
Elk) *antlers.* Cups protruding, tubular. Golden-brown when alive.
Not in Bermuda.

TAN LETTUCE-LEAF CORAL   **Pl. 11**
Agaricia agaricites
Colonies tan, sometimes leafy, sometimes encrusting or amorphous. May have thin, delicate, *leaflike plates* with cups on both
sides or may encrust sides of other corals. May form flat plates over
30 cm (1 ft.) in diameter in deep water. Pattern of cups distinctive.
Columella present. To 36 septa per cup.

LAMARCK'S LETTUCE-LEAF CORAL   **Pl. 11**
Agaricia lamarcki
A deepwater species, forming *flat plates in water deeper than 8 m*
(27 ft.). Prominent columella. 22–26 septa per cup. Several other
Agaricia species are similar; see plate for distinctive arrangement
of cups.

SUNRAY LETTUCE-LEAF CORAL   **Pl. 11**
Helioseris cucullata
Common in water deeper than 8 m (27 ft.). Forms large flat plates.
No columella.

TUBE CORAL *Cladocora arbuscula*   **Pl. 7**
Mass of *small white tubes,* each ending in a cup about 3.5 mm
(⅛ in.) in diameter. Branches have fine longitudinal ridges continuous with septa. About 36 septa per cup.

LARGE GROOVED BRAIN CORAL   **Pl. 9**
Colpophyllia natans
Convex boulders 1 m (3¼ ft.) or more in diameter. Brown, with
greenish valleys. Wide hills. Valleys large, deep, 1.5–2 cm (¼–¾ in.)
wide. *A thin lengthwise groove on each hill.* Colony often eroded
at base, forming overhangs. 8–12 toothed septa per cm.

PILLAR CORAL *Dendrogyra cylindrus*   **Pl. 7**
Groups of *pillarlike spires* to 3 m (10 ft.) high. Often covered with
olive-drab hairlike polyps in daytime. Winding narrow valleys;
thick toothless septa.

STOKES' STARLET CORAL   **Pl. 10**
Dichocoenia stokesi
Small, heavy, hemispherical boulders — to 30 cm (1 ft.) in diameter, usually less. *Oval cups* with toothless septa *project from surface.* Alternately thick and thin septa, 20 per cm.

SHARP-HILLED BRAIN CORAL   **Pl. 9**
Diploria clivosa
Usually encrusting, rarely hemispherical. Brown, with greenish
valleys. *Sharp* narrow *hills* — to 1.5 mm (1/10 in.) wide. Valleys
much wider — to 6 mm (¼ in.). Alternating wide and narrow
septa, about 35 per cm. Not in Bermuda or Brazil.

DEPRESSED BRAIN CORAL   **Pl. 9**
Diploria labyrinthiformis
Large, hemispherical, yellow to brown heads. Flat wide hills — to
2 cm (¾ in.) wide. Valleys much narrower. *A depression runs the
length of each hill.* 14–17 septa per cm. Common in rear zone.

COMMON BRAIN CORAL *Diploria strigosa*   **Pl. 9**
Medium-sized, hemispherical, greenish brown colonies. *Rounded*
(not sharp) *hills; almost as wide as valleys* — to 4.5 mm
(3/16 in.) without depressions. 15–20 septa per cm.

FLOWER CORAL *Eusimilia fastigiata*   **Pl. 10**
Short thick branches, each with a *large cup at the end.* Cups oval,
to 3.5 cm (1½ in.) long, usually less than 2 cm (¾ in.). 15–18 toothless septa per cm.

STAR CORAL *Favia fragum*   **Pl. 10**
Small hemispheres or ovals — no more than 5 cm (2 in.) in diameter. Yellow-brown. *Cups* usually angular, oval, less than 6.5 mm
(¼ in.) across, *widely separated by flat-topped walls.* 36–40 septa
per cup, with small irregular teeth. *On rocks or dead coral* in shallow water.

ROUGH STAR CORAL *Isophyllastrea rigida*   **Pl. 8**
Small, green, brown, or purple hemispherical boulders with short
stalk. Cups irregular, large — 1 cm (½ in.) or more in diameter.
Valleys whitish, slightly sinuous, moderately elongate, usually not
connected to one another. 25–30 septa per cup; each septum with
6–8 large teeth, lower teeth largest.

CACTUS CORAL   **Pl. 8**
Isophyllia sinuosa forma *multiflora*
Small, greenish or grayish, hemispherical heads — usually less
than 15 cm (6 in.) in diameter. Some short sinuous valleys, but
most cups simple, unconnected, large with *large-toothed septa.*
8–12 septa per cm. Young colonies, to 13 cm (5 in.), are often
round, with valleys in a radial arrangement.

STALKED CACTUS CORAL   **Pl. 8**
Isophyllia sinuosa forma *sinuosa*
Small lavender or green hemispherical heads on *short stalks.* 1 or
several *winding valleys with lobes radiating from center.* 7–9 septa
per cm; each septum with 6–10 coarse teeth.

BRANCHING CORAL *Madracis mirabilis*   **Pl. 7**
Dark brown, *brittle,* short branches with blunt forks at tips. Forms
slightly convex pillow-shaped colonies, sometimes several meters
in diameter, in water usually deeper than 6 m (20 ft.). Branches no
thinner than 6 mm (¼ in.). *Spines between cups. Related species:*
Encrusting Madracis, *M. decactis* (Pl. 7), is a deepwater encrusting
form; may form small boulders, nodules, or even short clubbed
branches. Resembles Yellow Porous Coral (p. 85) but not porous
and cups separated, not adjoining (see Pls. 7 and 8 for comparison).

COMMON ROSE CORAL *Manicina areolata*   **Pl. 9**
Yellow, oval, with *undulating edges. Upper surface flattened.* Usually 7.5 cm (3 in.) long. Young colonies stalked. Older colonies
break free, but signs of stalk evident underneath. 18 septa per cm.
Almost exclusively in Turtle Grass beds or lagoon, lying free in
sand. *Related species:* Rare Rose Coral, *M. mayori* (Pl. 9), possibly
a variant of Common Rose Coral, is a *rare* brown brain coral.
Resembles Depressed Brain Coral (p. 83) but *hills deep-grooved.*
12 septa per cm.

TAN BRAIN CORAL *Meandrina meandrites*   **Pl. 9**
Tan, flat or hemispherical boulders over 30 cm (1 ft.) in diameter.
Alternating small and large septa meet at top of hill, septa of
adjacent valley in zigzag arrangement. About 7 large septa per cm.

CRENELATED FIRE CORAL   **Pl. 11**
Millepora alcicornis
Flat, vertical, yellow-tan plates *lacking visible cups.* Upper edge of
plates *crenelated, bumpy, white-tipped.* Common on most of reef,
especially near shore. Contact produces painful welt.

FLAT-TOPPED FIRE CORAL Pl. 11
Millepora complanata
Similar to Crenelated Fire Coral (above) but *colony top squared off,* not bumpy.

ENCRUSTING FIRE CORAL *Millepora squarrosa*
Purplish crusts on rocks and coral inshore. Wrinkled; tops of wrinkles white. Cups not visible.

BOULDER CORAL *Montastrea annularis* Pl. 8
Commonest Caribbean coral. *Boulders* 1.5 m (5 ft.) or more in diameter. Green, tan, or brown lobate heads, often showing white damaged areas. *Cups shallow, circular,* about *2-2.5 mm ($\frac{1}{12}$ in.) in diameter.* Radiating septa in 3 cycles, first 2 fusing in center with columella. Fine regular teeth on septa. Forms shinglelike colonies in deep water.

LARGE-CUPPED BOULDER CORAL Pl. 8
Montastrea cavernosa
Large boulders over 1.5 m (5 ft.) in diameter. *Cups large, distinctive, blisterlike,* to 8 mm ($\frac{3}{8}$ in.) in diameter. 48 septa per cup.

LARGE FLOWER CORAL *Mussa angulosa* Pl. 10
Thick short branches, each ending in 1 or several large cups. *Cup size distinctive — to 4 cm ($1\frac{1}{2}$ in.) or larger.* Septa have coarse teeth pointing obliquely upward. 8 septa per cm.

LARGE CACTUS CORAL Pl. 8
Mycetophyllia lamarckiana
Flat pancakelike colonies, usually with *scalloped edges* and discontinuous radiating ridges, like spokes in a wheel. Brown, with green overtones. *Many septa extend vertically from surface.* Many growth centers surrounded by radiating septa. 2 or 3 vertical rows of septa lengthwise in each valley. 8-10 septa per cm, each with 7-9 large teeth pointing obliquely upward. Several other *Mycetophyllia* species are similar.

IVORY BUSH CORAL *Oculina diffusa* Pl. 7
Lumpy horizontal branches, never vertical fingers. Covered with olive-drab coenosarc when alive. *Cups far apart, slightly projecting.* Branches less than 1 cm ($\frac{1}{2}$ in.) thick. Colonies extensively branched. 24 septa per cup. Usually in calm sandy areas. *Related species: O. valenciennesi* is similar, but its branches are thicker than 1 cm ($\frac{1}{2}$ in.).

YELLOW POROUS CORAL *Porites astreoides* Pl. 8
Sulfur-yellow, lumpy, encrusting colonies. To 60 cm (2 ft.), usually much smaller. Typically porous appearance under lens. Septa have small rough teeth. 12 septa per cup.

THIN FINGER CORAL *Porites furcata* Pl. 7
Forked, vertically branching colonies. Each branch to 1 cm ($\frac{1}{2}$ in.)

in diameter. Branches not clubbed at ends. Rare variant is bright purple. Can cover bottom for acres, forming shallow flats. Porous.

THICK FINGER CORAL *Porites porites*   **Pl. 7**
Commonest finger coral. *Branches* usually 2 cm (¾ in.) or thicker, *with swollen tips.* Forms clumps of thick branches, often with grayish polyps extended in daytime to give a fuzzy appearance.

LARGE-CUPPED FUNGUS CORAL   **Pl. 10**
Scolymia lacera
Solitary large-toothed cup to 7.5 cm (3 in.) in diameter. No branches. Septa radiate from cup center. In water deeper than 15 m (50 ft.).

SHALLOW-WATER STARLET CORAL   **Pl. 10**
Siderastrea radians
Hemispherical grayish heads with *black dotlike cups scattered over surface. Cups angular* rather than round; deep and narrow. Often forms small round pebbles to 2.5 cm (1 in.) in diameter in silty water, Turtle Grass beds. Forms crusts on rocks. 30–40 septa per cup.

ROUND STARLET CORAL *Siderastrea siderea*   **Pl. 10**
Large hemispherical boulders on reef, often over 60 cm (2 ft.) in diameter. Similar to Shallow-water Starlet Coral but *cups shallower* and *larger* — to 5 mm (¼ in.) across. 50–60 septa per cm.

RED or ORANGE CORAL *Tubastrea coccinea*   **Pl. 10**
Small clumps of *orange or red* coral. *Large yellow polyps* visible at night. Usually on shaded sides of other corals; on some reefs (for example, off Bonaire) encrusts whole rocks. No zooxanthellae. *Cups* to 9 mm (⅜ in.) in diameter; *project about 1 cm (½ in.)* from spongy encrusting base.

SOFT CORALS

Robert Kinzie III

The soft corals are members of Class Anthozoa, Subclass Alcyonaria. For many people the idea of a soft coral might seem to be a contradiction in terms. When we think of coral, we usually think of coral islands, with their wave-resistant reefs and sandy beaches. How could a soft-bodied organism stand up to the might of crashing waves, hurricanes, and constant erosion by wind and rain above sea level and by currents below it? But the familiar hard coral rock you are familiar with is only one sort of coral skeleton. The animals that secrete this rock have close relatives whose skeletons are as soft as jelly. All corals have mineral skeletons made of calcium carbonate, a chalklike material. The cohesiveness and extent of the skeleton determine whether the coral is hard or soft. The Caribbean excels in the abundance and importance of the soft corals called gorgonians — sea fans and sea whips. It is unclear why these beautiful corals should be so common in the Caribbean and so uncommon in other tropical seas.

The anthozoans are divided into 2 major groups based on the appearance of the polyp.

One group, descriptively called octocorals, has polyps with 8 pinnate arms. An astounding thing about this group is that no matter how different the lifestyles, ecological habitats, size, or nature of the species, all octocoral polyps are remarkably similar (see Pl. 12).

The second group of anthozoans (the zoantharians, including the hard corals) has already been discussed (see pp. 80–86). One zoantharian group, however, has a soft skeleton of sorts. This group is known as the antipatharians, or black corals. The name comes from the ancient belief that the dark, horny, central, axial skeleton of these animals was an aid against (*anti*) disease (*pathes*). Today jewelry is made from the proteinaceous skeletons of these zoantharians, which in some degree may account for their increasing rarity.

Except for the black corals and the skeletonless zoanthids, all the animals referred to as soft corals are octocorals (gorgonians). Interestingly, this group, almost synonymous with the term *soft coral,* includes some quite hard species (though not in the Caribbean), such as Blue Coral, red Organ-pipe Coral, and red or pink Precious Coral.

The peculiar sea pansies are members of a group of more or less soft octocorals, the pennatulaceans or sea pens. These colonial animals are specialized for living on soft bottoms, using a fleshy stalk that is embedded in the substratum. The sea pansy, *Renilla,* is not uncommon in some shallow-water areas. It looks like a flat-topped mushroom with polyps growing from the upper surface. The true sea pens, although they are usually restricted to deeper water in the Caribbean, may occasionally be encountered by scuba divers. They may be distinguished from deepwater gorgonians by the fact that they attach to soft sediment rather than to hard bottoms as the gorgonians do. Their polyps grow from the tip or from one side of the stalk only.

Excluding the aforementioned organisms, any soft coral you find when you are snorkeling or scuba diving in the Caribbean is likely to be a gorgonian.

The gorgonians are all colonial octocorals with skeletons composed at least partially of more or less (usually less) consolidated bits of calcium carbonate called spicules. The taxonomy or classfication of the gorgonians is based primarily on the microscopic structure of these tiny pieces of calcium carbonate. The amazing ability of the gorgonians to modify colony form, color, size, and relative proportions within a species makes the use of such details indispensable for proper classification.

You can get a pretty good idea of what spicules look like by simply taking a bit of dried gorgonian tissue, soaking it in a few drops of Clorox, and looking at what's left with a simple hand lens or magnifying glass. The procedure will reveal the colors and the spiny nature of the spicules. These spicules form part of all gorgonian skeletons. In one group, the scleraxonians, they are the main constituents of the skeletal structure.

The remaining gorgonians, called holaxonians, have in addition to the spicular skeleton a central (axial) skeleton made of a horny substance called gorgonin, a proteinaceous material like hair and fingernails but rich in iodine and bromine. The skeletons of dead gorgonians are often found in the flotsam on the high-tide line on Caribbean beaches, and their brown color and fibrous composition may lead you to confuse them with small bits of driftwood. However, by lighting a part with a match, you can quickly tell the difference. If it is a gorgonian, there will be no smell of burning driftwood.

In most cases the polyps that form each gorgonian colony are supported by the axial skeleton. It is the flexible nature of this skeleton that gives the names sea fans and sea whips to these animals. The living tissue covers the gorgonin skeleton, and inside this tissue are embedded the calcium carbonate spicules. The surface of the colony is covered with the polyps. Often many hundreds or even thousands make up a single colony. These polyps are all connected by a primitive nervous system (touch a single expanded polyp and you will see its neighbors gradually contract) and by a common digestive system (food eaten by one polyp is shared with its neighbors). The polyps may be expanded, giving the colony a fuzzy or even bushy appearance, or contracted, leaving only tiny slits or dimples to show where the polyps have retracted into the protection of the spicule-embedded tissue. Polyps may be more than 1 cm ($\frac{1}{2}$ in.) long, including tentacles; the shortest are about 1.6 mm ($\frac{1}{16}$ in.) long.

Feeding and Nutrition. Corals, both hard and soft, employ a similar nutritional mode, one of the most successful and unique in the oceans. They are voracious and efficient carnivores. Like some of the hard corals, gorgonians catch minute prey with their nematocyst-laden tentacles. Hard and soft corals, however, use different methods to capture prey. The nematocysts of the gorgonians are small and evidently less potent than those of many other reef cnidarians. Their tentacles are usually rather weak and stiff, unlike the sinuous tentacles of many hard corals. Another obvious difference is that most gorgonians extend their tentacles during the day, whereas many stony corals characteristically are retracted by day and feed actively only at night.

Since the zooplankton in the vicinity of reefs is much more

abundant at night than in daytime, it appears that the gorgonians are either somewhat stupid in comparison to hard corals — or that they are up to something entirely different. As already stated, many reef animals — including the hard reef-building corals, the shallow-water gorgonians and anemones, and even the Giant Clam of Pacific fame — harbor within their cells single-celled algae called zooxanthellae. These algae, like all photosynthetic plants, can use the energy derived from sunlight to turn water and carbon dioxide into food. However, they lack an adequate supply of some essential elements. They obtain some of these from the waste products of the polyp. Bathed in tropical sunlight, the zooxanthellae and their animal partners have created highly productive ecosystems, the coral reefs, in ocean waters that in other situations are notably unproductive. It appears, from their relatively feeble prey-catching ability and from the fact that their zooxanthellae-packed tentacles are extended during the sunlit but prey-poor daytime, that the gorgonians may be specialists at the photosynthetic end of the scale, while the stony corals tend to function toward the actively carnivorous end. As usual there are exceptions, but it seems that in general this is how the 2 related groups of colonial reef corals, hard and soft, avoid competition. Consequently, both are able to grow luxuriantly in very much the same habitats.

Reproduction. Like the stony corals, gorgonians generally reproduce sexually. Sperms and eggs unite to form the basis for a new individual and eventually a new colony. As far as is known (which isn't very far at all), a gorgonian colony is either entirely male or entirely female. It also seems that a male colony will stay male and a female colony will stay female. Although this seems a very complicated way to say what is taken for granted in most of the animals we are familiar with, the various combinations and permutations of maleness and femaleness in other reef organisms may be bewildering indeed.

In the few species of gorgonians whose reproduction has been studied, it appears that millions of sperms are, at certain times of the year, simply pumped out into the surrounding water. They then somehow locate a female gorgonian polyp of the same species, enter the gastrovascular cavity, and fertilize the eggs, which are attached to cells lining the cavity. Think for a moment of the probability of a thing the size of a sperm (1 sperm = 10 micrometers; 24,000 sperms = 1 in.) coming into contact with a gorgonian of the right species, the right sex, and the right sexual condition. No wonder so much energy is involved in the production of eggs and sperms.

The fertilized eggs become tiny motile planula larvae. After a period of several hours to a few days of searching, the planula makes its choice, attaches to the bottom, and in a matter of hours is transformed from a swimming, torpedo-shaped creature to a tiny protopolyp with a mouth slit surrounded by 8 tiny bumps destined to become tentacles. After a few days it looks like a typical gorgonian polyp, and within a week new polyps have started to bud from the first one. After a time the original polyp is no longer distinguishable from the others.

Although sexual reproduction is common to all gorgonians and is the most important method in most, some species, particularly those lacking the gorgonin axial skeleton, can produce whole colonies from fragments of the original colony. This is particularly useful when the substratum upon which the colony developed is Staghorn Coral, which often shifts and moves.

Growth. Because each colony is the result of the budding and rebudding of its component polyps, the shape of the colony is basically determined by the budding pattern, with environmental effects superimposed. The simplest sort of colony formation is for the initial polyp to bud-off daughter polyps laterally, eventually forming an extensive sheet of an encrusting growth form (*Erythropodium* and sometimes *Briareum* do this; see p. 93). This sheet is sometimes thrown into folds, or it develops fingerlike projections with the same internal arrangement (again, some growth forms of *Briareum* do this). This colony type is especially characteristic of the scleraxonians, which have no internal, horny skeleton. The internal support given by the gorgonin axial skeleton allows the branching to become more complex, resulting in tree-shaped colonies (many plexaurids show this type of colony formation). Remember, however, that the axial skeleton is nonliving and simply supports the outer layer of tissue that contains the polyps, their connections, and the carbonate spicules. When these arborescent colonies are found growing in a strongly directional current, they become almost 2-dimensional, forming flat, candelabrum-shaped colonies. You can often tell a lot about the area in which gorgonians are growing by their shape and orientation.

Other typical colony shapes are the featherlike colonies characteristic of the genus *Pseudopterogorgia*. The most familiar gorgonians are probably the flat sea fans. These species, closely related to the pseudopterogorgian plumes, are formed by the sprouting of tiny branches around the rim of the fan. These soon put out lateral branches in the same plane. When they contact each other, the branches grow together and eventually form the characteristic netlike structure. These flat colonies, like the candelabrum-shaped forms, are oriented to present their flat face to the current. A simple inspection of a bed of sea fans gives a very good indication of the currents. If a colony is turned 90°, it will soon begin to sprout side fans at right angles to the current. This suggests that orientation is very important in the ecology of these species.

How fast do gorgonians grow? The answer to this question is not a simple one. Gorgonians seem to be able to grow tissues very quickly to repair damage caused by the loss of part of the colony.

This is probably an important adaptation, since the bare axial skeleton, if exposed for long, will become infested with algae or other organisms, which will then prevent the repair of the wound.

An interesting observation has been made about the ability of gorgonians to regenerate damaged tissue. When 1 or 2 Flamingo Tongues attack a sea fan colony, their depredations can be traced as paths of damage or missing tissue on the face of the fan. As you look farther back along this trail from the spot where the snail is currently eating, you will be looking at older and older damage. You will also see that, unless some algae or fire coral has settled on the exposed axial skeleton, the tissue eaten by the snail is gradually being replaced. In fact, it seems as if the feeding rate of the snail and the regeneration rate of the gorgonian are nicely matched. Thus the Flamingo Tongue might almost be said to be a farmer rather than a predator. However, this apparent balance is sometimes upset. Several snails, sometimes more than a dozen, may attack a single colony. In such cases the regenerative powers of the gorgonian are no match for the appetites of the Flamingo Tongues, and the whole colony is rapidly reduced to a bare skeleton.

The growth of gorgonians may be measured in terms of the colony's height increase. The normal rate seems to be 2–4 cm ($\frac{3}{4}$–$1\frac{1}{2}$ in.) per year. However, if each branch of a multibranched colony grows at this rate, the total increase in tissue for the whole colony becomes substantial. As the colony grows, the gorgonin axial skeleton increases in diameter by adding treelike rings. The approximate age of a colony can be estimated by counting these rings at the base. Don't try this on a living gorgonian, though, since you would have to kill it to see the rings.

Contributions to the Reef System. In the Caribbean, where the gorgonians are so important in terms of number and size, it is not surprising that they play significant roles in the dynamics of the reef. Although they are not true reef-builders, as the hard corals are, their spicules may in some areas constitute a significant fraction of the sand. Researchers in the Dry Tortugas have estimated that more than 1 kg ($2\frac{1}{4}$ lbs.) of spicules are deposited per square meter each year. This carbonate material may be moved up onto beaches as sand, may be cemented into the reef structure itself, or may be lost to the system by gradually moving down the slope into deep water.

In addition to contributing to the sand budget, gorgonians are also structurally important in that they provide resting and hiding places for many other reef organisms. Several species of fishes hide in the branches of gorgonian colonies. Other animals, notably the Coon Oyster and the Winged Pearl Oyster, actually attach themselves to gorgonian colonies and use them as scaffolding on which to carry on filter-feeding activities up off the bottom. Another animal that uses gorgonians as a feeding platform is the Basket Star.

Many smaller organisms, including barnacles, bryozoans, worms, and sea squirts, attach themselves to gorgonian colonies, using them as permanent substrata. Most of these epibionts cause little or no damage to the host gorgonian.

Fire corals, *Millepora,* are potentially harmful pests to the gorgonians. When a damaged area of the axial skeleton is exposed, there is a chance that a larva of a fire coral might settle on the newly uncovered area. If the fire coral colony gets a foothold, the fate of the gorgonian is sealed. The fire coral will gradually spread over the skeleton, inexorably killing and pushing back the gorgonian tissue. Eventually nothing will be visible except the fire coral colony. The only remaining trace of the original gorgonian will be its shape, recalling the underlying skeleton — treelike, plumelike, or fanlike.

As abundant as gorgonians are, one might think that they would be prey to many carnivorous reef animals. The effects of the Flamingo Tongue have already been mentioned. Smaller relatives, *Simnia* species, behave in a similar fashion, though they rarely if ever damage gorgonian colonies. Snails of the genus *Coralliophila* are frequently found partially embedded in the basal tissues of some gorgonians. They, too, appear to cause little damage to the host. The Fireworm eats gorgonian tissue. This habit seems to be particularly common when the branches of the colony are packed with eggs. It may be that the rich nature of the food makes this source, which otherwise is only infrequently eaten, attractive.

Several fishes have been seen nibbling at the surface of gorgonians. Although some may have been eating only the mucus that is secreted by the colonies, polyps have been found in the stomachs of a few species. Whether these are ingested accidentally or are actually sought is not known.

Considering their abundance, the fact that gorgonians are only infrequently damaged by predators is surprising. It has been suggested that they manufacture noxious materials, thus making themselves distasteful to potential predators. It is also thought that substances, perhaps in the mucus that often coats gorgonians, may protect them from being overgrown by smothering or encrusting organisms, such as algae and sponges.

Common Bushy Soft Coral, a common gorgonian, has been found to contain high concentrations of chemicals called prostaglandins, which can function like mammalian hormones. That they can act as birth-control agents in humans has led several drug companies to consider harvesting this marine resource. This fact should serve as a reminder that protection of the reef as a possible source of materials useful to man may become a matter of urgency.

Gorgonians contribute to reefs in many ways. As producers of sand, they add to the reef structure; as hiding and resting places, they greatly contribute to the spatial complexity and richness of the reef habitat; as food and substratum for other organisms, they contribute energy to the ecosystem. The gorgonians, remarkably adapted to the reef system and its inhabitants, are truly the hallmark of the Caribbean reefs.

Common Species

All the corals described below are members of Order Gorgonacea, except for the white encrusting soft corals, *Telesto* species, which belong to Order Telestacea.

DEADMAN'S FINGERS or   **Pls. 12, 13;**
CORKY SEA FINGERS *Briareum asbestinum*   **Fig. 3, p. 9**
Sometimes encrusting but commonly produces vertical stalks to 3 cm (1¼ in.) thick and often more than 15 cm (6 in.) long. When extended, large brown polyps give branches a *fuzzy, sometimes flowing look.* When polyps are retracted, reddish branches resemble wart-covered fingers. No axial skeleton. *Briareum,* like *Erythropodium,* is a scleraxonian. Central spicules red; surface spicules in white ring around red core. Only other scleraxonian you may find if you scuba dive is Deepwater Lace Coral (Pl. 12), a deepwater species that is dark brown or black and forms lacy, fanlike, 2-dimensional colonies with many short branches.

BROWN ENCRUSTING SOFT CORAL
Erythropodium caribaeorum
Polyps to 1.5 cm (¾ in.) or longer, giving colony a fuzzy appearance. When polyps are retracted, surface is usually reddish brown, somewhat shiny. Polyps often retract, leaving star-shaped apertures. Tissue usually only a few millimeters thick; spicules reddish or maroon. *Always encrusting.*

KNOBBY CANDELABRA *Eunicea* species   **Pls. 12, 13**
About 15 species; many difficult to identify. Common in both shallow and deep water. Most tan or dark brown, flat or arborescent gorgonians with thick branches and projecting light-colored or white calyxes are species of *Eunicea.* (1) *E. mammosa* (Pls. 12, 13) and (2) *E. succinea* are abundant on shallow reefs; distinct from other species; bushy, or branched in 1 plane; *branches knobby, with rounded calycylar lips; distinctive yellow-brown, with a distinctive odor.* (3) Tournefort's Knobby Candelabrum, *E. tourneforti,* forms bumpy dark brown or black candelbrum-shaped colonies.

SEA FANS   **Pl. 18;**
Gorgonia species   **Fig. 2, p. 8**
Color varies widely. 2 shallow-water species, (1) *G. ventalina* (Pl. 18) and (2) *G. flabellum,* which are difficult to distinguish in the field; both have flat branchlets.

SPINY CANDELABRA *Muricea* species   **Pls. 12, 13**
2 common shallow-water species, (1) *M. muricata* (Pls. 12, 13) and
(2) *M. atlantica,* commonly *branch in a single plane* and look
flattened; *prickly to the touch,* due to long spicules forming scales
into which the polyps retract; yellow, brownish, or tan. 2 other
species, (3) *M. elongata* and (4) *M. laxa,* occur below 30 m
(100 ft.); to 1 m (3¼ ft.) or higher; branches prickly, very thin —
often only 1-2 mm (¹/₁₆ in.) thick — and colony gray or brown.

SEA PLUME *Muriceopsis flavida*   **Pl. 13**
The only featherlike gorgonian likely to be seen that is not a
Pseudopterogorgia. Easily distinguished in having branchlets that
are clearly *cylindrical* in cross section. Branchlets to 3 mm (¹/₁₂ in.)
thick, rough to the touch.

TAN BUSHY SOFT CORAL *Plexaura flexuosa*   **Pl. 12**
General colony shape quite similar to that of Common Bushy Soft
Coral (below), but colonies usually *tan or yellowish,* less
frequently brownish or purplish. Branches feel dry, slightly
rough. Tissue seems more friable than in Common Bushy Soft
Coral.

COMMON BUSHY SOFT CORAL   **Pl. 12**
Plexaura homomalla
A common bushy shallow-water species. Branches usually more
than 1 cm (½ in.) thick. *Brown* when polyps extended; dark, almost black, when retracted. Branches feel soft; if squeezed too
hard, will produce a brown cloud. *Caution:* Sometimes causes skin
irritations, so don't carry this squeezing experiment too far.
The species from which prostaglandins have been obtained (see
p. 92).

SEA RODS *Plexaurella* species   **Pl. 13**
About 6 species; distinct from other gorgonians but difficult to
distinguish from one another. Branches thick — 10-15 mm (½-
⁵/₈ in.) in diameter — usually smooth, and gray or tan. *Resemble
broom handles;* stiff and fairly brittle. In most species polyps retract into calyxes which close tightly, leaving a slit on surface of
branch. Sometimes tissue surrounding calyx is slightly raised,
never sharply projecting or prickly. Commonest species is *P. grisea*
(Pl. 13).

FALSE PLEXAURAS *Pseudoplexaura* species   **Pl. 13**
Only a few species but difficult to distinguish from one another
and from gorgonians of other genera. Typically tree-shaped, often
like an upside-down funnel-shaped umbrella. *Many branches very
long,* with a few side branches; very flexible and thin. Most *species
slippery, even slimy.* Pores into which polyps retract are often *gaping holes.* Colonies purple, yellow, or gray; can be large — to 2 m
(6½ ft.) high.

SEA FEATHERS   Pls. 12, 13, 18;
Pseudopterogorgia species   Fig. 15, p. 33
About 12 species in Caribbean; most are difficult to identify.
(1) Forked Sea Feather, *P. bipinnata* (Pls. 12, 13), and (2) the
slightly deeper-living Deepwater Sea Feather, *P. elizabethae* (Pl.
18), are common in deep water in many areas. Scuba divers may
encounter several species, but snorkelers are most likely to see only
2 species: (3) Slimy Sea Feather, *P. americana,* may form large
plumelike colonies; easily recognized by touching its slimy surface,
when disturbed, may give off large amounts of mucus. (4) Smooth
Sea Feather, *P. acerosa* (Pl. 13; Fig. 15, p. 33), is large — to 2 m
(6½ ft.) wide — with a *smooth surface* that is never covered with
mucus; conspicuous plumes formed by long side branches.

SEA BLADES *Pterogorgia* species   **Pl. 30**
Several species. (1) Guadeloupe Sea Blade, *P. guadalupensis* (Pl.
30) has broad — to 10 cm (4 in.) — *flat bladelike branches* with
polyps that retract into longitudinal grooves along branch edges.
(2) Sea Blade, *P. anceps,* has *3- or 4-edged bladelike branches.*
Color varies in both species. (3) Yellow Sea Blade, *P. citrina,* forms
small colonies in rough-water areas; flat yellow blades, with polyps
that retract into individual calyxes along edges of blades, which
may be purplish.

WHITE ENCRUSTING SOFT CORALS *Telesto* species
The only octocorals in this list that are not gorgonians. Belong to
Order Telestacea. *Creeping stolons form mats from which the erect
branches rise.* Branches thin — about 2-4 mm (¹⁄₁₂-¹⁄₆ in.). Large
white polyps — to 5 cm (2 in.) long — extend from calyxes (cups)
along length of stalk. Colonies usually white or pale pink-brown;
may be covered with sponges. Often in harbors and bays, where it
encrusts pilings and other structures. Commonest species is
T. riisei.

5

Origin of the Coral Reef

The first attempt to comprehend the forces at work in the creation of coral reefs was made by Charles Darwin. His book *On the Structure and Distribution of Coral Reefs* rivals the *Origin of Species* in its biological perceptions and the timelessness of its theory. Although there have been refinements since 1842, when the book first appeared, Darwin's original concepts are still the foundation of our beliefs concerning the origin of coral reefs.

The development of these concepts required great breadth of vision. On his voyage aboard the *Beagle,* Darwin perceived not 1 but 3 major kinds of coral reefs. They appear to be so different as to have no relationship to one another.

The Three Kinds of Reefs. The first kind is the **fringing reef,** a mass of coral projecting from shore. It is characterized by a variety of coral types, often with no species obviously predominant. It is surrounded by patch reefs, which are simply aggregations of a few corals or coral boulders isolated from the main mass by areas of sand or Turtle Grass. The fringing reef is an area along the shore where rocks have provided a foothold for the settlement of the planula larvae, and colonies of coral have been able to grow. These reefs begin below the lowest low-water mark (since exposure to even a few hours of desiccation kills many corals) and extend seaward, sometimes for considerable distances. The fringing reef is always contiguous with the land mass; the seaward edge is not separated from the rest of the reef by a lagoon.

The **barrier reef,** the second major reef type, consists of a number of more or less clearly defined coral zones separated from the land mass by a lagoon. The lagoon is a shallow area with a floor of coral sand and debris and with areas of vegetation. It ranges from less than 150 m (500 ft.) to several kilometers in width. The lagoon of the Great Barrier Reef of Australia extends from 11 km (7 mi.) to 65 km (40 mi.) in width. Large lagoons separating barrier reefs from land masses are often called channels.

The third kind of coral reef is the **atoll,** an incomplete ring of sandy islands built up on coral reefs. In this case the lagoon is within the ring.

When Darwin observed examples of the 3 kinds of reefs, he noted that they appeared in different areas of the oceans and had different relationships to land masses. Most atolls are in the Indian and Pacific Oceans; they are rare in the Atlantic, although one exists off the coast of Belize. They are often far from any continent or large island and are invariably surrounded by deep water. It is as if they have been thrust up from the depths.

Barrier reefs always appear near land — usually within 80 km (50 mi.) — and the lagoon is relatively shallow, as if the reef were on a shelf of land. Seaward of a barrier reef, the bottom usually slopes sharply into deep water.

The fringing reef is obviously an extension of the shore. What connection can there be between it and the barrier reef and the atoll?

In order to explain the existence of these diverse reef types Darwin offered the subsidence of land hypothesis. He suggested that barrier reefs began as fringing reefs along the shores of volcanoes thrust high above sea level. Over millions of years the land subsided, the volcanoes sinking lower and lower into the sea. Coral grows best within the zone of light penetration — within 50 m (165 ft.) of the surface. As the land subsided, the coral growth kept up with the apparent rise of the sea level; thus the reef remained only a few meters below the surface. The outermost portion of the reef, with best access to the plankton being carried landward by ocean currents, grew faster because it had more food available. The result was a wall of coral that grew higher and higher. It was increasingly separated from its island by the conical nature of the volcano, which becomes narrower toward its peak. The barrier reef, then, originated as a fringing reef along shore; as the island receded beneath the sea, the reef became more and more distant from shore. The landward portion of the reef, unable to keep up because of a lack of food, died, hence the formation of the lagoon between land and reef. (See Fig. 34.)

The logical extension of this hypothesis is to continue the descent of the island until it disappears under the sea. Although the land mass is passive, the coral reef is not: it continues to grow, getting higher along with the sea level. The result is an atoll, a ring of coral reefs, the descendants of the barrier reef, surrounding the submerged cone of an extinct volcano (the original island). Sand is trapped by the reefs; sandy islands, or cays, appear. There is no sign of the original igneous rock on these islands. Bore down through the sand and you will reach dead coral, now turned into limestone. The lagoon is the area of clear, tranquil water within the ring of islands. It can be very deep, because beneath the surface lies the crater of a volcano. This has given rise to legends of bottomless lagoons. Actually, most atoll lagoons are less than 200 m (650 ft.) deep.

An alternate hypothesis, called the glacial control theory, was proposed by Reginald Daly in 1919. This theory suggests that during glacial periods in the earth's history, much of the water budget of the earth was tied up in the huge ice caps covering parts of North America, Europe, and other continents. The generally cold

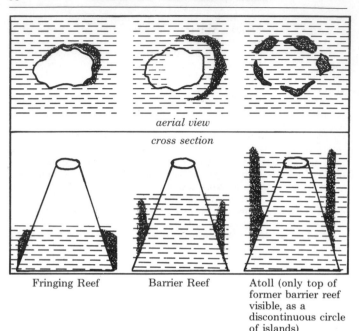

aerial view

cross section

Fringing Reef   Barrier Reef   Atoll (only top of
                                    former barrier reef
                                    visible, as a
                                    discontinuous circle
                                    of islands)

Fig. 34
Evolution of the 3 types of coral reefs according to Darwin

climate retarded evaporation, and rain was sparse. The sea level
fell at least 60 m (197 ft.) below what it is at present. The coral was
killed by the cold water, and the land masses were left unprotected. The ocean surf, during the thousands of years of glacial
dominance of the earth's climate, beat away at the shores, cutting
platforms in the rock. When the glaciers receded and the climate
warmed, the coral began to flourish, finding the wave-cut platforms suitable solid substrata. As the sea level rose from the melt-
water of the glaciers, the seaward edge of the platforms supported
the most rapid coral growth. Only the coral on the outer edge of
the platform could keep up with the rising water. This produced
the barrier reefs and their accompanying lagoons. Atolls formed on
the platforms surrounding drowned islands.

A number of other hypotheses have been offered, but current
research is focused on the controversy between Darwin's theory
and Daly's. Daly suggested that the sea level fell and then rose

again; Darwin believed that the primary movement was the subsidence of the land. Daly said that there was little or no sequential relationship between the 3 types of reefs; Darwin said that they evolved from fringing reef to barrier reef to atoll. Daly said that there was a flat platform of rock beneath barrier reefs and atolls; Darwin believed that under barrier reefs and atolls lay massive deposits of shallow-water corals — the remains of previous reefs that grew upward in a race to keep pace with the apparently rising waters.

The first major attempt to resolve this problem was made in 1904 by an expedition sent by the Royal Society of London. This group bored a hole beneath the sands of Funafuti Atoll in the South Pacific. They removed a core from a depth of 330 m (1114 ft.) *without ever reaching a reef base.* In the core were identified 28 genera of reef-building corals, 22 of which are now living on shallow-water reefs. No deepwater corals were in the sample. This substantiated Darwin's hypothesis, since no evidence of wave-cut shelves was found.

L. R. Cary, in 1931, made 3 borings progressively farther from the shore of a reef in Samoa. He concluded that the reef rested on a wave-cut platform, a conclusion that supported Daly's hypothesis. Two borings on Australia's Great Barrier Reef, in 1928 and 1938, discovered shore sand 120 and 140 m (400 and 450 ft.) below the reef surface, with no evidence of wave-cut shelves.

The conclusion to be drawn from research to date is that some reefs have evolved according to the method described by Darwin, and some have formed on wave-cut shelves, as Daly suggested. This compromise, marshalling evidence that made both sides happy, sat uncomfortably on the shoulders of its proponents until recent insights into the concept of plate tectonics clarified the picture. According to currently favored geological theory, the earth's crust consists of a number of massive plates which are sliding over the inner region (mantle). Certain areas girdling the globe, the midocean ridges, are regions of high volcanic activity, and outpourings of lava are raising the sea floor and pushing the plates apart. At other places the plates are colliding or, in some cases, sliding under one another; so the land is slowly subsiding. In yet other places the relative levels of land and sea remain more or less stable. Thus in some regions the land *is* subsiding as Darwin suggested, and in others the relationship between sea level and coral reef may be governed by other factors, such as glaciers thousands of kilometers away.

A Fourth Kind of Reef. In the Caribbean and tropical Atlantic waters the evolution of coral reefs was interrupted. These areas were fundamentally affected by recent glaciation; the last glacier receded less than 20,000 years ago. Although none of the recent glaciers reached even subtropical latitudes, the ocean water was cooled by its relative proximity to the glaciers and by the generally colder climate; thus the water temperature averaged below 20°C (68°F), the minimum long-term temperature for coral growth. The corals died and left the Caribbean shores unprotected. The soft limestone composing the islands was easily eroded, and wave-cut shelves appeared around the islands in the manner described by Daly. (The difference is in time scale. I am now referring to reefs that are less than 20,000 years old; the ancient Pacific reefs, millions of years old, are excluded.) When the waters warmed sufficiently to permit coral growth, flourishing reefs appeared on the seaward edges of the platforms, or banks, and lagoons formed inside these reefs. The platforms are not extensive enough to simulate true Pacific barrier reefs, and the lagoons are shallower — hence the term **bank/barrier reef** seems appropriate for the Atlantic-Caribbean version. These reefs are normally only hundreds of meters from the land mass, not thousands as is common in the Pacific. An exception is the so-called second largest barrier reef in the world, off the coast of Belize and easily accessible to Americans. It is about 200 km (125 mi.) long — versus 2000 km (1250 mi.) for Australia's Great Barrier Reef — and 11–12 km (7–8 mi.) offshore.

6

Ecology of the Coral Reef

Tropical seas are blue because the clear waters reflect the blue of the sky. The blueness is due to the absence of the green plants that give life to the sea. Such plants, called phytoplankton, microscopic algae that flourish in the cold seas beyond the tropics of Cancer and Capricorn, live out their lives in the upper 50 m (165 ft.) of the sea. This is the zone of light penetration, the photic zone. As the light penetrates farther into the depths, more and more light is absorbed until none exists. The longer light waves are absorbed first; so the reds (used most readily by plants during photosynthesis) are eliminated in the upper few meters. Everything below takes on an eerie bluish cast, since the blue light waves, being at the opposite (short) end of the spectrum from the red and being the most penetrating, predominate in deeper water.

The deep blue color and startling clarity of tropical seas tell us of the sparsity of phytoplankton in the water. In effect, the tropical seas are biological deserts. They lack the phytoplankton that make temperate and polar waters the meadows of the sea. Every ecosystem is based on plants that convert the sun's rays and the waste products of respiration into food. All living things ultimately depend on the sun for the energy they use to power their life functions. The distribution of energy in any ecosystem may be described by a trophic pyramid. Such a pyramid represents the amount of energy in the ecosystem, expressed not only in terms of calories but also in terms of mass of animal and plant tissue.

All plants, whether phytoplankton, trees, or grasses, are labeled producers. They produce the energy-containing compounds needed and used by consumers — herbivores and carnivores — for survival. Organisms that eat plants, herbivores, are called primary consumers, for they have the first crack at the energy produced by the plants. Secondary consumers, carnivores, eat primary consumers; tertiary consumers, also carnivores, eat secondary consumers (and sometimes primary consumers). Fig. 35 shows the trophic pyramid expressed in biomass, or grams of living tissue, and also in terms of specific organisms.

Notice that the closer an organism is to the bottom of the trophic pyramid, the greater the biomass it represents. The largest animals (elephant, hippopotamus) and the most abundant (mouse, rabbit, locust, beetle) are tied to the lowest levels of the trophic pyramid. They must browse all day to obtain enough food energy to sustain themselves. They can feed themselves adequately only by eating plants. But blue whales don't eat plants directly, and they are the largest animals on the earth today. Instead, they and most other large whales eat zooplankton, the incredibly abundant small animals that prey directly on the phytoplankton. In arctic seas zooplankton called krill or euphausiid shrimps form schools several meters thick and several kilometers wide. The whales spend their days swimming through these immense schools of krill with their mouths open, filtering out and swallowing tons of the shrimplike creatures.

Most zooplankton are microscopic. They not only sustain the whale; they also are the food of the coral polyp. With its whorl of tentacles armed with nematocysts, the polyp is one of the most effective predators of zooplankton. As the currents sweep over the reef, virtually every zooplanktonic organism is removed. But therein lies the rub: there weren't many of these organisms to begin with. We began with the premise that the clear blue tropical waters lacked phytoplankton. With few phytoplankton, there are even fewer zooplankton. *How can one of the most flourishing, highly populated biotic communities, the coral reef, survive in the almost plankton-free waters of the tropical seas?*

The Dilemma of the Inverted Trophic Pyramid. At a glance the normal food relationships found in all other ecosystems might appear to be reversed on the coral reef. For example, there seems to be an overabundance of consumers, such as fishes, both minnowlike silversides and large fishes such as groupers, parrotfishes, and damselfishes. Their biomass, plus that of the abundant snails, worms, brittle stars, and other invertebrates, seems to be substan-

Fig. 35

Trophic pyramid

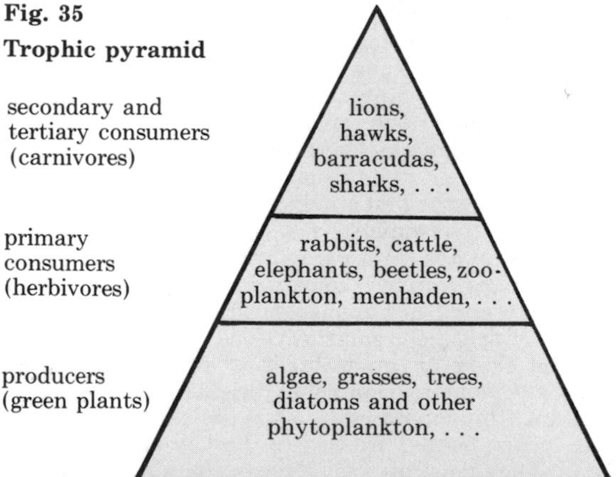

secondary and tertiary consumers (carnivores)

lions, hawks, barracudas, sharks, . . .

primary consumers (herbivores)

rabbits, cattle, elephants, beetles, zooplankton, menhaden, . . .

producers (green plants)

algae, grasses, trees, diatoms and other phytoplankton, . . .

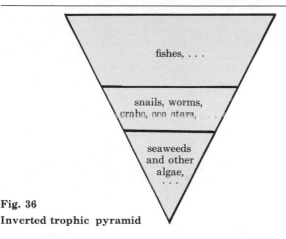

fishes, . . .

snails, worms,
crabs, sea stars,

seaweeds
and other
algae,
. . .

Fig. 36
Inverted trophic pyramid

tial, possibly even greater than that of the coral polyps themselves. Producers — plants such as the algae *Goniolithon* and *Halimeda* — are not as abundant as might be expected. A representation of the *apparent* biomass relationships would seem to warrant the trophic pyramid shown in Fig. 36.

But this presents us with a dilemma: If there are more consumers than producers, this conflicts with the pattern established by all other ecosystems and the laws of thermodynamics — in the inverted pyramid more energy would be taken out of the system than put into it. So somewhere in the ecosystem of the coral reef there must be more energy producers.

Enter the atomic bomb. After World War II the United States conducted its first major postwar nuclear tests off an obscure atoll, Eniwetok, in the Pacific. The government sponsored numerous studies of pre- and post-explosion flora and fauna to determine the effects of radiation on the biological environment. Among the scientists sent to Eniwetok were 2 famous ecologists, the brothers Howard and Eugene Odum, who performed one of the pre-explosion baseline studies. Their investigations produced some of the most challenging and creative hypotheses concerning the coral reef since Darwin had described the relationship of fringing reefs, barrier reefs, and atolls. They attacked the problem of the inverted trophic pyramid head-on, searching for the producers (the green plants) which they knew must be present in greater abundance than the animals that consumed them. They found them in 2 places.

First, the fleshy encrusting algae in the reef bottom were found to constitute a substantial proportion of the biomass of the reef —

weighing approximately twice as much as the primary consumers in the reef crest. In a slightly deeper zone the biomass of the bottom algae was 4 times that of the herbivores (primary consumers) and about 40 times that of the carnivores. The problem, then, was partially solved. When the algae living in the sand and encrusting the dead coral were weighed, they did constitute a substantial base for a normal trophic pyramid.

The Odums also found that there is a significant plant component inside *both* the polyp tissue and the skeleton of the corals themselves. Inside the coral polyp, in some of the cells of the gastrodermis, are numerous chlorophyll-bearing algae called zooxanthellae. It was suspected that the corals and the algae have a mutualistic relationship in which *excess food produced by the zooxanthellae could be consumed by the coral polyp.* The polyp might then be a miniature ecosystem in itself, with both producer and consumer in the same organism.

The biomass of zooxanthellae has recently been estimated at 50% of the total weight of some polyps. But research has shown that even if the polyp is getting food from its zooxanthellae, it still needs food from other sources. Nevertheless, assuming that the zooxanthellae have *some* role in coral nutrition, a miniature system can exist, one whose trophic pyramid may be represented as in Fig. 37. We will return to the role of the zooxanthellae later in this chapter, but first we need to look at some of the other sources of coral nutrition.

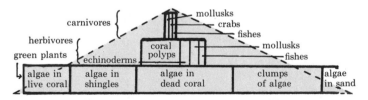

Fig. 37 Trophic pyramid of a coral reef — distribution of biomass

Resolving the Dilemma. Our understanding of the nutritional foundation of the coral reef remained at an almost superstitious Dark Ages level until the late 1950s. We knew that the apparent predominance of animals over plants in the coral-reef ecosystem could not possibly be valid, but there was no alternative explanation. The Odums' research kindled a flame that has spread to laboratories all over the world. Much has been learned about plant-animal relationships on the coral reef.

Corals are predacious animals. They extend their circlets of tentacles into the water at night, when zooplankton rise from the deep in their daily migration. The whole surface of the coral head becomes a trap for the plankton. Mucus covers everything, even the areas of coenosarc between polyps. As the tiny plankton float by, they become enmeshed in the mucus or paralyzed and entrapped by the dartlike nematocysts found all over the tentacles. The food organisms are transported in sheets of mucus that are beaten toward the mouth by minute hairlike cilia. Some corals also wipe the food-laden tentacles across the mouth. Within 30 seconds all food particles dropped on the surface of a colony of Shallow-water Starlet Coral are gone, swallowed in a sheet of mucus.

Some corals are capable of reversing the ciliary flow of mucus; others have ciliary currents that flow only away from the mouth. Both types are capable of carrying silt and waste away from the oral disk, down the column and off the corallum (coral head). The ability of corals to clear themselves of silt is a most important survival mechanism, since corals are sessile (attached), bottom-dwelling forms and are in danger of being smothered by bottom sediments. Shallow-water Starlet Coral, for example, can clear itself of silt just as fast as it can clear itself of food. This is important to its survival. Golfball-like colonies are often found on the bottom, in Turtle Grass beds, constantly subjected to siltation.

When hard corals take in food, the particles are held on the edges of the mesenteries by mesenterial filaments. These are relatively straight in the upper, pharyngeal region, but they become convoluted and more threadlike toward the base of the polyp. The filaments have both nematocysts and cilia on them and can secrete digestive enzymes. In most corals they can "creep" through the mouth or through temporary openings in the body wall. Some corals habitually feed by extruding the mesenterial filaments, initiating digestion just outside the mouth. Both touch and smell stimuli seem to evoke the extrusion of the filaments. The filaments can be extended more than 10 cm (4 in.) for more than an hour.

The efficiency of the coral polyps in removing plankton from the water is noteworthy. It has been estimated that the reef's filtering efficiency for diatoms is 91% and for zooplankton 60%. (There is some question as to whether corals eat phytoplankton at all. The diatoms, being phytoplankton, may be removed and eaten by suspension-feeders other than polyps. One observer has found 38,930 invertebrate plankton consumers, *exclusive of corals,* in a square meter of reef.)

In any case, most calculations reveal that the maximum amount of energy available to the corals from plankton is 6–13% of the total community expenditure. So, as effective as they are, the corals cannot obtain more than a small fraction of their nutritional needs from feeding on plankton. This is enough, however, to have a profound effect on the distribution, growth rate, and appearance of the corals. The richest zones of the reef are those at the seaward edge. The back reef exhibits various signs of impoverishment. No coral species is especially dominant in the back reef because the small edge of extra energy that is necessary to overgrow or otherwise outcompete other species is missing. Very few plankton have survived the predation of the fore-reef and reef-crest inhabitants seaward.

Even the shape of the coral changes as it inhabits deeper regions and is forced to rely more on plankton and less on the photosynthetic activities of its symbionts. Boulder Coral, for example, is rather spherical and boulderlike near the surface and flattened in the deepest parts of its vertical range, giving it a progressively larger polyp surface area relative to skeletal mass. The interplay of light reduction (and the consequent diminution of photosynthetic activity of the zooxanthellae) with increased reliance on plankton has affected the manner in which the polyps design the coral head.

Another source of food is the water itself. Dissolved molecules can be absorbed through the polyp's body wall by means of tiny fuzzlike projections called microvilli. Small quantities of important nutrients, such as glucose and certain amino acids, can be absorbed by means of the microvilli.

Since only a few of the food requirements of the coral have so far been accounted for, we must search for the rest within the polyp tissue and inside the coral head. The search leads us to recent research into the role of the zooxanthellae.

Zooxanthellae are 1-celled organisms with chloroplasts (which carry on photosynthesis) and 2 whiplike flagellae. The flagellae are found in grooves (sulci) arranged in characteristic fashion, one around the horizontal waist of the cell and the other running vertically around it with the flagellum trailing behind. Organisms of this type are called dinoflagellates. There are many kinds of dinoflagellates, most of which are free-living members of the phytoplankton. An infamous species is *Gymnodinium breve* (Fig. 38), which produces a toxin that kills massive numbers of fishes and invertebrates. It is the organism that causes red tides.

Fig. 38

Gymnodinium breve

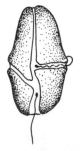

The name "zooxanthella" refers to the fact that these organisms live inside animals and are yellow-brown in color (*zoo-* = animal, *xanth-* = gold). More than 80 species of invertebrates are inhabited by zooxanthellae. Regardless of the host organism, all zooxanthellae look alike and all bear the same specific name, *Zooxanthella* (*Symbiodinium*) *microadriaticum*. They are spherical and 8–12 microns in diameter when in the host; in culture they may exhibit as many as 16 different forms, but the forms are the same regardless of the host from which they have been taken. Despite these similarities, some researchers question whether all zooxanthellae should be assigned the same name.

Consider the fact that in hard corals, at least, the planula larva leaves its parent polyp with its own culture of zooxanthellae taken from its parents. This direct transmission of zooxanthellae from generation to generation means that every species of coral transmits a single genetic line of zooxanthellae through time. But the corals have been steadily evolving over millions of years. Hundreds of species have derived from ancestral forms. Their symbionts have likewise made evolutionary adjustments to their environment. The zooxanthellae have had to adjust to their changing environment even though this environment is the *inside* of the body of the polyp. Evolution of this sort is biochemical rather than morphological. The result can be the evolution of new species just as valid as morphologically different ones.

New techniques, using radioactive tracers, are helping us discover the mechanisms by which the corals obtain sustenance from their zooxanthellae. In one experiment, polyps were exposed to radioactive carbon dioxide; after 1–5 weeks labeled food molecules were located *in the tissues of the polyps*. This experiment has been repeated on the reef itself, with similar results, proof that food manufactured by the zooxanthellae becomes part of the polyp tissue.

Studies done on the reef are more realistic and more useful. One such study, in which opaque and clear domes were used to cover sections of the reef, revealed that after $3\frac{1}{2}$ months in the shade the corals expelled their zooxanthellae and died. The colonies under the transparent domes survived.

Related observations suggest that corals with large polyps, such as Large Flower Coral, are relatively efficient at capturing zooplankton and have low metabolic rates. They are therefore less dependent on zooxanthellae for food. Corals with small polyps are relatively inefficient at capturing zooplankton and have high metabolic rates. They appear to be more dependent on their zooxanthellae. The fact that Large Flower Coral and Large-cupped Fungus Coral — the Caribbean corals with the largest polyps — live on the deeper, darker levels of the reef seems to corroborate this hypothesis.

Research done in the 1970s revealed that various nutrients are released by the zooxanthellae and are used by the polyps as food. The relationship between the coral and its zooxanthellae is of a type called mutualism: both organisms benefit. The coral obtains food and oxygen; the zooxanthellae obtain shelter and the polyp's waste products. The efficiency of the relationship is clearly expressed in the manner in which the zooxanthellae recycle the polyp's wastes. Two waste products are involved: ammonia and carbon dioxide.

Coral polyps release ammonia molecules as a waste product of protein metabolism (just as humans produce the ammonia-related molecules urea and uric acid, which become urine when diluted with water). The major constituent of ammonia is nitrogen. Plants require nitrogen to build their own proteins. The zooxanthellae locked inside the polyp have everything they need for survival except nitrogen. Thus the polyp provides the missing ingredient, just as the homeowner provides fertilizer for his lawn (the 10 in 10-6-4 fertilizer refers to the amount of nitrogen, usually extracted from urea, that it contains).

Carbon dioxide is a waste product of respiration, along with water molecules. When carbon dioxide and water combine, they form carbonic acid. Acid can dissolve the calcium carbonate skeleton of the coral or, more realistically, slow down the production or deposition of the calcium carbonate spicules that compose the coral's skeleton. But carbon dioxide and water are the main ingredients in photosynthesis. By performing photosynthesis the zooxanthellae remove excess carbon dioxide and water. This reduces the acidity inside the polyp and thus enhances the coral's ability to lay down its skeleton. In fact, the only corals that can produce enough calcium carbonate to form a reef are those species that contain zooxanthellae.

Here is a remarkable phenomenon, a mutualistic relationship between a plant and an animal — a relationship so important that neither participant can survive well without the other. So intimate is this ancient relationship that if you add coral polyp extract to a culture of zooxanthellae, the zooxanthellae will release 3 times as much sugar into the surrounding medium as was in it originally!

Competition. As in any ecosystem, every reef organism vies with every other for food, protection, and survival. Nothing that happens on the coral reef is accidental. The scattered distribution of one or another species of coral, fish, or alga may appear to be a random phenomenon. Further observation reveals the contrary. Every organism is located according to some grand design. The design is not a vast mosaic where every detail is precisely planned. Rather, it is manifested in the creation of narrow niches into which only certain species will fit.

On the back reef many coral species appear to be distributed randomly. But there is no Large Flower Coral, though it is common in deeper areas. Only one of the many species of lettuce corals is present. As the back reef rises toward the crest of the reef, a shallow area of rubble appears, virtually devoid of coral. This zone in turn becomes a forest of Elkhorn Coral (Pl. 7).

What causes such substantial changes in the distribution of corals, fishes, and plants on the reef? Do we have any insights into the master plan determining the distribution of organisms?

The reef consists of boulders, "heads," and branched colonies of corals cemented more or less permanently to the bottom. Species of fishes, worms, sea urchins, and algae are distributed according to the availability of protective niches inside the reef and of food sources supplied or regulated by the rocklike mass of reef.

Parrotfishes are large fishes that are common on the reef. Their jaws have dozens of rows of fused teeth that are used to bite off chunks of coral, and they have a pharyngeal mill, a muscular organ that grinds up the chunks. The fishes swallow the polyps and release fragments of coral skeleton from the anus. They need the reef for food, but survival depends on more than food. At night, when parrotfishes are most vulnerable, they choose a crevice in the reef and close it off with a protective cocoon of mucus to make a safe "bedroom."

Along with squirrelfishes and a number of other organisms, the Long-spined Black Urchin hides in crevices in the daytime and feeds at night. So dependent are these creatures on the shelter provided by the reef that they have created a barren zone about 9 m (30 ft.) wide, where they have eaten every blade of Turtle Grass. Beyond this zone only the swift or the brave dare to venture. The farther they stray from the protective crevices of the reef, the more vulnerable they are to the jaws of predators. As you swim across the lagoon, look for a sudden cessation of Turtle Grass below you. You will know that you are near the back reef. Look around. It is likely that you will see a barracuda on station, waiting for the unwary to stray from the protection of the reef.

Populations of animals depend on the number of crevices available to hide in, the amount of food, and their own fecundity. Two patterns regulate population size on the reef. Some species, such as the Hardhead Silverside, a minnow, produce large numbers of offspring. Such large populations are characterized by high mortality rates and short generation time. Great genetic variability is a function of large populations. More organisms mean a greater chance for changes to appear. This genetic variability is characteristic of opportunistic species, organisms that are tied relatively loosely to their environments because of the great variety within the species. After storms, for example, great damage to the reef is often in evidence everywhere. Normal patterns have been disrupted. Many biological niches, ordinarily inhabited by particular species, are empty due to death. Organisms with the ability to reproduce rapidly and profusely will colonize these niches and occupy them for a time — but more specialized and highly adapted species will win out in the long run. Highly specialized species usually have a low reproductive rate, a small population size, and increased inbreeding. A great degree of specialization enables them to maintain maximum competitive advantage over neighboring species. Their response to unusual events is poor, but their precise specialization enables them to win out if conditions return to normal.

Corals are highly specialized animals with a low reproductive rate. In some species planula larvae are so scarce that they have never been observed. In other species only a few larvae are released during brief seasons. The very high degree of specialization has advantages and disadvantages. If the environment changed more or less permanently, the coral would be at a competitive disadvantage and would risk extinction. This kind of permanent modification of the environment seems to be occurring at the only mainland American coral reef, located in the Florida Keys. Silt from construction a considerable distance north of the Keys is flowing south in quantities great enough to change the nature of the reefs. The less silt-resistant species, such as Elkhorn and Staghorn Corals, are disappearing, and more resistant species, such as Shallow-water Starlet Coral, are replacing them. If the siltation continues at high levels, whole reefs will disappear.

On the other hand, the high degree of specialization enables corals to occupy every possible niche. Some species, such as Lamarck's Lettuce-leaf Coral and Large Cactus Coral, can live in deep water where there is less light and become dominant there. Others can resist storm waves and will therefore live close to the surface. Because of their high degree of specialization, corals can cover much of the reef down to depths of near total darkness. In an evolutionary sense, then, corals are successful competitors, provided that environmental conditions remain stable.

The growth patterns of some corals enable them to overshadow other species. Light-deprivation is tantamount to death on the reef, for most reef-dwelling corals depend on the photosynthesis of their zooxanthellae to survive. Visualize, then, a fierce competition, even among the boulderlike coral colonies — a competition for food, light, and space. You might think that the rapidly growing, broad-branched corals, such as Elkhorn, would be the triumphant species on the reef. They are among the most efficient predators, they grow fastest, and they produce much shade with their antlerlike growth habit. The truth is that they do not dominate the reef except on the turbulent, wave-wracked reef crest. Instead, the relatively innocuous-looking Boulder Coral is dominant in 2 major sections of the reef, the buttress zone and the fore-reef terrace.

Rate of growth, shading ability, and effectiveness as a predator and as a silt remover are some of the factors that determine dominance. But there are too many unanswered questions for us to believe that we understand coral distribution completely. An exciting new factor was recently discovered by Judith Lang, who did her doctoral research primarily at 12–36 m (40–120 ft.) underwater along Jamaica's north coast. She discovered that the coral colonies will attack and eat each other. Yes, the polyps of each colony will actually feed on their neighbors, extruding their mesenterial filaments like swords and spears to defend or extend their territories. There is even a pecking order. Lang discovered that certain species are able to prey on other species, being invulnerable to the defense responses of their victim. Visualize 2 coral colonies growing next to each other. At the junction between the 2 coral heads one species has a white area where the mesenterial filaments of the other have lain, digesting all of the surrounding tissue and killing the polyps. The white area is an area of death, and the dominant colony will eventually overgrow the other, smothering and eating it in a kind of slow-motion struggle over months and years. See Table 1 for a comparison of the aggressiveness of some common species of corals.

Competitive exclusion of this type occurs notably in the densely populated mixed or buttress zones, 3–15 m (10–50 ft.) deep, where the corals crowd one another, sometimes covering 90% of the bottom. It is less apparent in deeper water and on the back reef, where the corals are farther apart. It is striking to note that the less competitive corals are the ones that are dominant on much of the reef. If *Montastrea* and *Acropora* are vulnerable to many other species (see Table 1), how is it that they are among the major

Table 1. Coral Hierarchy

Large Flower Coral[a] = Large-cupped Fungus Coral[a]
dominate
Tan Brain Coral = Cactus Coral = Stalked Cactus Coral
dominate
Large Cactus Coral
dominates
Soolymia cubensis = Rough Star Coral
dominate
Boulder Coral
dominates
Elkhorn Coral = Staghorn Coral
dominate
Agaricia species = Sunray Lettuce-leaf Coral

Note: An equals sign indicates that the species are equal in dominance.
a. Large Flower Coral and Large-cupped Fungus Coral are deepwater, large-polyp species; they are the most dominant corals.

reef-building corals? There are more elements to be considered before we have the answer to this question. (Lang suggests one possibility: aggressiveness of newly settled juvenile polyps may be critical, and competition among mature corals may not be a major factor.)

Sex, Reproduction, and Larval Dispersal. It takes a colony of Star Coral at least 8 years to reach sexual maturity; the Pacific Fungus Coral takes 10 years. Most branching corals grow faster than the massive species and reach sexual maturity a few years sooner.

Depressed Brain Coral, Common Rose Coral, and Star Coral are hermaphrodites, producing ripe eggs and sperms at the same time. Thus self-fertilization is possible, but this unlikely event has never been proven. In nature most hermaphrodites do not use the simple alternative of self-fertilization. Instead, these male-female organisms mate, cross-fertilizing each other to produce offspring with a variety of characteristics. The resulting population comprises many unique individuals, thereby providing a reservoir of adaptations, enabling the species to cope with environmental changes.

Some corals form unisexual colonies — that is, one whole coral head is composed of sperm-producing male polyps, and another has only egg-producing females. Elkhorn Coral, Large-cupped Boulder Coral, and Shallow-water Starlet Coral have been observed to contain eggs only. No one has ever seen sperm-bearing colonies. That they exist is very likely, and we can expect their discovery some day.

Fertilization is internal in many corals. The sperms swim in through the mouth and enter the gastrovascular cavity to fertilize the eggs hanging from the mesenteries. The planula larvae mature inside the polyp. They remain attached to the septa, breaking free and swimming out of the mouth when they reach maturity. Many corals release planulae once a year; Fragile Lettuce-leaf Coral and Common Rose Coral produce young only in the summer. Some corals, however, release planulae all year long. There is little advantage to producing larvae only at one season, as the tropical seas are relatively constant and do not have the tremendous upsurge of new life, the great increases in phytoplankton and zooplankton, of the temperate zone springtime. Even species with large polyps often produce only a few thousand planulae in a breeding season. Almost all of these are eaten by reef animals within a few hours of their release.

Upon their release the planulae swim upward toward the light, using hundreds of cilia for propulsion. Within a few days of their free-living existence the survivors reverse themselves and swim downward, eventually settling on the bottom to become polyps, each beginning a new colony. This occurs only if the planulae land on a suitable substratum: only a hard, clean, silt-free bottom will do. If these conditions are not met, the planula dies. Sometimes it survives for several weeks and is still able to produce a new colony. The longer the survival time, the greater the chances are for larval dispersal and the wider the potential distribution of the coral species. Larval dispersal is the major force in the spread of coral. Once the planula has landed, the coral can never move again. It loses its potential to invade suitable niches a distance away. Only when storms break off coral chunks that are swept into uncolonized areas will it have another chance.

The tendency of newborn planulae to swim upward and thus remain in the ever-moving stream of plankton aids dispersal. However, there must be a balance between the amount of energy available for dispersal and the amount left over for growth and survival of the parent coral colony. Only so much energy can be diverted toward the production of larvae. As many as possible must be produced to maximize the odds that at least some of them will survive their dangerous planktonic existence.

But the planulae enter the westward flow of surface water pushed by the ever-present trade winds, move across the Caribbean, and enter the Gulf Stream. There is a constant migration of larvae from the equatorial region toward the periphery of the Caribbean. This flow of life is more effective than one would think. For example, the *maximum* life span of the planulae of 4 corals found in Bermuda is 17–23 days. Bermuda is 1700 km (1100 mi.) from Little Bahama Bank (where corals grow in profusion). The warm waters of the Gulf Stream flow at 2.5 knots. They can carry the larvae to Bermuda in 15 days, well within survival time. This probably is how Bermuda, an island too far north to be expected to have coral, supports a number of reefs. Even if the water gets too cold one year, planulae from the Bahamas would ensure new growth the next. It is interesting to note that Bermuda lacks Elkhorn and Staghorn Corals even though conditions seem as suitable for these corals as for the massive species that grow there in some abundance. Possibly, Elkhorn and Staghorn planula larvae do not have a long enough life span to survive the migration.

Storms. A coral reef is a living thing. It grows ever outward, thrusting its buttresses into the full force of the sea. But the sea fights back. Storms batter the reef. Hurricanes have a devastating influence, and few reefs escape their fury for more than 20–30 years. Even minor storms, or those passing at considerable distances, can generate huge swells. When these reach land, they become powerful combers, bursting on the reef crest with a force that uproots and tears apart the Elkhorn Coral, stirring up clouds of silt that inundate the fore reef.

If you approach the reef crest from behind, you can swim over the rubble zone and look at the reef crest safely. Notice that many large colonies of Elkhorn Coral are lying on their sides or are broken. The damaged or flattened coral is not defeated, however; many colonies will continue to grow. Some of the coral pieces and

uprooted coral heads are not their usual rich tan color but instead
are gray and pallid; they are dead and have become rubble. Over
time the spaces between them will be filled with the alga *Halimeda,* living and dead, sea urchin spines, and foraminiferan tests,
until they are cemented together into a whole — the reef flat.

One investigator studied a shallow area where 57% of the bottom
was covered by coral. A hurricane destroyed virtually all of the
colonies. After $4\frac{1}{2}$ years only about 20% of the bottom had been
recolonized by new corals. Algae and other opportunistic species
(sponges and colonial anemones, for example) tend to take advantage of the bonanza of bare hard bottom after a storm. They soon
cover the area, making it impossible for the coral planulae to invade and settle. Even if they find a suitable patch of bottom to
settle on, it would take approximately 10 years for the resulting
coral colony to reach sexual maturity. If only a few planulae successfully settle and develop into coral colonies, the concentration
of sperms produced by these few colonies is too low for effective
fertilization. A much longer time elapses before normal conditions
return.

Estimates of recovery time after severe storms range from 20
years to more than 50. Although certain coral species may appear
in considerable numbers after 5–10 years or more, this does not
mean that the reef has recovered. Only when the original species
diversity has been established, when the mix between slow-growing massive corals and the faster-growing branching species is back
to normal, can one consider the reef to have recovered.

Coral Eaters. Catastrophes such as storms or massive increases
in silt deposition leave an obvious swath of destruction on the reef.
But there are more insidious constant threats to coral — namely,
the hordes of organisms that eat coral tissue and bore into the reef.
It might appear that building a rock-hard wall around itself and
having a deep hole to hide in would make the polyp invulnerable.
But a number of urchins, worms, fishes, snails, and mussels have
evolved methods of penetrating even these formidable defenses.

When polyps are destroyed by a predator, a small area of skeleton is exposed. This break can be repaired if the coral head has
enough energy and the area is not large. Small coral heads grow
rapidly compared to older, larger colonies, but they have relatively
little energy to repair torn tissue resulting from the attack of a
predator. Large heads may receive too many wounds to be able to
repair in a short time. Once the skeleton has lost its thin cover of
living coral tissue, it is vulnerable to colonization by a number of
organisms. Algae and sponges will settle wherever a hard surface
appears. Some of these are burrowing forms and will begin to penetrate the coral head.

One of the most vicious animals on the reef is the Fireworm. I
once saw a particularly large specimen wrapped around a thick,
vertical branch of Deadman's Fingers. The worm had started at

the tip of the branch and had swallowed the first 5 cm (2 in.), digesting all living tissue by secreting enzymes over the coenosarc (living tissue). The soupy mixture of enzymes and partially digested coral tissue was then sucked up by the pharynx of the worm, leaving a dead, white swath. Evidence suggests that this worm prefers the tips of Staghorn Coral, eating an average of 1 tip in 24 hours. Algae overgrow the damaged area, which never recovers.

The small Green Reef Crab simply uses its claws to pluck polyps from their cups. On the finger-coral flats, every space, hole, and tiny cave between the coral branches seems occupied. The abundance of this crab makes it an important predator of coral even though feeding on polyps may be incidental to its usual scavenger habits.

Certain snails eat coral. The Short Coral Snail and snails of the genus *Calliostoma,* such as the Chocolate-lined Top Snail, have been implicated in coral predation (see p. 50).

Of the fishes that eat coral the parrotfishes are most prominent. In a study done in Bermuda it was estimated that for every acre of reef 920 kg (1 ton) of solid coral skeleton is converted into fine sand every year, primarily by parrotfishes.

Less important predators are the Atlantic Spadefish, primarily a feeder on shellfish, and the Yellowtail Damselfish, which usually browses algae from coral surfaces. Like the butterflyfishes, these fishes take vigorous bites out of the coral, incidentally eating the polyps in their quest for other prey. Circular white patches and long white rasped areas are signs of browsing on coral heads by the Yellowtail Damselfish and parrotfishes, respectively (see Fig. 39).

Many fishes that feed on coral tissues do so accidentally. They are considered to be herbivorous, in search of algae. The fact that corals may contain as much as 50% zooxanthellae, which are in reality algae, may help explain the common use of coral tissues as food by otherwise herbivorous fishes.

Feeding on coral is usually done by browsing, more like cattle feeding on grass than predators attacking animal prey. This is advantageous to the coral because this feeding behavior tends to be spotty, leaving a white scar here and there on the surface of the coral head. As a result, living coral tissue has an opportunity to grow back over the area before colonization by sponges or algae begins. It normally takes 2–3 months to repair the damage. During this time larvae of the encrusting colonial anemones of the genus *Palythoa* and the Chicken Liver Sponge are particularly prone to landing on the unprotected skeletal surface and colonizing it. When this happens, there sometimes is a whole succession of forms growing on the formerly bare area, often expanding the size of the wound. Worms, other sponges, and boring or surface-feeding mollusks may find a foothold on the vulnerable area, replacing the original colonizers.

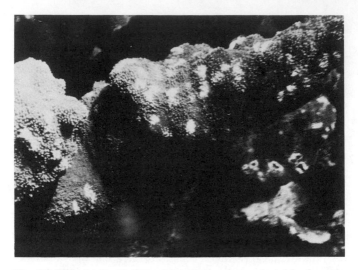

Fig. 39 Elkhorn Coral. The white spots were produced by browsing parrotfishes.

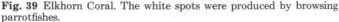

Heads of boulder and starlet corals show the damage wrought by predation most readily. In the case of Boulder Coral the lobed, irregular shape of the heads leads to shallow depressions on their surface. These tend to accumulate debris, causing suffocation of the polyps. White scars result. They are soon colonized by algae, snails, urchins, and other organisms and are expanded. That is why flattened heads of boulder corals are particularly scarred. Round Starlet Coral usually forms perfectly hemispherical heads and so is not as susceptible to scarring as the boulder corals, although the top of the dome is often the site of an ever-widening scar.

The back reef may be particularly susceptible to damage. First, it is nearest the shore, where siltation is maximum. Second, zooplankton are scantier here than on the reef front; thus the vigor of the corals is reduced just enough to make them vulnerable. In addition, parrotfishes and butterflyfishes are common here.

Even plants seem to be able to prey on coral. Blue-green microscopic tangled strands of single plant cells (*Oscillatoria*) form a narrow band around heads of star corals, boulder corals, and brain corals. Surrounded by these strands of algae, the polyps die.

Boring Organisms. Among the destructive forces on the reef the borers are paramount. They alone can alter the shape of the reef by undermining coral heads, causing them to break free when buffeted by waves or storms. The broken coral rolls downward along the sloping fore reef or falls back onto the rubble zone. In the former case the broken piece of coral may roll into water too deep to allow it to compete. Its precise "fit" into its niche prohibits it from adapting to other niches, and it dies. If the coral is washed backward it ends up in the graveyard of corals, the rubble zone, where in its weakened state it is overcome by siltation and colonization by algae.

The boring sponges of the genus *Cliona* cannot prey on intact living coral but must enter through a dead area of the colony. Once they have penetrated, they bore their way deep into the coral head, riddling the coral with many tunnels. Often sponges grow on the dead basal portions of branching colonies of Staghorn Coral or finger coral, for example, and extend into living branches, attacking from within. Nine species of boring sponge have been found on Staghorn Coral in Jamaica. There are several species of boring mollusks; the date mussels (similar in appearance to date pits) are the commonest.

The Black Date Mussel and the Mahogany Date Mussel are the most important Caribbean species. It is not known precisely how they penetrate and burrow into the coral. Recent studies suggest that a young mussel settles on the surface of the coral and waits for the coral to grow around it. As the coral continues to grow, the mussel burrows *outward,* maintaining contact with the outside. Apparently it rotates the posterior of its valves against the coral and secretes a chemical that aids in dissolving the calcium carbonate.

The date mussels and the boring sponges attack branching species more frequently than they attack massive corals. This possibly occurs because the branching corals grow most rapidly and thus have skeletons that are more porous (as in the case of Elkhorn and Staghorn Corals) or because they normally produce skeletons that are less compact (as in the case of the finger coral species).

In shallow water the Red Rock Urchin excavates shallow burrows in coral. The Reef Urchin is sometimes found on the fore reef and may bore into deeper-dwelling corals. Usually these urchins find depressions in coral heads and enlarge them by rotating their spine-covered bodies. The Long-spined Black Urchin may be very common on the reef. One observer reported an average of 8.7 urchins per square meter. They were estimated to have ground away 9.3 kg (over 20 lbs.) of reef per square meter per year.

The human animal is the most opportunistic of all species. His lack of commitment to one environment has led him to be adaptable to virtually all. When the environment does not suit him, he changes it. Peripheral areas bear the brunt of this expansion. Islands in the Caribbean and the sandy keys of southern Florida that were nearly uninhabited 60 years ago are now echoing to the throb of fast-paced, tourism-inspired development. Condominiums, monster hotels, and international airports are evident everywhere when one arrives at much-vaunted "tropical paradises." The bauxite industry spreads a thin coat of red dust over parts of northern Jamaica. Massive areas of St. Croix, Curaçao, Trinidad, Aruba, and other islands have sprouted gigantic tank farms and oil refineries. Many of the Florida Keys are so bulwarked and manicured that one is hard-pressed to find the original limestone beaches, so hard to walk on yet so lush with life in every crevice.

The catalogue of permanent human damage to the delicate reefs is long. The airfield at Castle Harbor, Bermuda, has permanently destroyed local reefs. Siltation associated with dredging has caused the destruction of corals in Water Bay, St. Thomas. Sewage has brought death to the corals in Kaneohe Bay, Hawaii. Large amounts of sewage fertilized the waters, causing such rapid plant growth that the natural cycles of plants and animals were disrupted. This resulted in the death of many fishes and other organisms as masses of dead plants rotted on the bottom, robbing the water of its oxygen. An alga, *Dictyosphaeria,* forming sheets of bubblelike cells, invaded the central part of Kaneohe Bay and covered parts of the bottom, killing the coral. Its abnormal growth was due to increased nutrients brought in by sewage.

Thermal effluents from power plants in Biscayne Bay, Florida, and Oahu, Hawaii, have caused the deaths of corals as far as 1.5 km (almost a mile) from the plants. The hot water was more than could be tolerated by many other tropical organisms. Research in Biscayne Bay has shown that many algae and invertebrate larvae die if exposed to temperatures above 32°C (90°F) for a few days. Many bays reach this temperature when shorefront power plants add their thermal effluents to already warm summer waters.

A desalination plant on St. Thomas has killed corals to a distance of 200 m (over 600 ft.).

Heavy metals, washed into the ocean by rainwater through storm sewers and released from bottom sediments by dredging, have been found in toxic concentrations on Florida reefs.

Oil pollution is a serious new hazard. It has even reached the marine laboratory on a tiny, obscure, uninhabited island off the coast of Virgin Gorda (itself sparsely populated) in the British Virgin Islands. This island was deliberately chosen for its remoteness. Yet, to the horror of the researchers, so much bunker oil (heavy tarlike crude oil) was released from ships and floated up on the beaches that it was necessary to keep a constant supply of kerosene on hand to wash the oil from their bodies.

Considerable research has been done on the effects of oil pollution. Floating oil, if present all the time, will certainly coat the corals exposed during low spring tides. Not only is the coral killed but the reproductive capability of nearby living polyps is reduced; recolonization becomes difficult, sometimes impossible, as long as the oil remains. A 1.6 km (1 mi.) long reef off Elath, Israel, has been destroyed by oil spills.

The polyps are destroyed, ironically, by their own defense mech-

Fig. 40 Underwater graffiti. Algae, sponge larvae, and other organisms will soon colonize the defenseless damaged areas of this head of Boulder Coral, which may die as a result of the thoughtless damage.

anisms. The oil irritates the polyp, which responds by producing copious amounts of mucus. Normally a whole flora of bacteria lives on the mucus in a balanced relationship with the coral. But when mucus is produced in huge quantities, it attracts hordes of other bacteria. They, in turn, engulf the mass of mucus and polyps, eating everything, polyps included. Thus a beautiful coral reef is reduced by bacteria to a mass of black bacterial slime. This slime has been seen on many reefs, including those in Bermuda.

To the aforementioned affronts to nature must be added the destruction caused by the building of hotels, industries, and even cities at the water's edge. Lagoons must be dredged and reefs blown apart to create and deepen channels for seagoing ships bringing in hundreds of tourists or thousands of barrels of oil every day. The silt from these enterprises is carried by longshore currents to other reefs.

New beaches are built by dredging sand and pouring it over rocky areas and marshes. These barren sandy beaches replace thriving biotic communities. Man has conquered his environment, creating sandy beaches where once there were nasty rocky shores. Or has he?

7

Sponges

Sponges, members of Phylum Porifera, are the most primitive of the many-celled animals. They consist of only a few kinds of cells arranged in layers. In many cases each cell acts independently of the others, its contribution to the whole sponge appearing to be coincidental. It reminds one of a city where each shoemaker is concerned with his own survival, yet all the inhabitants of the city are well shod. This lack of integration places sponges in the position of bridging the gap between colonies of 1-celled animals (colonial protozoa) and all other (truly multicelled) animals. No higher animals have evolved from sponges. They constitute a blind alley in animal evolution. For these reasons they are assigned to a separate subkingdom, Parazoa.

Each sponge has an outer skin or epidermis and a central mass, riddled with chambers containing special cells. These cells, called choanocytes, have a sticky collar and a hairlike flagellum. Choanocytes create a current of water by beating their flagella back and forth. The water enters through millions of pinholes in the skin (dermal pores) and passes through spaces lined with choanocytes (flagellated chambers). Plankton stick to the collars of the choanocytes and are used for food. Special cells, resembling amebas, carry food particles to the other cells of the body mass. The water, now devoid of its plankton, passes through canals that fuse to form large exhaust holes, the oscules. In the case of tube- and vase-shaped sponges, the exhaust canals (excurrent canals) fuse to form a large central cavity, the atrium, which opens to the outside through one large osculum rather than many smaller ones.

The water circulates in this sequence: dermal pores → incurrent canals → flagellated chambers (plankton removed here) → excurrent canals → atrium → osculum → outside.

When the water currents from the outgoing (excurrent) canals empty into the atrium (the way tributaries empty into rivers), the rate of flow increases. The water current coming from a large osculum can sometimes be detected 1 m ($3\frac{1}{4}$ ft.) above the sponge.

If sponges consist mostly of holes, how can some species appear so massive? A loggerhead sponge, for example, can be bigger than a beer barrel. The answer is that sponges have an internal skeleton of needles called spicules. These can have many shapes, with 3, 4, 5, or more rays coming from a central axis. Under a microscope they look like slivers of glass. There are often tough, stringy threads of protein called spongin fibers interwoven among the spicules. Some sponges, however, have only spongin and no spicules. These fibers and spicules form a dense network; thus the sponge is tough and rubbery. Various kinds of ameboid cells travel independently, like ghosts, slipping throughout this network and carrying out roles related to building spicules, transporting food, and removing wastes.

Some sponges encrust the bottom of any solid object and take its shape. Among these are the Chicken Liver Sponge, the Variable Sponge, the Fire Sponge, and the Black Chimney Sponge.

Many species of sponge form distinct shapes. They can be vaselike, tubular, spherical, or fingerlike. It is amazing that an animal so diffuse as a sponge can form a characteristic shape. After all, it has no nervous system, no digestive system, no circulatory system — in fact, no systems at all. Each cell or layer of cells functions more or less independently. Yet when a larval sponge (a flagellated ball of cells called a parenchymula) lands on a rock, it divides into 2, 4, and eventually thousands of cells. The aggregation develops into the shape distinctive of the species, though a sponge has no eyes, nose, or mouth and does not even have the means of being aware of itself. Proof of this uncanny ability of individual cells to act together was obtained early this century when a fully grown sponge was macerated and strained through fine mesh cloth. The result was complete disaggregation, just a dish full of individual cells, each completely separated from the others. After a day the cells had slithered, crawled, and wandered back together. Eventually they formed an almost complete duplicate of the original, with chambers, canals, and so forth.

Reproduction and Ecology. In some Caribbean sponges reproduction is a very brief activity; the whole process is limited to about 2 weeks. Males release large numbers of sperms, which invade females through their water circulation system and fertilize the eggs. Close synchronism between sperm release and egg ripening ensures that most eggs are fertilized. In the case of the Giant Bowl Sponge sperms make up 10–20% of total body weight during this period.

The Black Ball Sponge produces few eggs and sperms. It uses little energy for reproduction. Furthermore, its larvae are not brooded internally but are emitted as flagellated parenchymula, left to swim among the plankton and thus exposed to the possibility of predation. However, once established, this species has a high survival rate compared to the Giant Bowl Sponge.

Both the Giant Bowl Sponge and the Black Ball Sponge are specialist species. They have very specific habitat requirements and are distributed in narrow niches, the Giant Bowl Sponge in the deep fore reef and the Black Ball Sponge in shallow lagoons with nutrient-rich waters free of sediment. They have relatively large populations, live long, grow slowly, and expend relatively little energy on producing larvae.

This lifestyle contrasts greatly with that of a species of *Mycale*. This sponge reproduces throughout the warm, calm months, from May to October. Both sexes are present in the same sponge, and much energy is devoted to reproduction and brooding of young inside the sponge. These sponges colonize areas rapidly through the release of many well-developed larvae. Some of these land on sandy areas and are suffocated. Most do not survive. Those that successfully settle on the reef are subject to so much competition that an annual mortality rate of over 40% has been reported. They are especially susceptible to storms, which tear them from the substratum or bury them in silt.

Mycale is a generalist species. It exhibits wide habitat and depth range and low population density. It grows rapidly and has a short life span and an extended reproduction period. Its larvae are well developed and settle indiscriminately on any surface, producing large populations of young sponges, most of which die in their first year. *Mycale* is insensitive to most factors that limit populations of the specialist species — for example, temperature, current, and turbidity. Its metabolic rate is also several times faster.

The generalists and the specialists may have different lifestyles, but in the end the results are more or less the same: lots of sponges. In the long run they produce relatively constant populations. The specialists have adapted to narrow niches where they can compete effectively. They direct most of their energy toward survival of the individual and are long-lived, slow-growing species. *Mycale*, the generalist, invades a broad range of habitats and expends its energy producing short-lived populations throughout the reef.

Role. Sponges are attractive and conspicuous inhabitants of any Florida–West Indian coral reef. Some, such as the tube and vase sponges (*Spinosella*), the Orange Softball Sponge, and the Red Finger Sponge, add bright colors. Some have interesting shapes: the perfect vaselike form of the Stinking Vase Sponge, the bathtub shape of the Tub Sponge, the barrel form of the Common Loggerhead Sponge.

Sponges contribute in important ways to the ecology of the reef. They can effectively filter out plankton by pumping many liters of water through their flagellated chambers every day. But more important, they are able to use particles that are too small for other organisms to filter from the water. It has been shown that 80% of the particles consumed by 3 species of Jamaican sponges are so small that they cannot be seen with an ordinary microscope. Only 20% of the food of these sponges is the kind of plankton eaten by competing filter-feeders of other phyla. The choanocytes can engulf particles smaller than bacteria, and cytoplasmic strands stretching across excurrent canals form a network that traps whatever passes through the flagellated chambers. Ameboid cells then pick up the pieces and carry them off. These very tiny particles are more nutritious than ordinary plankton, containing 7 times the available carbon. Some sponges can live on bacteria and smaller particles alone; they don't have to rely on the sparse zooplankton. Sponges, then, are well adapted to living in the impoverished waters of tropical seas. They can live in deeper water than many other reef-dwelling animals because they do not depend on light-requiring phytoplankton. Only a few species harbor mutualistic zooxanthellae, the 1-celled plants so important in the survival of reef corals (see p. 110). In fact, it is the fore reef that often maintains the most flourishing sponge population. Deepwater sponges often exhibit massive growth, a phenomenon called gigantism.

Perhaps the major factor that limits the size of sponge populations is space on which to settle. On the teeming coral reef unpopulated surfaces are at a premium. Each hole in the skin (coenosarc) of the coral made by the rasping teeth of a parrotfish is almost immediately colonized by sponge larvae and other juveniles that constantly flit through the water in a settle-or-die competition that only a few survive. Often a damaged head of coral affords enough room on its unprotected surface to permit colonization by sponges that grow so rapidly they overshadow the coral, preventing light from reaching its zooxanthellae, destroying and eventually overgrowing the whole coral head.

Sponges prey on coral in a more direct way. Species of *Cliona,* the boring sponges, burrow into the coral, riddling it with holes. These parasitic sponges do not gain sustenance from the tissues of the coral. They are space parasites; they grow inward until much of the coral head has been replaced with sponge tissue. At first the only sign of their presence is a group of 5 mm ($\frac{1}{4}$ in.) holes lined with sponge tissue (red in the case of *C. lampa*), with a tiny osculum in the center of each mass of red tissue. The sponge feeds by filtering particles from the water. Eventually it may form a crust on the outside of the coral head. Even if the coral is pushed over by a storm surge and rolls down the fore-reef slope, the sponge continues to live and grow on the dying coral head. Eventually little is left of the coral as the triumphant sponge lives on.

Another boring sponge, the Yellow Boring Sponge, can actually penetrate the living coenosarc of the coral. It excavates cavities inside the coral head, producing yellow chimneys that extend through and above the coral surface.

Just as *Cliona* sponges and the Yellow Boring Sponge can destroy corals, so can the Orange Sponge support the coral, helping it maintain its normal position, though riddled with burrows made by boring sponges. The Orange Sponge grows on the underside of the coral, causing its edges to grow upward in folds above the sponge oscules. Thus both the sponge and the coral benefit: the sponge has a continually expanding surface on which to grow, and the coral is shielded from attack by *Cliona,* which can enter only through the nonliving underside of the coral.

Sponge-dwellers. A remarkable number and variety of organisms use the recesses of the sponge as a haven, for several reasons. There is safety deep inside the atrium of a tube sponge or within the recesses of the flagellated chambers. A steady supply of food enters via the current passing through the sponge. Sponges themselves are not very desirable as food. Some are smelly, some produce noxious secretions. If the sponge dwellers can live with these unpleasant attributes, they are relatively safe, for of the thousands of fishes on the reef only a few nibble on sponges for food and inadvertently eat their inhabitants. Angelfishes and filefishes are the major sponge predators. A few other animals, such as sea slugs, eat sponges, but they are too small to disturb the animals living inside.

In every outside crevice and deep within the atrium is a characteristic fauna. Brittle stars sometimes carpet the inside of the atrium, and they commonly inhabit the crevices of branching sponges. Two species, the Angular Brittle Star and Suenson's Brittle Star, live almost exclusively in or on sponges and soft corals.

Colonial anemones, *Parazoanthus,* live on the outside of a variety of sponges, such as *Iotrochota, Spinosella, Agelas, Xestospongia,* and others (see p. 246), and make the sponges look as if they are covered with tiny mushrooms, each about 5 mm ($\frac{1}{4}$ in.) in diameter.

A number of tiny fishes, predominantly gobies and blennies, live in or on sponges. They peer from the inner recesses of sponges and retreat inside them at signs of danger. Several species live so deep inside the sponge that their fins are frayed from constantly rubbing against sharp spicules.

Other common inhabitants of sponges are the Bicolor, Sponge, and Dusky Cardinalfishes, the Marbled Blenny, and the Greenband, Smallmouth, Yellowline, Sponge, and Frillfin Gobies. Juvenile Gulf Toadfish can often be found inside sponges in Florida.

Myriads of small shrimps and related arthropods live in the atrium and flagellated chambers of sponges. One investigator found 49 juvenile Spiny Lobsters in a single tube sponge of the genus *Spinosella.*

Pistol shrimps are the dominant crustaceans in sponges (see p. 155). In 3 large Common Loggerhead Sponges a researcher found a minimum of 5633 and a maximum of 16,352 pistol shrimps belonging to 2 species, *Synalpheus brooksi* and *S. mcclendoni.* Other crustaceans include the Common Rock Mantis Shrimp (a "thumb buster" stomatopod — see p. 153), and cleaning shrimps of the genus *Periclimenes.*

Many other animals find protection, temporary or permanent, inside the inviting nooks, crannies, and internal spaces of sponges. These include barnacles, crabs, clams, tunicates, flatworms, amphipods, isopods, and many others. Thus sponges are the habitat of whole communities.

In small sponges without hollow atria, such as the Red Finger Sponge, most of the animals living inside are threadlike worms of Family Syllidae. Since they eat the sponge tissue, the red color of their host is visible inside their bodies, causing them to match the color of the sponge. Tens of thousands of these reddish worms live inside the fingers of the Red Finger Sponge, their total mass constituting a significant portion of the weight of the sponge. The constant eating of internal tissues by the Sponge Threadworm is said to be responsible for the slow growth of its host, the Giant Bowl Sponge.

Uses. The bath sponge of yesteryear seems to have survived commercial competition with the artificial, cellulose sponge which can be manufactured for a few pennies. The natural sponge has a narrower niche than before, however; it is delicate enough to be useful in washing automobiles without damaging their finish. In the 1930s there was a massive movement of the Greek sponge-fishing industry to Florida, where the American commercial sponge, the Sheepswool Sponge, *Hippospongia lachne*, was present in exploitable quantities. At present the demand for natural sponges is great enough to keep a small sponge-fishing industry prosperous.

Sponges are also an important source of new medicines. The Fire Sponge has yielded 8 antibiotics. Many other sponges produce substances with bacteria-killing or cancer-inhibiting properties.

Although the discovery of useful medicines in sponges would give the phylum new luster in our eyes, its fate may depend not on new-found glory but on its very innocuousness. Common Bushy Soft Coral, for example, had a brief moment in the sun when it was found to produce a substance identical with a human sex-related hormone. It was harvested so ruthlessly by a pharmaceutical company that it was made practically extinct in some Bahama waters.

Other animals have learned to use the unpleasant properties of sponges to their own advantage. Several crabs pluck pieces of sponge from a rock and place them on their own backs. The sponge thrives, covering the whole carapace of the crab; when stationary, the crab is virtually invisible under its camouflage (see p. 151).

Classes. Of the 4 classes of sponges, only 2 are normally encountered in the southern Florida–West Indies region.

Class Demospongia is characterized by glassy (siliceous) spicules and/or spongin fibers. It includes the massive sponges, the tube, finger, and vase sponges, and the encrusting and boring forms visible in and around the coral reef and its environs, in both shallow and deep water.

A new class, Sclerospongia, was proposed in 1970. In it are placed about half a dozen species of sponges found in the deep fore reef of Caribbean coral reefs. These sponges have the glassy spicules and spongin of Demospongiae but are encased in an outer skeleton of chalklike calcium carbonate. Many oscules project from the outer skeleton, each surrounded by a starlike pattern of converging excurrent canals.

Although most sclerosponges are deepwater forms, rare specimens have been found at 1 m ($3\frac{1}{4}$ ft.). All live in caves except for *Ceratoporella nicholsoni*, which occurs out in the open beyond 60 m (200 ft.). This sponge can reach 1 m ($3\frac{1}{4}$ ft.) in diameter and can be abundant in deep water. Thus it is an important competitor for space with corals.

Common Species

Vance P. Vicente

The characteristics most widely used in sponge taxonomy are largely related to anatomy: size; type and arrangement of pores, oscules, spicules, and fibers; shape; surface characteristics. Other properties are sometimes useful: color, consistency, smell, symbiotic associations, and habitat. The descriptions below are based on characteristics easily recognizable by the unaided eye. The list is intended to be used as a guide in the field. For more detailed species descriptions, consult Weidenmayer's book, *The Shallow-water Sponges of the Western Bahamas* (see p. 272). All sponges described here are members of Class Demospongia.

Finger, Branching, and Bushy Sponges

RED FINGER SPONGE *Haliclona rubens* **Pl. 19**
Brick-red; firmly spongy. Usually either 1 erect cylindrical branch or a few cylindrical branches to 3 cm ($1\frac{1}{4}$ in.) thick, but sometimes fan-shaped, flattened, or encrusting. Oscules 1–5 mm ($\frac{1}{16}$–$\frac{1}{4}$ in.) wide, scattered over surface or in rows. Coral reefs, rocky areas; commonest in Turtle Grass beds.

BLUE-GREEN FINGER SPONGE *Haliclona viridis*
Green with shades of blue, brown, or gray. Branching, often bluntly, like a cockscomb; encrusting or massive. Softly spongy, limp, easily torn. Releases a *light green exudate* when squeezed underwater. Oscules to 6 mm ($\frac{1}{4}$ in.) wide, flush or raised in lobes or chimneylike processes. Turtle Grass beds, sometimes rocky areas.

BLACK BUSH SPONGE *Iotrochota birotulata*
Blackish, covered with thin *bright green layer* when alive. Bushy, with branches erect, sprawling, or growing in all directions; branches may be fused. Oscules rare, inconspicuous. Usually covered with orange colonial anemone, *Parazoanthus swiftii,* often in winding rows. Coral reefs.

PURPLE BUSH SPONGE   Pl. 20
Pandaros acanthifolium
Dark purple. Black when dried. Releases a *purplish-red exudate*
when squeezed underwater. 1 erect branch or fan-shaped or stocky
bushes attached to substratum by a short stalk. Surface has *coarse
conules.* Oscules inconspicuous, in depressions, to 3 mm ($\frac{1}{8}$ in.)
wide. Tough spongy consistency. Coral reefs; below 5 m (17 ft.).

Spherical Sponges

ORANGE SOFTBALL SPONGE
Cinachyra kuekenthali
Orange. Spherical or stalked with a rounded top that has a *depression containing oscules.* To 20 cm (8 in.) in diameter. *Related species: C. alloclada* is smaller; forms almost perfect hemispheres to
fist size. Deep.

Tube Sponges

PIPES-OF-PAN SPONGE *Agelas schmidti*   Pl. 19
Reddish brown. Typically with *laterally fused cylinders.* Thick-
walled, with a large oscule in each cylinder and smaller — to 5 mm
($\frac{1}{4}$ in.) — oscular openings scattered over surface. Colonial anemones, *Parazoanthus* species, common on surface. Coral reefs.

YELLOW TUBE SPONGE *Aplysina fistularis*   Pl. 19
Bright yellow, thick-walled tubes; turn black when removed from
water. Thin narrow diaphragm within oscular opening. May have
thin *fingerlike projections* to 1 cm ($\frac{1}{2}$ in.) long on surface of upper
portion of tubes and *around oscule.* Shallow to deep; rocky areas,
coral reefs.

GIANT TUBE SPONGE *Aplysina lacunosa*   Pl. 20
Color variable — yellow, bluish, or purplish — but purple-black
when dried. 1–3 or more *long, erect, hollow cylinders* — to 1 m
($3\frac{1}{4}$ ft.) high, to 10 cm (4 in.) in diameter — usually united at base,
sometimes close to each other. Stiffly spongy. Surface deep-grooved
with convoluted ridges and folds. Usually deep — 20–50 m (65–
165 ft.). *Related species: A. archeri* is similar but has shallow
grooves.

GLOBULAR TUBE SPONGE
Callyspongia fallax forma *fallax*
Beautiful reddish purple or bluish purple. Shape variable, most
often basally united, hollow, short, *globular lobes* — to 15 cm
(6 in.) long, to 4 cm ($1\frac{1}{2}$ in.) wide. Can form hollow tubes with
globular swellings. Compressible. Coral reefs, sometimes shallow
pools.

Table 2. Rapid Identification of Sponges[a]

Color	Body Form	Species
Red or orange	Round balls	Orange Softball Sponge
	Fingerlike branches	Red Finger Sponge
	Encrusting	Fire Sponge
	Encrusting, boring	Red Boring Sponge
Black or gray	Vase-shaped	Stinking Vase Sponge
	Massive, sometimes pillow-shaped	Pillow Stinking Sponge
	Flat, amorphous, with thin chimneys	Black Chimney Sponge
	Branching	Black Bush Sponge
	Encrusting (small smooth masses)	Formosan Sponge
	Massive, cake-shaped	Loggerhead Sponge
	Massive, barrel-shaped	Common Loggerhead Sponge
Brown	Encrusting	Chicken Liver Sponge
	Massive, sometimes with short branches	Variable Stinking Sponge
	Encrusting or massive	Touch me not Sponge
Purple (dark)	Branching	Black or Purple Bush Sponge
Lavender or violet	Branching cylinders	Lavender Tube Sponge
		Iridescent Tube Sponge
Yellow	Branching cylinders	Yellow Tube Sponge
	Boring	Yellow Boring Sponge
Green or dark blackish green	Fingerlike branches	Green Finger Sponge
	Encrusting, amorphous, with thin chimneys	Black Chimney Sponge

a. Sponges are so variable in shape and color that this chart is useful in the field only to give the observer an idea of the commonest species. For a serious attempt at classification, consult pp. 127–133.

IRIDESCENT TUBE SPONGE   Pl. 20
Spinosella plicifera
Iridescent blue, pink, purple, or orange. Single or clustered taper-
ing cylinders to 30 cm (1 ft.) high. *Can glow in daylight.* Spongy.
Surface often covered with raised, wrinkled ridges. Coral reefs.

LAVENDER TUBE SPONGE   Pl. 19
Spinosella vaginalis
Purplish, bluish, reddish, or grayish. *Tubes united at bases or
fused laterally.* Spongy hollow cylinders average 15–30 cm
(6–12 in.) high. May have large conules. Sometimes covered with
colonial anemone, *Parazoanthus parasiticus.* Coral reefs.

Vase and Tub Sponges

STINKING VASE SPONGE   Pl. 21
Ircinia campana
Brown, but sometimes reddish or greenish brown. Surface has
conules to 4 mm (³/₁₆ in.) high. Forms *broad vases* to 60 cm (2 ft.)
high. Spongy. Oscules inside concave or vase-shaped central depression. Collected specimens have terrible fetid odor. Lagoons,
coral reefs; often shallow.

GRAY CORNUCOPIA SPONGE   Pl. 20
Niphates digitalis
Bluish to grayish green, tube- or cone-shaped, with sharp fringed
rim. Surface feels rough, usually covered with colonial anemones,
Parazoanthus species; inside velvety. To 18 cm (7 in.) high. Rocky
inshore areas among algae; coral reefs.

STRAWBERRY SPONGE *Mycale* species   Pl. 20
1 or several fleshy, thick-walled, stocky, hollow cylinders fused laterally or at bases. Looks like a single, double, or triple group of
black or dark reddish brown urns covered with cone-shaped warts
or spines on outside. Thick vertical folds on surface separated by
narrow V-shaped depressions containing irregularly scattered
small holes. Large opening in top of sponge. Looks crimson only
under strong light. When removed from water, exudes large quantities of blood-red slime, which stains fingers crimson and gives rise
to former species name, (*Thorecta*) *horridus* (*Thorecta* means "armored warrior"). Usually less than 20 cm (8 in.) high. Coral reefs;
below 10 m (33 ft.).

GIANT BOWL SPONGE *Verongula gigantea*
Skin grass-green to olive-green, with yellow and brownish red
areas. Inside bright lemon-yellow; black when dried. Surface with
ridges outlining *rounded to polygonal depressions* to 1 cm (½ in.).
Bowl-shaped, often asymmetrical, with contorted walls. Walls to

70 cm (28 in.) high, to 1.5 cm ($\frac{5}{8}$ in.) thick at rim and 10 cm (4 in.) thick at base. Deep coral reefs.

BASKET or TUB SPONGE *Xestospongia muta*   **Pl. 20**
Brown or pink. Solid, brittle, not spongy. Irregular large knobby protuberances on surface, several centimeters in diameter and height. Often has deep vertical wrinkles. Shaped like a cup, vase, bowl, bell, or open-top barrel. *To bathtub size.* Coral reefs; below 5 m (17 ft.).

Encrusting Sponges

VARIABLE SPONGE *Anthosigmella varians*   **Pl. 20**
Light brown, tan, or greenish, with *smooth velvety surface;* oscular rim and crust edge paler than rest of sponge. Oscules sometimes raised in chimneylike or lumpy processes. Can form patches larger than 20 m² (215 ft.²). Other forms massive, amorphous. Rubbery; when dried, hard like wood. Massive form common in shallow lagoons, on flats where it may be exposed at low tide, on sand, rocks, Turtle Grass beds. Encrusting form in rocky areas.

CHICKEN LIVER SPONGE *Chondrilla nucula*   **Pl. 19**
Thin — to 3 mm ($\frac{1}{8}$ in.) — brown rubbery crust over hard substrata, including live corals. *Smooth slippery surface resembles fresh liver.* Oscules to 3 mm ($\frac{1}{8}$ in.) wide, dark or black, conspicuous only in undisturbed live specimens. Lagoons, Turtle Grass beds; shallows.

BLEEDING SPONGE *Oligoceras hemorrhages*
Brown or dark olive, easily torn, softly spongy. Tiny white-tipped conules. If torn, "bleeds" a beautiful *red exudate.* Can form crusts or lobate colonies to 25 cm (10 in.) in diameter, to 5 cm (2 in.) high. Oscules numerous, often on tops of lobes, to 5 mm ($\frac{1}{4}$ in.) in diameter. Turtle Grass beds. *Similar species:* Stinking Sponge, *Ircinia felix* (Pl. 18), is lighter, has larger conules, is not easily torn, has black oscular rims, and does not release a red exudate.

BLACK CHIMNEY SPONGE *Pellina carbonaria*
Dark green but looks black. May be buried in sand, coral rubble, seagrass beds, and most shallow substrata from which *chimneys* (oscular processes) *arise.* Skin easily detached. Lagoons.

FIRE SPONGE *Tedania ignis*   **Pl. 19**
Orange or red. Crust to 1 cm ($\frac{1}{2}$ in.) thick on Red Mangrove roots, rocks, coral rubble, seagrass beds. Oscular processes volcanolike; oscules to 1 cm ($\frac{1}{2}$ in.) in diameter, conspicuous only in undisturbed specimens. Thin delicate skin (translucent, sometimes whitish) covers surface. Compressible but easily torn. *Can be very irritating to skin upon contact.*

Amorphous and Massive Sponges

FORMOSAN SPONGE *Erylus formosus*
Purplish gray to black crust, massive or amorphous. Inside white
to grayish. *Surface smooth,* becomes wrinkled when sponge is
lifted from water. Easily detachable skin. Oscules to 1 cm (½ in.)
wide, often recessed on tops of lumps and ridges. Coral reefs; 3–
20 m (10–67 ft.) deep.

PILLOW STINKING SPONGE   **Pl. 2**
Ircinia strobilina
Gray, with *large conules* to 8 mm (⅜ in.) high. Shaped like a
stubby cylinder (wider than high) or pillow. If cylindrical, oscules
to 5 mm (¼ in.) in diameter, scattered in groups on top surface
(rarely gathered in center of top). If pillow-shaped, *oscules
large — to 1 cm (½ in.) — lined up along top crest of pillow.* Emits
characteristic fetid odor if removed from water. Lagoons, usually
on rocky bottoms.

TOUCH-ME-NOT SPONGE   **Pl. 19**
Neofibularia nolitangere
Brown. Brittle and crumbly, *not spongy.* Adults large, doughnut-
shaped or very thick encrustations to 60 cm (2 ft.) wide. Oscules to
1.5 cm (⅝ in.) wide, irregularly distributed. Many black brittle
stars often visible on surface, which may be covered with sediment
or algae. *If touched, causes severe rash, swollen fingertips, or severe itching over whole body.* Coral reefs; usually 10–15 m (33–
50 ft.) deep; under ledges in shallow water.

COMMON LOGGERHEAD SPONGE   **Pl. 21**
Spheciospongia vesparium
Black or grayish black. Usually forms *large round barrel* or cake-
shaped hemispherical mass with *flattened top.* Rubbery, not
spongy. *Cluster of large black holes in center of the flat top.*
Clearly visible clustered pores on sides. Surface irregular, lumpy,
but never conulose. Many pistol shrimps and porcellanid crabs
inside. To 1 m (3¼ ft.) across. Shallow, sometimes huge specimens
awash; seagrass beds, sandy sediment, rocky areas.

Boring Sponges

RED BORING SPONGE   **Pl. 20**
Cliona delitrix
Red crust dotted with white colonial anemone, *Parazoanthus
parasiticus.* May look brown in deep water due to lack of red light.
On massive coral heads, sometimes overgrowing and killing whole
coral colony. Colonizes dead coral bases. Coral reefs; below 10 m
(33 ft.). *Related species:* (1) *C. lampa,* found at shallower depths,

more often produces red-lined tunnels. (2) *C. langae* forms a brown crust on corals and rubble (see p. 50). Both species similar to Red Boring Sponge.

YELLOW BORING SPONGE   Pl. 20
Siphonodictyon coralliphagum
Yellow lumps and short wide tubes, each with 1 large osculum, or yellow crust growing on or projecting from coral. Can penetrate live coral coenosarc. Riddles and overgrows coral head, often killing it. Usually below 10 m (33 ft.).

8

Segmented Worms

Paul G. Johnson and Barry A. Vittor

The coral reef seems to transform its inhabitants into colorful flamboyant versions of their more mundane terrestrial brethren. This transformation is nowhere more apparent than in the segmented worms, Phylum Annelida. On the reef the worms look like flowers in a garden, colorful fans, and miniature Christmas trees. Thousands of invisible threadworms live inside sponges, and many dead coral heads are riddled with worm burrows. But these biologically important species, together with the sediment-dwelling forms so important as food for fishes and invertebrates, pale in comparison with the more spectacular filter-feeding species.

There are 4 classes of segmented worms: leeches (Class Hirudinea); worms with few bristles (Class Oligochaeta), such as earthworms; primitive, rarely seen worms (Class Archiannelida); and worms with many bristles (Class Polychaeta), the commonest marine forms.

Polychaetes, the subject of this chapter, have evolved numerous physical adaptations, all from the basic body plan depicted in Fig. 41. The head is termed the prostomium and includes the eyes, antennae, and palps. The peristomium, or first body segment, often carries tentacles or other filamentlike structures. Each segment has a pair of paddlelike appendages used for swimming or crawling. Projecting from these are many bristles, or setae, giving rise to the name of the class (*poly* = many; *chaeta* = bristles). These setae can be long and poisonous, presenting a ferocious, invulnerable wall of needles around the worm; they can be extended over the back of the worm to form a protective mat; or they can be short, an aid in crawling and burrowing.

The most striking adaptation of a number of reef-dwelling polychaetes is the crown of branched tentacles, or radioles, which are used to strain plankton from the water. The radioles form an outwardly expanding or inverted (Christmas-tree-like) funnel that focuses downward toward the mouth. Microscopic, moving, hairlike cilia create a current that sweeps water through the funnel, and the feathery radioles filter out small particles. If you look closely, you will see a calcareous plate extending above and behind the fan. This is the operculum (a trap door of a sort), which is snapped down like a lid over the tube as soon as the eyespots on the radioles detect a shadow. The operculum is armored with horns, antlers, or star-shaped, massed needles.

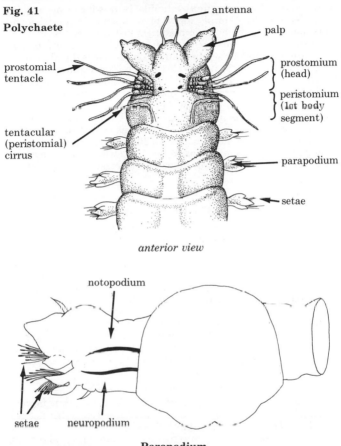

Fig. 41
Polychaete

antenna

palp

prostomial tentacle

prostomium (head)

peristomium (1ot body segment)

tentacular (peristomial) cirrus

parapodium

setae

anterior view

notopodium

setae   neuropodium

Parapodium
cross section

Feeding methods vary. Most tube-dwellers are filter-feeders; some extend long filaments, which look like strands of spaghetti, over the bottom, picking up organic material (detritus) and carrying it to the mouth by ciliary action. This is called detritus-feeding. Another method of feeding is demonstrated by the Sponge Thread-worm, which lives in the chambers and tunnels of sponges, eating the sponge tissues. Members of Family Eunicidae bore into dead and dying corals, riddling them with burrows and thereby weakening the corals, which eventually crumble. Burrowing forms may be deposit-feeders. They simply ingest mud or sand, flood it with enzymes, and digest the organic materials in the sediment.

The free-living worms (errant polychaetes) are usually predators. One of the most ferocious animals on the reef is the Fireworm, which attacks anything it can catch, including sea anemones 10 times its size. It everts its pharynx over a portion of its prey, secreting digestive juices that dissolve the tissues; these are then sucked up by the pharynx. The Fireworm is often seen on the reef. It has no need to hide because its body margins are white masses of long, poisonous setae. Be careful not to touch this worm, for its barbed setae easily penetrate the skin and are difficult to remove. Wearing gloves may give you a false sense of security: when you remove the gloves, the setae embedded in them will penetrate your fingertips.

Common Species

Polychaetes, with the exception of particularly large common forms, can be hard to identify in the field. The purpose here is to acquaint the nonspecialist with those varieties that are most frequently encountered and that can be identified on the basis of obvious external characteristics. Tube type (if any), coloration, length, unusual appendages, habitat, and other criteria may be used to establish at least the family of the worms included here. The serious student should seek more complete literature on polychaete systematics to identify other species.

Polychaetes are divided into 2 groups of families on the basis of lifestyle rather than physical characteristics. Because these categories are artificial, they are hard to relate to the ecology and phylogeny (evolution) of the class.

1. **Sedentary polychaetes** are adapted to existence in one place. Usually build tubes or burrows. Often have elaborate fanlike or elongate tentacles. Body often divided into 2 or 3 distinct regions. Parapodia and setae often reduced.

2. **Errant polychaetes** are free-living and move about in search of food. Predatory, carnivorous. Most have well-developed parapodia to aid in swimming and burrowing. Usually have a toothed, eversible pharynx used to capture other worms or small invertebrates.

Sedentary Polychaetes

HORNED or FEATHERED CHRISTMAS TREE WORM
Spirobranchus giganteus giganteus   **Pl. 28**
Family Serpulidae. One of the largest and most visible serpulids on the reef; common name derives from shape of the expanded bran-

chial crown. Body to 12 cm (5 in.) long, divided into thorax and abdomen, housed in a sturdy convoluted *calcareous tube* attached to rocks, coral. Protruding from tube are *paired whorls of branchial crown,* as well as plate-shaped operculum on a fleshy stalk. Branchial crown important in respiration and filter-feeding. Operculum armed with 2 or 3 *branched antlerlike processes.* Tube smooth and porcelainlike inside; deep lavender, shading to white at rim. Outside chalky white, rough, irregular; often encrusted with organisms. Animal strikingly colored: antlers deep carmine-red, operculum yellow, body flesh-colored, spectacular crown yellow, red, or blue. Usually solitary on reef face, where currents provide continuous supply of plankton, but many may be found close together on coral head. Throughout West Indies from 50 m (165 ft.) to shore.

STAR CHRISTMAS TREE WORM *Pomatostegus stellatus*
Family Serpulidae. Similar to Horned Christmas Tree Worm (above); identifiable by its distinctively shaped operculum, consisting of 3-5 disklike horny plates mounted one on top of another on a hollow central axis; under each plate are *rows of starlike diverging spines and a circle of spines.* Branchiae spiraled, about $1\frac{1}{2}$ turns, bright rose to chocolate-brown, lightly barred with white. Body flesh-colored, with yellow cross-stripes that shine like silk when held to light. Tube hard and calcareous. Caribbean, south Florida.

SPINY FEATHER DUSTER WORMS *Hydroides* species
Family Serpulidae. To 4 cm ($1\frac{1}{2}$ in.) long, usually smaller. White calcareous tube stout, rough, often irregularly coiled, and attached to surface of shells, rocks. Branchial plumes orange, fan out to either side of opercular stalk. Operculum ornate, with 10 or 11 large, equal-sized, horny spines, all curving inward and ending in sharp points. Spines mounted in depression of a basal funnel of fused, radially symmetrical, toothlike structures. Bases of large spines hinged, so when worm withdraws into tube, *opercular spines expand outward into a circle of daggerlike projections,* protecting tube entrance. 10-15 species throughout Caribbean; common species include *H. uncinata, H. crucigera, H. elegans.* Accurate species identification requires detailed study of operculum and setae.

BANDED FANWORMS *Sabella* species   **Pl. 28**
Family Sabellidae. Thick-bodied sabellids in rocky habitats on leeward side of coral reefs or protected tide pools. Common in West Indies, Bermuda, south Florida. (1) Five-spotted Feather Duster Worm, *S. melanostigma* (Pl. 28), has a regular arrangement of *4 or 5 pairs of black eyespots* along each tentacular filament; eyespots easily visible to unaided eye (see plate). Body yellowish brown, with distinctive pattern of black spots in double rows on either side

(pattern most noticeable on anterior segments). Expanded branchial crown brown at base, grading to uniform yellow toward end of filaments. Unlike most sabellids, this species, if disturbed, will leave its tube quickly and build a new *mucus-silt tube* elsewhere. (2) *S. micropthalma* has *more eyespots, which are irregularly distributed along filaments*. Body pale yellow, without paired spots. Filaments unbanded in both species.

ELEGANT FANWORM *Hypsicomus elegans*   **Pl. 28**
Family Sabellidae. Body pale purplish brown, heavily shaded along middorsal line. Membrane at base of tentacular crown usually purple. Branchiae yellow, occasionally spotted or banded with purple. White, yellow, purple-spotted, and red forms have also been found. To 6 cm (2½ in.) long, 1.8 cm (¾ in.) of which forms the branchiae. *Oblique lateral row of setae on collar just below tentacular crown.* Tube dark, tough, sometimes long and tortuous; penetrates clumps of shells or rocks. Commonest on older parts of reef with little live coral, and on underside of loose rocks on shallow landward side of reef. Prefers well-shaded areas. Common in rocky and reef habitats throughout coastal southeastern U.S., Bermuda, West Indies.

RED-BANDED FANWORM *Potamilla fonticula*   **Pl. 28**
Family Sabellidae. Large tube-dwelling feather-duster to 7 cm (2¾ in.) long, 3 cm (1¼ in.) of which forms the tentacular crown, which is white or red, with a *dark red band midway along branchial filaments*. Row of minute eyespots on most branchiae, not visible without magnification. Branchia bases united by delicate low weblike membrane. Body flesh-colored, with 2 brown ventral stripes running length of worm. About 20 thoracic segments in adult. Tube tough and horny, to 15 cm (6 in.) long, 1.5 cm (¾ in.) wide. Free end of tube tapered; consists of fine mud and mucus. Among loose rocks or in clumps in quiet water. Florida Keys, Virgin Islands, Puerto Rico. *Related species: P. reniformis* has *1 pair of eyes* at base of tentacular crown.

MAGNIFICENT BANDED FANWORM   **Pl. 28**
Sabellastarte magnifica
Family Sabellidae. A common, strikingly colored fanworm. Body to 12 cm (4¾ in.) long, including 9 cm (3½ in.) tentacular crown, which is made up of many closely set filaments and may have a *spread of 20–25 cm (8–10 in.).* Usually a shade of brown, with several series of colored spots arranged in bands — brown banded with light tan spots, chocolate-brown banded in white, dark purple with brown spots, or dark mahogany-red banded with light brown — but rarely almost white, with indistinct barring like watered silk. Tube cylindrical, formed of mucus cementing fine particles of mud; lined internally with hardened mucus. *Often in clumps* near leeward side of rocks or on floor of small tide pools;

the many expanded branchial crowns resemble a field of flowers. Juvenile cannot be differentiated from Black-spotted Fanworm (below) in the field.

BLACK-SPOTTED FANWORM *Branchiomma nigromaculata*
Family Sabellidae. Small — rarely longer than 2.5 cm (1 in.). Body speckled with dark spots; *branchiae have many minute black eyespots.* Cannot be differentiated from juvenile Magnificent Banded Fanworm (above) in the field.

MEDUSA WORM *Loimia medusa*
Family Terebellidae. 2 body regions: thorax (brick-red, usually thick, with dorsal bundles of setae and ventral pads, bearing hooked setae) and abdomen (thinner, with reduced parapodia). Tube mucous-lined, covered with debris, secured to rocks or buried vertically. *Numerous feeding tentacles project from tube.* White, banded or checkered purple, these tentacles can spread out a meter or more over the bottom in search of food particles, which are carried to the mouth by way of a ciliated groove. Tentacles retract when touched. Widely distributed in tropics and subtropics. *Similar species: Eupolymnia nebulosa* has white tentacles.

Errant Polychaetes

FIREWORM *Hermodice carunculata*   **Pl. 28**
Family Amphinomidae. *Caution:* Harmful to touch (see p. 256). To 30 cm (1 ft.) long, usually smaller. *A large, transversely pleated, cushionlike growth (the caruncle) extends from prostomium to 3rd or 4th segment.* This sensitive olfactory organ is used to locate food by tasting water. Large, bushy, paired branchiae on 1st segment, continue along body. Body greenish to chocolate-brown, with bright red branchiae contrasting with bundles of white setae. A predator; seen most often on reef in early morning or evening, when it makes its feeding excursions. Feeds mainly on corals, colonial anemones, other sedentary animals (see p. 114). Often in crevices or under rocks on coral reefs and in Turtle Grass beds. Southeast Florida, Caribbean, Bahamas.

RED-TIPPED FIREWORM *Chloeia viridis*   **Pl. 28**
Family Amphinomidae. Closely associated with reefs; may be found creeping over and between rocks on bottom, scavenging for food, or occasionally swimming near surface. Usually 20–30 cm (8–12 in.) long, *heavy and flattened.* Dorsal side of adults striped with red and brown bars. Gills conspicuous, have regular fernlike branches. Long white setae along margin of body can penetrate your skin, so do not touch. West Indies.

ROUGH SCALEWORM *Hermenia verruculosa*
Family Polynoidae. Stout, *grub-shaped.* Flattened ventrally, arched dorsally, slightly tapered anteriorly and posteriorly. Large

specimen may be more than 3 cm (1¼ in.) long, 9 mm (⅜ in.) wide, including setae. 26 segments in mature specimen. Bilobed prostomium partially covered by enlarged 1st pair of scales. 4 eyes, anterior pair surrounded by broad red bands. Dorsum rough, granulated, with dark bands of globular bumps. Setae amber, stout, forked; project conspicuously from body. *Body accumulates a covering of fine sand,* which obscures dorsal elytrae (scales). Lives in interstices of coral; when disturbed, moves rapidly into crevices.

LUMINESCENT THREADWORM *Odontosyllis enopla*
SPONGE THREADWORM *Haplosyllis spongicola*
ZEBRA WORM *Trypanosillis vittigera*
Family Syllidae. Small threadlike worms. Abundant in Caribbean but difficult to find due to small size and cryptic habits. Body elongate, with *beaded dorsal cirri projecting from parapodia* like strings of pearls. Feed on sedentary organisms by everting pharynx armed with 1 or more teeth; once prey is punctured, pumping pharynx sucks out juices. (1) The Luminescent Threadworm and some other species perform a spawning ritual in which the body becomes filled with eggs or sperms, and worms swarm in plankton at night to discharge gametes. During this ritual the Luminescent Threadworm displays a striking luminescent pattern of flashes similar to that of fireflies. Females, swimming in tight circles on surface, light up at intervals of 10–20 seconds and produce a circle of light to which male is attracted. Male flashes briefly as he swims to center of circle to spawn. (2) Sponge Threadworm *lives in small passageways of sponges,* probably eating tissues of host. Tiny — less than 6 mm (¼ in.) long. Color similar to that of host sponge, whose tissues are visible in the gut of the transparent worm (see p. 126). (3) Zebra Worm is flattened. Common. Reproduces asexually by simple budding. New individuals bud-off from posterior end of body.

ATLANTIC PALOLO WORM *Eunice schemacephala*
Family Eunicidae. Large — to 16 cm (6¼ in.) long, only 5 mm (¼ in.) wide. Head bilobed, with 5 antennae and pair of kidneyshaped eyes. Peristomium has a pair of cirri. Color of worm variable; often dark iridescent reddish brown, with *white bands grading to large white spots on posterior segments.* Parapodia thick; following 8th body segment, red comblike gills rise from dorsal cirri. In burrows inside coral and rocks (as are many other eunicids). Complex jaws permit this worm to rasp tunnels in coral heads, occasionally damaging live coral. When spawning, millions of worms swarm at surface, looking like thick vermicelli soup. Posterior end, filled with sperms or eggs, breaks off and swims to surface; anterior end remains on bottom. Swarming has been observed at 3.6–9 m (12–30 ft.) off Dry Tortugas.

Plates

PLATE 1

The Mixed Zone (1)

1. **TAN BUSHY SOFT CORAL,** *Plexaura flexuosa.* Tan branches with elongate forks.

2. **BOULDER CORAL,** *Montastrea annularis.* Green or tan lobed heads.

3. **CRENELATED FIRE CORAL,** *Millepora alcicornis.* Yellow or tan, with white bumpy tips.

4. **BLUE CHROMIS,** *Chromis cyanea.* Bright iridescent blue fish.

5. **COMMON BRAIN CORAL,** *Diploria strigosa.* Round; greenish brown hills.

6. **FLOWER CORAL,** *Eusimilia fastigiata.* Yellow; large cups at ends of short branches.

7. **ROUND STARLET CORAL,** *Siderastrea siderea.* Gray or tan; cups look like tiny dots.

8. **BRANCHING CORAL,** *Madracis mirabilis.* Cushionlike clumps of brittle, short, brown, forked branches.

9. **LARGE GROOVED BRAIN CORAL,** *Colpophyllia natans.* Brown or tan; wide hills and valleys; thin groove along hilltops.

10. **STAGHORN CORAL,** *Acropora cervicornis.* 1 antlerlike branch shown.

11. **BLACK DURGON,** *Melichthys niger.* Black triggerfish with large dorsal fin.

12. **FLAT-TOPPED FIRE CORAL,** *Millepora complanata.* 2 flat-topped blades shown.

13. **COMMON BUSHY SOFT CORAL,** *Plexaura homomalla.* Brown; forks shorter than in Tan Bushy Soft Coral.

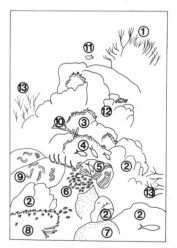

PLATE 2

The Fore-reef Terrace

1. IRIDESCENT TUBE SPONGE, *Spinosella plicifera.* Dull purple with iridescent light blue overtones.

2. KNOBBY CANDELABRA, *Eunicea* species. Thick, bushy, knobby, yellow-brown branches.

3. STOPLIGHT PARROTFISH, *Sparisoma viride.* Gray with red belly; large scales outlined in black.

4. CRENELATED FIRE CORAL, *Millepora alcicornis.* Tan, smooth; no visible cups; pointed white branch tips.

5. LARGE-CUPPED BOULDER CORAL, *Montastrea cavernosa.* Cups distinct, blisterlike, greenish with bright green centers.

6. TAN LETTUCE-LEAF CORAL, *Agaricia agaricites.* Flat leaflike plates with concentric rings of cups in connected valleys.

7. FLOWER CORAL, *Eusimilia fastigiata.* Yellow or tan; cups large, oval, at ends of short branches.

8. BLACK WIRE CORAL, *Stichopathes lutkeni.* Brown or cream; wirelike. Black corals (antipatharians) are found only in deep water.

9. PILLOW STINKING SPONGE, *Ircinia strobilina.* Gray; large pointed warts.

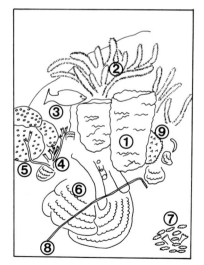

PLATE 3

The Mixed Zone (2)

Top

1. GRAY or MANGROVE SNAPPER, *Lutjanus griseus.* Dark horizontal splotch over eye; tail edged in black.

2. SEA ROD, *Plexaurella grisea.* Long, thick, smooth, gray or tan branches joined at base.

3. BOULDER CORAL, *Montastrea annularis.* Green or brownish; multilobed boulder form in shallow water.

4. LARGE CACTUS CORAL, *Mycetophyllia lamarckiana.* Flat scallop-edged colony; valleys radiate from center.

5. LARGE GROOVED BRAIN CORAL, *Colpophyllia natans.* Tan or brown; wide hills and valleys; thin groove along hilltops.

6. THICK FINGER CORAL, *Porites porites.* 2 cm ($\frac{3}{4}$ in.) thick fingers; may be covered with grayish fuzz (polyps).

7. YELLOW POROUS CORAL, *Porites astreoides.* Bright yellow; encrusting or shapeless bumpy mound.

8. LARGE-CUPPED BOULDER CORAL, *Montastrea cavernosa.* Greenish; cups large, blisterlike.

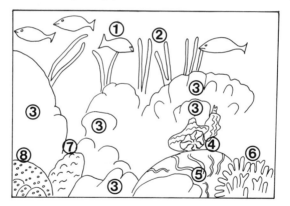

Bottom

At the center the clumps of long, transparent, white-banded tentacles with light shining through them belong to a **Ringed Anemone,** protruding from a **Boulder Coral** crevice. Branches of **Crenelated Fire Coral** are silhouetted behind and to the right of the anemone. The bowl-shaped sponge on the right may be a **Stinking Vase Sponge.** Beneath it, in the right corner, is a thick lumpy colony of **Tan Lettuce-leaf Coral.** Several other forms of this coral extend across the foreground, surrounding the columnar head of Boulder Coral. Behind and to the left of the anemone are 10 brown-and-yellow banded arms of a **Banded Sea Lily.** To the left of the sea lily are 2 large flat plates of a **lettuce coral.**

PLATE 4

Coral Reef Community (1)

Top

A **Spotted Eagle Ray** glides over a sandy plain on the fore-reef terrace. In the background is a colony of **Garden Eels,** which will withdraw into their burrows as the ray reaches them.

Center

Pillar Coral is often covered with olive-drab polyps, giving it a hairy appearance. Along the bottom of the photo (left to right): **Common Bushy Soft Coral, Pillar Coral, Large Grooved Brain Coral,** a dark head of **Boulder Coral,** and a light head of **Large-cupped Boulder Coral.**

Bottom

Photographer Jo Furman placed a mirror on a reef and caught this territorial display as a **Bluestriped Grunt** attacked its image.

PLATE 5
Coral Reef Community (2)

Top

THE FORE-REEF SLOPE. This head of **Boulder Coral** has been eroded, probably by sponges burrowing into its dead undersection. Its base is brittle, and a storm surge (deep wave) may send it tumbling down the fore-reef slope. Note the shinglelike growth habit, characteristic in deep water. Schools of **Blue Chromis** are in the background.

Bottom

SOFT CORALS. *Top left:* **Sea feather** — pale yellow or light purple. *Center left:* **Common Bushy Soft Coral** — brown, tan, or yellowish; bushy. Just below it is a bumpy head of **Boulder Coral.** *Center right:* **Sea fan** — usually purple or yellow; oriented at right angles to current. In front of it is a multilobed head of **Boulder Coral.** *Bottom center:* **Sea rods** — grayish, yellow, or straw-colored; many thick branches joined at bases.

PLATE 6

The Fringing Reef and a Turtle Grass Bed

Top

A ROCKY LEDGE NEAR SHORE. In daytime the **Blackbar Soldier-fish** can sometimes be seen in shadowy areas under overhangs. In the lower left corner is a **French Grunt.** The **Long-spined Black Urchins** seek shadows in daytime; at night they leave the protection of overhangs to feed in nearby Turtle Grass beds.

Center

A ROCKY AREA NEAR A TURTLE GRASS BED. Two **Long-spined Black Urchins** (1 with some white spines) are next to a **Sea Egg.** To the right of the Sea Egg is the common alga, *Halimeda opuntia,* which forms dark green mats on the lagoon floor. Above the urchins are several leafy heads of **Tan Lettuce-leaf Coral.** Above this coral are branches of **Thin Finger Coral.**

Bottom

CORALS AND ANEMONES ON A FRINGING REEF. The 2 large ruglike anemones are **Sun Anemones.** Between them is a head of **Depressed Brain Coral.** Above this coral and surrounding the right-hand Sun Anemone is a lumpy mass of **Boulder Coral.** Along the upper-right margin of the same anemone is a small piece of **Crenelated Fire Coral.** Just above and alongside the anemone is a white margin on the Boulder Coral. (This may be an example of competition between the 2 sessile organisms. The coral cannot overgrow the anemone, because the anemone may digest the coral polyps within reach of its mesenterial filaments.) To the left of the anemones is a clump of **Thick Finger Coral.** Note its fuzzy appearance. This species is one of the few that partially extend their polyps in daytime. At the left of the photo are branches of **Staghorn Coral.**

PLATE 7

Hard Corals (1): Branched

1. STAGHORN CORAL *Acropora cervicornis*   p. 82
Cups tubular. White or tan.

2. ELKHORN CORAL *Acropora palmata*   p. 82
Cups tubular. Flattened, moose-antler-like. Yellow or tan.

3. PILLAR CORAL *Dendrogyra cylindrus*   p. 83
Long thick pillars — to 10 cm (4 in.) wide, 3 m (10 ft.) high. Often covered with fine, furry, olive-drab polyps.

4. IVORY BUSH CORAL *Oculina diffusa*   p. 85
Thin blunt branches with well-spaced, large, protruding cups. When alive, coenosarc olive-drab.

5. THICK FINGER CORAL *Porites porites*   p. 86
Usually well-formed fingers to 2.5 cm (1 in.) wide, 7.5 cm (3 in.) long, always with swollen tips. Specimen shown has abortive fingers.

6. THIN FINGER CORAL *Porites furcata*   p. 85
Fingers no thicker than 1 cm ($\frac{1}{2}$ in.); tips not swollen. Usually gray or tan, rarely purple.

7. Close-up of **porous coral or finger coral** cup arrangement and porous skeleton.

8. BRANCHING CORAL *Madracis mirabilis*   p. 84
Brittle branches to 5 mm ($\frac{1}{4}$ in.) thick (thinner than in Thin Finger Coral), in mounded colony. Cups near branch bases farther apart than ones near tips; spaces around cups spiny. Brown or yellow. Deeper than 6 m (20 ft.).

9. ENCRUSTING MADRACIS *Madracis decactis*   p. 84
Lumpy crust when at depth of 15 m (50 ft.) or so. Tiny spines around cups. Similar to Yellow Porous Coral but not porous and not sulfur-yellow.

10. TUBE CORAL *Cladocora arbuscula*   p. 83
Small clump of thin white tubes — to 3.5 mm ($\frac{1}{8}$ in.) in diameter, 9.5 mm ($\frac{3}{8}$ in.) high.

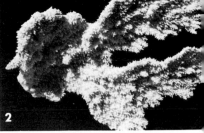

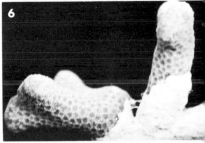

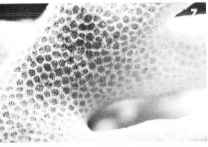

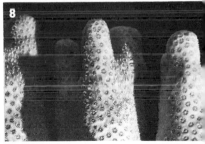

PLATE 8

Hard Corals (2): Boulder, Encrusting, and Cactus

1. BOULDER CORAL *Montastrea annularis*   p. 85
Small to huge — to 3 m (10 ft.) high — greenish or brownish boulder. Colonies often lobed, may have white scars. Forms flat shingle in deep water. Common.

2. Close-up of **Boulder Coral** cups (see p. 6).

3. LARGE-CUPPED BOULDER CORAL   p. 85
   Montastrea cavernosa
Cups to 8 mm (⅜ in.) in diameter, usually project slightly, giving a blistered appearance. Can form large boulder. Flattened in deep water.

4. YELLOW POROUS CORAL *Porites astreoides*   p. 85
Bright sulfur-yellow, with bumps on surface. Small irregular boulder, or crust on other corals, rocks. Porous.

5. Close-up of **Yellow Porous Coral** cups and porous skeleton.

6. ROUGH STAR CORAL *Isophyllastrea rigida*   p. 84
Brown with contrasting light-colored closed valleys. Small hemispherical boulder. Fleshy when alive.

7. STALKED CACTUS CORAL   p. 84
   Isophyllia sinuosa forma *sinuosa*
Small — to 20 cm (8 in.) across — lavender or green head on short stalk. 1 or several winding lobed valleys radiate from center. Fleshy when alive.

8. CACTUS CORAL   p. 84
   Isophyllia sinuosa forma *multiflora*
Cups large, sometimes fused into short valleys. Septa large-toothed. 12 septa per cm. Greenish; fleshy when alive.

9. LARGE CACTUS CORAL   p. 85
   Mycetophyllia lamarckiana
Flat colony, usually scallop-edged. Large-toothed septa run lengthwise in valleys; punctuated by growth centers where septa radiate outward for short distance. Hills radiate from center. Dark green or brownish. Usually in deep water.

10. Close-up of **Large Cactus Coral.** Note large teeth on septa. Groups of short radiating septa are growth centers.

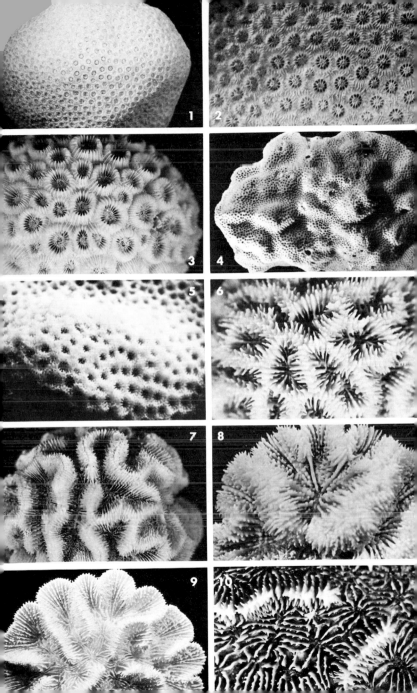

PLATE 9

Hard Corals (3): Brain and Rose

1. LARGE GROOVED BRAIN CORAL   p. 83
Colpophyllia natans
Large hemispherical boulder with broad hills and valleys about equal in width. Pale brown; valleys greenish. Thin groove on hill ridges. Steplike extension from about halfway down septa to valley floor. Usually eroded at base, forming overhang that shelters squirrelfishes.

2. Close-up of **Large Grooved Brain Coral.** Note groove along hills.

3. DEPRESSED BRAIN CORAL   p. 83
Diploria labyrinthiformis
Yellowish or brownish hemisphere. Hills have distinctive shallow depression; hills broader than valleys, vertical-sided. Can form large head. Common.

4. Close-up of **Depressed Brain Coral.** Note vertical-sided hills and shallow grooves.

5. SHARP-HILLED BRAIN CORAL   p. 83
Diploria clivosa
Usually an irregular crust, can form hemisphere. Sharp-crested hills much narrower than valleys. Inshore; uncommon in deep water.

6. COMMON BRAIN CORAL *Diploria strigosa*   p. 83
Medium-sized yellow, brown, or greenish hemisphere. Rounded hills slightly narrower than valleys.

7. RARE ROSE CORAL *Manicina mayori*   p. 84
Small brown hemisphere 15 cm (6 in.) or less across. Stalkless. Resembles Depressed Brain Coral but has deep vertical-sided grooves in hills. Uncommon.

8. COMMON ROSE CORAL *Manicina areolata*   p. 84
Juveniles stalked, attached to bottom; older colonies free on sand. Usually oval, to 7.5 cm (3 in.), with undulating edges. Yellow. Common in Turtle Grass beds.

9. TAN BRAIN CORAL *Meandrina meandrites*   p. 84
Large light tan boulder. 2 heads shown: boulder-shaped specimen (left) from shallow water; flattened form (right) from deep water.

10. Close-up of **Tan Brain Coral.** Large toothless septa alternate with smaller septa. Septa of adjacent hills fuse to form thin zigzag line. Septum edges beaded under magnification. Septa to 1 mm ($\frac{1}{16}$ in.) thick.

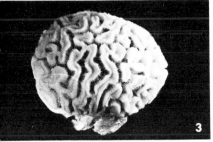

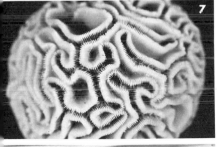

PLATE 10

Hard Corals (4): Star, Flower, Fungus, and Orange

1. STOKES' STARLET CORAL p. 83
Dichocoenia stokesi
Tan hemispherical head usually less than 15 cm (6 in.) across. Cups elongate, with raised edges.
2. Close-up of **Stokes' Starlet Coral.** Note cuplike valleys and alternating thick and thin septa.
3. SHALLOW-WATER STARLET CORAL p. 86
Siderastrea radians
Gray or tan hemisphere on fringing reef; marble-sized ball in Turtle Grass bed; crust in rocky shallows. Common in shallow water.
4. Shallow-water Starlet Coral (below) and **Round Starlet Coral,** *Siderastrea siderea* (above), for comparison. Round Starlet Coral can form a large hemispherical boulder, usually below 3 m (10 ft.); cups rounder, wider than in Shallow-water Starlet Coral. See p. 86 and Pl. 1.
5. STAR CORAL *Favia fragum* p. 83
Loaf- or moundlike head to 5 cm (2 in.) long. Yellow or brown. Cups widely spaced without raised edges; separated by thick, dense, flat walls. Shallow; often encrusts rocks.
6. LARGE-CUPPED FUNGUS CORAL p. 86
Scolymia lacera
Solitary round colony to 7.5 cm (3 in.) across. Large-toothed septa; when alive, septa fleshy, hide teeth. Deep water.
7. LARGE FLOWER CORAL *Mussa angulosa* p. 85
Groups of 3 or more large cups — to 10 cm (4 in.) long, 5 cm (2 in.) wide, usually smaller — on 1 or several stalks. Coarse-toothed septa extend over cup rims and down outside of stalks. Usually below 6 m (20 ft.).
8. Live **Large Flower Coral** underwater. Note fleshy look, common to many large-toothed corals. See cactus corals, Pl. 8.
9. RED or ORANGE CORAL *Tubastrea coccinea* p. 86
Cups orange or red, tubelike, to 9 mm ($\frac{3}{8}$ in.) wide. Polyps large, yellow, extended at night. Clumps of 15 or more cups grow on shaded sides of other corals, except off Bonaire, where they grow extensively, sometimes covering whole coral heads.
10. FLOWER CORAL *Eusimilia fastigiata* p. 83
Clump of 2 or 3 large elongate — to 3.5 cm ($1\frac{1}{2}$ in.) — cups on short stalks. Tan or yellow. Thick toothless septa extend over edges and down outside of cups. Often at bases of brain and boulder corals.

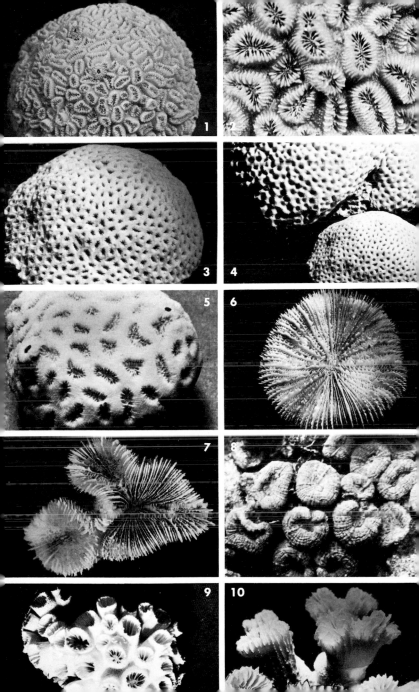

PLATE 11
Hard Corals (5): Fire and Lettuce

1. CRENELATED FIRE CORAL p. 84
Millepora alcicornis
Smooth. Cups pinhole-sized. Upper edges of flat vertical plates pointed, bumpy, or crenelated. Yellow. Common in shallows.

2. FLAT-TOPPED FIRE CORAL p. 85
Millepora complanata
Smooth. Cups pinhole-sized. Upper edges of flat plates squared off, sometimes rippled. Yellow. Common in shallows; may occupy large areas in subtidal zone just offshore.

3. Close-up of **Crenelated Fire Coral.** Note microscopic polyps extending from pinhole-sized cups.

4. TAN LETTUCE-LEAF CORAL p. 82
Agaricia agaricites
Tan or brownish. In shallow water, usually leaflike (may form fragile leaves with cups on 1 surface), but can be a clump or small, veined, boulderlike colony. In deep water, forms flat horizontal shingle. 4–7 cups per cm.

5. Close-up of **Tan Lettuce-leaf Coral.** Note long rows of cups and discontinuous valleys. Many other *Agaricia* species are similar: if valleys continuous, 5–8 cups per cm, and columella prominent, specimen is *A. undata;* if 3–5 cups per cm, septa alternately long and short, and columella prominent, Lamarck's Lettuce-leaf Coral, a deepwater species that forms large — to 56 cm (22 in.) across — flat plates; if similar to Lamarck's but septa equal-sized (usually), Graham's Lettuce-leaf Coral.

6. FRAGILE LETTUCE-LEAF CORAL
Agaricia fragilis
Close-up. Cups somewhat more scattered than in Tan Lettuce-leaf Coral, and in continuous valleys. Columella weak. 5–8 cups per cm.

7. SUNRAY LETTUCE-LEAF CORAL p. 82
Helioseris cucullata
Distinctive ridges beneath small groups of cups. Valleys discontinuous. Septa sharp, raised. No columellá.

8. Close-up of **Sunray Lettuce-leaf Coral.** Note cups, which are on 1 surface only.

9. LAMARCK'S LETTUCE-LEAF CORAL p. 82
Agaricia lamarcki
Live specimen shown. Note characteristic white polyp mouths against dark background.

10. COMPETITION BETWEEN CORALS. A juvenile **Tan Brain Coral,** *Meandrina meandrites* (p. 84), is growing next to a colony of **Sunray Lettuce-Leaf Coral.** The brain coral has resisted being overgrown by extending its mesenterial filaments and digesting polyps of the lettuce coral that were within reach. A defensive ridge has formed between the two.

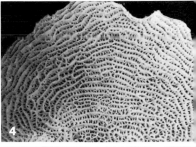

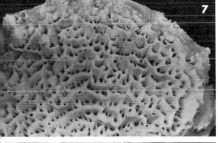

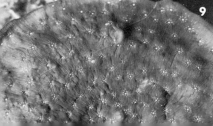

PLATE 12

Soft Corals (1): Live

1. Close-up of a **soft coral** polyp. Each polyp has 8 pinnate (minutely branched) tentacles. In contrast to hard corals, many soft corals extend their polyps in daytime.

2. Close-up of **knobby candelabrum** branches. Note close-set tubular cups with rounded lips. Polyps are partially extended.

3. KNOBBY CANDELABRUM *Eunicea mammosa*   p. 93
Small tan colony less than 20 cm (8 in.) high, growing in 1 plane. Looks fuzzy because polyps are extended. Relatively few branches. Tournefort's Knobby Candelabrum has thick — to 1.5 cm ($^5/_8$ in.) — tan or brown branches and strongly projecting cups with upturned lower lips; to 60 cm (2 ft.) tall.

4. DEEPWATER LACE CORAL   p. 93
Iciligorgia schrammi
Brown or black, but looks red when photographed with artificial light. Polyps on margins of flattened branches. Branched in 1 plane. Common below 21 m (70 ft.).

5. TAN BUSHY SOFT CORAL *Plexaura flexuosa*   p. 94
Bushy but tends to spread in 1 plane. Branches often forked, to 4.5 mm ($^1/_6$ in.) thick at ends. Cups round, not slitlike; shallow lip below each. White, yellow, brown, or tan.

6. FORKED SEA FEATHER   p. 95
Pseudopterogorgia bipinnata
A small sea feather. When alive, violet or bright yellow. Deep water. See also Pl. 13.

7. DEADMAN'S FINGERS *Briareum asbestinum*   p. 93
Branches to 1 cm ($^1/_2$ in.) thick, 60 cm (2 ft.) tall. Purplish gray; often covered with long hairlike polyps, giving a furry brown look. Note naked branches at bottom. See also Pl.13.

8. COMMON BUSHY SOFT CORAL   p. 94
Plexaura homomalla
Bushy but tends to grow in 1 plane. Dark brown to blackish. Branches to 5 mm ($^1/_6$ in.) thick. Cups pitlike, not slits. Common in shallows.

9. SPINY CANDELABRUM *Muricea muricata*   p. 94
Broad fan-shaped colony branched in 1 plane; to 30 cm (1 ft.) high. Yellow or tan. Lower lip of cup prominent, spiny; forms spiny upward-pointing triangle. End branches short, tapered, flattened, to 6 mm ($^1/_4$ in.) thick. See also Pl. 13.

PLATE 13
Soft Corals (2): Dried

1. SEA PLUME *Muriceopsis flavida* p. 94
Tall and plumelike. Branchlets slender, to 7.5 cm (3 in.) long, extend in all directions (not 2-dimensional as in sea feathers). Cups crowded, on all sides of branches; when dried, cups are low warts with elongate pores. In Caribbean, brown or buff; elsewhere, purple tinged with yellow.

2. SPINY CANDELABRUM *Muricea muricata* p. 94
When dried, white or tan. Lower lip of cups spiny. See also Pl. 12.

3. SEA ROD *Plexaurella grisea* p. 94
Long, thick — to 1.2 cm (½ in.) — smooth, straight, usually forked branches. Cups oval; long axis of cups runs along branch. Gray.

4. POROUS FALSE PLEXAURA p. 94
Pseudoplexaura porosa
Large — colony to 2.25 m (7½ ft.) across. Bushy. Branches forked, tapered, round, to 4 mm (³⁄₁₆ in.) thick; tips soft and slimy. Cups crowded, flush with surface, wide and gaping, giving porous look. When alive, light yellow, brownish, or reddish purple; when dried, light brown or buff.

5. KNOBBY CANDELABRUM *Eunicea mammosa* p. 93
Small yellow-brown colony with stout branches and crowded swollen cups. See also Pl. 12.

6. DEADMAN'S FINGERS *Briareum asbestinum* p. 93
Irregular upright branches united at bases; no side branches. See also Pl. 12.

7. DOUBLE-FORKED SEA ROD p. 94
Plexaurella dichotoma
Large — to 78 cm (31 in.) high — bushy colony. Blunt, usually twice-forked branches to 1.5 cm (³⁄₄ in.) thick. Cups slitlike. When alive, yellowish brown; when dried, grayish yellow or tan.

8. FORKED SEA FEATHER p. 95
Pseudopterogorgia bipinnata
Short — to 57 cm (23 in.) — and broad. Branches in 1 plane. Main branches fork into large secondary branches. Pairs of branchlets extend at right angles from main branches at 4–10 mm (³⁄₁₆–½ in.) intervals. Cups slitlike, in single or staggered double row on sides of branches. When alive, violet or bright yellow; when dried, pale violet. Deep water — 14–55 m (46–180 ft.). See also Pl. 12.

9. SMOOTH SEA FEATHER p. 95
Pseudopterogorgia acerosa
Tall — to 2 m (6½ ft.). Cups are tiny pores staggered on branch edges. When alive, light purple, purple-red, or light yellow; when dried, tan or white. Not slimy like Slimy Sea Feather.

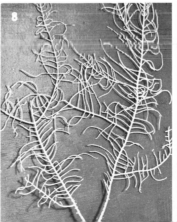

PLATE 14

Sea Anemones (1): Colonial and True; False Corals

1. ENCRUSTING COLONIAL ANEMONE p. 76
Palythoa caribaeorum
Flat, leathery, tan or white mat to 1 m (3¼ ft.) or more across, encrusting rocks or dead coral. Polyps to 1 cm (⅜ in.) across. When closed, polyps slitlike; when open, round, fringed with tiny tentacles. Common on fringing reefs.

2. GREEN COLONIAL ANEMONE p. 77
Zoanthus sociatus
Flat, rubbery, bright green mat encrusting rocks, coral, rubble, or sand. Polyps fleshy, to 2.5 cm (1 in.) tall. Each disk to 1.3 cm (½ in.) across, edged with 2 circles of about 30 stubby tentacles each. Not below 5 m (16 ft.).

3. ST. THOMAS FALSE CORAL p. 76
Rhodactis sanctithomae
Many polyps crowded in thick, fuzzy, olive-green or purplish mat. Most of each disk covered with tiny leaflike tentacles; margin flat, edged with tiny, pointed, whitish tentacles. When animal withdrawn, disk looks like smooth inflated mound. Usually 5 cm (2 in.) or less across disk.

4. FLORIDA FALSE CORAL *Ricordia florida* p. 76
Polyps crowded in small clump — often less than 30 cm (1 ft.) across — encrusting rocks or dead coral. Polyps to 2.5 cm (1 in.) across. Polyp tentacles look like iridescent green or orange warts crowded over disk. 1 or several mouths, often near center of disk; each looks like a larger wart.

5. PALE ANEMONE *Aiptasia tagetes* p. 74
Brownish translucent polyps often crowded in colony. Column long, thin. Nearly 100 alternating long and very short tentacles. On rocks, Red Mangrove roots, dead coral. Small — to 5 cm (2 in.) tall, usually shorter.

6. ROCK ANEMONE *Anthopleura krebsi* p. 74
Greenish or rust striped tentacles surround darker disk with white slitlike mouth. On intertidal rocks. Small — to 3 cm (1¼ in.) across disk.

7. COLLARED SAND ANEMONE p. 75
Phyllactis flosculifera
Olive or greenish brown disk almost buried in intertidal sand; often disappears under sand at low tide. Few to many long tentacles around mouth, often not visible in daytime. Disk covered with radiating furrows. To 8 cm (3¼ in.) across disk.

8. RED WARTY ANEMONE p. 74
Bunodosoma granuliferum
Usually brown or brick-red, with several rings of short, tapering, white-spotted olive-green tentacles. Projecting mouth bright red. Often closed in daytime, looks like red lump under overhangs, in crevices. To 8 cm (3¼ in.) across disk.

PLATE 15

Sea Anemones (2): True and Tube-dwelling

1. MAROON ANEMONE *Actinia bermudensis*   p. 73
All maroon, with several rows of short tapered tentacles. Circle of bright blue warts at margin. Small — to 5 cm (2 in.) across disk.

2. BEADED ANEMONE *Phymanthus crucifer*   p. 75
Disk flat, fringed with about 200 short tapering tentacles. Color variable: buff, sand, olive, or even reddish, often with light and dark stripes and rows of warts radiating from central mouth. Sand-dwelling. To 15 cm (6 in.) across disk.

3. SUN ANEMONE *Stoichactis helianthus*   p. 75
Disk round, covered with uniformly stubby, olive or tan and whitish tentacles. Often many specimens are crowded together and look like a rug. To 15 cm (6 in.) across disk.

4. TRICOLOR ANEMONE *Calliactis tricolor*   p. 74
Tentacles short, thin, furry, light-colored, in a fringe around disk. Column purple or yellow-brown, with several rows of raised dark warts just above base. On snail shells inhabited by hermit crabs, usually Star-eyed and Red Hermits. To 5 cm (2 in.) across disk.

5. BANDED TUBE-DWELLING ANEMONE   p. 77
Arachnanthus nocturnus
2 rings of tentacles: inner ring of short, stubby, incurved tentacles; outer ring of long, brown-and-white banded, tapering tentacles that stream with current. In parchmentlike tube projecting from sand. To 2 cm ($^3/_4$ in.) across disk.

6. RINGED ANEMONE *Bartholomea annulata*   p. 74
Many long, transparent, brownish tentacles ringed with white bands. Column long, thin, rarely seen. To 12.5 cm (5 in.) across disk. See also Pl. 3.

7. STINGING ANEMONE *Lebrunia danae*   p. 75
Brown or olive and white. Looks like a mass of tentacles; disk often poorly defined. 2 types of tentacles: whitish, multiforked false tentacles predominant in daytime; medium-length, greenish or brownish, tapering tentacles predominant at night. To 30 cm (1 ft.) across disk. Stings.

8. GIANT CARIBBEAN ANEMONE   p. 75
Condylactis gigantea
Thick, 20 cm (8 in.) long, purple-tipped tentacles shown. Most conspicuous anemone. Tentacles thick, tapered, tan, faintly ribbed with lighter color; tips often pink or purple. Column often orange, may be olive or pale blue. On reefs. To 30 cm (1 ft.) across disk. See also Pl. 18.

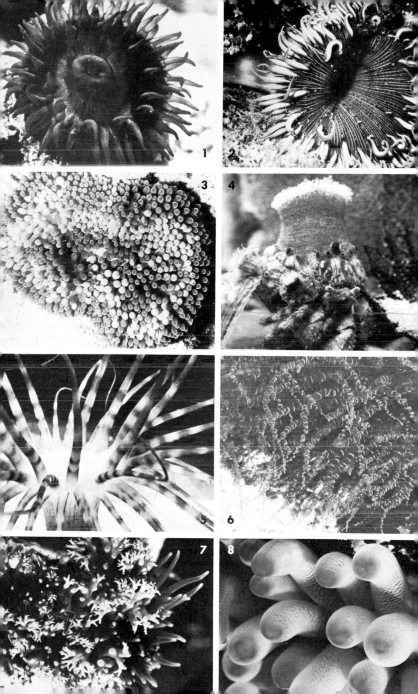

PLATE 16

Jellyfish and Siphonophores

1. MOON JELLY *Aurelia aurita* p. 66
Large — to 25 cm (10 in.) across — transparent blue-purple jelly-fish. Tiny inconspicuous tentacles around margin. Distinctive circular masses of reproductive tissue in 4-leaf clover pattern at center of disk.

2. SEA WASP *Carybdea alata* p. 66
Squared-off, transparent jellyfish to 3.8 cm (1½ in.) long, with 4 tentacles, 1 at each corner of bell. Swims rapidly in horizontal position, trailing tentacles, which may be longer than 30 cm (1 ft.). In small schools at night; in daytime, often in shallow water off north coast of Jamaica. Stings.

3. UPSIDE-DOWN JELLYFISH p. 66
Cassiopeia xamachana
Large — to 30 cm (1 ft.) across — boldly patterned, olive and white jellyfish. Shown with oral surface (underside) up, mutualistic zooxanthellae being bathed in sunlight. Note oral arms with frilly zooxanthellae-containing lappets.

4. SEA NETTLE *Chrysaora quinquecirrha* p. 67
Transparent whitish jellyfish with 4 long frilly oral arms suspended from underside. Long — to 1 m (3¼ ft.) — clearly visible tentacles. Bell covered with distinctive whitish dots, may have reddish or whitish overtones. Stings.

5. Aboral (top) view of **Upside-down Jellyfish.** Note several dark-colored lappets beyond bell margins.

6. BLUE BUTTON *Porpita porpita* p. 68
Small — to 2.5 cm (1 in.) across — bluish jellyfish-shaped siphonophore with black margin. Dark lines radiate from center of float to margin. 1 large feeding polyp suspended from center of underside; many short blue fishing polyps hang from margins.

7. BY-THE-WIND SAILOR *Velella velella* p. 68
Flat, purple, disk-shaped float to 7.5 cm (3 in.) across, with gelatinous sail. Margin edged with short tentacles. Underside arranged in concentric ridges covered with stocky reproductive polyps. This siphonophore has a large central feeding polyp. Note also the parasitic **snail** crawling up left edge of sail.

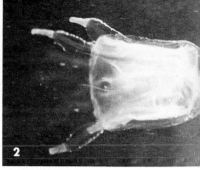

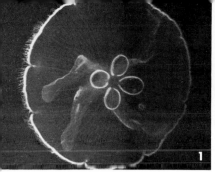

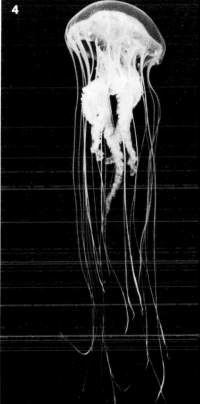

PLATE 17

Coral Reef Community (3)

1. CRENELATED FIRE CORAL, *Millepora alcicornis.* Causes painful welt if rubbed against. White spots near middle of colony possibly caused by Fireworm.

2. THREESPOT DAMSELFISH, *Eupomacentrus planifrons.* Juvenile (shown) yellow with blue-rimmed black spots; adult brown. Shown defending its territory (whole area in photo) against other fishes.

3. THICK FINGER CORAL, *Porites porites.* One of the few hard corals that sometimes extend polyps in daytime; looks fuzzy.

4. IRIDESCENT TUBE SPONGE, *Spinosella plicifera.* Normally purplish blue. White specimen may be dead and bleached (but usually overgrown almost immediately after death) or a live albino.

5. ROUND STARLET CORAL, *Siderastrea siderea.* Often a hemispherical head; cups shallow. Colony below it is same species but mostly dead, encrusted with fouling organisms.

6. MAGNIFICENT BANDED FANWORM, *Sabellastarte magnifica.* Clump of flowerlike gill-fans extending from mud and mucous tubes. When approached, fans withdraw instantaneously.

7. KNOBBY CANDELABRUM, *Eunicea mammosa.* Thick, flexible, tan branches covered with wartlike bumps under cups from which polyps extend.

8. RED FINGER SPONGE, *Haliclona rubens.* A few large oscules.

9. SEA ROD, *Plexaurella grisea.* Clump of long straight branches; most branching near base.

10. STAGHORN CORAL, *Acropora cervicornis.* Large beds in mixed zone.

11. LONG-SPINED BLACK URCHIN, *Diadema antillarum.* Hides on reef in daytime. Be careful not to rub against spines of a partly hidden urchin.

12. TAN LETTUCE-LEAF CORAL, *Agaricia agaricites.* Here, a thick mass behind Red Finger Sponges; in deep water, a flat plate.

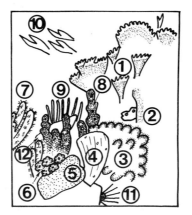

PLATE 18
Coral Reef Community (4)

Top Left
To the left of the **Giant Caribbean Anemone** are maroon fingers of **Red Finger Sponges.** The black fingers above them are another species of **finger sponge.** Plates of **Crenelated Fire Coral** tower upward to the left of the sponges, and **Flat-topped Fire Coral** is at the left of the photo. The greenish gray sponge at the upper right is a **Stinking Sponge,** with **sea rods,** *Plexaurella grisea,* behind it. Along the bottom of the photo (left to right): a few spines of a hidden **Long-spined Black Urchin,** a mass of **Red Finger Sponge,** a juvenile **Threespot Damselfish,** and a crust of **Fire Sponge.**

Top Right
At the center are arms of a **Beaded Sea Lily** (do not confuse this species with the Orange Sea Lily, whose arms are totally orange). A crust of **Fire Sponge** is in the foreground. The yellow tubes are coral-destroying **Yellow Boring Sponges.** Behind the sea lily are arms of a **Suenson's Brittle Star.**

Bottom
1. **STAGHORN CORAL,** *Acropora cervicornis.* Note whole bed of this coral.
2. **DEEPWATER SEA FEATHER,** *Pseudopterogorgia elizabethae.*
3. **BOULDER CORAL,** *Montastrea annularis.* Main reef-building coral.
4. **INDIGO HAMLET,** *Hypoplectrus indigo.* To 12.5 cm (5 in.). Serranidae.
5. **BLUEHEAD,** *Thalassoma bifasciatum.* Only supermale blue. Labridae.
6. **BLUE CHROMIS,** *Chromis cyanea.* To 12.5 cm (5 in.). Pomacentridae.
7. **TAN LETTUCE-LEAF CORAL,** *Agaricia agaricites.* On sides of Boulder Coral.
8. **LARGE CACTUS CORAL,** *Mycetophyllia lamarckiana.* Flat; valleys radiate from center.
9. **SEA FAN,** *Gorgonia ventalina.* To 1 m (3¼ ft.) or wider.
10. **YELLOW BORING SPONGE,** *Siphonodictyon coralliphagum.* Thick yellow tubes project from a coral; rest of sponge in coral.
11. **CRENELATED FIRE CORAL,** *Millepora alcicornis.* Tan; tips white.
12. **SEA ROD,** *Plexaurella grisea.* A soft coral; thick, branched.

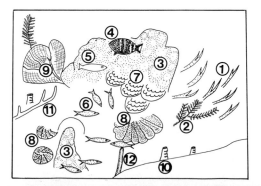

PLATE 19

Sponges (1)

1. RED FINGER SPONGE *Haliclona rubens*   p. 127
Encrusting or branched; branches to 30 cm (1 ft.) or higher. Color distinctive. Oscules large, scattered, flush or raised.

2. YELLOW TUBE SPONGE *Aplysina fistularis*   p. 128
1 or several thick-walled tubes united at bases; to 10 cm (4 in.) high. Narrow diaphragm inside opening. Often thin projections around top.

3. LAVENDER TUBE SPONGE   p. 130
  Spinosella vaginalis
Clustered thin-walled tubes joined at bases; to 1 m (3¼ ft.) high. Rim jagged. Bluish or grayish. Outside covered with *Parazoanthus parasiticus,* a colonial anemone; inside velvety with vertical rows of holes. Note also the **Suenson's Brittle Star** arms.

4. A large cluster of **Lavender Tube Sponges.** Note also the school of yellow **Blueheads** and the **Bicolor Damselfish.**

5. CHICKEN LIVER SPONGE *Chondrilla nucula*   p. 131
Shiny brown sheet covering bottom, encrusting dead coral, rocks, even *Halimeda* (shown).

6. PIPES-OF-PAN SPONGE *Agelas schmidti*   p. 128
Usually 5 or 6 fused, thick-walled, orange cylinders covered with elongate holes or series of 2 or 3 holes connected by canal.

7. FIRE SPONGE *Tedania ignis*   p. 131
Encrusts coral, rocks, cave walls. Oscules scattered. Tissue easily torn; *not covered with anemones.* Irritating when touched. Note also the **Cardinalfish** (lower center) between the valves of the **Rough File Clam,** a scalloplike animal with long tentacles.

8. TOUCH-ME-NOT SPONGE   p. 132
  Neofibularia nolitangere
Massive, irregular; may have short, thick, chimneylike tubes with large openings. Dark brown; may look reddish in bright light. Not shiny. Inside walls of openings rough, with many tiny white Spongeworms barely visible. 3–46 m (10–150 ft.) deep. Irritating when touched; can produce severe dermatitis in sensitive individuals. Despite its harmful effects on humans, angelfishes, such as this **Gray Angelfish,** readily eat it.

PLATE 20

Sponges (2)

1. GIANT TUBE SPONGE *Aplysina lacunosa*   p. 128
Hollow thick-walled cylinder to 1 m ($3\frac{1}{4}$ ft.) or higher; usually single, occasionally 2–4 joined at bases. Yellow, pinkish lavender, or red-brown. On deep reefs.

2. STRAWBERRY SPONGE *Mycale* species   p. 130
Urn-shaped, with pointed warts. Small — usually less than 20 cm (8 in.) high. Looks black or brown underwater unless light is strong. On reefs. Note also the 2 **Red Finger Sponge** branches framing the red Strawberry Sponge cylinder.

3. BASKET or TUB SPONGE *Xestospongia muta*   p. 131
Often bowl- or tub-shaped; to 1 m ($3\frac{1}{4}$ ft.) or more across top. Brown. Hard, irregular, with large protuberances on outside.

4. GRAY CORNUCOPIA SPONGE   p. 130
   Niphates digitalis
Cone-shaped, with thin fringed rim. Inside velvety; outside corrugated, usually covered with *Parazoanthus* anemones. Note also the **Arrow Crab** in the unusual saddle-shaped opening.

5. PURPLE BUSH SPONGE   p. 128
   Pandaros acanthifolium
Branched or bushy, with coarse conules. Looks black. Note the purple-red exudate on the fingers.

6. RED BORING SPONGE *Cliona delitrix*   p. 132
Red crust dotted with brownish *Parazoanthus* anemones; looks brown in deep water. Occasionally with large protruding oscules. Kills deep-reef coral.

7. VARIABLE SPONGE *Anthosigmella varians*   p. 131
Smooth, hard, velvety tan or greenish. Usually flat crust or amorphous lumpy mass. When dry, feels like wood.

8. IRIDESCENT TUBE SPONGE   p. 130
   Spinosella plicifera
Wrinkled tube to 30 cm (1 ft.) high, with large opening rimmed in iridescent blue. See also Pl. 2.

9. YELLOW BORING SPONGE   p. 133
   Siphonodictyon coralliphagum
Only yellow tubes of sponge are visible on this riddled head of **Boulder Coral;** most of sponge is inside coral. Destroys deep-reef coral.

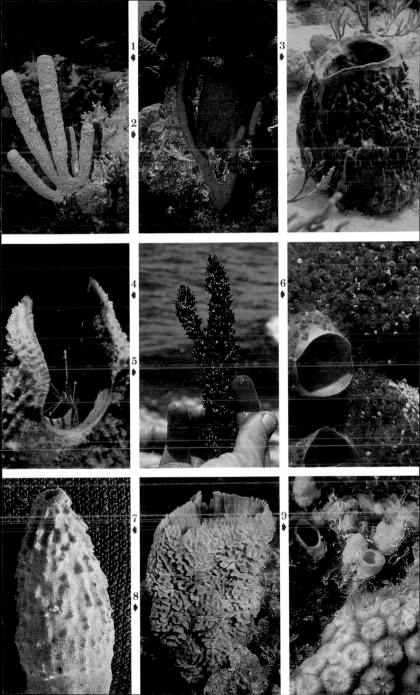

PLATE 21
Sponge-dominated Scenes

Top Left
The large gray vase-shaped sponge is a **Stinking Vase Sponge.**
Look for pointed conules, to 4 mm ($^{3}/_{16}$ in.) high, covering the outside. In the crevice at the right of this sponge are the long red
tentacles of a **Rough File Clam.** Directly below the vase sponge is
a **Bicolor Damselfish,** swimming over a **Red Boring Sponge.**
The 2 heads of coral to the right are **Boulder Coral.** A **Horned
Christmas Tree Worm** projects at the left of the Red Boring
Sponge. At the far left is a branch of a **Red Finger Sponge.** In the
lower left corner is a **Black Ball Sponge,** which is gray, with
clusters of large black oscules. This species is hard and has a few
oscules on conical elevations; the oscules close when touched.

Top Right
The damaged area of the **Round Starlet Coral** has been colonized by algae, sponges, and the **Painted Tunicate.** Further
damage is being wrought on its base by a **Red Boring Sponge,**
which, in turn, has been colonized by *Parazoanthus parasiticus,*
a colonial anemone (see p. 77). Note also the 3 **Suenson's Brittle
Star** arms on the Red Boring Sponge.

Bottom Left
The purple sponge is a **Giant Tube Sponge.** The red sponge at the
lower left is a **Red Boring Sponge,** which has virtually covered
and killed a small head of coral. The fish is a **Princess Parrotfish;** note that the white stripes reach its mouth and eye, which
differentiates it from the more common Mottlefin Parrotfish. Behind the parrotfish is a branch of a **Red Finger Sponge.** The
small coral in the lower right corner is a **lettuce coral.** The top of
a **Banded Butterflyfish** is just visible in the upper left corner,
above the tube sponge.

Bottom Right
The **Common Loggerhead Sponge** has groups of conspicuous
black oscules on its flattened or depressed top. Though similar to
the Pillow Stinking Sponge, which is also found in shallow sandy
areas and Turtle Grass beds, this loggerhead sponge lacks pointed
conules on its surface and has groups of pores on its sides. Note also
the **Crenelated Fire Coral** in the foreground and the **French
Grunts.**

PLATE 22
Fishes (1): Damselfishes and Others

1. YELLOWTAIL SNAPPER *Ocyurus chrysurus*
Yellow stripe; yellow, deeply forked tail. Over reefs. May gather around diver to search for bread. To 76 cm (2½ ft.). Lutjanidae, p. 225.

2. SERGEANT MAJOR *Abudefduf saxatilis*
5 vertical stripes. Males dark when guarding eggs or in crevices. Common everywhere. To 18 cm (7 in.). Pomacentridae, p. 228.

3. FOUREYE BUTTERFLYFISH
Chaetodon capistratus
Black band through eye. False eyespots near tail. Eats organisms in coral crevices. To 15 cm (6 in.). Chaetodontidae, p. 228.

4. BROWN CHROMIS *Chromis multilineata*
Dark blotch at base of pectoral fin. Tail deeply forked. Loose schools above patch reefs and at outer edge of large reefs. Eats plankton. To 14 cm (5½ in.). Pomacentridae, p. 228.

5. DUSKY DAMSELFISH
Eupomacentrus dorsopunicans
Juvenile (shown) blue, with blue-rimmed black spot on yellow-blue dorsal fin. Adult brown, with thin dark vertical bars. Defends territory in rocky reef areas, tide pools. Small — to 15 cm (6 in.). Pomacentridae, p. 228.

6. BLUEHEAD *Thalassoma bifasciatum*
Supermale (shown) has blue-headed pattern. Female, male, and young are yellow, with or without black stripes. Yellow forms are cleaners. To 15 cm (6 in.). Labridae, p. 229. Note also the **Rock Beauty,** an angelfish, in the background; to 30 cm (1 ft.).

7. MARGATE *Haemulon album*
Rear of dorsal fin pearly gray; tail blackish. Near coral rubble. Eats small fishes, crustaceans. To 60 cm (2 ft.). Pomadasyidae, p. 226.

8. FLYING GURNARD *Dactylopterus volitans*   p. 223
Brownish with dark brown bands. Crawls on pelvic fins, which are folded when at rest. To 45 cm (1½ ft.). Dactylopteridae.

PLATE 23

Fishes (2): Groupers, Sea Bass, and Others

1. YELLOWFIN GROUPER *Mycteroperca venenosa*
Color variable: pale to almost black in shadow. Pectoral fin with broad yellow margin. To 1 m (3¼ ft.). Serranidae, p. 223.

2. RED HIND *Epinephelus guttatus*   p. 223
White to olive; red spots on head, body. Similar to Rock Hind but lacks black blotches on back and spotted tail. To 45 cm (1½ ft.). Serranidae. Note also 2 parasitic isopods, **Anilocra laticaudata** (see p. 216), near eye.

3. HARLEQUIN BASS *Serranus tigrinus*
Near bottom on coral, grass; often hovers. Eats crustaceans. Small — to 10 cm (4 in.). Serranidae, p. 223.

4. CONEY *Cephalopholis fulva*
Blue spots on body; 2 distinct black spots on back just behind dorsal fin. Color variable, may be half black and half white. To 30 cm (1 ft.). Serranidae, p. 223.

5. SCHOOLMASTER *Lutjanus apodus*
Yellow and gray, usually with bright blue streak under eye. Reefs, mangrove channels. Eats small fishes; like all other snappers, has large canine teeth. To 60 cm (2 ft.). Lutjanidae, p. 225.

6. FRENCH GRUNT *Haemulon flavolineatum*   p. 226
Commonest grunt. Yellow stripes on silver, or blue stripes on yellow-orange. Diagonal stripes on afterbody. School bunches up if approached. To 30 cm (1 ft.). Pomadasyidae. Note also 3 **Yellow Goatfish,** with 1 yellow stripe and yellow tail.

7. PORKFISH *Anisotremus virginicus*
Vertical black and white stripes. Nocturnal. Eats brittle stars, worms, mollusks. Young are cleaners. To 30 cm (1 ft.). Pomadasyidae, p. 226.

8. NASSAU GROUPER *Epinephelus striatus*
Black spots around eyes. Vertical olive-brown bands. Dark saddle between dorsal fin and tail. To 1.2 m (4 ft.). Serranidae, p. 223. Note also **Sharknose Goby** cleaning behind eye (see Pl. 27).

PLATE 24

Fishes (3): Parrotfishes and Others

1. RAINBOW PARROTFISH *Scarus guacamaia*
Green teeth. Greenish with orange and bronze highlights; rear half of male light green. Young striped. Shallow reefs. To 1.2 m (4 ft.). Scaridae, p. 230.

2. STOPLIGHT PARROTFISH *Sparisoma viride*
Female (shown) has red belly, white crescent on tail, scales outlined in black. To 54 cm (21 in.). Scaridae, p. 230. Note **Spanish Hogfish** in background.

3. A **parrotfish,** *Scarus* species, sleeping in a mucous cocoon (see p. 210).

4. HORSE-EYE JACK *Caranx latus*
Eyes large. Tail yellow. A row of black bony scutes near tail. Lacks blue stripe of common Bar Jack. Eats small fishes, shrimps. To 60 cm (2 ft.). Carangidae, p. 225.

5. BLUE TANG *Acanthurus coeruleus*
Light-colored spine at tail base. Young bright yellow. Often in small schools, a beautiful sight. Browses on algae. To 30 cm (1 ft.). Acanthuridae, p. 232.

6. ORANGESPOTTED FILEFISH
Cantherhines pullus
Usually brown, with small, scattered, brown-centered orange spots. Eats sponges, algae, many invertebrates. To 19 cm (7½ in.). Balistidae, p. 234.

7. SMOOTH TRUNKFISH *Lactophrys triqueter*
Mosaic pattern of hexagons becomes dots on back. Mouth black. No spines on head or front of anal fin. To 30 cm (1 ft.). Ostraciidae, p. 235.

8. FAIRY BASSLET *Gramma loreto*   p. 232
In southern Caribbean, half of body purple; in northern Caribbean, yellow extends almost to head. In caves, crevices. Eats plankton. Tiny — to 7.5 cm (3 in.). Grammidae.

PLATE 25
Fishes (4): Angelfishes and Others

1. SHARKNOSE GOBY *Gobiosoma evelynae*
Yellow V on snout and head. Mouth behind snout, sharklike. A cleaner (photo may be of a cleaning station on Large-cupped Boulder Coral). Tiny — to 3.8 cm (1½ in.). Gobiidae, p. 231.

2. SPOTTED MORAY *Gymnothorax moringa*   p. 218
Body spotted brown and white. Dorsal fin yellow. Large teeth. Shallow reefs, rocky areas. Rarely seen, hides in crevices; nocturnal. To 90 cm (3 ft.). Muraenidae.

3. FRENCH ANGELFISH *Pomacanthus paru*
Blackish gray. Body scales golden-edged. Yellow bar at base of pectoral fins. Reefs. To 38 cm (15 in.). Chaetodontidae, p. 228.

4. GRAY ANGELFISH *Pomacanthus arcuatus*
Bluish blotches at bases of curved yellow bars differentiate juvenile (shown) from French juvenile; retains color pattern until longer than 10 cm (4 in.). Specimen shown is hiding in vacant conch shell. A cleaner. Chaetodontidae, p. 228.

5. QUEEN ANGELFISH *Holacanthus ciliaris*
Tail and pectoral fins yellow. Dark forehead "crown" ringed with bright blue. Reefs. To 30 cm (1 ft.). Chaetodontidae, p. 228.

6. BLACKBAR SOLDIERFISH *Myripristis jacobus*
Distinct black bar. Eyes large. Nocturnal; in daytime, under reef overhangs. To 20 cm (8 in.). Holocentridae, p. 222. Note **Longspine Squirrelfish** at right; long spine on anal fin; deep water.

7. SHORTNOSE BATFISH *Ogcocephalus nasutus*
Pectoral fins lack spots. Swims or crawls over sandy areas to search for snails, clams, worms. To 38 cm (15 in.). Ogcocephalidae, p. 221.

8. BLUESTRIPE LIZARDFISH *Synodus saurus*
Bluish longitudinal lines; otherwise similar to Sand Diver. On sand, propped up on ventral fins from which it launches itself to attack small fishes; often buried in sand. To 45 cm (1½ ft.). Synodontidae, p. 220.

PLATE 26

Fishes (5)

1. QUEEN TRIGGERFISH *Balistes vetula*
1st spine on dorsal fin locked in place by the 2nd, or "trigger."
Flaps dorsal fin back and forth to swim. Eats crabs and sea urchins. To 60 cm (2 ft.). Balistidae, p. 234.

2. LONGLURE FROGFISH p. 220
Antennarius multiocellatus
Color variable; usually a white vertical streak at beginning of dorsal fin, a white saddle behind dorsal fin. Thin projection above upturned mouth topped with fluffy "lure," which is waved to entice minnows. Small — to 11 cm (4½ in.). Antennariidae.

3. FLAMEFISH *Apogon maculatus*
Black spot under rear of dorsal fin. 2 thin, white, parallel lines through eye. Nocturnal; in daytime, in crevices. Small — to 12.5 cm (5 in.). Apogonidae, p. 224.

4. JACKKNIFE-FISH *Equetus lanceolatus*
1 black stripe on body. Pectoral and rear dorsal fins colorless. No white spots. Rocky areas, reefs. To 23 cm (9 in.). Sciaenidae, p. 227.

5. PEARLY RAZORFISH *Hemipteronotus novacula*
Greenish. Builds low sand mounds into which it dives if threatened. Hovers over sandy bottoms, body curved. Small — to 38 cm (15 in.), usually smaller. Labridae, p. 229.

6. PORCUPINEFISH *Diodon hystrix* p. 235
Spines shorter on forehead than on body. Spotted; no bars. Usually hidden in coral crevices, deflated, head and large eyes visible. To 90 cm (3 ft.). Diodontidae.

7. BIGEYE *Priacanthus arenatus*
Reddish, may have silver pattern. Margins of tail and anal fin blackish. Nocturnal. To 38 cm (15 in.). Priacanthidae, p. 224.

8. Close-up of **Blackbar Soldierfish** or **Squirrelfish;** both Holocentridae, p. 222. Note parasitic isopod, ***Anilocra,*** above eye; parasite always orients toward front of fish (see p. 216).

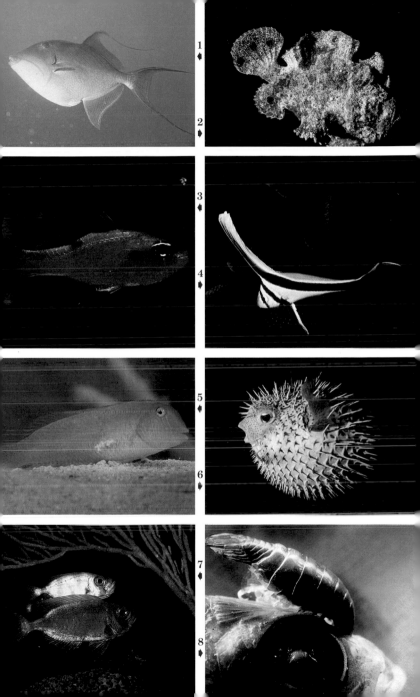

PLATE 27
Feeding Behavior of Fishes

Cleaning Symbiosis (see p. 246)

1. A **Bigeye** approaches a cleaning station on a head of **Depressed Brain Coral** and hovers motionless above a tiny — 4 cm (1½ in.) — **goby** (just visible on the top of the coral head, directly below the mouth of the Bigeye). The goby is a Cleaning Goby or a Sharknose Goby (both have an underslung sharklike mouth, black stripes, and a bright yellow V over the eyes).

2. The goby (visible between the coral head and the Bigeye) immediately ascends.

3. The goby begins picking off parasites and damaged tissues at the bottom of its host's eye. Note that the Bigeye has changed color.

4. The Bigeye opens its mouth wide to allow the goby to clean inside and to have access to the gills, usually a haven for parasites. The goby will eventually clean the oral cavity and leave via a gill opening. Bigeyes normally eat fishes the size of the goby.

A Feeding Stingray

5. A **Southern Stingray** swims over the bottom by undulating its pectoral fins.

6. The stingray plunges to the bottom, vigorously undulating its pectoral fins and stirring up the sand.

7. Having located its prey, the stingray lowers its pectoral fins and raises its body, manipulating the prey into its mouth.

8. Note the small **flounder** in the mouth of the stingray, which fed on the flounder for 10–15 minutes. (Stingrays normally eat clams, crabs, small fishes, worms, and other bottom-dwelling forms hidden under sand.)

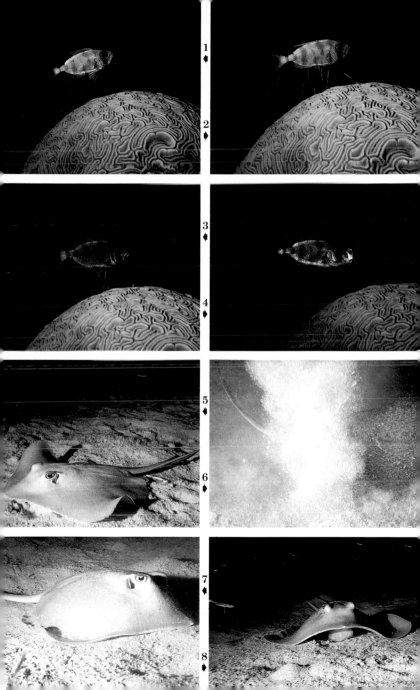

PLATE 28

Worms

1. HORNED or FEATHERED CHRISTMAS   p. 136
   TREE WORM *Spirobranchus giganteus giganteus*
Paired yellow conical whorls. Red or blue gills extend from convoluted white calcareous tube, which is usually attached to rocks, coral. Tiny pink antlers on operculum. Common.

2. Calcareous tube of **Horned Christmas Tree Worm;** note white operculum. Note also **lettuce coral** at right and **Red or Orange Coral** polyps at left.

3. RED-BANDED FANWORM *Potamilla fonticula*   p. 138
Large feather duster worm with white or red gills extending from tough parchmentlike tube; tube to 15 cm (6 in.) long. Dark red band midway along gills.

4. ELEGANT FANWORM *Hypsicomus elegans*   p. 138
Gills usually yellow, banded with purple. Tube parchmentlike, long, dark, tortuous. Calm shaded reef areas.

5. MAGNIFICENT BANDED FANWORM   p. 138
   Sabellastarte magnifica
Large. Brown or red-brown circlet of gills to 25 cm (10 in.) across, usually much smaller. In clumps of many worms, muddy tubes projecting 20–25 cm (8–10 in.) from bottom. Common.

6. FIVE-SPOTTED FEATHER DUSTER WORM   p. 137
   Sabella melanostigma
Small. 4 or 5 pairs of black eyespots along each gill. Tube muddy. Often in clumps.

7. FIREWORM *Hermodice carunculata*   p. 139
Large. Olive; edges banded with red and white. White band consists of thousands of glassy needlelike setae; if touched, become embedded in flesh. Common and predacious on reefs and most other habitats.

8. RED-TIPPED FIREWORM *Chloeia viridis*   p. 139
To 30 cm (1 ft.) long, usually smaller. White with brown stripe and tan bars. Setae long, numerous, needlelike.

PLATE 29

Shrimps and Lobsters

1. BANDED CORAL or BARBER POLE SHRIMP   p. 157
Stenopus hispidus
Often perches or "dances" on coral, where it sets up a cleaning station. To 5 cm (2 in.) long.

2. SPOTTED CLEANING SHRIMP   p. 156
Periclimenes yucatanicus
Note white-ringed brown spots (absent in Pederson's Cleaning Shrimp). Common cleaning shrimp, commensal with Ringed and Giant Caribbean Anemones and other large anemones. Tiny — to 2.5 cm (1 in.) long.

3. RED SNAPPING SHRIMP *Alpheus armatus*   p. 155
Male has larger claw than female. To 5 cm (2 in.) long. A mated pair (male closer to viewer) shown in commensal relationship with **Ringed Anemone.**

4. SHORT-CLAWED SPONGE SHRIMP   p. 155
Synalpheus brevicarpus
Major claw smooth, reddish, enlarged, cylindrical. A snapping shrimp; when cocked claw is released, snaps shut with loud popping sound. Inside sponges. To 2.5 cm (1 in.) long. Female shown; note eggs glued to swimmerets under abdomen.

5. SPINY LOBSTER *Panulirus argus*   p. 157
No claws or rostrum. 2 hornlike spines arch over eyes. A few pairs of white spots scattered on abdomen. To 60 cm (2 ft.) long, 14 kg (30 lbs.), usually much smaller.

6. SLIPPER LOBSTER *Scyllarides nodifer*   p. 158
No antennae; antennules flattened. Similar to Spanish Lobster, which has 4 reddish purple spots on 1st abdominal segment.

7. PEPPERMINT or VEINED SHRIMP   p. 156
Lysmata wurdemanni
Longitudinal red lines edged with white. A cleaning shrimp. Often inside sponges; shown on **Staghorn Coral.** To 4 cm (1⅝ in.) long.

8. RED-BACKED CLEANING SHRIMP   p. 156
or SCARLET LADY *Lysmata grabhami*
Yellow, with scarlet dorsal surface. Antennae long, white, often protrude from coral crevices. A cleaning shrimp. To 5 cm (2 in.) long.

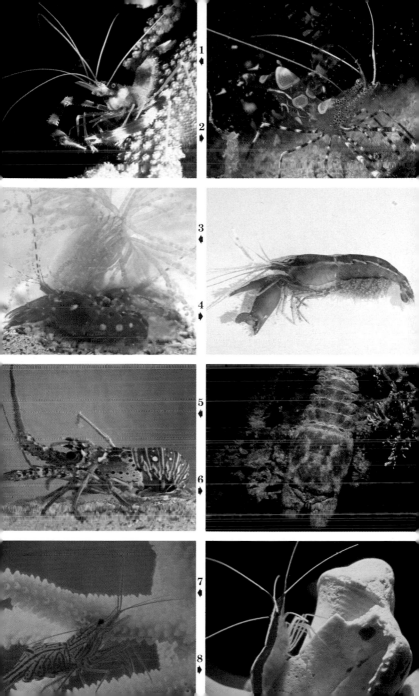

PLATE 30

Crabs and Cnidarians

1. STAR-EYED HERMIT CRAB *Dardanus venosus* p. 159
Claw tips black; legs banded red and tan. Pupil of eye star-shaped.
Often in conch and Tulip Snail shells. Large — carapace to 2.5 cm
(1 in.) long.

2. ARROW CRAB *Stenorhynchus seticornis* p. 163
Yellow-and-brown striped, with purple or blue claws. Carapace to
6 cm (2½ in.) long.

3. LESSER SPONGE CRAB *Dromidia antillensis* p. 162
Last pair of legs dorsal, longer than preceding pair. Claw tips crimson. Covered with sponges, colonial anemones, or tunicates. Carapace to 7.5 cm (3 in.) long.

4. SPOTTED PORTUNUS or p. 166
   SPOTTED SWIMMING CRAB *Portunus sebae*
Posterior legs paddle-shaped. Long lateral spines and 2 distinct
red-brown spots on carapace. Carapace to 10 cm (4 in.) long.

5. RED or ORANGE CORAL *Tubastrea coccinea* p. 86
Close-up of polyps. See p. 7 and Pl. 10.

6. GIANT CARIBBEAN ANEMONE p. 75
   Condylactis gigantea
Largest Caribbean anemone — to 30 cm (1 ft.) across disk. Each
thick tan tentacle often tipped with pink or purple bulb. Column
often orange, sometimes green or purple-tinged. Most are host to
tiny **Pederson's Cleaning Shrimp** (center of photo).

7. PORTUGUESE MAN-OF-WAR *Physalia physalia* p. 67
Iridescent bluish purple float with trailing tentacles to 10 m
(33 ft.) long. Short convoluted tentacles are sections of long fishing
tentacles.

8. GUADELOUPE SEA BLADE p. 95
   Pterogorgia guadalupensis
Bushy, with broad flat blades. Polyps in grooves along branch
edges. Don't confuse with Yellow Sea Blade, which has fewer and
thinner branches, sparser growth habit.

PLATE 31

Brittle Stars, Octopus, and Squids

1. SPINY OPHIOCOMA *Ophiocoma echinata* p. 181
Aboral surface usually dark brown, sometimes mottled. Spines long, conspicuous. Large — arms to 15 cm (6 in.) or longer.

2. RUBY BRITTLE STAR *Ophioderma rubicundum* p. 183
Disk solid purplish red or mottled with white. Spines flattened against indistinctly banded arms. Medium-sized — to 2 cm ($\frac{3}{4}$ in.) across disk.

3. OERSTED'S BRITTLE STAR p. 185
Ophiothrix oerstedii
Aboral surface gray, bluish gray, or brown; covered with long barbed spines. Glassy spines on finely banded arms.

4. SLIMY BRITTLE STAR *Ophiomyxa flaccida* p. 183
Disk covered with smooth opaque skin. Arms long, slender, with tiny spines. Feels slimy. To 2 cm ($\frac{3}{4}$ in.) across disk.

5. RETICULATED BRITTLE STAR p. 183
Ophionereis reticulata
Disk bluish or bone-white with webbed pattern. Arms banded with brown.

6. SEAWEED or FOUR-EYED REEF OCTOPUS p. 149
Octopus hummelincki
Body covered with flat, bladelike, fuzzy-ended papillae. Pair of false eyespots (ocelli) vividly circled in bright blue; 1 visible under each bulging true eye. In algae beds. Small — to 20 cm (8 in.) from tip of arm to tip of opposite arm.

7. ATLANTIC OVAL or REEF SQUID p. 148
Sepioteuthis sepioidea
Usually swims forward, with tentacles bunched together, by undulating long lateral fins. Small schools on back reefs and in lagoons. To 25 cm (10 in.) long. Shown at night capturing a shrimp near surface.

8. PLEE'S STRIPED SQUID *Loligo pleii* p. 148
Wavy maroon stripes. Arrow-shaped tail fins extend over posterior third of body. To 60 cm (2 ft.) long. Similar to Northern Squid, which lacks stripes.

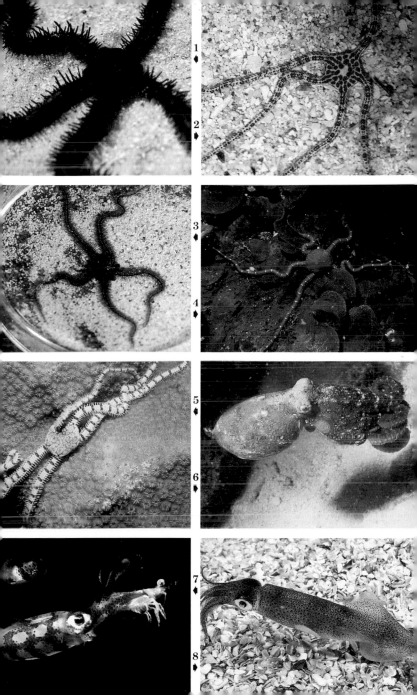

PLATE 32

Echinoderms

1. BEADED SEA LILY *Nemaster discoidea*   p. 205
Usually hidden in coral crevices with arms protruding. Deep water.
Tip of 1 arm shown; note beaded silver-gray pinnules.

2. ORANGE SEA LILY *Nemaster rubiginosa*   p. 205
Calyx usually hidden, but many of its 20 curled yellow arms often
visible projecting from crevices. Usually a black stripe on each
arm. Commonest crinoid. Deep water. Underside shown; note leglike cirri.

3. BANDED SEA LILY *Tropiometra carinata*   p. 205
Yellow-and-brown banded arms form fan. Shallowest crinoid;
sometimes visible to snorkelers. Southern Caribbean, especially
Barbados, Colombia. 10 feathery arms shown projecting from pil-
ing crevice.

4. BASKET STAR *Astrophyton muricatum*   p. 179
In daytime, a tightly coiled mass of tendrils, often hidden in soft
corals. Shown at night, when it expands to 18 cm (7 in.) or more,
forming a plankton-entrapping fan.

5. REEF URCHIN *Echinometra viridis*   p. 190
Test reddish; spines rose-colored at base, becoming green, then
chocolate-tipped. Usually on reefs below 5 m (17 ft.). Small — to
5 cm (2 in.) wide.

6. RED ROCK URCHIN *Echinometra lucunter*   p. 190
Several blackish-looking specimens with red undertones shown in
a tide pool. Note also, at the right between 2 urchins, the **Magpie,**
a snail typically found with this urchin just below intertidal zone.

7. VARIABLE or GREEN SEA URCHIN   p. 192
    Lytechinus variegatus
Spines short, white or greenish; test usually greenish. On Turtle
Grass beds, often in profusion, sometimes with similar Sea Egg,
which has a black test and white spines.

8. RED SPINY SEA STAR *Echinaster sentus*   p. 175
Distinctive red color, blunt arms, and large pointed spines. Under
coral in shallow flats. Usually less than 10 cm (4 in.) wide.

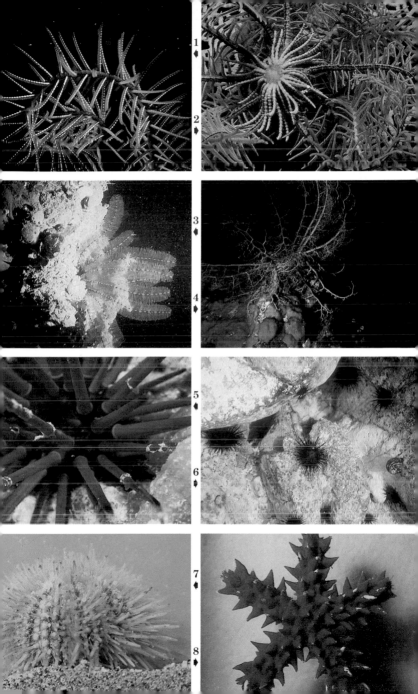

PLATE 33

Sea and Brittle Stars

1. COMET SEA STAR *Linckia guildingii*   p. 175
Arms long, thin, parallel-sided. Usually 5 arms; 1 large and 4–6 small arms common in juveniles. Covered with smooth low nodules. Beige, tan, or rarely reddish. To 23 cm (9 in.) from tip of arm to tip of opposite arm.

2. HARLEQUIN BRITTLE STAR   p. 182
Ophioderma appressum
Arms long, look minutely serrated; banded green and gray, or brown and white. Disk usually olive-green with white or black spots, sometimes brown or gray; to 2.5 cm (1 in.) across.

3. RETICULATED or CUSHION SEA STAR   p. 176
Oreaster reticulatus
Thick, inflated, covered with netlike array of contrasting-colored tubercles. Adult variable, often tan with red tubercles; juvenile green. In Turtle Grass beds. Large — to 50 cm (20 in.) across.

4. Oral view of **Harlequin Brittle Star.** Arm spines short, conical, in bundles of 5, closely pressed to arm. Radial shields triangular. Note distinctive pattern of bursa openings.

5. NETTED SEA STAR *Luidia clathrata*   p. 176
5 arms, with dark wavy lines parallel to both sides of black central stripe. Surface velvetlike. Buried under sand. Large — to 30 cm (1 ft.) across.

6. BROWN SPINY SEA STAR   p. 175
Echinaster spinulosus
5 long tapering arms covered with short, often contrasting-colored spines. Reddish, greenish, or tan. On mud in mangrove channels. To 15 cm (6 in.) across.

7. NINE-ARMED SEA STAR *Luidia senegalensis*   p. 176
9 long, tapered, pointed, purple arms covered with minute spines. Surface velvetlike. Buried under sand. Large — to 30 cm (1 ft.) across or larger.

8. LIMP or WEAK SEA STAR *Luidia alternata*   p. 176
5 very long, flaccid, tapered arms covered with long fragile spines. Cream, with brown or black blotches; sometimes indistinct dark bands. Under sand. Large — to 36 cm (14 in.) across.

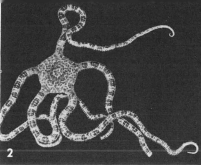

2

3

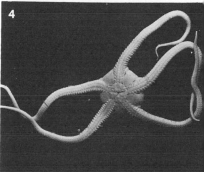

4

5

6

7

8

PLATE 34

Sea Urchins (1): Keyhole
and Other Regular

1. FIVE-HOLED KEYHOLE URCHIN p. 192
Mellita quinquiesperforata
Tan or gray, quite round, sharp-edged. Covered with fuzzlike spines. 5 "keyholes" (lunules) pierce test. 5 "petals" on aboral surface, vague when alive, distinct when dried. To 10 cm (4 in.) across.

2. SIX-HOLED KEYHOLE URCHIN p. 191
Leodia sexiesperforata
Dried specimen shown; spines have fallen off. 6 "keyholes" (lunules). 5 "petals" on aboral surface. Sandy beaches. To 10 cm (4 in.) across.

3. WILLIAMS' VARIABLE SEA URCHIN p. 192
Lytechinus williamsi
Test white or light green, visible between spines. Spines white, thinner and longer than in the more common Variable Sea Urchin. Podia distinctively purple-tipped. Deep water. Smaller than Variable Sea Urchin — to 5.5 cm (2¼ in.) across.

4. CLUB or PENCIL URCHIN p. 191
Eucidaris tribuloides
Test light brown, flecked with white. Spines thick, cylindrical, blunt-tipped, relatively sparse. To 5 cm (2 in.) across, larger in Bermuda and Brazil.

5. REEF URCHIN *Echinometra viridis* p. 190
Test red or maroon. All spines same color: tip brown, shaft green with rose near test, base ringed with white. Spines finer and longer than in Red Rock Urchin. Usually on deepwater coral. To 5 cm (2 in.) across.

6. HEART or MUD URCHIN *Moira atropos* p. 192
Tan, furry. 5 deep, narrow, slitlike ambulacra. Posterior almost vertical. Under mud. To 5.7 cm (2¼ in.) long.

7. RED ROCK URCHIN *Echinometra lucunter* p. 190
Test red or dark red. Spines red or blackish, to 2.5 cm (1 in.) long. Rocky shores just below low-tide line, almost always in rock crevices or tide pools. To 6.5 cm (2½ in.) across.

8. SEA EGG *Tripneustes ventricosus* p. 193
Round, with black test and short white spines. Turtle Grass beds. Large — to 13 cm (5 in.) across. Note also the **Fireworm** attacking the urchin.

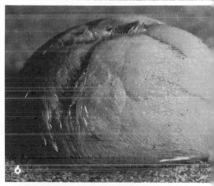

PLATE 35
Sea Urchins (2): Large and Irregular

1. GREAT RED-FOOTED URCHIN p. 193
Plagiobrissus grandis
Tan, oval, with about 20 long spines protruding from anterior dorsal surface. Test covered with thin spines; tract of bristlelike spines runs length of ventral surface. Thick red podia surround mouth and anus. Buried under sand. Large — to 23 cm (9 in.) long.
2. Ventral view of **Great Red-footed Urchin.** Note thick podia around mouth, midventral tract of bristlelike spines, and tuft of spines around anus.
3. SEA PUSSY or CAKE URCHIN p. 192
Meoma ventricosa
Reddish brown, covered with short bristly spines. Distinct pattern of 5 groovelike ambulacra: posterior pair angle sharply backward; the 1 anterior ambulacrum shallow, indistinct when animal alive. Under sand mounds. Large — to 12.5 cm (5 in.) long.
4. Dried **Sea Pussy** test. Note shallow anterior ambulacrum, angular line pattern around upper third of test.
5. FLAT SEA BISCUIT *Clypeaster subdepressus* p. 190
Yellowish, reddish, or dark brown. Relatively flat (compared to Inflated Sea Biscuit), with rounded margins; oval or pear-shaped, widest from posterior to middle. Spines fuzzlike. "Petals" small compared to Inflated Sea Biscuit's. Turtle Grass beds. Large — to 15 cm (6 in.) long, 1.5 cm ($\frac{5}{8}$ in.) high.
6. Dried **Flat Sea Biscuit** test. Note oval shape and relatively small "petals."
7. INFLATED SEA BISCUIT p. 190
Clypeaster rosaceus
Yellowish, reddish, greenish brown, or dark brown. Moundlike, with rounded margins; oval. Underside shallowly depressed at center. Large expanded "petals" cover more than $\frac{2}{3}$ of aboral surface. On sand in Turtle Grass beds, often camouflaged with grass, seashells. Large — to 15 cm (6 in.) long, 5 cm (2 in.) high.
8. Dried **Inflated Sea Biscuit** test. Note oval shape and large "petals."

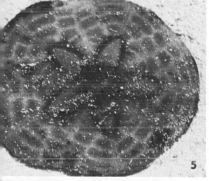

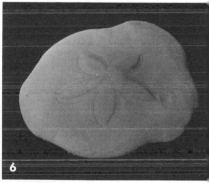

PLATE 36

Sea Cucumbers

1. BROWN ROCK SEA CUCUMBER p. 200
Holothuria glaberrima
Smooth-skinned. Light to dark brown. Tentacles black, bushy.
Podia dark brown, scattered over sole. On and under rocks and
among seaweed on wave-dashed beaches. To 15 cm (6 in.) long.

2. THREE-ROWED SEA CUCUMBER p. 201
Isostichopus badionotus
Dorsal surface smooth or warty. Striped, spotted, or blotched; orange and brown, dark brown, cream, or blackish. About 22 peltate
tentacles. Podia brown, in 3 rows on sole; central row widest and
split by seam (see below). Turtle Grass beds. Large — to 45 cm
(1½ ft.) long.

3. FURRY SEA CUCUMBER p. 199
Astichopus multifidus
Unique — dorsal surface covered with soft, pointed, 1 cm (½ in.)
long podia. Typical podia with disklike tips cover sole. Brown,
gray, or mottled brown and gray. Deep water near reef. Large — to
45 cm (1½ ft.) long.

4. BURROWING SEA CUCUMBER p. 200
Holothuria arenicola
Tan or gray; 2 rows of brown blotches on dorsal surface. Tentacles
tan, peltate. Podia small, inconspicuous. Forms mounds in sandy
and grassy areas. To 15 cm (6 in.) long.

5. FIVE-TOOTHED SEA CUCUMBER p. 199
Actinopyga agassizii
Dorsal surface brown, mottled; sole lighter. 25–30 tan peltate tentacles. Podia brownish, scattered on sole. Turtle Grass beds. To
30 cm (1 ft.) long. *Top:* Close-up of posterior. Note the 5 squarish
calcareous teeth in the anus.

6. An extended **Burrowing Sea Cucumber.** Note the characteristic double row of brown blotches.

7. GOLDEN SEA CUCUMBER *Holothuria parvula* p. 201
Back arched, with large pointed warts. Golden-brown, with bright
yellow podia on flattened sole. Under rocks in shallow water.
Tiny — to 3.5 cm (1¾ in.) long. Preserved specimen shown.

8. A **Three-rowed Sea Cucumber** (left) and a **Donkey Dung
Sea Cucumber,** *Holothuria mexicana* (right), crawling across the
glass of an aquarium. Note the scattered brown podia on the white
or pink sole of the Donkey Dung Sea Cucumber (p. 200).

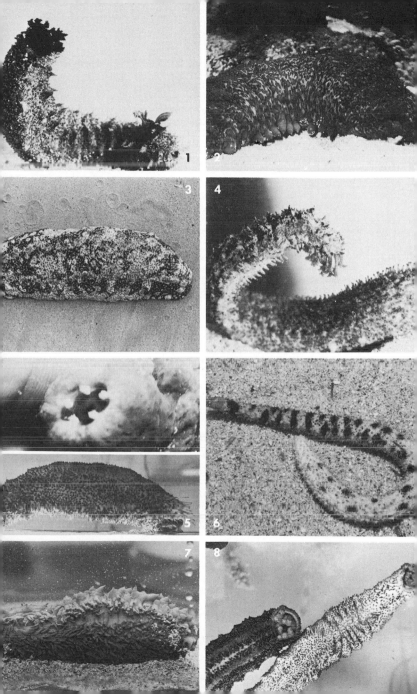

PLATE 37
Echinoderms and a Commensal Fish

1. BEADED SEA STAR *Astropecten articulatus*   p. 174
Aboral surface brown, purple, or maroon. Beads at ray margins yellow or tan. Bases of upper beads lack spines. Muddy bottoms. To 15 cm (6 in.) across.

2. SPINY BEADED SEA STAR   p. 174
   Astropecten duplicatus
Aboral surface reddish brown, brown, gray, or spotted tan. Bead color may match aboral color. Large pointed spines project from upper beads (visible in dried specimen shown). To 20 cm (8 in.) across.

3. PYGMY SEA CUCUMBER *Pentacta pygmaea*   p. 201
Chocolate-brown. 10 tentacles. Podia yellow or pink, in 3 rows. 2 double rows of blunt tubercles on dorsum. On rocks or Turtle Grass in shallow water. Small — to 5 cm (2 in.) long.

4. DONKEY DUNG SEA CUCUMBER   p. 200
   Holothuria mexicana
Specimen shown has been removed from water, placed on beach; thus is contracted. Skin leathery, thick, smooth or warty. Conspicuous deep wrinkles. Podia brown, scattered on rose or white sole. Common in Turtle Grass beds. Large — to 40 cm (16 in.).

5. BEADED SEA CUCUMBER *Euapta lappa*   p. 198
Fragile, sticky. Thick, squarish beadlike segments. Brown, with thin yellow and black stripes along body. Tentacles tan, feathery. Under rocks. Large —to 1 m (3¼ ft.) long.

6. BLACK-AND-WHITE SEA LILY   p. 205
   Nemaster grandis
To 40 black-and-white, 25 cm (10 in.) long arms. Often fully exposed in daytime. Deep water. Specimen shown is on **Giant Tube Sponge,** projecting from head of **Large Grooved Brain Coral.**

7. PEARLFISH *Carapus bermudensis*   p. 221
Silvery and pinkish, somewhat translucent. Appears to lack fins. Snout extends beyond lower lip. In cloaca and respiratory tree region of Five-toothed Sea Cucumber (see Fig. 62). To 16 cm (6¼ in.) long. Carapidae.

8. SEA EGG *Tripneustes ventricosus*   p. 193
Dried bleached test shown. Note bumps, which are articulation points of spines. 5 rows of tiny holes are ambulacra; podia extend from holes. Often in Turtle Grass beds.

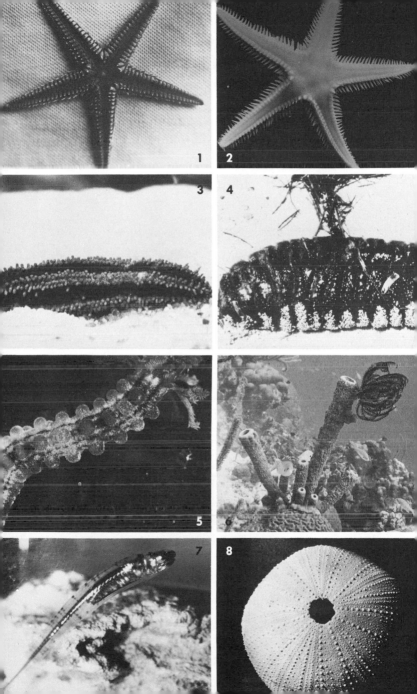

9

Mollusks

The members of Phylum Mollusca are generally an unprepossessing lot: bivalves are usually buried under the surface of the sand, and gastropods move at a snail's pace, often camouflaged by a fuzzy outer covering or encrusting organisms. Not so the mollusks of the coral reef: the most exciting and beautiful molluscan forms can be found on the reef and its environs.

Snails are represented by the huge Queen Conch, with its flaming pink aperture; the voracious, predatory Tulip Snail, whose red flesh contrasts with its symmetrical tan shell; and the Flamingo Tongue, the most beautiful of all, its bright orange leopard-spotted mantle aglow against a purple sea fan, which is its prey.

Common reef bivalves include the Winged Pearl Oyster, which commonly lives on soft corals, and the file clams, *Lima* species, which can be found in crevices between corals. If you are lucky, you will see one of these scalloplike animals swimming erratically, with hinge foremost, trailing streaming orange tentacles behind.

But it is the octopods and squids that cause one to lose one's breath at the moment of discovery. To happen upon a meter wide octopus as it crawls from the recesses of one coral head to hide under another brings to mind horror stories of man-eating, ship-capturing monsters. Perhaps it will help you, as you draw back in shock, to know that octopuses are among the shiest of animals, content to hide all day and to feed on nothing larger than crabs at night.

Of the 6 classes in Phylum Mollusca, only 3 are common on coral reefs:

1. **Snails, limpets, nudibranchs, and sea slugs** (Class Gastropoda) exhibit a great variety of forms. Most members of the class move along the bottom on a flat foot, usually with a spiral or domed shell carried on the back. Nudibranchs have lost the shell completely.

2. **Clams, oysters, and mussels** (Class Pelecypoda; also known as Lamellibranchia and Bivalvia) are bivalves, animals with soft bodies enclosed within 2 shells.

3. **Octopods and squids** (Class Cephalopoda) have tentacles extending from the head. Octopods usually crawl along the bottom; squids swim in schools.

Why do we place these very different organisms in the same phylum? What do they have in common? Three features reveal their common ancestry.

First, all mollusks have a mass of tissue, the mantle, surrounding the viscera (internal organs).

Second, the mantle usually secretes a shell. The shell may enclose the mollusk's body, or it may be enclosed within the body, as in the case of the relatively inconsequential penlike shell of a squid. With the exception of nudibranchs and octopods there is some sign of a shell in or around every mollusk.

Third, all mollusks have a foot, a muscular organ usually used for propulsion. It may be the hatchet-shaped distensible foot of a clam, which when filled with blood becomes a long, pointed organ. A pocket at one end fills with blood, like a balloon, forming an anchor. The clam then contracts the stretched muscles of the foot and pulls itself into the sediment. A snail secretes a trail of mucus so slippery and dense that it can crawl over a razor's edge unharmed, its "stomach foot" (*gastro* = stomach, *pod* = foot) protected by the mucus. Octopods and squids use tentacles that extend from the head like an Indian's headdress. Each tentacle (the octopus has 8, the squid 10) is soft and muscular. The ventral surface is covered with round suction cups so effective that, when the octopus has applied itself to the underside of a rock, you might tear off a tentacle before you dislodge the animal.

The mantle of an octopus or squid is tough and muscular, and it is alternately contracted and relaxed to force water into and out of the mantle cavity, bathing the gills. Under stress, the animal forcibly contracts the mantle; a powerful stream of water is expelled from the siphon, jetting the animal backward.

The mantle of clams and snails is made of soft, filmy tissue, and its primary function is to secrete the shell.

Many bivalves are filter-feeders. They extend a double siphon to suck in and expel seawater. Tiny hairlike cilia on the flat, layered gills beat back and forth, creating a current that pulls in the water. Microscopic plankton stick to the mucus-covered gills as the water sweeps by, and the cilia sweep them to the mouth.

Snails probably originated as browsers of algae growing on rocks and coral. They have a tonguelike organ, the radula, composed of hundreds of chitinous (plasticlike) teeth. It is rasped on any surface, scraping off the algae. But snails are a diverse group. Evolution has provided them with the means for invading other biological niches. The radula is used by oyster drills to bore a neat round hole through the shell of bivalves. The radula is then inserted through the hole and used to tear the flesh from the prey animal until its shell is empty. The cone snails have reached a high point in the evolution of the radula. It has become a poison dart that is thrust into worms or fishes, paralyzing them instantly. The prey is then swallowed whole.

Octopods and squids have an inverted hawk's beak. They use it to bite a crab just behind the eyes, injecting poison with the bite and thereby paralyzing the crab.

Snails and Sea Slugs

Most gastropods are found, not on the coral reef, but in the Turtle Grass beds of the lagoon. The conchs are large herbivores; their shells are used commercially as curios and to make cameos. But these snails are threatened primarily because of their suitability as food rather than the attractiveness of their shells. Each shell is neatly incised with a 2 cm (¾ in.) long hole just above the attachment of the columellar muscle. Once this muscle is severed by a fisherman, the body falls from the shell.

The only snails of importance on the reef are the Flamingo Tongue and the camouflaged, hard-to-find coral snails. These are among the few predators of corals; they insert an elongate proboscis into the coral cup and suck out the polyp's tissues.

Common Species

The measurements given below for snails are the distance between the tip of the spire and the bottom of the aperture.

Snails

STOCKY CERITH *Cerithium literatum* **Fig. 42**
To 2.5 cm (1 in.). Whitish with *brown markings in rows* (like print). Shoulder below each suture has 9–12 prominent sharp nodules. Turtle Grass beds, shallow water. *Related species:* (1) Ivory Cerith, *C. eburneum,* is narrower, lacks sharp nodules. 4–6 rows of 18–22 *small rounded beads* on each whorl. White or speckled brown. (2) Middle-spined Cerith, *C. algicola,* is more elongate than Stocky Cerith; *sharp nodules* less pronounced, *project from middle of whorls* (not from just below sutures). Whitish, with brown lines or blotches.

Fig. 42
Stocky Cerith

CHOCOLATE-LINED TOP SNAIL Fig. 21, p. 51
Calliostoma javanicum
To 3 cm (1¼ in.). *Top-shaped;* flattened bottom contains *funnel-shaped umbilicus.* 9 or 10 flat whorls covered with thin dark beaded lines. Brownish, mottled with red and orange. On coral.

SHORT CORAL SNAIL Fig. 21, p. 51
Coralliophila abbreviata
To 2.5 cm (1 in.). Shell grayish white; aperture pink or violet. Shell solid, with 5 or 6 shouldered whorls (last one large) and *several heavy vertical folds from base to spire.* At bases of sea fans. *Related species:* Caribbean Coral Snail, *C. caribaea,* is smaller — to 2 cm (¾ in.). Shell has *slanting vertical folds* and weak revolving lines. Whitish; aperture purplish. Coral reefs, lagoons.

FLAMINGO TONGUE *Cyphoma gibbosum* Fig. 14, p. 32
To 2.5 cm (1 in.). Shell smooth, glossy pink or orange, with elongate aperture and *ridge around middle.* When seen alive, usually on a sea fan, the mantle (a thin film of tissue) extends around shell. *Mantle bright orange with black-ringed leopardlike spots;* color will not last because mantle is withdrawn upon death, so living specimens should not be collected.

TULIP SNAIL *Fasciolaria tulipa* Fig. 11, p. 22
To 23 cm (9 in.). Reddish brown to gray, with *interrupted brown spiral lines.* Shell smooth. When alive, tissues red. In Turtle Grass beds. *Related species:* Banded Tulip Snail, *F. hunteria,* is smaller — to 7.5 cm (3 in.) — with more distinct uninterrupted brown spiral lines.

QUEEN CONCH *Strombus gigas* Fig. 10, p. 21
The large — to 30 cm (1 ft.) — edible conch. White, often covered with thin brown plasticlike periostracum. *Aperture and flaring lip usually bright pink* in fresh specimens. Turtle Grass and sandy bottoms. *Related species:* (1) West Indian Fighting Conch, *S. pugilis,* is shiny orange; *lacks upper flare on aperture.* (2) Hawkwing Conch, *S. raninus,* is gray or whitish, with streaks of black or brown; aperture lavender. *Lacks obvious spines on shoulder of each whorl.* Both species smaller than Queen Conch.

Sea Slugs

SPOTTED SEA HARE *Aplysia dactylomela* Fig. 12, p. 23
Large — to 40 cm (16 in.). *Body olive-drab, with black ringlike spots.* Rabbit-ear-like structures (rhinophores) extend from head. Long groove runs length of back, bordered by 2 flaps. Emits a purple cloud when disturbed. Usually found browsing on algae in Turtle Grass beds; young may be under rocks. *Related species:* (1) Black-rimmed Sea Hare, *A. parvula,* has a *black-rimmed body*

with gold or olive undertones; no spots. (2) Black Sea Hare, *A. morio,* has an almost completely *black body.* (3) Ragged Sea Hare, *Bursatella leachii pleii,* is tan or brown; covered with *elongate filmy flattened papillae,* giving animal a hairy or woolly appearance. (4) Warty Sea Cat, *Dolabrifera dolabrifera,* to 10 cm (4 in.), is light or dark green, tan, or black; sole light green, with tan spots; *body covered with pointed warts.* Under stones and in tide pools.

LETTUCE SEA SLUG *Tridachia crispata*   Fig. 21, p. 51
To 5 cm (2 in.). Mass of *white-rimmed frills* cover back. Body usually green (sometimes blue), with cream-colored spots. Feeds on algae in Turtle Grass beds.

Clams and Oysters

Most bivalves live buried in sand or attached to rocks and are therefore not often visible on the coral reef. Among the few common pelecypods on the reef are the flamboyant, red-fleshed file clams and the dramatic Spiny or Thorny Oyster and Winged Pearl Oyster.

Fig. 43

Winged Pearl Oyster

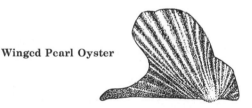

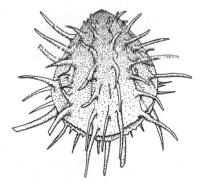

**Spiny or
Thorny Oyster**

Common Species

ROUGH FILE CLAM *Lima scabra* **Pl. 19**
2.5–7.5 cm (1–3 in.) long. Outside brown; plasticlike covering over longitudinal ridges with *rasplike or filelike surface*. Inside shiny white. Live animal orange or red, with long streaming tentacles. The other 2 *Lima* species are similar but smaller.

WINGED PEARL OYSTER *Pteria colymbus* **Fig. 43**
3.8–7.5 cm (1½–3 in.) long. Brownish purple. *Long thin extension of shell runs along straight flat hinge.* Shell surface wrinkled; may have radiating brown lines. Wings round, notched. Inside pearly.

SPINY or THORNY OYSTER **Fig. 43**
Spondylus americanus
7.5–12.5 cm (3–5 in.) long. Shell round, inflated, with *many long spines projecting in all directions*. Some spines flat, with wedge-shaped tips; others needlelike. Surface under spines white, yellow, brown, purple, or red, with many radiating ribs. Often embedded in coral; specimens on beaches often worn.

Octopods and Squids

Cephalopods are among the most intelligent of invertebrates. Most octopods brood their young, blowing jets of oxygenated water over them and protecting them until they can fend for themselves. Both squids and octopods can change color almost instantaneously. Most squids swim in schools; most octopods are solitary. Squids usually swim headfirst by gently moving their lateral fins in a rippling fashion. Octopods, on the other hand, crawl along the bottom in their never-ending search for crabs. When startled or attacked, they bring their whole arsenal of tricks into play. First they change color, turning black, perhaps to frighten the predator. If this doesn't work, the squid might instantly become virtually transparent, almost invisible in the water. The octopod becomes camouflaged, matching the bottom. If the predator advances farther, the cephalopod gives it the old one-two. The one: a cloud of black dye is released, simulating another prey animal and confusing the attacker. The two: at the same time the cephalopod forcibly ejects a stream of water through its siphon, jetting backward with great velocity under cover of the dye.

The eye of cephalopods is much like man's in its ability to focus and form images. But the lens moves back and forth like that of a camera rather than changing its shape like a human lens. The animal clearly sees its surroundings and can almost instantly match the color of its environment by sending nervous messages to cells in its skin called chromatophores. These contain bags of dye in 3 primary colors. When the bags are expanded, the color becomes intense. When contracted, the cells become nearly colorless, as the dye is reduced to a tiny dot. Camouflage is achieved by the expansion of some chromatophores and the contraction of others until the color of the background is matched.

Octopods and squids have separate sexes. During courtship the male, using a specially adapted tentacle, removes a packet of sperms from its own body and places it inside the female's mantle cavity. Squids lay chains of egg capsules in festoons over the bottom. Octopods lay eggs in caves, the female broods them, blowing oxygenated water over them with her siphon. Recent studies of the Seaweed or Four-eyed Reef Octopus have revealed that the female spawns only once in her life. While brooding her young she eats little, and her feeding habits change. Instead of boring a hole in snails to remove the tissue she wrenches the animal from its shell, often not eating it after all her work. About 10 days after her eggs hatch, she dies. What is so exciting to scientists is that a gland in the eye socket seems to be responsible for her rapid aging and death. If the gland is removed, the octopus resumes her normal habits and lives for many months. The optic gland has been compared to the human pituitary gland.

Squids have a thin, plasticlike, internal shell called a pen. Most octopods have lost the shell completely. A common deepwater cephalopod, the Common Spirula, has embedded in its body a coiled, gas-filled shell that gives it buoyancy. When the animal dies and decays, the shell floats to the surface and drifts ashore. Look for the shell, with its chambers separated by mother-of-pearl septa, in seaweed on the beach.

The Atlantic Oval or Reef Squid, because of its gregarious and fearless habits, provides much joy to snorkelers and scuba divers. Small schools of this wonderful animal appear suddenly in the corner of your eye as you swim over lagoon or reef, sometimes in water less than 2 m (6½ ft.) deep. You are startled not so much by their sudden appearance as by the realization that they are staring at you with as much interest as you are exhibiting toward them. Approach slowly, and they will hold their ground, staring all the more intently. When you are about 1.5 m (5 ft.) away, they will swim slowly backward in unison, their fins rippling and their tentacles bunched up. Swim faster, and they will match your velocity, keeping the same precise distance. Stop, and they will stop too. This game can go on for 15 minutes or more, until one of the parties tires. If you rush at them in a threatening manner, they will change color and back off a little more rapidly.

Common Species

Four squids and 5 octopods are commonly found in shallow water in our study region. Several obvious diagnostic features are used to differentiate squids and octopods in the field. A squid has 10 arms, a long tapered body, and is pelagic (free-swimming). An octopod has 8 arms, a bulbous body, and is most often seen scuttling from one hiding place to another in rocks or reefs. The measurements given below are for the distance from the posterior of the body to the tip of the longest arm, unless otherwise specified.

Fig. 44

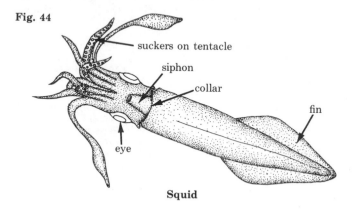

suckers on tentacle

siphon

collar

fin

eye

Squid

Squids

PLEE'S STRIPED SQUID *Loligo pleii*   **Pl. 31**
To 60 cm (2 ft.), including arms. Body long and slender, with long, narrow, slightly wavy, dark maroon bands along sides; rest of body covered with small maroon dots. *Triangular fins on last third of body.*

BRIEF THUMBSTALL SQUID *Lolliguncula brevis*
To 25 cm (10 in.), including arms. *Short rounded fins on last third of body* form a flat round disk. Upper arms very short. Dorsal surface covered with easily visible round purple dots. Underside of fins white.

PICKFORD'S SQUID *Pickfordiateuthis pulchella*
Tiny — to 4 cm (1½ in.). Body broad, with *2 small round disklike fins separated from each other* and not joined posteriorly. Eyes large. Over Turtle Grass beds in shallow water.

ATLANTIC OVAL or REEF SQUID   **Pl. 31**
Sepioteuthis sepioidea
To 25 cm (10 in.). *Long, more or less oval fins that start just behind mouth.* Skin yellowish, with purple dots, but color variable, most often appearing light purple. Swims with short tentacles

bunched, so they look like the front end of the head. Conspicuous fins along body have a rippling movement used for propulsion except when frightened. In schools of 4–6, moving slowly in back reef area.

COMMON SPIRULA *Spirula spirula*
Only the shell is commonly found; the living animal is rarely seen. *Fragile white shell is a chambered cone coiled in a flat spiral, usually less than 2.5 cm (1 in) in diameter.* Each chamber divided from its neighbor by a shiny white, concave, fragile wall with a tiny dot in its center. Shell develops inside the body of a small, short-armed deepsea squid. When animals dies and decays, air-filled shell floats to surface, eventually to be washed ashore.

Octopods

BRIAR or REEF OCTOPUS *Octopus briareus*
To 54 cm (1½ ft.). Arms thick at bases. Longest arm about 5 times body length. *2nd and 3rd pairs of arms longer than the others.* Pinkish or greenish to red-mottled. Usually intertidal, under coral heads; occasionally in tide pools.

SEAWEED or FOUR-EYED REEF OCTOPUS   Pl. 31
Octopus hummelincki
Small — to 20 cm (8 in.). Covered with flat, bladelike, fuzzy-ended papillae. Eyes project conspicuously from body. *Round pale to purplish blotch or circle next to each eye* gives a 4-eyed appearance. The false eyespots may be vivid, making this species easy to identify. When crawling, animal is reddish, yellow-brown, or whitish, mottled with golden-yellow. When swimming, changes to uniform light brown. In beds of sargassum weed and other brownish algae.

JOUBIN'S OCTOPUS *Octopus joubini*
Small — to 15 cm (6 in.) — with *short arms* (only slightly longer than body). Skin smooth, with a few scattered warts. Dark brown or blackish. Often within bivalve shells.

WHITE-SPOTTED or GRASS OCTOPUS
Octopus macropus
To 1 m (3¼ ft.), including longest arm. Blue-green, brownish gray, or pinkish orange, with *large white spots.* When disturbed, becomes brick-red and spots become prominent. First arm is longest.

COMMON ATLANTIC OCTOPUS *Octopus vulgaris*
The largest of the shallow-water octopods, with a maximum radial spread of about 2.2 m (7 ft.). To 90 cm (3 ft.), including longest arm. Longest arm about 4 times body length. Front and rear pairs of arms shorter than side arms; *front pair shortest.* Skin smooth, usually white, mottled with bluish green.

10

Shrimps, Lobsters, and Crabs

Malcolm Telford

Crabs, lobsters, and shrimps — members of Phylum Arthropoda, Class Crustacea — are in countless numbers on the reef, much as their relatives, the insects, dominate terrestrial habitats.

Virtually every large sea anemone has a tiny, purplish cleaning shrimp hidden inside its tentacular crown, while pairs of pistol shrimps live out their lives underneath the protective umbrella of the anemone's nematocyst-bearing tentacles. Crabs are often camouflaged and hard to see, but if you shake a clump of Thin Finger Coral, perhaps a dozen tiny Green Reef Crabs will fall out of its crevices. Urchin Crabs hide under the ominous spines of the Long-spined Black Urchin. A pair of long antennae extending from under a coral head gives evidence of the presence of a Spiny Lobster. An exciting underwater treat is to see a red-and-white Banded Coral or Barber Pole Shrimp dancing on the tip of a coral head, performing the intricate ritual that signals its availability to clean passing fishes. Even when they are out of sight, you will be able to hear the crustaceans: listen for the pops and clicks of pistol and snapping shrimps near any coral head.

Crustaceans live in a hard shell. Rapid movement is made possible by joints in their armor, the ringlike segments of a lobster's abdomen and its jointed legs. Living encased in a shell offers protection but presents problems, too. Growth is difficult, for the shell must be cast aside periodically to allow the body to increase in size. This is regulated by a complex hormone interaction. After a period of feeding and fat accumulation, hormones from the eyestalk region cause the edges of the carapace (shell) to split. The crab, shrimp, or lobster then crawls out, leaving behind the shell, a perfect replica of itself. The soft and vulnerable animal hides while producing another hormone that prevents water loss and causes the animal to swell, its tissues filled with excess water. Still hidden, it lays down a new shell on its bloated body. When the shell hardens, another hormone causes the crustacean to lose water, deflating it, and its reduced body rattles around in the new, enlarged carapace. Now the animal has room to grow until it fills its armored shell and once again has to molt.

Almost all crustaceans have separate sexes, but a few shrimps start life as males and after one reproductive period become females. In most instances mating is seasonal and involves an elaborate courtship ritual. Many crabs mate when the female is still soft from molting. Premolt females release a sex attractant. Drawn to the female, the male may attend his lady for some days before she molts, often carrying her beneath him during this time. After she has molted, the male turns the female on her back, folds back her abdomen to expose the genital openings, and inserts his copulatory appendages. The sperms of most crustaceans do not have a movable tail and must therefore be placed accurately.

Like fleas, ticks, mosquitoes, and other terrestrial parasites, some crustaceans have adapted to living on the body of a host. In most cases the relationship is harmless, as with the tiny pea crab that lives on the Sea Pussy or Cake Urchin. The crab eats detritus on the body of the urchin, perhaps actually benefiting the urchin by keeping it clean. The 6 mm ($\frac{1}{4}$ in.) crab obtains shelter among the bristles and hollows of the urchin's body.

The Elkhorn Coral or Gall Crab has a more pronounced effect on its host, usually Elkhorn Coral. The female crab stimulates the coral to grow a chamber that eventually encloses the crab in a permanent prison. She maintains a flow of water through the chamber and uses hairy appendages to filter out plankton. The tiny male crab roams around freely and periodically enters the female's chamber to mate with her.

A shocking underwater experience is to pick up a conch and turn the shell over, only to discover that you are holding a very active, large, red hermit crab — the Red Hermit, which is the largest of the West Indian hermits.

Several species of crabs cover their carapaces with living organisms, providing both camouflage and a source of food in some cases. The Giant Decorator Crab, the Sponge Spider Crab, the Lesser Sponge Crab, and the Round Sponge Crab are difficult to find because their backs are covered with assorted growths of algae, hydrozoan polyps, sponges, and other encrusting organisms. There is no doubt that they are deliberately planted there. The Lesser Sponge Crab and Round Sponge Crab are actually covered with tiny curved bristles that are useful in anchoring the sponges.

A shrimp or lobster has an elongate body made up of 3 regions: head, thorax, and abdomen (see Fig. 45). The head and thorax are fused to form a cephalothorax and are covered by a single piece of hardened cuticle, the carapace. The head bears 5 pairs of appendages: 2 pairs of sensory antennae (the smaller first pair, the antennules, are branched; the second pair are not), followed by 3 pairs that are jaws and other mouth parts. The next 8 pairs of appendages belong to the thorax. The first 3 aid in feeding; these are called maxillipeds (little jaw legs) and are located around the mouth. The next 5 pairs of thoracic appendages are the walking legs. The first, second, and third pairs may have pincers (claws), or chelae. The first pair of pincers may be very large; they serve no locomotive function but are used to capture food. The abdomen

Fig. 45

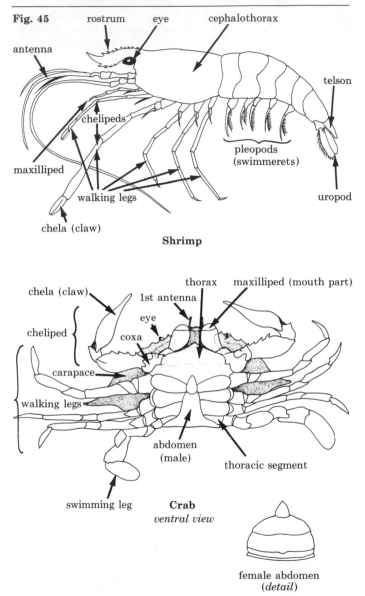

rostrum   eye   cephalothorax

antenna

chelipeds

maxilliped

walking legs

chela (claw)

telson

pleopods
(swimmerets)

uropod

Shrimp

chela (claw)

cheliped

carapace

walking legs

coxa

eye

1st antenna

thorax   maxilliped (mouth part)

abdomen
(male)

thoracic segment

swimming leg   **Crab**
ventral view

female abdomen
(*detail*)

consists of 6 segments, usually with appendages, but this is a variable feature. The appendages are usually flattened and are used for swimming and/or carrying eggs. The final pair of abdominal appendages are often large and flat; with the terminal piece of the body (telson), they make up the tail fan.

Crabs have a reduced abdomen, which is folded under the cephalothorax (see Fig. 45).

Common Species

There are 26,000 species in Class Crustacea; they are arranged in 8 subclasses and 31 orders. Only 2 orders, Stomatopoda and Decapoda, are important on the reef. Order Decapoda is so complex that it has been divided into 7 sections.

Mantis Shrimps

Order Stomatopoda. Head unlike that of any other crustacean because it is jointed. Anterior part, bearing eyes and antennules, moves independently. Carapace covers only posterior part of head and first 3 segments of thorax. Second pair of thoracic appendages greatly enlarged, used as raptorial legs (adapted to seize prey). Mantis shrimps have such sharp raptorial legs that they can cut other shrimps in half when they strike. Terminal joint or finger of second leg may have strong teeth and is *folded along a sharp-edged groove in preceding joint.* Some species lurk near the entrance to their burrows; others creep up on their prey and strike them down with incredible rapidity, like the familiar Praying Mantis, after which they are named. More than 60 species in the Florida-Caribbean region.

ROCK MANTIS SHRIMPS   Fig. 46, p. 154
Gonodactylus species
To 10 cm (4 in.) long. Species are difficult to identify, but any shallow-water mantis shrimp *without teeth on its raptorial fingers* probably belongs to this genus. Telson has 3 or 5 ridges; 4 ridges on last abdominal segment. Common Rock Mantis Shrimp, *G. oerstedi* (Fig. 46), is variable in color, often dark mottled green to black but may be cream with green mottling; *central ridge on telson and base of unarmed finger of claw swollen.* In coral crevices. Avoid picking up finger corals and other corals with many crannies; if you touch a hidden mantis shrimp, it may lash out with its razor-sharp finger, splitting yours. This is the source of one of the common names for these shrimps: thumb busters.

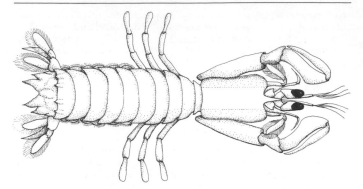

Common Rock Mantis Shrimp

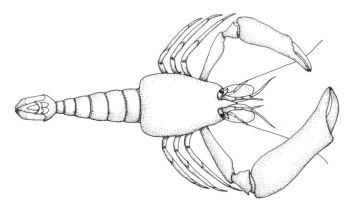

Fig. 46   Common Watchman Shrimp

Ten-legged Crustaceans

Order Decapoda. By far the most conspicuous and largest group of
crustaceans. 5 pairs of walking legs on thorax. Some legs have pincers; 1 pair of pincers usually very large. Divided into 2 groups:
those that swim readily or habitually (Suborder Natantia) and
those that crawl (Suborder Reptantia). Natantia comprises all
shrimps and prawns, arranged in 3 sections; Reptantia comprises
lobsters, crabs, and their allies, arranged in 4 sections, only 3 of
which are represented around coral reefs.

Caridean Shrimps and Prawns

Section Caridea. The largest group of shrimps; several families, about 1700 species. 2 distinguishing features: first 2 pairs of legs have pincers, and side plates of second abdominal segment overlap those of the first.

COMMON WATCHMAN SHRIMP   Fig. 46, p. 154
Pontonia mexicana
To 3 cm (1¼ in.) long. A symbiont of pen shells and other mollusks. Colorless and translucent, with claws as long as body. Usually found in pairs, lurking just inside opening of host's shell. Family Palaemonidae. Several other, similar *Pontonia* species occur wherever suitable hosts are found. All species from North Carolina to Gulf of Mexico and Caribbean.

SNAPPING SHRIMPS   Pl. 29
Alpheus species
Also called pistol shrimps. *One claw grossly enlarged.* Movable finger can be temporarily locked in open position while muscles in massive palm start contracting to generate tension. Lock mechanism suddenly releases, and claw snaps shut with a noise like a pistol shot. Used to warn other shrimps trespassing on occupied territory; also to stun small fishes which are then dragged into shrimp's lair and eaten. Family Alpheidae. (1) Common Snapping Shrimp, *A. heterochaelis,* to 3 cm (1¼ in.) long, has deep notches in upper and lower margins of palm and grooves and depressions along its length. *Rostrum small; edges of carapace beside eyes rounded, without spines.* In reefs and oyster beds from North Carolina and Bermuda to Brazil. (2) Red Snapping Shrimp, *A. armatus* (Pl. 29), to 5 cm (2 in.) long. Beneath tentacles of Ringed Anemone (see plate and p. 37). (3) Banded Snapping Shrimp, *A. armillatus,* to 3 cm (1¼ in.) long, is similar to Red Snapping Shrimp, but *abdomen banded with white and greenish tan.*

SPONGE SHRIMPS   Pl. 29
Synalpheus species
To 2 cm (¾ in.) long. Like the snapping shrimps (above), these shrimps are also called pistol shrimps. Several species live inside sponges, where they feed on worms, debris, and possibly the sponge itself. Family Alpheidae. (1) Long-clawed Sponge Shrimp, *S. longicarpus,* lives in brown sponges from North Carolina and Florida Keys to Trinidad. Short broad *rostrum with 3 teeth,* the lateral ones over the eyes. *Large claw smooth, almost cylindrical,* with markedly unequal fingers. (2) *S. minus* is smaller — to 1.2 cm (½ in.) long—with a less inflated pistol claw. In green sponges. (3) Short-clawed Sponge Shrimp, *S. brevicarpus* (Pl. 29), is similar but *light green with red-tipped large claw.*

PEPPERMINT or VEINED SHRIMP   **Pl. 29**
Lysmata wurdemanni
To 4 cm (1½ in.) long. *Translucent with longitudinal red lines*
edged with white. Also called Red Cleaning Shrimp. Among
sponges and tunicates, especially along wharf and jetty supports in
Florida, Gulf of Mexico, and Caribbean. This species and many
others of the genus act as cleaning shrimps, picking tissue debris
and microorganisms off fishes that actively seek them out (see p.
247). Family Hippolytidae. *Related species:* Red-backed Cleaning
Shrimp or Scarlet Lady, *L. grabhami* (Pl. 29), is similar but *bright*
yellow with a broad red stripe on back and a thin white stripe
along the crown of back; long antennae white.

PEDERSON'S CLEANING SHRIMP   **Pl. 30**
Periclimenes pedersoni
A tiny — to 2.5 cm (1 in.) long — shrimp. *Transparent, with pur-*
plish overtones. On many anemones, especially Ringed and Giant
Caribbean Anemones. Family Hippolytidae. *Related species:*
Spotted Cleaning Shrimp, *P. yucatanicus* (Pl. 29), is similar but
whitish with brown and black circles and rings; legs and antennae
banded white and brown.

Penaeid or Commercial Shrimps

Section Penaeidea. Pincers on first 3 pairs of legs, all about same
size. Abdomen, which may be large, bent only slightly downward.

WHITE SHRIMPS   **Fig. 47**
Penaeus species
Large; often abundant. The shrimps most sought commercially for
food. Several species common from Carolinas to Brazil, where
adults occur in marine habitats and young in brackish bays or
estuaries. Family Penaeidae. (1) White Shrimp, *P. setiferus,* the
largest penaeid — to 18 cm (7 in.) long — is almost transparent
with a bluish tinge; *anterior half of carapace grooved.* (2) Brazilian Shrimp, *P. brasiliensis,* often found in mixed shoals with
White Shrimp, has *lateral grooves extending entire length of cara-*
pace. (3) American Pink Shrimp, *P. duorarum,* and (4) Brown
Shrimp, *P. aztecus,* are similar commercial species.

Stenopodidean Shrimps

Section Stenopodidea. Unlike the penaeids, these shrimps, commonly called coral shrimps, have the third pair of pincers greatly
enlarged; skeleton relatively thick and spiny. More cylindrical, less
compressed than penaeids. First 3 pairs of legs have pincers, the
third pair much longer and stronger than the others. Most often
around coral reefs, where several species act as cleaners.

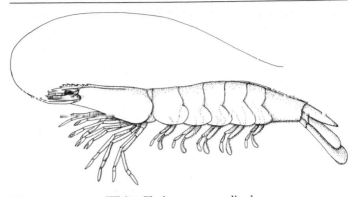

Fig. 47   **White Shrimp** — generalized

BANDED CORAL or BARBER POLE SHRIMP   Pl. 29
Stenopus hispidus
To 5 cm (2 in.) long. *Whitish, banded with bright red.* On coral
reefs of Florida and West Indies; in crevices at shallow to moderate
depths.

Spiny and Slipper Lobsters

Section Palinura. Abdomen (the part we eat) well developed. No
transverse lines across outer lobes of tail fan. Front of carapace
short; rostrum indistinct or absent. *Walking legs without pincers,*
but in some species the end joint is folded back and lies alongside
the preceding one.

SPINY LOBSTER   Pl. 29
Panulirus argus
To 60 cm (2 ft.) long. Unlike northern lobsters and crayfishes, *has
neither pincers nor rostrum.* Carapace more or less cylindrical and
armed with many strong sharp spines, including a very prominent
one bent forward over each eye. Antennae long, extend backward
for full length of body. Bases of antennae large and spiny; when
moved up and down rapidly, produce a rattling or squealing sound
that warns other lobsters to stay out of occupied territory. May be
brightly colored: carapace yellow and reddish brown or even blue;
legs lined with yellow; abdomen yellow-spotted. By day, hide in
crevices in reefs where, all too often, they fall prey to greedy
spear-gun hunters. North Carolina to Brazil, but sadly depleted in
some popular tourist regions.

SCYLLARIDES species   Pl. 29; Fig. 48

Lobsterlike in appearance but greatly flattened. *Bases of antennae enormously enlarged into flat plates edged with sharp pointed teeth.* No claws or pincers. Slipper Lobster, *S. nodifer* (Pl. 29; Fig. 48), to 30 cm (1 ft.) long, is sandy-colored, mottled with purple-brown. Most likely to be seen at night on surface of reefs or in inshore surf zone. Throughout our region but not really common anywhere.

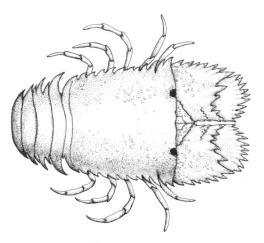

Fig. 48   **Slipper Lobster**

Hermit, Porcelain, and Mole Crabs

Section Anomura. These crabs have a well-developed asymmetrical abdomen bent beneath them. Uropods do not always form a tail fan but are usually present. Fifth thoracic legs unlike the others in appearance and high up toward the back. Common in the Florida-Caribbean region. The hermit crabs have an asymmetrically coiled abdomen that fits into an empty shell for protection.

FLAT-CLAWED HERMIT CRAB   Fig. 49, p. 160

Pagurus operculatus

Carapace to 1.2 cm (½ in.) long. Width of large claw at least ¾ of its length, with a *fleshy frill on lower side of wrist joint.* Brightly colored: legs and small claw orange; large claw whitish; arm purple; eyestalks and bases of antennae banded with purple, but antennae themselves orange. In shallow water in Florida and West Indies to Barbados.

PAGURISTES species   Fig. 49, p. 160
Carapace to 2.5 cm (1 in.) long. About half a dozen species in our area. Gray's Hermit Crab, *P. grayi* (Fig. 49), has *spooned fingertips* and inconspicuous hairs on hand that do not conceal spines; throughout Florida and Caribbean.

RED HERMIT CRAB   Fig. 49, p. 160
Petrochirus diogenes
Largest hermit — carapace to 8 cm (3¼ in.) long. Right hand slightly larger than left. Fingertips hard and stony (*petro* = stony, *chirus* = finger). Both claws covered with *large granules arranged in groups separated by semicircular fringes of flat hairs.* Mostly rusty red; antennae banded with white along filaments and striped on bases. North Carolina to Brazil, frequently in Queen Conch Shell.

STAR-EYED HERMIT CRAB   Pl. 30
Dardanus venosus
Large-sized hermit — carapace to 2.5 cm (1 in.) long. Left claw much larger than right and with numerous granules fringed by hairs. Pattern of granules outlined by network of fine red lines like blood vessels. Spoon-shaped fingertips black and horny. 2nd legs have a longitudinal ridge with granular crossbars on ventral side. Cornea of each eye greenish blue with dark central spot and *radiating lines forming a star. Related species;* Bar-eyed Hermit Crab, *D. fucosus,* is similar; identify by *horizontal black bar* (instead of a star) in its cornea. Occurs with Star-eyed Hermit from Bermuda to Florida and throughout Caribbean to Brazil.

SMOOTH-CLAWED HERMIT CRAB   Fig. 49, p. 161
Calcinus tibicen
All hard parts of this little hermit — carapace to 1.2 cm (½ in.) long — are *hairless and smooth.* Left claw much larger than right, fingertips hard and sharp-pointed. Claws reddish, brown, or maroon with *white fingertips;* terminal sections of legs white or yellow banded with red; carapace red with small white spots. An olive-green variant with pale blue spots found in some areas. In shallow water from Florida to Brazil.

ROUGH-CLAWED PORCELAIN CRAB   Fig. 49, p. 161
Pachycheles ackleianus
Tiny — carapace to 9 mm (⅜ in.) long. Identify by *stout, rough, robust claws.* Cephalothorax rich orange-brown; broad white stripe on midline of carapace; ventral surface pale creamy white. Claws have irregular rows of large flat tubercles without hairs; fingers close along their full length. On sponges and coral heads; intertidal zone to considerable depths. Gulf of Mexico through Caribbean to Brazil.

Fig. 49

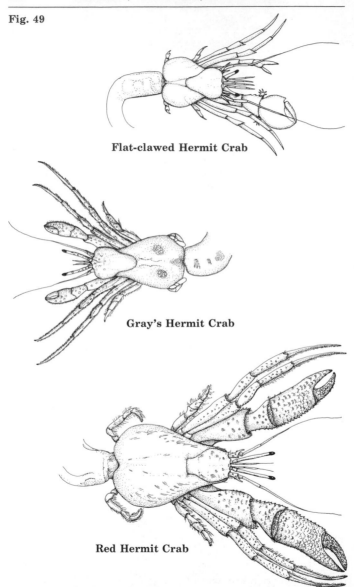

Flat-clawed Hermit Crab

Gray's Hermit Crab

Red Hermit Crab

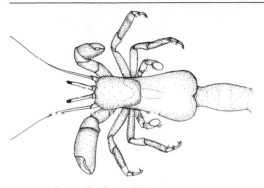

Smooth-clawed Hermit Crab

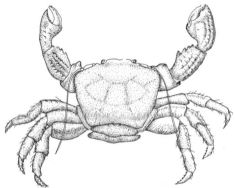

Rough-clawed Porcelain Crab

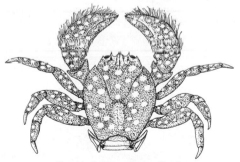

Spotted Porcelain Crab

SPOTTED PORCELAIN CRAB   **Fig. 49, p. 161**
Porcellana sayana
Carapace to 2.2 cm (⅞ in.) long. Nearly as wide as long, with 3
pointed teeth on front. Terminal joints of walking legs end in a
single spine. *Orange-red with numerous pure white and violet
spots, each ringed with intense blood-red lines.* Underside white
mottled with red; claws pure white. Palms of claws fringed with
long yellow hairs. Often free-living but most commonly found as
symbiont of hermit crabs, especially Red Hermit, with whose color
it blends. Also found near or on Queen Conch, where it withdraws
into host's shell when disturbed. Many related species. North Carolina to Brazil.

True, Short-tailed or Tail-less Crabs

Section Brachyura. The most complex and most numerous group
of crustaceans; more than 4500 species. Abdomen small, thin,
folded tightly beneath thorax; no uropods. In males, abdomen
pointed and narrow; only 2 pairs of abdominal appendages, used in
copulation. In females, abdomen broad and rounded; 5 pairs of
abdominal appendages, used for carrying eggs. The crabs described
below are divided into 4 groups on the basis of morphological characteristics: (1) last 2 pairs of legs reduced; last pair dorsal;
(2) mouth area triangular; (3) mouth area square; a rostrum;
(4) mouth area square; no rostrum.

1. LAST 2 PAIRS OF LEGS REDUCED; LAST PAIR DORSAL

Sponge Crabs

LESSER SPONGE CRAB *Dromidia antillensis*   **Pl. 30**
Carapace to 7.5 cm (3 in.) long, convex, covered with tan hairs.
Last pair of legs bent over back, hold sponge to back until sponge
gains purchase and becomes permanently attached. Robust crim-
son-tipped claws. Sponges, tunicates, and/or colonial anemones on
back provide camouflage and protection. *Similar species:* Round
Sponge Crab, *Dromia erythropus,* is larger, wider, covered with
stiff, blackish hairs; *tips of legs hairless, light red.*

2. MOUTH AREA TRIANGULAR

Purse and Box Crabs

PURSE CRAB *Persephona punctata*   **Fig. 50, p. 164**
Carapace to 5 cm (2 in.) long, *almost circular* in outline with eyes
and front protruding. Posterior margin has *3 large conical teeth.*
Entire margin marked with small granular bumps. Color variable,
usually whitish to gray, occasionally bluish, with large red-brown
spots or circles in irregular rows. 2 other *Persephona* species are
less common in our area.

SHAMEFACED or BOX CRABS   Fig. 50, p. 164
Calappa species
Easily recognized by flattened claws with a *palisade of teeth along upper surface.* Hooked knob on outer side of one claw, a guide for claw when used like a can opener on a mollusk shell. Spend much time buried in sand up to their eyes. About 6 species in our area. Flaming Shamefaced or Box Crab, *C. flammea* (Fig. 50), the commonest, has carapace to 8 cm (3¼ in.) long. Sandy white or gray, mottled and streaked with purple-brown flamelike pattern; claws purple-striped, with bright red streaky patches on inner surfaces; tips of legs and teeth of carapace yellow. All species in shallow sandy areas from Massachusetts to Brazil, including Bermuda.

3. MOUTH AREA SQUARE; A ROSTRUM

Spider Crabs

ARROW CRAB   Pls. 20, 30
Stenorhynchus seticornis
Carapace to 6 cm (2½ in.) long. *Long and narrow, with rostrum drawn out into a tapered point;* legs also long and slender. Beautiful: golden, yellow, or cream lined with brown, black, or iridescent blue; slender claws blue to violet; legs reddish or yellow. Coral reef crevices, shallow or deep, from North Carolina and Bermuda to Brazil.

GREEN REEF CRAB   Fig. 50, p. 164
Mithrax sculptus
Carapace to 2.5 cm (1 in.) long, dark green, with *4 rounded ridges leading to toothed lobes on margins.* Legs hairy, sandy gray. Wide-gaping claws meet at deeply spooned tips; blunt tooth near base of movable finger. Almost every stone, shell, and coral fragment seems to shelter this crab in some reefs; with each rising tide Bonefish and other fishes come swarming in to feed on them. Scattered from Florida and Bahamas throughout West Indies to Brazil; on reefs, gravel, and Turtle Grass beds; especially abundant on shallow finger coral flats and reefs. *Related species:* About 20 *Mithrax* species in our area, some very large. Spooned claws with blunt tooth are characteristic. *M. coryphe* is similar to Green Reef Crab but pale sand-colored; only *3 marginal lobes;* equally abundant in the same range, but the 2 species seldom occur together.

SPONGE SPIDER CRAB   Fig. 50, p. 165
Macrocoeloma trispinosum
Carapace to 3.5 cm (1½ in.) long. Carapace and rostral horns liberally covered with hooked hairs into which fragments of sponge are inserted by crab; entire body may be covered by growing sponge. Usually yellow, orange, or reddish brown beneath protective sponge crust. May have algae or other encrusting organisms

Fig. 50

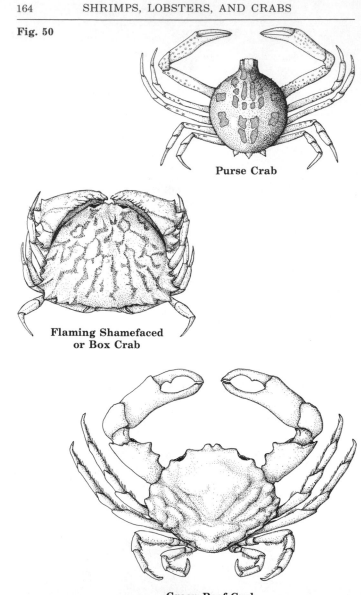

Purse Crab

**Flaming Shamefaced
or Box Crab**

Green Reef Crab

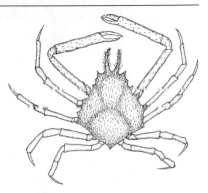

Sponge Spider Crab   Giant Decorator Crab

growing on back. *Posterior has 3 conical spines.* In shallow to deep water from North Carolina and Yucatan to Brazil. 7 other *Macrocoeloma* species in our area.

GIANT DECORATOR CRAB   **Fig. 50, p. 165**
Stenocionops furcata
Carapace to 15 cm (6 in.) long. *Rostral horns long, curved inward.* Chelipeds nearly twice as long as walking legs. Often covered with encrusting organisms.

4. MOUTH AREA SQUARE; NO ROSTRUM

Swimming Crabs (Family Portunidae):
Last pair of legs flat, paddle-shaped

BLUE CRABS *Callinectes* species   **Fig. 51, p. 167**
Carapace to 9 cm (3½ in.) long, *much wider than long, with a sharp spine at each lateral angle.* These, the most pugnacious crabs, rear up with claws poised for attack when approached. About 6 species in our area. (1) Common Blue Crab, *C. sapidus* (Fig. 51), the most abundant, can be identified by having only *2 teeth between eyes* (other species have 4). Beautiful blue-gray, shading to bright blue on claws; white underneath. Fingers red-tipped; leg joints orange. Common throughout eastern seaboard and West Indies, where it is an important food item. (2) Ornate Blue Crab, *C. ornata,* is similar but carapace greenish, covered with brown hairs; walking legs blue with coral tips. (3) Dana's Blue Crab, *C. danae,* has a blue-gray carapace embellished with a *scroll-work of white lines.*

PORTUNUS or SWIMMING CRABS   **Pl. 30**
Portunus species
Similar in shape and behavior to blue crabs; difficult to differentiate in the field. Most easily identified common portunid is (1)
Spotted Portunus or Spotted Swimming Crab, *P. sebae* (Pl. 30);
carapace to 7.5 cm (3 in.) long; tan, with 2 distinct *white-ringed
red or brown spots* on posterior. (2) Sargassum Swimming Crab, *P.
sayi,* is smaller; on sargassum weed, matching its colors.

*Stone Crabs (Family Xanthidae):
Broad-fronted; oval to hexagonal*

STONE CRAB *Menippe mercenaria*   **Fig. 51, p. 167**
Carapace to 9 cm (3½ in.) long. Smooth, heavy, thick-shelled, with
4 blunt teeth along sides and with stout claws. Dark blue to purple
when young; red-brown, spotted with gray or white when older.
Legs red, banded or spotted with yellow; fingers of claws very dark
brown or black. Choice species of commerce; found in fish markets
from North Carolina to Yucatan, Bahamas, and Greater Antilles.
Young crabs in moderately deep water; older ones migrate to
muddy bays and harbors where they burrow. *Related species: M.
nodifrons* is smaller — carapace to 4.8 cm (1⅞ in.) long — redder,
with small granular *tubercles or pimples on front;* common from
Florida to Brazil and throughout West Indies.

CORAL CRAB   **Fig. 51, p. 168**
Carpilius corallinus
The largest — carapace to 13 cm (5 in.) long — and one of the most
handsome West Indian crabs. Shell almost completely smooth,
with a *single blunt lateral tooth.* Entire crab is a rich *red with fine
yellow or white lines and spots;* fingers of claws dark red or purple.
Once was common from Bahamas to Brazil on shallow reefs and
Turtle Grass beds, but trapping and skin divers have taken their
toll; becoming scarce, and big specimens are now rare.

ELKHORN CORAL or GALL CRAB   **Fig. 51, p. 168**
Domecia acanthophora
Elkhorn Coral often has a small filter-feeding crab living with it in
resting places formed by modified growth of the coral. This tiny
little crab — carapace to 1 cm (½ in.) long — is almost *colorless,
slightly reddish on front,* with numerous black spines on carapace
and claws. On corals and sponges from North Carolina to Brazil
(see p. 37).

SMALL REEF CRAB   **Fig. 51, p. 168**
Melybia thalamita
Very small — carapace to 8 mm (⅜ in.) long — and inconspicuous.
With a hand lens, a *row of spines is visible along top edge of long
upper section of legs.* Eyes more widely spaced than in Elkhorn

Coral Crab (above); no black spines. On corals and sponges from Florida to Brazil.

Rock Runners, Spray Crabs, and Marsh Crabs (Family Grapsidae):
Carapace squarish; eyes close to corners

URCHIN CRAB *Percnon gibbesi*   Fig. 51, p. 108
Carapace to 2.5 cm (1 in.) long. Body flattened, disklike. Carapace brown, flesh, or pink, with a *median blue stripe and an iridescent greenish line around front.* Legs brown with golden banding and splotches of gold at joints. Near coral, usually near or under Long-spined Black Urchin; also on rocks in spray zone.

Fig. 51

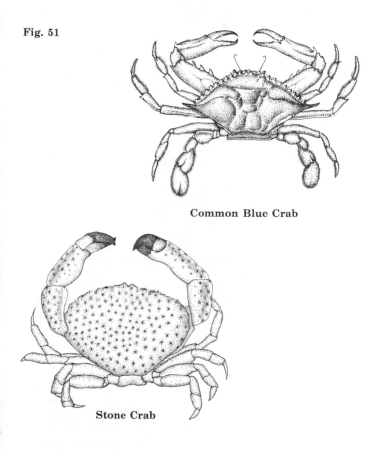

Common Blue Crab

Stone Crab

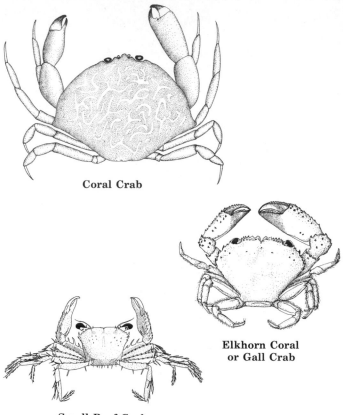

Coral Crab

**Elkhorn Coral
or Gall Crab**

Small Reef Crab

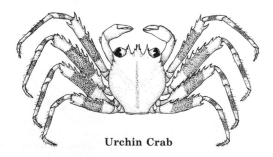

Urchin Crab

11

Echinoderms

There are various theories about the origin of Phylum Echinodermata — the spiny-skinned animals. One theory, based primarily on the fossil record, suggests that they originally were stalked, 10-armed, radially symmetrical (arranged like the spokes of a wheel around a central axis), and attached to the bottom of ancient seas. Attachment has a profound influence on the body plan of an organism, for it eliminates the advantage of having a "front." A sessile (attached) organism must wait for food to drift toward it. The food can come from any direction — hence the basic body design of most bottom-dwelling, attached animals: radial symmetry.

But millions of years of evolutionary plasticity and experimentation have resulted in a number of changes in the echinoderm body plan. One of the earliest was a reduction in the number of arms from 10 to 5, as the ancestral animals lay on one side, eventually losing the arms and the internal body structure of that side. This change to a pentamerous plan (5 body divisions) is clearly reflected in all 5 classes:

1. **Sea stars** (Class Asteroidea) are essentially the ancestral form turned over: the mouth faces down instead of up. Most have 5 arms or multiples of 5 and move slowly across the sea bottom on hundreds of tube feet projecting from grooves in each arm.

2. **Brittle or serpent stars** (Class Ophiuroidea) look a good deal like the sea stars, but the thin, whiplike arms move in a serpentine, sinuous motion in contrast to the movements of the stiff, ponderous arms of the sea stars.

3. **Sea urchins** (Class Echinoidea) have no arms. Long spines are substitutes, but the echinoids demonstrate their affinity to the other classes in the form of grooves or patterns of 5 petal-like figures, symbolic of their 5-armed ancestry. They walk on spines or tube feet that project between the spines, looking like animated pincushions.

4. **Sea cucumbers** (Class Holothuroidea) are echinoderms that have advanced to a point where they have given up their ancestral radial symmetry. They are bilaterally symmetrical and have evolved a front and rear. These animals move slowly over the bottom or burrow under it, their anterior ends bearing a mass of tentacles endowed with sense organs. They have developed a "forward-backward" axis, with their sensory apparatus located at the

Fig. 52

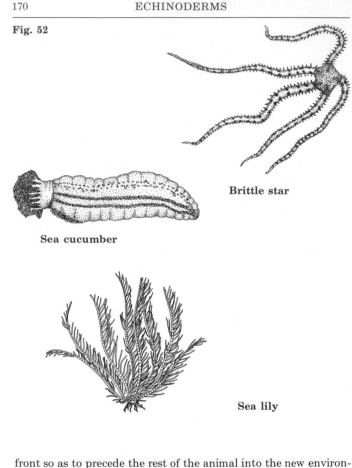

Brittle star

Sea cucumber

Sea lily

front so as to precede the rest of the animal into the new environment. Inside the tubelike body are 5 glistening white longitudinal muscles — a clue to the fact that sea cucumbers are echinoderms.

5. **Sea lilies or feather stars** (Class Crinoidea) are stalked and sessile forms that appear more or less identical to fossils imprinted in the mud of ancient (Ordovician) seas. They reach out in all directions with feathery arms to strain plankton from the water, their oral surfaces facing upward. The attached crinoids appear to be heading for extinction; only a few modern species are left. But a relatively recently evolved group, capable of walking and even swimming, has become quite successful and is common on the deep reef.

Identification begins with spiny or warty skin and some portion of the body in 5 parts. For example, whereas a uniform cover of spines often hides the pentamerous body plan in the test (shell) of a sea urchin, one can turn it over, mouth side up, and see 5 white teeth in the mouth.

An evolutionary trick used to great advantage by echinoderms throughout the phylum is the remarkable power of regeneration. All echinoderms can replace substantial portions of the body when they are lost or destroyed. A serpent star may lose one of its arms, but in a few weeks it will be as good as new. A sea cucumber in an uncomfortable or threatened position will spew out its innards (a phenomenon referred to as evisceration). This may repel an enemy (or attract a predator to the offal), providing the animal with a chance to escape. It will soon regenerate new insides.

Another universal characteristic of Phylum Echinodermata is the presence of a unique hydraulic system, the water-vascular system. It consists of a circular ring canal around the animal's esophagus and 5 radial canals emanating from the ring canal like the spokes of a wheel. Attached to these radial canals are podia, tube feet that are extended by hydraulic pressure in the system. When the tube feet are retracted, they remain in this state more or less indefinitely with virtually no expenditure of energy. Thus, when a sea star attacks an oyster, it can wrap its arms around the bivalve and contract the hundreds of podia projecting from each arm, creating an inexorable pull.

The radial symmetry of the animals in this phylum makes it necessary to refer to the surfaces of the body in terms of the mouth, rather than the traditional front, back, top, and bottom of bilaterally symmetrical organisms. Thus in asteroids (sea stars) the portion containing the mouth, called the oral surface, faces down, and its obverse, the aboral surface, faces up. The crinoids, however, have an upward-facing oral surface and an attached or bottom-facing aboral surface. Some "irregular" sea urchins have evolved bilateral symmetry, with a mouth near the front and a posterior anus; and these sea urchins, together with the sea cucumbers, have a true anterior-posterior axis.

Sea Stars

Sea stars are usually found on sandy bottoms or in Turtle Grass beds, generally in water deeper than 1 m ($3\frac{1}{4}$ ft.), or under rocks or coral.

Two of the commonest species, the Nine-armed Sea Star and the Reticulated or Cushion Sea Star, are relatively easy to spot as they glide over the bottom. Margined sea stars, *Astropecten* species, often burrow under the sand. The Nine-armed Sea Star and the margined sea stars favor a soft bottom and often bury themselves in their search for burrowing mollusks or other echinoderms. These sea stars can locate their prey deep under the sand. They are voracious predators, especially of mollusks.

Both the margined sea stars and the Nine-armed Sea Star have made another adjustment to the muddy sediment on and in which they live. They can eat organic particles by removing them from the sediment through the movement of microscopic hairs called cilia. Their adaptation to soft sediment is also exhibited by unusual pointed podia that lack suckers. This permits them to thrust the podia deep into the substratum in their search for prey. Bilobed ampullae (looking like the rubber bulb on a nose dropper) make the podia especially strong and permit the sea stars to pull themselves under the sand relatively rapidly.

The Reticulated Sea Star has suckers on its podia and does not burrow. It finds its prey on the surface of the sand.

The sea stars without suckers on their podia (the Nine-armed Sea Star and *Astropecten* species) swallow their prey whole. Shells and other indigestibles are cast out of the mouth. The Reticulated Sea Star and the other sea stars can insert the cardiac portion of the stomach through the "gape" between the valves of a mollusk. After this has been done, the filmy stomach walls secrete enzymes that digest the mollusk tissues into a froth, which is soon absorbed through the stomach walls. When the sea star moves on, a set of clean, empty valves is left behind. I once saw a sea star pluck a snail from the wall of an aquarium, overcoming the suction of the snail's foot which was pressed against the glass. Dozens of podia pulled at the snail. Within 5 minutes it had been pulled from the glass with an almost audible pop and turned around. Within 5 more minutes the sea star had forced its diaphanous stomach into the aperture of the snail's shell, and enzymes were being secreted. It is a most remarkable method of feeding, since the sea star has no eyes or nose and indeed does not even have a "front." Nor does it have a brain, in the sense of an accumulated mass of nervous tissue. One or 2 rings of nerves around the esophagus are the only coordinating mechanism.

There is a widespread belief that sea stars are able to feed on bivalves by using their hydraulic system to exhaust the bivalves' muscles and pull their shells open. It has been shown, however, that the whole process occurs so rapidly that it is unlikely that the sea star has to wait for the bivalve to exhaust its strength. In fact, a sea star can insert its stomach through a gape of 0.1 mm — thinner than this line: _____. Since their shells do not close perfectly, most bivalves are at the mercy of a sea star even in the absence of its "ultimate weapon," the water-vascular system.

Sea stars reproduce by external fertilization. There is no sexual dimorphism (both sexes look alike). Gametes are simply broadcast into the water from pores along or between the arms, and eggs and sperms meet only by chance. However, several mechanisms in-

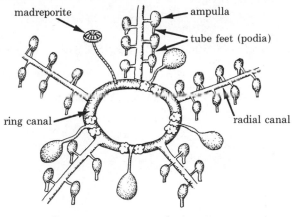

Fig. 53   **Sea star water-vascular system**

crease the likelihood of a meeting. Hundreds of thousands of eggs and millions of sperms are released during a relatively short season. Whereas maturation of the gonads is seasonal, actual shedding of gametes is stimulated by the presence of opposite-sexed gametes. If sperms are detected by a female sea star, her ovary wall contracts, expelling the eggs.

The fertilized eggs hatch into bilaterally symmetrical larvae called bipinnaria. The unfertilized and fertilized eggs and the larvae compose a substantial portion of the plankton around the coral reef during reproductive seasons.

Common Species

In the following accounts **r** is the distance from the disk center to the interradial margin (the point of the V formed by 2 rays, or arms); it is the distance from the disk center to the ray tip. It = r means that the ray length is about equal to the disk radius; R = 4r, that the ray length is about 4 times the disk radius; R = 12r, that the ray length is about 12 times the disk radius; and so forth. If R = r, the rays are short relative to the disk diameter; if R = 12r, on the other hand, the rays are very long relative to the disk diameter.

COMMON BLUNT-ARMED SEA STAR *Asterina folium*
Small — to 2.5 cm (1 in.). Olive or bluish green; juveniles white. Looks like a flattened disk with wavy edges. *Rays reduced to rounded bulges on disk edge.* On underside of rocks or coral frag-

ments at or just below low tide; also on fringing reefs. Bermuda, Florida, West Indies. Common, but difficult to find unless searched for diligently. R = 1.2–1.3r.

HARTMEYER'S BLUNT-ARMED SEA STAR   Fig. 54
Asterina hartmeyeri
Small (about half the size of Common Blunt-armed Sea Star, above) — to 1 cm (½ in.). White or pinkish white. Differentiate from Common Blunt-armed by shape of rays, which are somewhat longer and more distinct. West Indies.

Fig. 54

Hartmeyer's Blunt-armed Sea Star

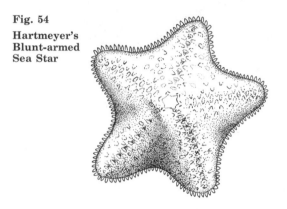

BEADED SEA STAR *Astropecten articulatus*   Pl. 37
Medium-sized — usually to 15 cm (6 in.). Color variable: aboral surface brown, purple, or maroon, but regular beads (marginal plates) at margins of rays always contrasting, usually yellow or tan. *Lacks large erect spines or tubercles on inner margin* of basal superomarginal plates; if viewed from above, appears to have no marginal spines. Soft bottoms. Florida, West Indies. R = 4–6.5r.

SPINY BEADED SEA STAR   Pl. 37
Astropecten duplicatus
May be slightly larger than Beaded Sea Star (above) — commonly to 20 cm (8 in.) — and less flattened, spinier, more compact, with a smaller disk. *A large erect spine (or at least a tubercle) on inner margin of some or all basal superomarginal plates.* Reddish or brown, sometimes gray or light brown or brown spotted on tan. Superomarginals often color of aboral surface — for example, reddish brown. Soft bottoms in shallow water — usually deeper than 1 m (3¼ ft.), commonest around 5 m (17 ft.). Often in groups. Buried when seeking prey (mollusks), sometimes on surface of soft

sediments. Florida Keys, West Indies, coast of Central America. R = 4-6.5r.

BERMUDA SEA STAR *Coscinasterias tenuispina*
Medium-sized — to 27 cm (11 in.), usually much smaller. *Purple, with yellow spines.* Like Comet Sea Star, this species reproduces by autotomy, breaking apart into several individuals. Daughter organisms regenerate new rays in haphazard fashion; some have 5 arms, others 6, 7, 8, or more (7 more common than 5). Rays usually at various stages of regeneration, so sizes vary. Soft bottoms in Bermuda; rare or absent elsewhere in our area. Probably accidentally introduced from Europe. R = 4-6r.

RED SPINY SEA STAR *Echinaster sentus*   Pl. 32
Medium-sized — adults 7.5-15 cm (3-6 in.). Rays short, straight-sided, blunt-ended, covered with *large pointed spines.* Bright or deep red, rarely reddish brown. In finger-coral flats, under coral debris, sometimes in knee-deep water. Florida, Caribbean. R = 4r. *Related species: E. echinophorus* is also red but has slender tapering rays and smaller and more spines. Jamaica, Brazil, Yucatan. R = 4.5-6r.

BROWN SPINY SEA STAR   Pl. 33
Echinaster spinulosus
Medium-sized — to 16 cm (6¼ in.). Rays long, tapering, not slender. Reddish or greenish brown, *often covered with short contrasting-colored spines,* sometimes in rows running length of ray. Spines may be same color as rest of body, making this sea star resemble Forbes' Asterias, *Asterias forbesi,* the common northern sea star. Soft bottoms in mangrove channels, especially in Florida Keys. In contrast with other species, Brown Spiny Sea Star seeks light rather than being repelled by it and is therefore found in the open. R = 4-6r.

COMET SEA STAR   Pl. 33;
Linckia guildingii   Fig. 55, p. 176
Medium-sized — to 23 cm (9 in.). Rays long, thin — length 9-10 times diameter. *Rays parallel-sided, not tapered, with blunt tips.* Rounded nodules or tubercles randomly distributed on aboral surface; surface smooth to touch. Flesh-colored, beige, tan, or rarely reddish. Ambulacra bordered by rows of round granules. Shallow water, on sandy bottoms and reef flats, under rocks near low-tide mark. Bermuda, Florida, Caribbean. R = 8-12r. Adults not as common as juveniles because before adulthood animal may reproduce by autotomy (breaking apart, producing 2 or more daughter organisms, each of which regenerates missing parts). Often 1 broken-off mature ray regenerates 4 or more tiny rays, giving a cometlike appearance, with parent ray as tail of comet (see Fig. 55). Adults capable of producing eggs and sperms and reproducing sexually. *Similar species: Ophidiaster guildingii* is smaller —

Fig. 55

Comet Sea Star

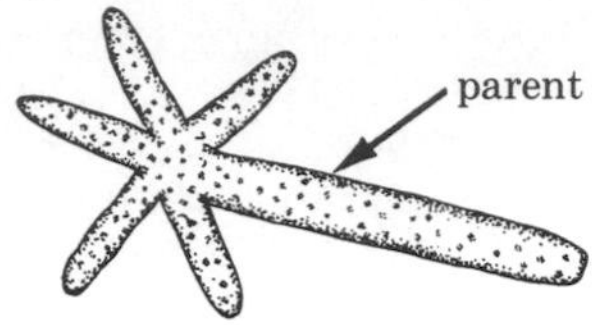

parent ray

usually no larger than 10 cm (4 in.) — and usually blotched with purple, pink, or red. Surface similar to that of Comet Sea Star but with 7 longitudinal rows of smooth tubercles covering aboral surface. Florida, West Indies. R = 8–12r.

LIMP or WEAK SEA STAR *Luidia alternata*   **Pl. 33**
Large — to 36 cm (14½ in.). Bristling with long — to 5 mm (¼ in.) — thin tan spines projecting beyond typical velvetlike surface. Rays wide at base, *bluntly tapered, limp, easily autotomized* (broken from disk). Animal sags when lifted; rays easily twisted, giving animal a rag-doll flaccidity. Usually blotchy dark brown, with tan areas or with indistinct black or purple bands; underside tan. Lies buried in sand with outline of body or 1 ray just visible. Turtle Grass beds, lagoons. Florida, West Indies. R = 7r.

NETTED SEA STAR *Luidia clathrata*   **Pl. 33**
Large — to 30 cm (1 ft.), usually somewhat smaller. Covered with velvetlike spines characteristic of *Luidia* species. Cream, tan, or bluish gray. Dark brown or blackish stripe down each ray, with *netlike or wavy dark lines* parallel to it. Usually buried under sandy sediment in lagoons to deep water — 2 m (6½ ft.) to 90 m (300 ft.) or deeper. Bermuda, Florida, West Indies. R = 6r.

NINE-ARMED SEA STAR *Luidia senegalensis*   **Pl. 33**
Large — often over 30 cm (1 ft.). Aboral surface purple, bluish, or greenish gray, covered with minute spines, *velvetlike* to touch. 9 long, narrow, sharply tapering rays. On sandy surfaces or just under surface covered with thin film of sand. Lagoons and Turtle Grass beds, deeper than 2 m (6½ ft.). West Indies, rare in Florida. R = 12r.

RETICULATED or CUSHION SEA STAR   ⎮ **Pl. 33**
Oreaster reticulatus
Large — to 50 cm (20 in.); juveniles to 15 cm (6 in.). Commonest, most spectacular sea star of Turtle Grass beds. *Thick inflated body covered with netlike array of large contrasting-colored tubercles.* Juveniles light green; adults variable, usually tan or rust, with dark brown or red tubercles. Disk to 7.5 cm (3 in.) high. Body rigid, but tips of rays often curled upward. Walks on thick podia over sand bottoms of Turtle Grass beds, especially around 2 m (6½ ft.) depth. Throughout our area; has been overcollected by souvenir hunters, so may be locally rare. R = 2r.

Brittle or Serpent Stars

Gordon T. Taylor and Richard D. Bray

Brittle stars are everywhere on the coral reef and its environs; there does not seem to be a hole that they do not usurp for a home. Tube- and vaselike sponges are favorite habitats, and one sponge can have dozens, even hundreds, of brittle stars hiding in its inner recesses. Brittle stars, with over 1800 species worldwide, compose the second largest class of echinoderms. In the West Indies and southern Florida 21 species are common. Their cryptic habits, however, make them seem rare — and contribute to their survival. Brittle stars shun light. Tiny receptors in their spines and podia allow them to detect gradients of light. They seek the darkest shadows and tend to press themselves against surfaces, taking on the irregular shape of a crevice or hole. This, combined with dark or mottled coloration, makes them practically invisible to the casual observer. At night, when predation pressure is reduced, many species leave the protection of their shelters to feed.

Brittle stars resemble the more familiar sea stars (p. 171). They are different, however, both behaviorally and anatomically. A sea star walks ponderously over the bottom on hundreds of tube feet, its arms held more or less rigid. A brittle or serpent star sinuously moves its long delicate spiny arms in a swimming or serpentine motion. Its tube feet are reduced; their function is primarily sensory. Another important difference is the attachment of the arms. The arms of a sea star are not differentiated from the disk; they merge imperceptibly with it. The arms of a brittle star project from the well-defined margin of the central disk; you can clearly see the origin of each arm.

Most brittle stars exhibit the traditional pentamerous (5-part) body plan of all echinoderms and have 5 arms. Some species, however, have 6 or 7 or many arms that branch repeatedly, ending in a network of fine tendrils.

The main features of the oral surface (bottom side) of the disk are the 5 triangular jaws, each with a central column of teeth. These seize prey or tear tissue from carrion or gather sediment containing microscopic food organisms.

The arms are covered with rows of plates; those on the sides are armed with spines. The tube feet (podia) project from the bottom of each arm and are protected by 1 or 2 modified spines called podial scales. There is no ambulacral groove. The podia lack the suction apparatus (ampullae) of the sea stars and are largely sensory. In some species they are used to pass particles of food to the mouth, with or without the aid of a secreted mucous string. One exception is the Reticulated Brittle Star, which has been observed walking on its podia.

Brittle stars have the simplest digestive system of all of the echinoderms. Above the muscular jaws is the mouth, which opens into a short esophagus. This leads to the saclike stomach, which completes the digestive system. There are no intestines, digestive glands, or anus. The stomach does the job of the intestines and digestive glands, and the mouth acts as the anus when digestion and absorption of nutrients is complete.

Brittle stars feed on a variety of food ranging from bacteria and microalgae to larval fishes. They employ many feeding methods, most of which can be observed in the Florida–West Indian reef-dwelling species. Many species sift sand and digest out microorganisms, tiny invertebrates, and decaying organic matter. Others are predators that actively seek, capture, and consume invertebrates and small vertebrates. A number of suspension-feeders, such as the Basket Star, strain plankton from the water. These animals often climb onto a sea fan or other gorgonian coral and extend a complex web of tendrils from their arms, forming an effective net. Plankton is caught as it sticks to strings of adhesive mucus, or is trapped in long, barbed spines. The Basket Star usually curls into an indistinguishable ball in the daytime, continuing to grasp its perch on a sponge or soft coral. Only at night is the exquisite network of tendrils easily seen. Other suspension-feeders bury their disks in the sand, extending their arms upward into the water column.

The arms of brittle stars contain neither digestive nor reproductive organs; thus their loss is relatively inconsequential. Brittle stars shed 1, 2, or more arms when under the slightest stress and regenerate new arms as readily. If you try to grasp a brittle star by 1 or 2 arms, you will be left holding the writhing arms detached from the disk.

Major organs of brittle stars are sacs called bursae. These are hollows (invaginations) of the disk at the base of each arm. They extend into the body and open to the exterior through slits. Every species has such openings, genital slits, 1 on each side of the arm, except members of Family Ophiodermatidae, which have 2 on each side. The inner surface of the thin-walled sacs is covered with microscopic hairlike cilia. These constantly move back and forth, creating water circulation within the bursae; presumably this aids in respiration and the removal of metabolic wastes.

The gonads are also located on the walls of the bursae, but they line the side facing the body cavity. The sperm and egg cells must pass through the walls of the bursae when ripe. Then the cilia-driven water currents expel them through the genital slits to the outside. Egg and sperm cells meet by chance; hence millions are wasted. In many species adults offer no parental care, and the fertilized eggs develop while floating in the water column as part of the plankton, at the mercy of many predators. Most species have separate sexes (but a number of species are hermaphroditic). Males and females look alike; since fertilization is external, sex recognition is unnecessary, and no sex differences have evolved.

Different species spawn at different times, but most reproduce during the spring and summer. The fertilized egg develops into a bilaterally symmetrical larva with long larval arms, the pluteus. It matures floating in the surface waters, then sinks to the ocean floor, becoming a miniature replica of the adult. It may, however, differ from the adult in color, proportions, and distribution of such external structures as scales, granules, and spines. Some species brood their young on the walls of the bursae, releasing juvenile brittle stars through the genital slits. These juveniles do not pass through the planktonic larval stages.

Some brittle stars can be found inside sponges and on soft corals in the deep fore-reef zone. Species that live within the atrium of tubular sponges have at least 2 survival advantages: shelter from predators and a food-bearing current created by the sponges. Bring a light with you even in the daytime to help locate brittle stars living deep inside holes in sponges. Brittle stars that normally hide in sponges, beneath coral rubble, or in living coral by day may leave their shelter at night to seek elevated feeding sites, such as sea fans or Turtle Grass. These species may feed on epifauna and epiflora on the elevated feeding sites, on the host organism itself, or on plankton carried by passing currents, which is caught in their long spines and podia. Some species of Family Ophiotrichidae produce mucus that may entrap the plankton.

Common Species

You can easily distinguish between the major families and identify some of the larger species of brittle stars in the field. For many species you must use a hand lens to make a positive identification. The characteristics of the juveniles of many species change with maturity. The descriptions that follow are based on adult specimens to avoid confusion. Be wary of using color as the sole criterion for identification because it can vary with habitat, diet, and geographical distribution. The pattern of coloration is reasonably consistent, but the actual colors that make up the pattern may vary within a species. Use at least one characteristic in addition to color, and be aware that there is a certain amount of variability in all characteristics described.

BASKET STAR   Pl. 32
Astrophyton muricatum
Large — to 3 cm (1¼ in.) or more across disk. Many divided arms; when extended at night, diameter may be more than 18 cm (7 in.). *Arms repeatedly branched into many fine tendril-like tips.* Disk 5-cornered star. Aboral surface orange, pink, or tan; oral surface lighter. Coiled into flat disk in daytime; expanded and netlike at night. On soft corals below 6 m (20 ft.) on reefs.

Table 3. Identification of Common Brittle Stars

Features	Genus and Family
Arms extend into elaborate netlike pattern of tendrils.	*Astrophyton,* Family Gorgonocephalidae (p. 179)
Disk and arms covered with smooth *opaque* skin.	*Ophiomyxa,* Family Ophiomyxidae (p. 183)
Disk and arms covered with thin *transparent* skin. Disk seems to be mounted on jaw-arm complex (see *Ophiocnida,* below).	*Ophiactis,* Family Ophiactidae (p. 180)
Smooth or minutely serrated arms; 4 genital slits per interbrachium.	*Ophioderma,* Family Ophiodermatidae (pp. 182–183)
Large, with long spines on arms. No radial shields.	*Ophiocoma,* Family Ophiocomidae (pp. 181–182)
Long arms edged with glassy spines. Often inside sponges or on soft corals.	*Ophiothrix,* Family Ophiotrichidae (pp. 183, 185, 186)
Disk covered with large scales. A few spines on arms.	*Ophiozona,* Family Ophiolepididae (p. 186)
Disk covered with small scales. Arm spines long but pressed to arm.	*Ophionereis,* Family Ophiochitonidae (p. 183)
Disk covered with small scattered papillae. Disk appears to be mounted on jaw-arm complex.	*Ophiocnida,* Family Amphiuridae (p. 181)

FIVE-ARMED OPHIACTIS *Ophiactis quinqueradia*
Small — to 7 mm (¼ in.) across disk; arms to 4 cm (1½ in.) long. *Disk and arms covered with thin transparent skin. Disk appears to be mounted on top of jaw-arm complex.* Radial shields large, bladelike, granular. Arm spines short, flat, conical, granular. *5 arms,* long and slender. Aboral arm plates ellipsoid, granular. Entire aboral surface usually dark brown or mottled; arms banded; oral surface tan. Usually inside sponges. Young in sponges and coralline algae, adults in crevices of coral.

SAVIGNY'S OPHIACTIS *Ophiactis savignyi*
Similar to Five-armed Ophiactis (above) but usually has 6 arms and usually green and white.

LOBATE BRITTLE STAR *Ophiocnida scabriuscula*
Disk lobed, covered with small scattered papillae; a series of papillae around perimeter of disk. Disk appears to be mounted on jawarm complex. Radial shields small, needle-shaped. Arms long, slender. 3 short, blunt, flattened arm spines per lateral plate. Aboral arm plates rectangular. Disk brown, with lighter radial shields; arms tan, banded with brown. Usually buried in sand near shore.

SPINY OPHIOCOMA *Ophiocoma echinata*   **Pl. 31**
Large — may be over 3 cm (1¼ in.) across disk; arms to 15 cm (6 in.) long. *Spiny; dark brown.* 2 genital slits per interbrachium. Spiny arms, no radial shields, oral and dental papillae present. 2 podial scales per podium. *Arm spine closest to mouth club-shaped.* Aboral surface dark brown, sometimes mottled with lighter shades; arms may be banded in shades of brown; oral surface white. Conspicuous in shallow water under rocks or in coral.

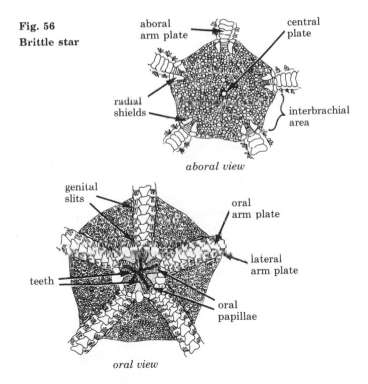

Fig. 56
Brittle star

aboral
arm plate

central
plate

radial
shields

interbrachial
area

aboral view

genital
slits

oral
arm plate

lateral
arm plate

teeth

oral
papillae

oral view

BANDED OPHIOCOMA *Ophiocoma pumila*
Somewhat smaller — to 1.5 cm (³/₄ in.) across disk; arms to 15 cm
(6 in.) long — and less conspicuous than Red Ophiocoma (below)
and Spiny Ophiocoma (above). Spines relatively short, about 3
times as long as arm segment. Arms long, slender. Uppermost
spines pointed, others blunt. Each podium has a single ovoid
podial scale. Usually disk light brown, arms banded in shades of
brown. Juveniles may be greenish. In coral crevices or among
coralline algae, close to low-water mark.

RED OPHIOCOMA *Ophiocoma wendti*
To 3.2 cm (1¼ in.) across disk; arms to 16 cm (6¼ in.) long. Similar
to Spiny Ophiocoma (above), but arm spines even longer — about
8 times as long as arm segment. Arm spine closest to mouth not
club-shaped. Aboral surface black or dark brown; *oral surface (especially podia) bright red;* no white anywhere.

HARLEQUIN BRITTLE STAR   Pl. 33; Fig. 57, p. 184
Ophioderma appressum
To 2.5 cm (1 in.) across disk. Similar to Chocolate Brittle Star
(below), but aboral arm plates undivided. Arm spines about ²/₃ as
long as arm segment and cigar-shaped; the one closest to mouth
longer and wider than others. Disk usually olive-green but may be
brown or gray with white and/or black spots; arms banded green,
gray, or brown and white. *Arms minutely serrated.* West Indian
reefs.

SHORT-ARMED BRITTLE STAR *Ophioderma brevicaudum*
To 2 cm (³/₄ in.) across disk. Similar to Chocolate Brittle Star
(below), but radial shields not apparent. Divided aboral arm plates
thick, irregular in shape. *Arms relatively short* (about 3–4 times
disk diameter), with thick scales at bases. Aboral disk light gray to
green; arms lightly banded; oral surface lighter. In rubble at low-
water mark.

SHORT-SPINED BRITTLE STAR *Ophioderma brevispinum*
Usually 1 cm (½ in.) or less across disk. Similar to Chocolate Brittle Star (below), but aboral arm plates undivided, bell-shaped;
radial shields not apparent. Also similar to Harlequin Brittle Star
(above), but smaller and less common. *Arm spines short,* about ½
as long as arm segment, somewhat cylindrical, at 30–45° angle
from arm axis. 2 color patterns: (1) disk mottled with light green
and white, arms banded in shades of green; (2) disk orangish green,
arms banded with orange, gray, or green. *Arms look serrated.*

CHOCOLATE BRITTLE STAR   Fig. 57, p. 184
Ophioderma cinereum
Large — to 3.5 cm (1³/₈ in.) across disk. Arms relatively short, only
4 times disk diameter. Disk covered with granules. *4 genital slits
per interbrachium. Arms look smooth due to short bladelike*

spines flattened against them. Oral but no dental papillae. Aboral arm plates divided into 2 or more subplates per segment. Ellipsoid radial shields. Color varies, usually medium brown, with or without darker specks on disk; arms indistinctly banded.

BLACK-SPECKLED BRITTLE STAR *Ophioderma guttatum*
Largest West Indian brittle star — to 3.5 cm (1⅜ in.) across disk, arms to 15 cm (6 in.) long. Similar to Chocolate Brittle Star (above), but radial shields not apparent. Aboral arm plates thin, divided into interlocking subplates. Disk granules flattened on top. Arm spines flat, blunt, rectangular. Disk and arms brownish, green, or tan, with many small dark spots. *Arms look minutely serrated.*

SMOOTH BRITTLE STAR *Ophioderma phoenium*
To 2.3 cm (⅞ in.) across disk. Similar to Ruby Brittle Star (below) in having undivided aboral arm plates. Minute ovoid radial shields, sometimes only 1 per arm base. Trapezoidal aboral arm plates. Disk and arms rust or yellowish brown. *Arms look smooth.*

RUBY BRITTLE STAR *Ophioderma rubicundum*   **Pl. 31**
To 2 cm (¾ in.) across disk. Similar to Chocolate Brittle Star (above), but has *undivided rectangular aboral arm plates.* 2 ovoid radial shields per arm base. *Disk usually solid purplish red or mottled with white;* arms indistinctly banded with same colors. *Arms look smooth.*

SLIMY BRITTLE STAR   **Pl. 31; Fig. 57, p. 184**
Ophiomyxa flaccida
To 2 cm (¾ in.) across disk. *Disk and arms covered with smooth opaque skin.* 5 tapered unbranched arms. Aboral surface of disk has club-shaped radial shields beneath skin and a chain of elliptical plates around perimeter. Arms long, slender, with short pinnate spines. Serrated oral papillae, no podial scales. Color varies: Disk mottled with off-white and orange or dark green and gray; arms banded with same colors. *Feels slimy; arms look smooth.* Sandy areas of back reef; Turtle Grass.

RETICULATED BRITTLE STAR   **Pl. 31; Fig. 57, p. 184**
Ophionereis reticulata
To 1.5 cm (⅗ in.) across disk. Disk covered with minute, fine scales. Radial shields small, elongate, diamond-shaped. Arms long, slender. Aboral arm plates divided into 3 subplates. Arm spines short, blunt, conical. Ground color bluish or bone-white; usually a fine brown reticulate (webbed) pattern on disk; brown bands on arms. In clean sand under coral slabs in shallow to deep water.

ANGULAR BRITTLE STAR *Ophiothrix angulata*
To 1.2 cm (½ in.) across disk; arms to 7 cm (2¾ in.) long. *Spines on arms glassy.* Disk and radial shields covered with *short 2- and 3-pronged spines.* Arm spines are 5 times as long as arm segment;

Fig. 57

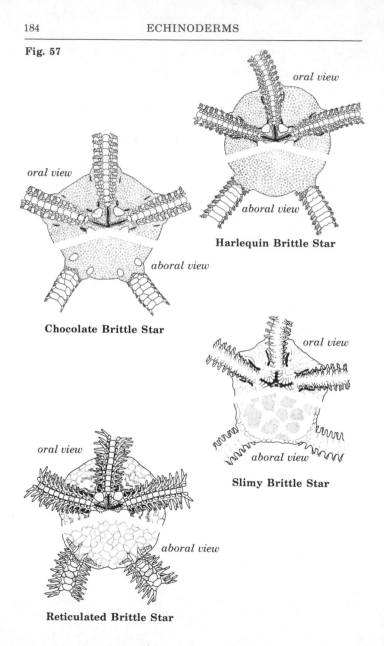

oral view

oral view

aboral view

Harlequin Brittle Star

aboral view

Chocolate Brittle Star

oral view

aboral view

Slimy Brittle Star

oral view

aboral view

Reticulated Brittle Star

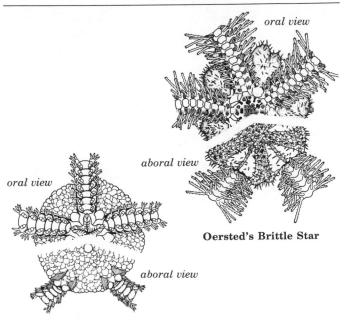

oral view

aboral view

Oersted's Brittle Star

oral view

aboral view

Scaly Brittle Star

hollow, thin, barbed, somewhat flattened. Color varies: aboral surface mottled purple and white, with banded arms or with white radial stripes; or disk and arms tan with a radial red stripe; or some other pattern. *Usually inside sponges.*

STRIPED BRITTLE STAR *Ophiothrix lineata*
To 1.2 cm (½ in.) across disk; arms to 12 cm (4¾ in.) long. *Spines on arm glassy.* Aboral disk surface, excluding radial shields, covered with short papillae. Arm spines relatively thick and flattened, approximately 4 times as long as arm segment. Color varies: aboral surface may be brown or deep purple, with faint black radial stripes on each arm and black stripe, bordered by white stripes, running down each arm; oral surface off-white. Inside sponges or on soft corals.

OERSTED'S BRITTLE STAR   Pl. 31; Fig. 57, p. 185
Ophiothrix oerstedii
Larger than other *Ophiothrix* species — more than 1.4 cm (¾ in.) across disk; arms longer than 8 cm (3¼ in.). *Spines on arms glassy.* Aboral disk, except radial shields, covered with long, barbed spines. Arm spines 4 times as long as arm segment, lowest spine wing-

shaped. 2 papillae-covered podial scales per podium. Aboral surface gray or grayish blue on disk; fine zebralike banding on arms; *no radial stripes;* oral surface much lighter than aboral. Turtle Grass beds; sometimes other sandy areas of back reef.

SUENSON'S BRITTLE STAR Pls. 18, 19, 21
Ophiothrix suensonii
To 1.3 cm (½ in.) across disk. *Spines on arms glassy.* Short spinelets around perimeter of radial shields; long barbed spines on aboral surface of disk. *Radial shields large, occupy most of disk surface.* Arms spines extremely long — about 6 times as long as arm segment — slender and barbed. Lowest arm spine hookshaped. Lavender or bright red, with gray radial shields and bold black or purple radial stripes on oral and aboral arm surfaces. *Inside sponges or on soft corals.*

SCALY BRITTLE STAR Fig. 57, p. 185
Ophiozona impressa
Disk covered with large, irregular, rough scales; no spines. Radial shields triangular. Arms short, with a few short, blunt, cigarshaped spines. Bone-white with brown mottling and brown bands on arms; aboral surface white or cream. In sand and beneath coral rubble.

Sea Urchins

The sea urchins are among the most conspicuous inhabitants of lagoons and Turtle Grass beds. They are abundant and obvious. Their spines obviate the need for protective coloration. They are slow-moving grazers, feeding on blades of Turtle Grass and disintegrating organic detritus on the surface of the sand; they can also scrape the thin film of algae from the surface of rocks. They have invaded virtually every shallow-water niche, with whole populations living under the sediment, invisible except to those who know where to look for them. Some have forsaken the selective grazing techniques of the surface dwellers and are deposit-feeders, passing the sand through their digestive tracts and digesting the organic matter that had been mixed with the sand grains. Most urchins, however, use their podia to remove detritus from the sediment selectively, even when buried under it.

Adult sea urchins have few enemies. Their formidable appearance notwithstanding, a number of organisms have evolved strategies to cope with the bristling mass of spines to reach the internal tissues. The Emperor Helmet Snail, a huge snail whose shell may be 25 cm (10 in.) long, attacks the most dangerous of all Caribbean urchins, the Long-spined Black Urchin, by first crushing the poisonous spines with its tough foot and then piercing the test with its proboscis. Once entry is made, the filelike tongue scrapes away the internal tissues. Several species of fishes and crabs also successfully attack urchins.

Sea urchins have made remarkable adaptations to their various modes of existence. The surface-dwelling forms have retained the radial symmetry characteristic of the phylum. Indeed, they are the most perfectly symmetrical members of the phylum. The urchins that have become adapted to an existence under the surface of the sediment have evolved a shape more efficient for burrowing. Many species have become flattened. The ultimate development in this direction is exhibited by the Five-holed Keyhole Urchin: a 7.5 cm (3 in.) specimen may be only 6 mm ($\frac{1}{4}$ in.) thick, with sharp margins.

An even more remarkable adaptation by burrowers is the loss of radial symmetry and the development of bilateral symmetry. The animals have developed a spadelike shape with a bluntly narrowed anterior end that enables them to penetrate sand more easily. These irregular urchins have also adapted internally. The anus has shifted from the center of the aboral surface and opens posteriorly and even ventrally. The mouth has shifted anteriorly. In the Great Red-footed Urchin and the Sea Pussy or Cake Urchin the test projects down from the ventral surface, like a perpetually open lower jaw. As a result the animals can plow through the sediment like bulldozers, forcing sand into the digestive tract with every forward motion.

Thus a regular, or radially symmetrical, urchin is considered to have an oral-aboral axis. The "top" of such an animal is its aboral surface. An irregular, or bilaterally symmetrical, urchin has an upper region called the dorsal surface. So the anus of a regular urchin, such as the Red Rock Urchin, is on its aboral surface, and the anus of an irregular urchin, such as the Sea Pussy, is posterior and ventral.

In irregular urchins the degree of bilaterality seems to match the degree to which they penetrate the substratum. Those found at or near the surface of the sand, such as the sea biscuits and keyhole urchins, retain the primitive, centrally located mouth. Sea biscuits are usually only partially buried and are often even completely visible in Turtle Grass beds. Keyhole urchins live just under the surface of the sediment in sandy areas. They can cover themselves with sand when living directly on the surface.

I will never forget collecting burrowing urchins at Discovery Bay, Jamaica. My guide took me to the edge of the lagoon near the back reef. He anchored the boat near a sandy area devoid of algae, relieved only by small mounds of sand projecting from the bottom. No sooner had we dived to the bottom, about 2 m ($6\frac{1}{2}$ ft.) down, than he waved his hands over one of the mounds, as a magician waves his wand. Presto! A large brown Sea Pussy appeared. To find this animal, look for hillocks of sand topped with white particles that are larger than the sand grains. Wave your hand close to one of these mounds so as to set up a current to wash away the surface sediment, and you will uncover a Sea Pussy. I must admit I was enthralled with the new trick. When I returned to the lab that day I left behind about half an acre of uncovered, starkly bare Sea Pussies.

That same day my friend promised to demonstrate a real feat of the field echinoid specialist: to show me a living specimen of one of the most highly evolved of the Caribbean sea urchins, the Great Red-footed Urchin. After about 20 minutes of searching he called me over in great excitement (I had been happily uncovering Sea Pussies). When I arrived, he pointed downward. I could see nothing. When I swam down so that my face mask was about 15 cm (6 in.) from the bottom, I saw about 10 rods, each about as thick as a toothpick, projecting in an irregular row about 6 mm ($\frac{1}{4}$ in.) from the sand. They were translucent spines, the color of the sand. How he was able to find these almost invisible clues so quickly surprised both of us. With a series of vigorous waves of his hand he set up a strong current and raised a cloud of sand. The sand soon settled and there, visible in all its glory, was a Great Red-footed Urchin. It was silvery gray and had very fine spines covering its 15 cm (6 in.)-long oval body. From the anterior end projected about 20 glassy spines, each the thickness and length of a toothpick. The Great Red-footed Urchin has 22 large, blood-red, rapidly moving tube feet around the mouth, a few more at the anus, and bristles about 2.5 cm (1 in.) long arranged in a tract along the midventral surface from mouth to anus. It crawls surprisingly rapidly, using this tract of brushlike bristles.

The dominant sea urchin on open sandy bottoms in water deeper than 2 m ($6\frac{1}{2}$ ft.) is the Long-spined Black Urchin. Its "diadem," or crown, is composed of spines that are as fierce as they look. They are often 15 cm (6 in.) long, needle-tipped, and covered with mucus containing a poison. The spines can rotate freely to point at any moving shadow or object that presents a threat. An adult Long-spined Black Urchin is virtually invulnerable, although it is said that the Jolthead Porgy and the Queen Triggerfish have mastered the art of grasping one of the long spines and flipping the urchin over so that its more vulnerable underside is exposed to the long incisors and bony jaws of these fishes.

In general the pain from Long-spined Black Urchin toxin ends quickly, and the spines dissolve in the human skin within 1–2 days. Certainly these slowly moving and conspicuous animals do not warrant the unreasoning fear they sometimes engender. It is easy to avoid them if a face mask is worn to allow vision underwater. If contact is made, the pain is no more intense than that of a bee sting.

A group of Long-spined Black Urchins has a rather fear-inspiring appearance (see Fig. 9, p. 20), yet some animals seek these aggregations for the protection they afford. The Urchin Crab seems to live almost exclusively beneath the spines of this sea urchin.

In Turtle Grass beds 2 similar species, the Variable or Green Sea Urchin and the Sea Egg, are in seeming competition for the same niche. There is some question as to how both species can so efficiently compete with each other. Why doesn't the fitter species render the other extinct? It may be that the 2 species do not use the same food source — that the Variable Urchin eats the encrusting algae, or maybe sponges or bryozoans, growing on the Turtle Grass blades, and the Sea Egg eats the blades. This hypothesis has not been validated, however.

The Reef Urchin and Williams' Variable Sea Urchin are interesting because their adaptation to deepwater living has made them longer-spined, smaller, and more fragile-looking than their more common shallow-water sister species (see the accounts of these 2 species on pp. 190 and 192). This increase in fragility may be due to a diminution of food with depth or perhaps to a lessened requirement for robustness with descent from the turbulent, storm-tossed shallows.

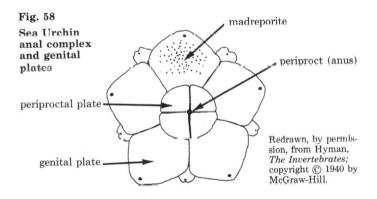

Fig. 58

Sea Urchin anal complex and genital plates

madreporite

periproct (anus)

periproctal plate

genital plate

Redrawn, by permission, from Hyman, *The Invertebrates;* copyright © 1940 by McGraw-Hill.

Common Species

BROWN ROCK URCHIN *Arbacia punctulata*
Less than 5 cm (2 in.) in diameter. Spines tan, purple, or reddish black, usually *grayish brown,* about 2 cm (¾ in.) long. Test brown. Commonest along east coast of U.S. to Cape Cod; may be found in Florida, Cuba, and Yucatan but not on most Caribbean islands, except Trinidad, Tobago, and others near Central America. Similar in habitat to Red Rock Urchin (p. 190) but lacks the red color, is somewhat smaller, has 4 periproctal plates. May also be in deep water on sandy or rocky bottoms. Eats detritus, algae.

GROOVED BURROWING URCHIN *Brissus unicolor*

Medium-sized — smaller, longer — averages less than 7.5 cm (3 in.) — and narrower than Sea Pussy (p. 192). Pale brown. 4 groovelike ambulacra project from middorsal region; *anterior pair extend at right angles from anterior-posterior axis* (anterior ambulacra point about 45° toward front in Sea Pussy). Place at which ambulacra converge (apical center) measurably forward of midline (more anterior than in Sea Pussy). Buried in sand under rocks on reef flats, often with Little Burrowing Urchin (p. 191).

INFLATED SEA BISCUIT   Pl. 35
Clypeaster rosaceus

Large. Inflated and thick: specimen 13 cm (5 in.) long may be 4.5–5.5 cm (1¾–2¼ in.) high. Densely covered with short spines. *5 symmetrical oval petals* extend over most of aboral surface. Yellowish, reddish, usually greenish brown to deep brown. Body oval, rising to a blunt peak at aboral center. Turtle Grass beds; on surface of sediment. Often camouflaged with shells, Turtle Grass blades.

FLAT SEA BISCUIT   Pl. 35
Clypeaster subdepressus

Large — average size 13–15 cm (5–6 in.). Much less inflated than Inflated Sea Biscuit (above): specimen 25 cm (10 in.) long may be only 2.5 cm (1 in.) high. Margins rounded. 5 relatively small petals extend about ½ length of radius or less; less distinct than in Inflated Sea Biscuit. Body widest from posterior to middle. On Turtle Grass beds; not as common as Inflated Sea Biscuit.

LONG-SPINED BLACK URCHIN   Pls. 6, 17;
Diadema antillarum   Fig. 8, p. 19

Length of *needle-tipped spines at least 3 times diameter of test, about 15 cm (6 in.) in adults. Spines black* (or banded brown and black, or white and brown in young specimens). Hides in coral crevices or aggregates in groups in lagoon during daytime; groups scatter and feed on algae and Turtle Grass at night. Buttress and mixed zones of reef; also Turtle Grass beds in lagoons. Spines contain toxin and cause beelike sting.

RED ROCK URCHIN *Echinometra lucunter*   Pls. 32, 34

To 6.5 cm (2½ in.), except off Bermuda and Brazil, where it reaches 8.5 cm (3¼ in.). Spines as long as diameter of test, about 2.5 cm (1 in.). *Spines red,* reddish black, or reddish brown. Some red almost always visible at base of spines. More than 4 periproctal plates. Rocky shores just below water's surface; tide pools. Can grind holes in rock to create a protective chamber.

REEF URCHIN *Echinometra viridis*   Pls. 32, 34

To 5 cm (2 in.). *Spines have thin white ring at base,* then rose or coral, then green with chocolate-colored tips; finer and longer than in Red Rock Urchin (above). Test reddish or maroon. Commonest in coral crevices at 5–12 m (17–40 ft.) or deeper but can be near shore in coral flats. Not usually with Red Rock Urchin on shallow rocky shores.

LITTLE BURROWING URCHIN *Echinoneus cyclostomus*
Small — averages 2.5 cm (1 in.). *Petals broad and shallow, reach margins.* Oval; cream or reddish yellow, with bright red tube feet. 4 genital plates on middorsal surface look like 4-leaf clover. Asymmetrical midventral peristome, behind which is oval periproct. Lives buried in coral sand under rocks on reef flats.

NOTCHED SAND DOLLAR *Encope emarginata*
To 14 cm (5½ in.). Flat, oval, with tiny bristlelike spines giving a fuzzy appearance. *Test perforated by 1 oval hole and 5 notches* (marginal lunules). Tan, brown, or greenish brown. Buried in sand off South America and nearby islands.

CLUB or PENCIL URCHIN   Pl. 34
Eucidaris tribuloides
Usually less than 5 cm (2 in.) in diameter, except off Bermuda and Brazil, where larger. *Spines thick, cylindrical, blunt-tipped, relatively sparse.* Test clearly visible between spines, light brown flecked with white. Spines usually covered with filamentous algae or encrusting animals. On reef in most zones, in coral crevices, but commonest on Turtle Grass beds, especially at 5–7 m (17–23 ft.). Eats sponges, algae, and Turtle Grass.

SIX-HOLED KEYHOLE URCHIN   Pl. 34; Fig. 59
Leodia sexiesperforata
To 10 cm (4 in.). Similar to Five-holed Keyhole Urchin (p. 192) but has *6 lunules.* Buries itself by rotating body from side to side; can submerge in 15 min.

Fig. 59

**Six-holed
Keyhole
Urchin**

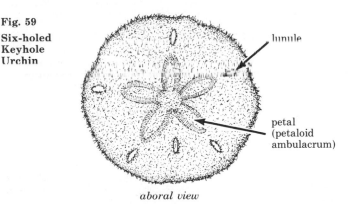

lunule

petal
(petaloid
ambulacrum)

aboral view

VARIABLE or GREEN SEA URCHIN Pl. 32
Lytechinus variegatus
To 7.5 cm (3 in.). *Profusely covered with 1 cm ($\frac{1}{2}$ in.) long greenish white or white spines,* sometimes purple-tipped (specimens off southeastern U.S. may have stout red or purplish spines; those from Bermuda have slender bright purple spines). *Test usually light green, podia white.* Radially symmetrical. Turtle Grass beds; often camouflages test with debris.

WILLIAMS' VARIABLE SEA URCHIN Pl. 34
Lytechinus williamsi
To 5.5 cm (2$\frac{1}{4}$ in.). Spines thinner and longer than in Variable Sea Urchin (above). Podia and *pedicellariae purple-tipped.* Test white or green. On lettuce corals or Staghorn Coral on fore reef, usually at 5–12 m (17–40 ft.); occasionally in shallow water on finger-coral flats.

FIVE-HOLED KEYHOLE URCHIN Pl. 34
Mellita quinquiesperforata
To 10 cm (4 in.). Tan or gray; round and flattened, with sharp edges. Test perforated with *5 lunules* (Six-holed Keyhole Urchin has 6). Silvery gray, covered with fuzzlike bristles. Abundant beyond breakers on sandy beaches, usually covered with a thin layer of sand or buried just beneath surface of sediment. Can force itself into sand in 1–4 min.

SEA PUSSY or CAKE URCHIN Pl. 35
Meoma ventricosa
Large — adults to 12.5 cm (5 in.) long. 4 groovelike ambulacra angled from center of dorsal surface. *5th (middorsal) ambulacrum an obscured depression* rather than a distinct groove. Lower portion of anterior ventral mouth projects from body as a shovel-like "lower jaw." Reddish brown and bristly, with some anterior bristles about 5 mm ($\frac{1}{4}$ in.). Just under surface of sand, creating hillocks. In sand fields of lagoons, deeper than 2 m (6$\frac{1}{2}$ ft.), commonest below 7 m (23 ft.); a few small specimens on sediment in Turtle Grass beds. Ingests sand. Will emerge from sediment at night in response to lowered nocturnal oxygen levels beneath sand. When disturbed, can secrete a yellowish substance that repels predators (stingrays and shamefaced crabs) and can kill small fishes.

HEART or MUD URCHIN Pl. 34
Moira atropos
Small — no larger than 6 cm (2$\frac{1}{2}$ in.). *Ambulacra deeply sunken into test; look like thin slits at surface.* Anterior ambulacrum long; paired posterior ambulacra angling backward from midline are short, do not reach margin. Pale brown or grayish, covered with thin furlike bristles. Inflated, *almost spherical.* Posterior abruptly terminates, so posterior margin almost vertical. Buried in mud in shallows.

GREAT RED-FOOTED URCHIN   Pl. 35
Plagiobrissus grandis
One of the largest urchins — to 23 cm (9 in.). Oval; tan or silvery
gray. About *20 anterior dorsal spines*, each 5–7.5 cm (2–3 in.) long;
raised when animal is alarmed but always point posteriorly to
some degree. Covered with many thin flexible spines. Ventral surface of adult has 2.5 cm (1 in.) wide brushlike tract of long bristles,
upon which it walks. Mouth and anus ventral, mouth surrounded
by jawlike projection. *Thick red podia concentrated around
mouth and anus.* Buried deep in sand of lagoons. Lacks burrow;
does not come to surface at night, so difficult to find. Adults can be
recognized by large size.

SEA EGG *Tripneustes ventricosus*   **Pls. 34, 37**
Usually 10–13 cm (4–5 in.) or larger. Profusely covered with 1 cm
(½ in.) long white spines. *Test black, dark purple, or brown.* Common on Turtle Grass beds; often covers test with debris. Eats algae
and Turtle Grass. Eggs eaten by West Indians.

Sea Cucumbers

At dusk, in back reefs and lagoons off Jamaica, Bonaire, and other
Caribbean islands, the skin diver can see a remarkable sight: in
water just 2–3 m (6½–10 ft.) deep a meter-long animal extends itself from under clumps of coral debris and, like a vacuum cleaner
hose, moves one end to and fro over the bottom, "vacuuming" the
surrounding area. It is clear that this is a sea cucumber, for it has
the typical elongate, tubelike body with anterior tentacles.

But those who have tried to collect a specimen have a sad story
to relate. Grasping the animal with both hands reveals a warty
skin. With such good purchase the collector feels optimistic — but
not for long. The animal has a firm grip on the underside of the
coral boulder and, as it contracts its body to retreat, the collector
finds the table turned. He is slowly being pulled into the dark
recesses that provide the animal's security.

Its strength and cryptic habits have made this huge, relatively
common animal so safe that it has only recently come to the attention of science. At this writing it has just been named: Thomas'
Giant Sea Cucumber, *Holothuria thomasae* (see p. 201). There
are probably no more than 3 preserved specimens in the world.

The sea cucumbers are a bizarre echinoderm class. They either
eat sediment or strain plankton from the water with anterior tentacles. They bear little resemblance to their radially symmetrical
ancestors, since they are elongate and have a well-developed anterior end endowed with sensory tentacles. The mouth has no
teeth, but in one common species the *anus* has 5 shiny white teeth
(see Fig. 66, p. 199). The richly equipped anus makes further contributions. In most large forms it is the opening through which

water is drawn to provide oxygen for the organs of the body cavity. Internal gill-like structures are periodically bathed with oxygenated seawater as the animal alternately contracts and relaxes the muscles of its body wall, "inhaling" and "exhaling" a stream of water. I timed the respiratory cycle of a large cucumber and found that the interval between successive expirations was 40 seconds.

The most remarkable behavioral characteristic of this class is the ability to eviscerate the internal organs when under stress. When shaken vigorously or placed under environmental stress, the animal will release, through its anus, its digestive organs and sometimes part of its respiratory tree and gonads. The response has obvious survival value, for when the predator sees the offal just released by the cucumber, it will stop trying to penetrate the tough skin and will begin eating the internal organs; as a result, the sea cucumber is able to retire to a crevice or burrow under the sand, where it will regenerate a new set of internal organs.

Another defense mechanism of several genera of large sea cucumbers is the capacity to shoot from the anus sticky tubules of Cuvier. When approached by a predator, the animal contracts its body and points its anus at the source of the disturbance. Attached to the base of one or both of the respiratory trees are masses of white, pink, or red blind tubules. Water is forced into the tubules, elongating them like elastic bands. Finally they burst from their point of attachment and are released through the anus. When they reach their target, they become sticky adhesive threads, thoroughly enmeshing small predators, such as crabs, and leaving them helpless. The Five-toothed Sea Cucumber emits a tuft of pink tubules which, though not sticky, are poisonous.

Sea cucumbers are usually brown or gray and live either on the surface of the sand or under rocks or coral debris. Some burrow under the surface of the sediment.

Fig. 60
Sea cucumber

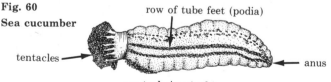

row of tube feet (podia)

tentacles

anus

ventral view (sole)

Holothuroids have an anterior-posterior axis. At the anterior end are many tentacles — usually 10–30, depending on the species. The tentacles, like the podia (tube feet), are extensions of the water-vascular system but are more elaborate and are always located at the anterior end (see Fig. 60). The podia vary in distribution. In some cases there are 3, 4, or 5 rows of podia, corresponding

Fig. 61 A head-
on view of a
Three-rowed
Sea Cucumber.

to their distribution in ambulacra, as in the sea stars and urchins.
In other cases the podia are randomly scattered over the body.
Sometimes the podia are most densely distributed on the flattened
portion of the body, which always faces the sediment and is called
the sole (as in the sole of one's foot) or trivium (because it comprises 3 ambulacral areas). Cucumbers with a sole have distinct
dorsal and ventral surfaces. If turned over, these animals always
right themselves.

Internally there is a large body cavity, or coelom, containing the
usual echinoderm distribution of organs. The ring canal surrounds
the pharynx; it is located anteriorly and gives rise to the 5 radial
canals that extend anteriorly to become the tentacles and then
continue posteriorly down the sides of the animal to form internal
ambulacra, from which the podia project.

The digestive tract has a long intestine, looped 3 times. Food is
digested by enzymes and then either carried to the rest of the body
by amebalike cells called coelomocytes or absorbed through the
walls of the intestine and diffused through the coelemic fluid.
There is no true circulatory system.

Most cucumbers are too large and thick-walled to absorb oxygen
through the body wall. Instead a pair of respiratory trees are located inside the body cavity. These trees have many branches,
each ending in a tiny bladder. One end of each respiratory tree is
attached to the cloaca, a large chamber near the anus. At each
inhalation the cloaca is filled with water, and the anal sphincter is
closed. Muscles contract, forcing the water into the respiratory
tree. Oxygen diffuses through the thin walls of the branches into
the coelemic fluid. The process is then reversed, and the water is
exhaled.

The Five-toothed Cucumber may have an internal resident. A
small fish may live in the trunk of one of the respiratory trees. The

Pearlfish may be as long as 15 cm (6 in.). It leaves the cucumber at
night to forage, returning at dawn to back its way through the
anus into the respiratory trunk (see Fig. 62). It is not known
whether the fish always returns to the same cucumber. Only a
small percentage of cucumbers harbors such a fish (see p. 249).

There is only one gonad, and the eggs or sperms it produces are
usually shed into the water, where a chance encounter with a ga-
mete of the appropriate sex results in fertilization. The zygote develops into a free-swimming larva that undergoes several metamorphoses, eventually becoming a miniature adult that lives on
the bottom.

Ecology. Large sea cucumbers often deposit well-formed fecal
casts, about 1 cm ($\frac{1}{2}$ in.) in diameter, near the anus. They look like
curled, sand-colored cylinders (see Fig. 63). These begin as sand
stuffed into the mouth by the oral tentacles and passed through
the long intestine. Organic matter is digested by enzymes and carried through the gut wall, usually by coelomocytes.

Holothuroids are sluggish, but when placed in aquariums, the
large cucumbers use their podia to crawl ponderously along the
glass surface. It is practically impossible to pull a Five-toothed
Cucumber from the glass because the suction of its many podia is
so strong. Even more sluggish are the plankton filter-feeders of
Order Dendrochirotida. These move so infrequently that one specimen remained in the same spot in an aquarium for 2 years.

The Three-rowed Cucumber has been reported to fill its digestive tract with sand and empty it 3 times a day. Someone once
calculated that the large cucumbers in a particular 4.4 km²
(1.7 mi.²) area of Bermuda would pass 500–1000 tons of sand
through their bodies annually.

Although they have no eyes, sea cucumbers are sensitive to light.
Intense light, such as that from a photographic floodlamp, causes
them to turn away and retract their tentacles. A deepwater species,
the Furry Sea Cucumber, is attracted to low levels of light.

A common cucumber that is rarely seen is the Burrowing Sea
Cucumber. This is the only large holothuroid in the Caribbean

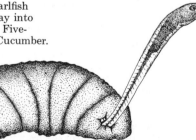

Fig. 62 A Pearlfish
backing its way into
the anus of a Five-
toothed Sea Cucumber.

Fig. 63 A Donkey Dung Sea Cucumber. Note the fecal casts near its anus.

that lives deep underground in a burrow. The sand excavated from the burrow is thrown up about its entrance in a large mound. Look for these mounds in shallow water, often in grassy areas (see p. 200).

The Furry Sea Cucumber is the only species of large sea cucumber reported to live almost exclusively in water deeper than 10 m (33 ft.) near Caribbean reefs. It is much more active than the others and has been reported to be able to *swim*. Under duress its normal crawling gait increases to a walk, and then, if the stimulus continues, it will bound along at the unheard-of speed of 2 m (6½ ft.) per minute. This is close to the record for all echinoderms. Swimming has been observed only once and is accomplished by undulation of the body. Scuba divers should be on the alert for this animal, as it needs careful study.

Common Species

Sea cucumbers are divided into 6 orders, 3 of which contain common shallow-water species:

1. **Apodids** (Order Apodida) have no podia. Tentacles simple, digitate, or pinnate.

2. **Aspidochirotids** (Order Aspidochirotida) have podia. Tentacles peltate.

3. **Dendrochirotids** (Order Dendrochirotida) have podia. Tentacles dendritic.

Fig. 64

Sea cucumber tentacles

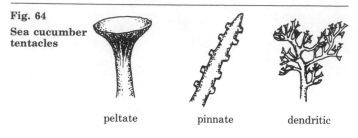

peltate   pinnate   dendritic

Apodids

WORM CUCUMBER *Chiridota rotifera*
Small, wormlike — less than 10 cm (4 in.); averages 6 cm (2½ in.)
long, 4 mm (³⁄₁₆ in.) wide. *Pink or reddish.* 20 palmate tentacles;
stems short, broad, with short fingerlike digits along edges. Tentacles in inner circle small and easily overlooked. No podia. Buried in
sand at water's edge and in tide pools, among algae and in dead
coral. Throughout our area.

BEADED SEA CUCUMBER *Euapta lappa*   **Pl. 37**
Large — to 1 m (3¼ ft.), usually 35 cm (14 in.). Elongate — largest
specimens no thicker than 2.5 cm (1 in.). Distinctly annulated with
thick squarish beadlike segments. Brown, with thin yellow and
black longitudinal stripes; may have white spots. *Long thick
feathery tentacles,* usually extended and visible. Ossicles penetrate
skin, make animal sticky. If touched, will stick to your hand. *Body
fragile,* easily fragmented. No tube feet. Nocturnal. Sticks to undersurface of flat rocks in shallow water, sometimes just below tide
mark. Bahamas, West Indies; not in Bermuda.

Fig. 65 The
peltate tentacles
of a Donkey Dung
Sea Cucumber.

Fig. 66 The anal teeth of a Five-toothed Sea Cucumber.

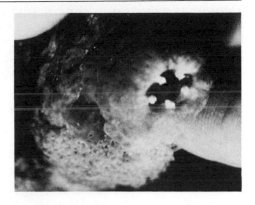

SEAWEED CUCUMBER *Synaptula hydriformis*
To 10 cm (4 in.). *Wormlike.* 2 color phases: red-brown and deep green. Brown form lives on brown algae, green form on green algae. A *few long, slender, simple digits on tentacles.* No podia. Gives birth to live young. Subtidal in tufts of seaweed; mangrove lagoons, sandy bottoms. Throughout our area; green form common in Bermuda, brown form predominates in Jamaica.

Aspidochirotids

FIVE-TOOTHED SEA CUCUMBER   Pl. 36; Fig. 66
Actinopyga agassizii
Large — 30 cm (1 ft.). 25–30 peltate tentacles. Color variable, often dark gray or brown or spotted. *5 conspicuous anal teeth* visible when animal exhales. Sole lighter than dorsum, with numerous scattered *pale podia.* In Turtle Grass beds in shallow water, with Three-rowed and Donkey Dung Cucumbers. Jamaica, Bahamas, Haiti; rare or absent in Virgin Islands and much of Antilles. Pearlfish may be in cloaca (see Fig. 62, p. 196).

FURRY SEA CUCUMBER *Astichopus multifidus*   Pl. 36
Large and broad — to 45 cm (18 in.) long, 9 cm (3½ in.) wide. Dorsal and ventral surfaces covered with many long — 1 cm (½ in.)—soft podia, which make animal *look and feel furry.* Dorsal podia pointed; ventral podia have typical disklike tips. Color variable: brown, gray, or mottled. Sole may be uniform white or gray, with densely crowded podia. A *deepwater species* — rarely above 2 m (6½ ft.), usually at 5–40 m (17–130 ft.) — on sandy plains between coral masses. Known for rapid movement (see p. 197) and rapid metabolism. Anus large, opens for exhalation as often as every 10 seconds. West Indies, Florida.

BURROWING SEA CUCUMBER *Holothuria arenicola* **Pl. 36**
Medium-sized — usually 10 cm (4 in.), can reach 25 cm (10 in.).
Tan or pale gray, sometimes stained with rusty yellow. *Double series of dusky spots or blotches on dorsum.* Tube feet small, scattered, inconspicuous. Buried in coral debris; also produces large mounds in sand flats with or without grass. Bermuda to Brazil (see p. 197).

FLORIDA SEA CUCUMBER *Holothuria floridana*
Almost identical with Donkey Dung Cucumber (below) but smaller — rarely more than 20 cm (8 in.) — and more slender. *20 yellow tentacles.* Usually gray or dark brown. Skin thinner and rougher (more warty) than that of the Donkey Dung. *Tube feet scattered, yellow.* Near mangrove swamps and in Turtle Grass beds. Florida (where it has almost completely replaced the Donkey Dung), Jamaica, western Caribbean, Dutch Antilles.

BROWN ROCK SEA CUCUMBER **Pl. 36**
Holothuria glaberrima
Medium-sized — usually 10–15 cm (4–6 in.). Skin smooth, ventral side with numerous dark brown podia. *20 bushy black tentacles.* Black, dark brown, rarely gray; uniform color without spots. On and under rocks in surf zone throughout our area except Florida.

GRAY SEA CUCUMBER *Holothuria grisea*
Medium-sized — to 20 cm (8 in.), usually smaller. Gray, deep pink, or mottled; covered with warts. Slightly flattened ventral surface densely covered with yellow podia; larger specimens almost completely cylindrical (lack sole). *23 bushy yellow tentacles; 11 small ventral ones gradually increasing in size dorsally.* Young among rocks or coral debris; largest sometimes in Turtle Grass beds, where they may be mistaken for Florida Sea Cucumber (above). Throughout our area except Bermuda; common in Jamaica.

IMPATIENT SEA CUCUMBER *Holothuria impatiens*
Medium-sized — averages 15 cm (6 in.). Flask-shaped; mottled gray, brown, or purplish. *Skin feels rough;* covered with low rounded warts, some with concentric brown lines. Anterior end may be darker than rest of body. About 20 tentacles. Under rocks in lagoons or open water, below 2 m (6½ ft.), often at considerable depths. Name may come from *readiness to eject copious amounts of sticky white Cuvier's tubules* when picked up. Reported as uncommon (possibly because usually hidden in crevices beyond wading depth). Florida, West Indies; not in Bermuda.

DONKEY DUNG SEA CUCUMBER **Pls. 36, 37;**
Holothuria mexicana **Fig. 63, p. 197**
Large — usually 25–40 cm (10–16 in.). Small individuals almost unknown. Commonest sea cucumber in our area. Ocher-yellow to dark brown, usually dark brown or gray, sometimes with sediment

on dorsum. Body often wrinkled, may have few warts on dorsum or smooth thick skin. *Brown tube feet scattered over flattened rose-colored sole* (sole may be white or brown in older specimens). 22 tan peltate tentacles. Turtle Grass beds in water deeper than 1 m (3¼ ft.), with Five-toothed and Three-rowed Cucumbers. Throughout our area except Bermuda and Florida.

GOLDEN SEA CUCUMBER *Holothuria parvula*　　**Pl. 36**
Tiny　averages 3.5 cm (1¼ in.). Golden brown, greenish yellow, or light brown, with numerous *bright yellow podia* on flattened sole. Fluorescent pigment may be visible on skin. Dorsum arched with many low warts. Under rocks in reef flats, shallow water, tide pools. When picked up and squeezed, *readily ejects harmless sticky white Cuvier's tubules.* Bermuda, West Indies.

SURINAM SEA CUCUMBER *Holothuria surinamensis*
Medium-sized — to 20 cm (8 in.), commonly about 10 cm (4 in.). Dark brown, yellowish brown, reddish chocolate, or purple-brown. May have a series of purple spots on dorsum. Body cylindrical, may be covered with small dull white papillae. Podia white, with yellow tips. About 20 short pale peltate tentacles. Often in tufts of algae or among finger-coral colonies. Common in Bermuda, Jamaica, Antigua, and throughout our area except Florida.

THOMAS' GIANT SEA CUCUMBER *Holothuria thomasae*
Huge — minimum length 1 m (3¼ ft.). Resembles vacuum cleaner hose. Yellowish brown to maroon, with brown, light brown, and whitish flecks. Covered with *rows of long pointed tubercles across dorsum,* with regions of smooth skin between rows. Podia short, brown. 20 yellow, pink, or brown peltate tentacles. Nocturnal, hides in daytime. Extends from under coral boulders and debris at dusk, remains active at night. Posterior firmly attached to underside of boulder. In lagoons and protected water with rubble-strewn bottom; deeper than 2 m (6½ ft.).

THREE-ROWED SEA CUCUMBER　　　　　**Pl. 36;**
Isostichopus badionotus　　　　　　　**Fig. 61, p. 195**
Large　to 45 cm (1½ ft.) or more. Body somewhat angular. Variable in color and form, but usually brown mottled with orange or black; striped; deep crimson in Tobago. *3 rows of dark brown podia on sole,* central row wider and split. In Turtle Grass beds, usually at 1–2 m (3–6½ ft.). Throughout our area, especially Bermuda and Jamaica.

PYGMY SEA CUCUMBER *Pentacta pygmaea*　　**Pl. 37**
Small — to 10 cm (4 in.), usually 5 cm (2 in.). Dorsum with 2 double rows of blunt tubercles. Chocolate-brown, with 3 rows of yellow or pink podia. 10 tentacles, 2 smaller than others. Shallow rocky bottoms or Turtle Grass beds in Florida Gulf Coast, Puerto Rico, Trinidad, Brazil.

Dendrochirotids

SURINAM PARATHYONE *Parathyone surinamensis*
Small — to 10 cm (4 in.), usually 7.5 cm (3 in.). Brown or gray, with *10 dark dendritic tentacles*. Podia whitish with yellowish tips, numerous, cover body. Ventral side not flattened (no sole). Near low-water mark on rocky shores, under rocks. Common in Bermuda; found throughout West Indies. *Similar species:* Brown Rock Sea Cucumber (p. 200) also has no sole but is more often gray, with fewer tentacles; ventral podia not concentrated.

Sea Lilies or Feather Stars

Richard D. Bray and Gordon T. Taylor

Some 345 million years ago a warm ocean covered much of the West Indies and North America. Long before the first dinosaur appeared, giant sharks pursued lobe-finned fishes in seas now replaced by mountains and plains. The bottom of these seas was a veritable garden, and growing like flowers on sand and mud were the sea lilies, or crinoids.

These animals had stalks, and their arms reached upward. They were immobile. They must have lived in an era of incredible abundance of plankton, for they abounded and became a dominant form. Movement was apparently unnecessary, for swarms of plankton must have floated by and been strained from the sea by the crinoids' many arms, each covered with sticky mucus and bristling with numerous pinnules, like teeth on a comb.

Time passed and the seas receded. Mud bottoms sank under the accumulated debris of the ages. The pressure turned the mud into shale. In this stone we now find the fossil remains of the once dominant stalk-bearing crinoids: doughnut-shaped, 1 cm (½ in.) wide imprints on ancient mud, each representing the cylindrical base of a stalk. They are crowded together and must have formed a dense underbrush of living crinoids.

As warm seas became cold, most crinoid species survived only in the tropics, where plankton is scarce. Only on the coral reef is food abundant. But competition is keen. Every advantage makes survival more likely. About 200 million years ago the crinoids evolved stalkless motile forms, members of Suborder Comatulida. Their arms became adapted to flapping up and down, so they evolved a modest swimming capability. These stalkless feather stars are today the commonest crinoids. They have come a long way from their stalk-bearing ancestors and have become so successful that their kind now radiates out from the region around the equator, invading new habitats. Furthermore, the number of species of comatulids is actually increasing. The ancient stalk-bearing forms

Fig. 67 A Black-and-white Sea Lily on Pillar Coral.

have retained a precarious foothold in great depths and cold seas, where detritus or plankton is still abundant. These usually have 10 or fewer arms. But the comatulids, with their ability to move to favorable positions, have evolved many arms and a greater plankton-catching ability, making them effective competitors on modern coral reefs.

The typical crinoid has an upward-facing cup called a calyx, composed of calcareous plates. The flat top of the calyx is the tegmen. On it are the mouth and anus. Arising from the edges of the calyx is a series of jointed arms. Some crinoids retain the primitive number of arms — 5 — but often the arms branch to yield as many as 200. Projecting from each side of the arms is a row of jointed appendages, pinnules, giving the arms a feathery appearance. The pinnules have minute tube feet, used to trap and transport food. Five ambulacral grooves extend from the centrally located mouth, one into each arm.

The stalk, a series of disks, is attached to the aboral pole (the underside) of the calyx. The stalk may bear 1 or several whorls of leglike appendages called cirri. Although the stalk is lost early during comatulid development, the cirri usually remain, clustered around a single aboral plate, the centrodorsal.

The loss of the stalk by the comatulids had far-reaching consequences for the crinoids. No longer were they restricted to an attached (sessile) existence; they could crawl and swim, using their arms. Swimming is an activity that probably enables crinoids to avoid predation. The mobility also frees them from their reliance on the vagaries of the current for their food supply. They can alter their position to maximize exposure to passing plankton.

Many crinoids have adapted to a nocturnal feeding pattern. Some comatulids feed during the evening and crawl into the protection of the reef structure during the day, reemerging shortly after sunset. It has been suggested that this daily pattern might be a response to possible predation or disturbance by reef fish.

Although male and female crinoids are morphologically similar, the sexes are separate. The reproductive structures are borne on the pinnules of each arm closest to the calyx. Fertilization and subsequent larval development are usually external. During development all larval crinoids assume the ancestral stalk-bearing condition, although the comatulids lose the stalk later in development.

Crinoids are suspension-feeders, dependent upon the water currents to provide their diet of plankton. The pinnular tube feet secrete a mucus that traps the food particles. These particles are conveyed to the ciliated food groove by the tube feet and are ultimately transported to the mouth.

Fig. 68
Sea lily

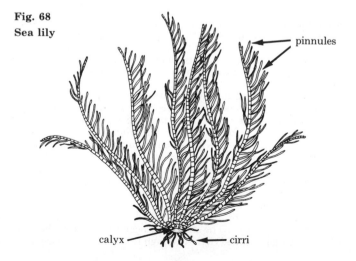

pinnules

calyx ←   → cirri

Common Species

SWIMMING SEA LILY
Analcidometra armata
10 thin small arms — usually to 9 cm (3½ in.). Gray-green, with red bands. Pinnules banded red and white or orange-yellow. Usually elevated above substratum, attached to sea feathers, where it strains plankton from water. Swims. Throughout West Indies.

RED SEA LILY *Comactinia echinoptera*
10 arms; 15-20 cirri. Reddish brown arms visible projecting from crevices only at night. Stout arms with pinnules in a plane on either side of arm, featherlike rather than at right angles to each other as in *Nemaster* species (below). Pinnules red, orange, yellow, or beaded red and white. Comb teeth on pinnules nearest calyx. On flat rather than hilly bottoms at 15-50 m (50-165 ft.).

GREEN SEA LILY *Ctenantedon kinziei*
10 arms; 50-90 cirri. Greenish; *paired black spots on arms.* Cryptic; hidden even at night. Can swim vigorously. At 15-50 m (50-165 ft.) on coral reefs.

BLACK-AND-WHITE SEA LILY
Pl. 37;
Nemaster grandis
Fig. 67, p. 203
To 40 arms, each to 25 cm (10 in.). *Arms and pinnules black; pinnules white-tipped.* Stands fully exposed on projections. Only crinoid visible with body completely exposed during day. At 10–50 m (33-165 ft.). Central and western Caribbean.

ORANGE SEA LILY *Nemaster rubiginosa*
Pl. 32
20 arms. Usually *orange, with median aboral black stripe* on each arm. Commonest crinoid on many Caribbean reefs. Look for 1 or several bright orange arms projecting from crevice; arms usually curled at tips. Pinnules orange, yellow, or rarely whitish with black tips. Calyx hidden in crevices, under coral, in sponge atrium. Calyx and arms often inhabited by a number of symbionts, including a small annelid worm and various shrimps. Usually at 10–50 m (33–165 ft.), but off Tobago as shallow as 2 m (6½ ft.). Caribbean and Bahamas. *Related species:* Beaded Sea Lily, *N. discoidea* (Pl. 32), is similar but lacks black stripe on each arm; smaller and more delicate than Orange and Black-and-white Sea Lilies; has beaded pinnules; usually silver-gray or gray-green; partially hidden in crevices at 20-40 m (67-130 ft.).

BANDED SEA LILY
Pl. 32
Tropiometra carinata
10 arms, longer than in most other crinoids — 20-30 cm (8-12 in.). Arms brown, with yellow bands. Calyx usually hidden in crevices; stout arms extended, visible. In shallow wave-agitated environments; at 1 m (3¼ ft.), usually deeper.

12

Fishes

Every fish on the reef is programmed to survive, its behavior imprinted in its genes, the product of millions of years of evolution. Two behavioral strategies are available to animals whose lives are beset with the desperate problems of survival: they can evolve a fixed pattern of automatic, reflexive responses, or they can use a slower, more flexible technique, developing a different response to every stimulus. On the reef or Turtle Grass bed the slashing jaws of the predator leave little opportunity for choice, and most fish behavior is automatic and invariable. When faced with a particular stimulus, where failure could easily mean extinction, the fish responds as his ancestors did — and survives. That is why when several chromis are whirling in a courtship dance, they are oblivious to predators; their automatic ancient pattern of reproduction demands that the ritual be completed. That is why a Nassau Grouper, using a now-obsolete defense mechanism, presses itself against the wall of a cave to escape a spearfisherman, even though this behavior makes it vulnerable to the spear. That is why a school of silversides draws together in the face of a predator rather than scattering in fear even if the predator looms just a couple of meters away. It is also the reason why the fearsome barracuda that appears suddenly just over your shoulder will not attack you, though you are relatively defenseless in the face of its deadly teeth. The barracuda is programmed to attack prey within a definite size range, and though you swim clumsily, your unprotected flesh vulnerable in the water, it will not — it cannot — attack. Unfortunately the shark has a wider range of prey size. But this does not signify intelligence. In fact, when its feeding response is stimulated, the shark will automatically attack anything nearby, even other members of its species.

Fish-watching becomes a fine art once you have overcome the distraction of the dazzling jewel-like appearance of so many tropical fishes. First you must learn to discern their patterns of behavior, the regular responses they make to their surroundings; then you can begin to understand their interactions, their feeding and courtship patterns, territoriality and survival techniques. You will be able to hover over the reef, watching a parrotfish chewing chunks from a coral head, and actually *hear* its teeth rasp the hard coral. You will see a Trumpetfish hanging, head down, motionless, almost identical to the vertical branches of a soft coral, waiting for

a small fish to pass nearby. You will see Bar Jacks plunge into a
school of minnows, the frantic constriction of the school, and then,
almost immediately after the attack, the relaxation of the school
and the resumption of normal behavior, even though the jacks are
still nearby. But you will also be able to see the Bar Jacks exhibit
more innovative behavior. They may be seen hovering over stingrays rooting in the sediment, as if waiting for small animals to be
exposed by the rays' activities.

The following is designed to help you focus on and understand
behavior patterns of fishes.

Feeding Activities. The coral reef seethes with life — a huge
number and great variety of organisms. On a wreck or jetty in cold
northern waters an assiduous diver may find 10-15 species of fishes
in this optimal habitat. One researcher in the Bahamas found
70-80 species on a single coral patch *3 m (10 ft.) in diameter!* Others have reported 150 species from an area of similar size. It is well
known that 2 kinds of organism cannot inhabit the same environmental niche. If competing species feed on exactly the same food
source in exactly the same manner at exactly the same time of day,
sooner or later one species will predominate and the other will
become extinct. The hundreds of coral reef species have evolved a
huge array of feeding strategies, each fitting into a niche subtly
different in some crucial way from that of its neighbors. It is difficult to believe that each of the 400 or so species of fishes on a reef
has a feeding mode different from those of the others when one
considers the limited kinds of food available: corals, algae, plankton, crawling and burrowing animals, and of course other fishes.

One type of differentiation is feeding time. There are daytime
feeders and nighttime feeders. Thus, 2 species can use the same
food source without competing directly. Many wrasses eat small
shrimps, other crustaceans, and worms in the daytime. At dusk
they are the first to settle on the bottom for the night, their bodies
sometimes awkwardly bent to fit a crevice between coral heads.
Soon after the wrasses have gone to sleep, the squirrelfishes leave
their shelters and come out to feed on the same prey, their big eyes
discerning the movements of the small arthropods and worms in
the dark.

Fishes that find their prey on the sea floor have an especially
large variety of feeding stratagems. Many eat tiny crustaceans living on or just beneath the surface of the sediment or on the surface
of a coral head. They have small mouths and usually hover close to
the bottom, inspecting it. Detecting a movement or an unusual
contour, they seize their prey in a characteristic plucking manner.
This method of feeding seems to have preadapted certain fishes to
be cleaners — that is, to employ a feeding pattern of removing ectoparasites from the flanks of larger fishes. Juvenile wrasses,
butterflyfishes, and damselfishes are known to participate in cleaning symbiosis. Whether it be a coral head or the body of a large

grouper makes little difference to a small Bluehead; on both there are tiny crustaceans available for the plucking. It has taken a million years of evolution to develop the ritual performed by both cleaner and client that turns a normally carnivorous fish into one that accepts the ministrations of the cleaner.

Most adult butterflyfishes have long snouts. They remove small animals from crevices deep in the coral. Because most other fishes lack elongate mouths, only a few can use this source of food. Most damselfishes feed on a variety of encrusting organisms, such as tunicates, along with the eggs of various animals attached to the coral. They do not compete very much with the butterflyfishes, as their mouth structure dictates that they feed on prey at the surface of the coral head. One species of butterflyfish seems to be directly competitive with the damselfishes. It has a blunt snout and must feed on the surface of the coral. Large damselfishes, such as the common Yellowtail Damselfish, also feed on coral. But a closer look reveals that the butterflyfish feeds by sucking mucus from the coral, leaving its tissues intact, whereas the damselfishes actually scrape off the living coral, leaving characteristic round dime-sized scars all over the coral head.

Most fishes that feed on really small organisms are daytime feeders, since they must have adequate light to locate their prey. The bottom-feeders use many techniques to locate worms and crustaceans in the sediment. A trunkfish plucks animals from the bottom, but if none are visible, it blows a jet of water, disturbing the sediment and snapping up any organisms dislodged.

The goatfishes also feed on small organisms in the sediment, feeling for them with a pair of long, sensitive barbels underneath the chin. A school of these fishes is often attended by several wrasses, which attempt to steal food not noticed by the goatfishes. Mojarras eat the sediment, removing its inhabitants with their gill rakers and passing the clean sand out through their gill openings.

A number of fishes have gone to great lengths to find food sources they can use without the danger of too much competition. The beautiful Blue, French, Gray, and Queen Angelfishes and their close relative, the Rock Beauty, eat sponges almost exclusively. The sharp spicules, the bad odor, and the sometimes irritating tissues do not seem to inhibit them. The Whitespotted Filefish is one of the few competitors; most other fishes give sponges a wide berth. Even more indicative of the desperate search for relatively noncompetitive food sources is the ability of the Jolthead Porgy and the Queen Triggerfish to attack successfully the most ferocious-looking of all reef inhabitants, the Long-spined Black Urchin. They have evolved hard bony jaws and a technique of flipping the urchin over to expose its relatively short-spined, vulnerable bottom.

Although there is often a substantial growth of algae on and near the reef, an herbivorous feeding mode evolved comparatively recently and is considered an advanced trait. It is exhibited by relatively few fishes. Herbivores must have a long digestive tract to perform the digestive functions necessary to deal adequately with plants, especially those algae infused with hard calcium carbonate. The "cattle of the sea," the plant-eaters, are primarily the Doctorfish and its close relative, the Blue Tang. Parrotfishes are also considered plant-grazers. It seems likely that grazing on plants has evolved from the selective plucking style of feeding discussed above. Corroboration of this supposition can be found by examining the families of herbivorous fishes. Virtually all families of herbivores have some carnivorous members. Herbivores often retain features similar to those of their carnivorous brethren. They are usually colorful daytime feeders with small mouths. Furthermore, when a grazing herbivore ingests a mouthful of leafy algae, it cannot but consume the many small animals that use the algae as a refuge. Thus, to a greater or lesser extent, plant-eating fishes are not exclusively herbivorous and may be considered omnivorous.

Damselfishes, especially the *Chromis* species, feed on zooplankton floating over the reef. They hover in loose schools, darting off on short forays to snap up tiny crustaceans. Minnows, such as the Reef Silverside, anchovies, and small clupeids (herrings) are also plankton-eaters but usually confine their feeding activities to nighttime. They, too, have small mouths; but whereas the bottom-feeder's mouth is usually directed downward, that of a plankton-eater is usually upturned (anchovies excepted). Because the upturned mouth shortens its snout, the plankton-eater is able to see tiny prey in the water immediately ahead.

Hovering close to the schools of plankton-eaters are their predators — the jacks, needlefishes, and barracudas. You may watch for hours as small schools of jacks thread their way among clouds of silversides, yet no aggressive behavior is exhibited. Only if you accidentally intrude by distracting the prey fishes with your presence, confusing the school, will you see a successful attack. It is likely that predators find it hard to catch small reef fishes during most of the day. At dusk and dawn the diagonal rays of the sun silhouette the fishes moving to and from their feeding grounds and resting places, making it easier for predators to locate them. If you want to see increased predatory activity, you should do your fish-watching at dawn or dusk.

One group of predators is successful throughout the day. These are the stalkers — long, thin fishes that drift slowly and motionlessly toward their prey until they are close enough for a sudden rush. Trumpetfishes and cornetfishes hang vertically in the water near soft corals, camouflaged by dark colors and vertical stripes. They drift toward unwary small fishes until they are able to suck them into their tiny mouths with massive inhalations of water. Barracudas and needlefishes have developed a similar technique and will hover motionless (horizontally, however) until an unwary

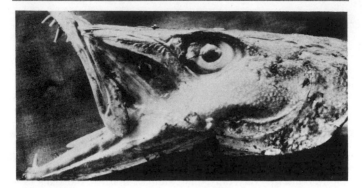

Fig. 69 The head of a barracuda. Note the long, pointed teeth characteristic of this predator.

fish strays too far from the school and presents an accessible target.

As twilight approaches, the plankton-eaters descend from midwater, moving toward the cover of the reef. Other daytime feeders join them, and there is a modest but noticeable migration toward the crevices and other havens of the reef. The surgeonfishes and tangs move in beautiful gray or blue, cloudlike schools, and groups of parrotfishes gravitate toward sheltering holes.

The nocturnal fishes have not yet emerged from their lairs, and for half an hour after dark the water column is relatively empty. Then, as if by a signal, the nighttime feeders emerge. The soldierfishes and bigeyes occupy the midwater levels vacated by chromis and other daytime feeders, their well-adapted eyes straining to locate relatively large zooplankton (bigger than many daytime plankton-eaters consume). The plankton has its own daily vertical migration, rising from the depths at night and reaching greatest abundance near the surface after midnight. By dawn the plankton has begun its descent, and the satiated soldierfishes and bigeyes return to their lairs.

The squirrelfishes and scorpionfishes, as well as moray and conger eels, hunt close to the bottom. The squirrelfishes locate crabs and shrimps with their large eyes, the morays slither in and out of crevices, locating their hapless victims, often sleeping fishes, by smell and touch. One contact with the delicate sensory receptors on the snout of a moray eel, and the prey fish is doomed. Some parrotfishes produce a cocoon of mucus (see Pl. 24) to sleep in, presumably to discourage predation by morays and other nighttime feeders.

Some fishes have become highly modified for a particular mode of feeding. For example, puffers and burrfishes have huge front teeth, permitting them to eat snails, urchins, and other hard-shelled animals.

Stingrays combine physical and behavioral adaptations. They feed on buried crustaceans, worms, and mollusks, uncovering them by scooping out depressions in the sand with their highly developed flattened pectoral fins. Sometimes they can be seen thrashing about on the bottom, raising clouds of sand and eating the sand-dwellers as they become exposed.

The "uglies" of the underwater world are the frogfishes and batfishes. These highly camouflaged animals squat on the bottom on leglike fins. The first spine of the dorsal fin is modified for use as a fishing rod and tipped with a wormlike lure. When a small fish approaches, the lure is waved enticingly. The batfishes do not have a long rod, only a small lure just above the upper lip. They are voracious predators and are often cannibalistic. The large, upward-slanting mouth engulfs small fishes with a single inhalation as soon as they come within range.

Territoriality. Territoriality refers to the tendency to occupy and defend a particular area, usually for the purposes of sustenance and reproduction.

There are many patterns of territoriality, as each species divides the reef for its own purposes. Some fishes are territorial all the time, some only during the reproductive period. Some fishes are territorial only toward their own species, some only toward other fishes with the same feeding mechanisms, even if they are of other species. Some act aggressively toward virtually every organism invading their domain.

Some butterflyfishes defend a territory against members of their own species, but only against those of the same size. Individuals, smaller or larger, are not targets of their aggression. As they grow, their color patterns change, and those with the same pattern are attacked; thus selection of target fishes is very precise. This high degree of selection acts as a spacing mechanism, ensuring the best use of the food supply. Because juvenile butterflyfishes do not have very long snouts, they are confined to foraging in relatively superficial coral crevices, whereas large mature fishes can probe more deeply. So only those of the same size are directly competitive.

Surgeonfishes are territorial when young but not when mature. Perhaps their small size makes the juveniles more vulnerable; as a result, it is advantageous to them to have a secure territory with nearby crevices for safety. Adults, with sharp lancets near their tails, are large enough to browse the reef freely.

A fish cannot expend more energy in defense of its territory than it draws from the food it finds there. One energy-saving mechanism that has evolved is the visual threat display. Much posturing and ritualized long-distance sparring is indulged in between invader and defender. Eventually, in almost all cases, the invader leaves before physical contact is made. Thus fishes are spared frequent and exhausting battles over feeding and reproduction areas.

In a recent study one species of territorial algae-grazing fish was shown to respond aggressively to 38 other species that invaded its territory. All the invaders were algae-feeders. Sixteen other species were not attacked. *These were all non-algae-feeders.* Somehow the defending fishes were able to determine the feeding style of fishes entering their territory, attacking only their competitors.

Most damselfishes are indiscriminate and pugnacious in the defense of their territory. The degree of aggressiveness, however, varies from species to species. For example, the midwater chromis are not at all territorial, and the common Sergeant Major is strongly territorial only during egg-laying and brood-care periods. Territorial behavior may be divided between the 2 main social groupings in damselfishes: solitary species and gregarious species.

The solitary species tend to choose small areas, which they aggressively defend against all comers throughout the year. The smallest territory is the tentacular crown of an anemone, which is inhabited by a mated pair of Pacific Damselfish. The Caribbean damsels, *Eupomacentrus* and *Microspathodon,* usually occupy a small irregular area, roughly a meter in diameter.

The territory of each damselfish becomes a miniature algae garden. The defender drives away the grazers, so no systematic foraging may take place. The damselfish may take random mouthfuls of algae, leaving a few sparse areas that quickly grow back, but it does not seriously overgraze the algae in its territory.

The gregarious species form either schools or shoals. Shoals of midwater chromis, for example, have no territory, at least not when feeding during the day. Schools group around a coral head or rock outcropping, hovering over it and moving up for food and down for shelter. The Sergeant Major forms small schools of as many as 20–30 individuals, often near a pinnacle of coral. They will jointly defend this area but show little or no territoriality among themselves.

Most damselfishes are solitary breeders, gluing their eggs to the coral, fanning and guarding them until they hatch. The Sergeant Major and the chromis, on the other hand, are colonial breeders; many females lay their eggs on the same coral head. The school shows less aggressive behavior toward its members but communally defends the brooding area against other species. In some species 2 or 3 males may fertilize the eggs of several females. Each male then guards one part of the communal egg mass.

In the case of damselfishes food is plentiful, so space availability — including shelter from predation — governs which and how many species are present. In one study of a complex reef so many niches were available that 24 damselfish species shared the resources of the reef.

Many other species of fishes exhibit territoriality. Perhaps the most conspicuous are the aggressive supermales of the normally docile Bluehead and parrotfishes. It is common to see a large colorful male Queen Parrotfish dart across one's path, followed by another, intent on driving the first from its territory.

Reproduction and Development. The variety of reproductive methods that the fishes of the coral reef employ rivals their extraordinary diversity. Some undergo a sex change, a procedure only recently developed by humans. Males become females, and females become males again. Sometimes the males brood the eggs and care for the young. The male seahorse goes one better: it broods the eggs in a pouch on its abdomen. The female's role is simply to deposit the eggs in the pouch; she is free thereafter.

Most fishes have some mechanism for coordinating the release of eggs and sperms. Gregarious fishes, such as mackerels and jacks, release their reproductive products as they travel in large schools. Along with her eggs the female releases a chemical called a pheromone, which stimulates the male to release his sperms. This is a primitive form of reproduction; it requires a huge number of eggs and a copious supply of yolk to sustain the larval fish in the absence of any care by the parents. The fertilized eggs float freely in the water as part of the plankton and are nutritious food for many predators. The lack of care after birth demands a huge expenditure of energy in egg production, on the assumption that numbers will compensate for protection. The result is the same as with more apparently efficient techniques involving parental care. Of the millions of fertilized eggs a mature male and female produce, an average of only 2 reach adulthood. If this were not so, births would outnumber deaths, and the ocean would rapidly fill up with that species of fish.

Shallow-water fishes often produce demersal (sinking) eggs, but some reef fishes release their eggs in the turbulent surface water at the lee edge of the reef, where predation is minimal. Flyingfishes bind sargassum weed into a round ball with silken thread, depositing hundreds of eggs inside the ball, which floats until the eggs hatch.

Many reef fishes have a long period of development, the larvae dispersing over large areas and colonizing distant reefs. Jacks, groupers, goatfishes, surgeonfishes, and lizardfishes have floating eggs and larvae of this type. Snappers, parrotfishes, damsels, and butterflyfishes have eggs that sink or eggs that hatch into larvae that immediately seek havens close to the area of their birth. Some damselfishes glue their eggs to the bottom and stand guard over them, so the young never face the rigors of a pelagic (free-floating) existence.

Larval type varies. Tarpons, eels, and a few other fishes undergo a unique leaflike larval stage called leptocephalus. The Tarpon larva is completely transparent, about 2.5 cm (1 in.) long, flattened and broad like a leaf, with a deeply forked tail and 2 bubblelike eyes. No internal organs are visible at all; the larva looks as if it is made of glass.

Most spawning takes place in the winter months, between February and April, especially among groupers, surgeonfishes, and parrotfishes. Jacks, snappers, and damselfishes spawn throughout the year, with a peak in the coldest months. Young fish of some species may enter tide pools, often around new moon, where they undergo a transformation from disk-shaped larvae to the various adult shapes. This may take 4–5 days.

Many fishes have elaborate courtship and spawning rituals. All these rituals are considered mechanisms, evolved over millions of years, that ensure fertilization and dissemination of the eggs.

Scuba divers can watch the spawning ritual of parrotfishes and wrasses. Adult male and female Yellowtail Parrotfish are of 2 distinct color patterns. Most are blotchy and brown with a yellow tail. A few large males are a bright aqua with red eyes and have been designated supermales. Yellowtail Parrotfish spawn all year at the reef front — the junction of the reef edge and sand — at 7.6–21.3 m (25–71 ft.) or deeper. Most spawning takes place in the afternoon, but observers have reported spawning activity as early as 11:25 A.M. About 200 blotchy brown fish gather in a loose school, some moving or lying on the bottom, most milling about. From time to time groups of 4–13 fish begin to swirl around one another in the school. They incline their bodies upward, then after a short pause, rush toward the surface for a distance of about 2.1–3.6 m (7–12 ft.). Spawning, which occurs at the peak of the rush, produces a cloud of white eggs and sperms. The spawning runs take as little as 2 seconds to complete, after which the participants slowly descend and disperse into the school. Soon afterward another group performs the rite, usually spawning in the same place as their predecessors, seeking out the white cloud which has still not completely dispersed.

After 5 or 6 runs spawning activity ceases for about 5 minutes. The school slowly drifts along the reef front; at intervals of about 60 m (197 ft.) milling commences again, and another spawning sequence is initiated. Research has shown that there is a preponderance of males in every spawning rush, 3–12 males to each female. It is likely that males make several runs for every run by a female. Since males and females look alike, it is possible that the female releases a chemical that attracts the males.

Occasionally a bright aqua supermale is seen swimming near the spawning aggregation but not participating in the ritual. Instead it attacks and nips several of the participants. There seems to be a courtship dance by male Yellowtail Parrotfish. They twitch their bodies briefly in the presence of the female. The aqua supermale exhibits this twitching behavior; but when the object of his display is examined later, it often turns out to be a male. Evidently the supermale may be quite aggressive and strong, but it is not so super when it comes to selecting a mate. When supermales are successful in attracting a female, they always spawn in male-female pairs, never in groups. Viewing this phenomenon is a rare experience, a triumph of fish-watching.

Other species, such as the Mottlefin Parrotfish, spawn most frequently in pairs of different-colored fish and only infrequently in large aggregations.

The Bluehead, contrary to its common name, is almost always yellow, sometimes with a series of horizontal dark brown blotches. Males and females 5-6 cm (2-2½ in.) long aggregate in schools of almost 80 over a coral head or boulder. Five to 10 or more fish swim upward about 60 cm (2 ft.) and release their sexual products. Occasionally a large supermale with a blue head appears. It displays for an individual yellow fish, erecting the dorsal fin fully, exposing an anterior black spot. Often the fish so ardently pursued is a male or immature female — they are indistinguishable. Like the supermale Yellowtail Parrotfish, the supermale Bluehead is often thwarted by its inability to discriminate between the sexes. On rare occasions everything is just right, and a female will rise with the supermale, and spawning will occur.

Although most spawning of Blueheads occurs in aggregations, many other wrasses, especially Slippery Dicks, Puddingwifes, and Clown and Blackear Wrasses, mate in pairs.

Sex reversal is common, even frequent, among species of wrasses, parrotfishes, and groupers. In all cases mature females become large males, often the aggressive supermales. Recent studies have shown that many supermales have senescent testes. This, coupled with their apparent ineffectiveness in spawning, probably means that they contribute little toward the total pool of fertilized eggs. In the light of the foregoing, why sex reversal is so common is an enigma.

Subterranean Fishes. There is a belt of barren sediment at the seaward edge of some Turtle Grass beds where parrotfishes and other herbivores have grazed off the grass. This band is the region where reef fishes, extending their range, go without risk to feed. Beyond this zone lies danger, as the haven of the reef is too far to reach quickly when a predator approaches.

This and other sandy areas in the lagoon are inhabited by a number of subterranean animals. Look for holes about 3.8 cm (1½ in.) in diameter that have been bulldozed by various alpheid shrimps. They use their large claws to shovel muddy sand from the crumbling walls of their burrows. Many species of gobies have become boarders. An Orangespotted Goby, Spotfin Goby, or Dash Goby may be seen at the mouth of one of these burrows, squatting on its pectoral fins. Approach, and both shrimp and fish will retreat. The goby will dive headfirst into the hole.

Larger burrows are excavated by the Sand Tilefish, which may reach 60 cm (2 ft.) in length. The large opening of the burrow is usually surrounded by a mound of sand and shells excavated by the fish. The Sand Tilefish can be seen hovering like a pale ghost near its burrow.

Parasites. The parasites eaten by the tiny cleaning fishes are usually too small to be seen with the naked eye, although sometimes 1 mm ($\frac{1}{16}$ in.) long copepods (tiny crustaceans) or monogenetic trematodes (ectoparasitic flatworms) are visible on the flanks of a newly caught fish. One crustacean parasite, however, often catches the fish-watcher's eye. It is an isopod — an oval, flattened, multijointed animal clearly visible above or below the eye of a fish. Usually of the genus *Anilocra,* this parasite holds on to the fish's skin with sharp claws, often damaging the skin and bone structure of the head but never enough to prevent its host from feeding. The male phase is short-lived, and the male animal is small; so whenever you see one of these isopods, it will probably be a female. Look for them on squirrelfishes and on groupers, where *A. laticauda* is particularly common, though many species of reef fishes may be parasitized. The isopod is usually bigger than the eye of the fish, often 2.5 cm (1 in.) long. (See p. 248.)

Taxonomy. One estimate of the number of living fish species is 21,585. Over 400 species may be found on a single coral reef; 50 species are visible in a single day's exploration. All fishes belong to 3 classes: Agnatha, primitive jawless fishes (grotesque deepsea or parasitic animals not found in our study area); Chondrichthyes, cartilaginous fishes such as skates, rays, and sharks; and Osteichthyes, the bony fishes, with about 21,000 of the total number of species.

It will soon be apparent, as you reflect on the fishes you have seen after a day's diving, that some resemble one another (the tangs and surgeonfishes, for example, are similar except for color) and that some show not the remotest resemblance. But the human mind demands that some sense be made of the welter of shapes and sizes flitting about the reef. This urge to integrate information is responsible for the creation of about 43 orders and 211 families of fishes within these orders, of which about 20 orders (60 families) will concern us. The most comprehensible taxonomic unit, then, is the family, names of which can be recognized by the suffix *-idae.*

Common Families

A hundred of the commonest fishes found on the reef and its environs are pictured on the next few pages and on Pls. 22–26. Each family below is briefly described, and for most families a representative species is illustrated. To identify a fish, it is best simply to leaf through the following drawings until you recognize a shape. After a while you will be able to turn directly to the appropriate family. As you begin to recognize the characteristics of the families, you will be able to identify fishes not found in this book. Sharks (Order Selachii in Class Chondrichthyes) are discussed on pp. 236–241.

Cartilaginous Fishes

Order Rajiformes

STINGRAYS Family Dasyatidae
Broad, flattened, cartilaginous; with gill slits underneath body. Poisonous spine on upper surface of tail. Lack caudal fin, thus called whiptail stingrays. **Southern Stingray,** *Dasyatis americana,* shown (see also Pl. 27). Gray, brownish, or olive, with white undersides. To 1.5 m (5 ft.) wide.

Fig. 70

Southern Stingray

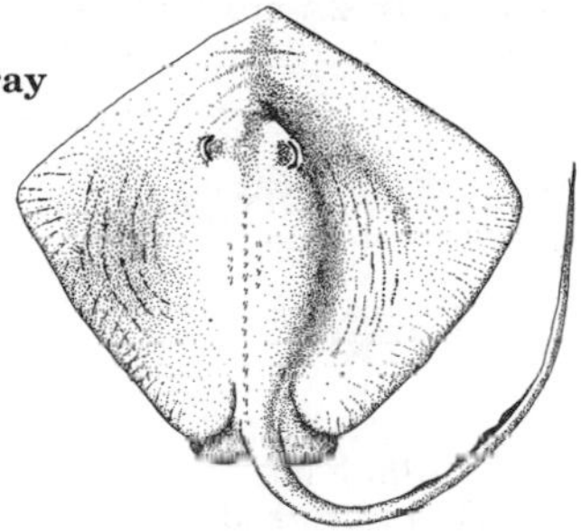

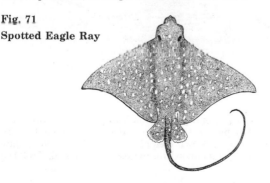

EAGLE RAYS Family Myliobatidae
Head distinct. Long whiplike tail with 1 or more venomous spines near base. Active; rarely buried in sand. **Spotted Eagle Ray,** *Aetobatus narinari,* shown (see also Pl. 4). Brown to olive with white spots and/or rings. To 2.1 m (7 ft.) wide.

Fig. 71

Spotted Eagle Ray

FINTAIL STINGRAYS Family Urolophidae
Thick, relatively short tail. Poisonous spine. **Yellow Stingray,** *Urolophus jamaicensis* (not shown). Dorsal surface covered with network of greenish or brownish lines on pale background. Platter-shaped. To 35 cm (14 in.) wide.

Bony Fishes

Order Elopiformes

TARPONS and LADYFISHES Family Elopidae
Silvery; may have large scales. In estuaries and among mangroves. Carnivorous. **Tarpon,** *Megalops atlantica,* shown. Jutting lower jaw; last dorsal fin ray prolonged as stout filament. Blue-black back, large silvery scales. To 2.4 m (8 ft.).

Fig. 72
Tarpon

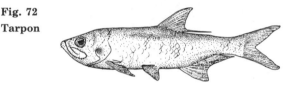

BONEFISHES Family Albulidae
Silvery, strong, hard. Deeply forked tail. Snout projects beyond lower jaw, so mouth is set downward. **Bonefish,** *Albula vulpes,* shown. Indistinct dark vertical bars on back. On sand flats, eating crabs, clams. To 90 cm (3 ft.).

Fig. 73
Bonefish

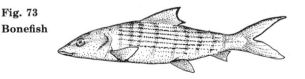

Order Anguilliformes

MORAY EELS Family Muraenidae
Gills are small round openings. Often a hump behind head. Large fanglike teeth. No pectoral fins. In crevices. **Spotted Moray,** *Gymnothorax moringa,* shown (see also Pl. 25). White lower jaw; brown to black markings on white-yellow background. To 90 cm (3 ft.).

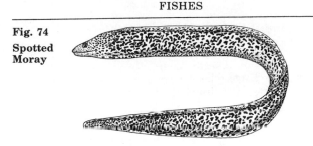

Fig. 74

Spotted Moray

CONGER EELS Family Congridae
Slitlike gills, large eyes, well-developed lips. Lack fanglike teeth.
Garden Eel, *Nystactichthys halis,* shown (see also Pl. 4). Tail ends
in hard point. Blackish olive, posterior becomes white; small orange spots over body. In colonies in deep water; animals vertical,
tails in sand. To 50 cm (20 in.).

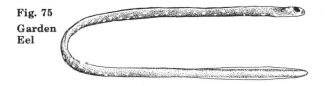

Fig. 75

Garden Eel

Order Clupeiformes

HERRINGS Family Clupeidae
Small silvery schooling fishes with 1 dorsal fin and deeply forked
tail. Do not confuse with silversides, which have 2 dorsal fins.
Redear Sardine, *Harengula humeralis,* shown. Silvery, with orange blotch at upper gill cover. Large schools near shore. To 23 cm
(9 in.), usually much smaller.

Fig. 76

Redear Sardine

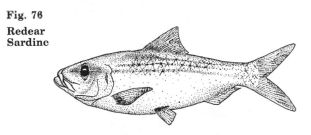

ANCHOVIES Family Engraulidae
Small translucent schooling fishes with silvery stripe down side of body. Snout projects beyond tip of lower jaw. **Longnose Anchovy,** *Anchoa lamprotaenia,* shown. Translucent, with silver stripe down side. Large schools near shore; commonest in bays along continent rather than islands. To 9 cm (3½ in.).

Fig. 77

Longnose Anchovy

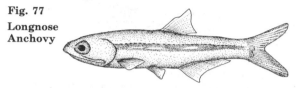

Order Myctophiformes

LIZARDFISHES Family Synodontidae
Well camouflaged — sand-colored with brown blotches or bars. Torpedo-shaped, with large upward-pointing mouth. On bottom, propped up on fins. **Sand Diver,** *Synodus intermedius,* shown. Brown bars and yellowish lines on sides. Fins orangish. To 50 cm (20 in.).

Fig. 78

Sand Diver

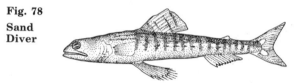

Order Lophiiformes

FROGFISHES Family Antennariidae
Grotesque, with lumplike body, blunt head, and leglike ventral and anal fins. Extensible "fishing rod and lure" above upper lip. **Longlure Frogfish,** *Antennarius multiocellatus,* shown (see also Pl. 26). Small, dark, sometimes spotted. To 11 cm (4½ in.).

Fig. 79

Longlure Frogfish

BATFISHES Family Ogcocephalidae
Flattened, with large armlike pectoral fins on which they walk.
"Lure" over upper lip, but no "fishing rod" (see preceding family).
Spiny. **Polka-dot Batfish,** *Ogcocephalus radiatus,* shown.
Brown, with dark round spots edged with white. Adult belly
coppery red. To 38 cm (15 in.).

Fig. 80

Polka-dot Batfish

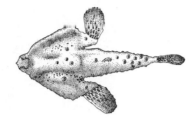

Order Gadiformes

PEARLFISHES Family Carapidae
Knifelike, tapering to point at tail. Inside host in daytime. **Pearlfish,** *Carapus bermudensis,* shown (see also Pl. 37). Pearly pink,
shiny. Inside Five-toothed Sea Cucumber in daytime (see Fig. 62);
forages freely at night. To 18 cm (7 in.).

Fig. 81
Pearlfish

Order Atheriniformes

NEEDLEFISHES and HALFBEAKS
Families Belonidae and Hemiramphidae
Long beak with sharp teeth. Silvery, elongate. Halfbeaks have a
reduced upper jaw. **Redfin Needlefish,** *Strongylura notata,*
shown. Back pale green; dorsal fin and upper tail fin with reddish
tips. At water's surface near shore. To 60 cm (2 ft.). **Ballyhoo,**
Hemiramphus brasiliensis, shown. Back dark green; sides silvery
white; upper lobe of tail orange. To 38 cm (15 in.).

Fig. 82

Redfin Needlefish

Ballyhoo

SILVERSIDES Family Atherinidae
Minnows with a silvery lateral stripe. 2 dorsal fins. In large schools
near shore. **Hardhead Silverside,** *Atherinomorus stipes,* shown.
Translucent, with a silvery stripe overlying a black one. Commonest minnow near shore. To 13 cm (5 in.), usually smaller.

Fig. 83

**Hardhead
Silverside**

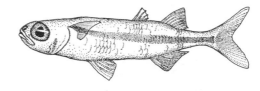

Order Beryciformes

SQUIRRELFISHES Family Holocentridae
Big-eyed and reddish. Dorsal fin spiny anteriorly, soft posteriorly.
In caves, overhangs during day. Nocturnal. **Squirrelfish,** *Holo-
centrus rufus,* shown. Reddish and white horizontal stripes. Diagonal white bar below eye. Often has white blotch on body. To 30 cm
(1 ft.).

Fig. 84
Squirrelfish

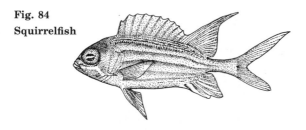

Order Gasterosteiformes

TRUMPETFISHES and CORNETFISHES
Families Aulostomidae and Fistulariidae
Tiny slanted mouth, long snout, barbel on chin. Posterior dorsal
and anal fins. Elongate. Often hang vertically in water. **Trumpetfish,** *Aulostomus maculatus,* shown. Brown or brownish red with
silvery or yellow horizontal stripes. Silvery lines on head. To 1 m
(3¼ ft.). **Cornetfish,** *Fistularia tabacaria,* also shown. Similar to
Trumpetfish but has a long filament extending from tail. Color
variable: blue, olive, or brown. To 1.8 m (6 ft.).

Fig. 85

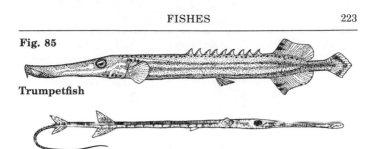

Trumpetfish

Cornetfish

Order Scorpaeniformes

SCORPIONFISHES Family Scorpaenidae
Spiny, with a row of spines extending from beneath eye toward
gill. Fin spines may be poisonous. Usually dark, mottled bottom-
dwellers. Large mouth. **Spotted Scorpionfish,** *Scorpaena plumieri,* shown. Head and body dark brown, bases of fins whitish.
Head blunt, eyes projecting. To 45 cm (1½ ft.).

Fig. 86

**Spotted
Scorpionfish**

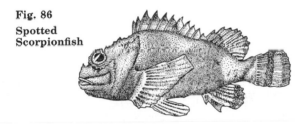

Order Dactylopteriformes

FLYING GURNARDS Family Dactylopteridae
Large pectoral fins, blunt head, large eyes. **Flying Gurnard,**
Dactylopterus volitans (see Pl. 23). Huge pectoral fins expanded
only when moving. Color variable, matches habitat. To 45 cm
(1½ ft.).

Order Perciformes

SEA BASSES and GROUPERS Family Serranidae
Large, with lobed tail, large mouth. Posterior dorsal fin large and
extended. Often in caves. **Red Hind,** *Epinephelus guttatus,* shown
(see also Pl. 23). Red spots, background pale to olive. Fins edged
with black. To 45 cm (1½ ft.).

Fig. 87
Red Hind

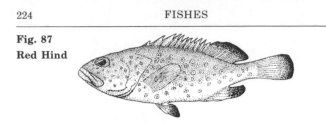

BIGEYES Family Priacanthidae
Broad body, with undershot jaw and large mouth facing upward.
Large eyes, reddish color, rough scales. Nocturnal; in caves during
day. **Glasseye Snapper,** *Priacanthus cruentatus,* shown. Long
spine at base of gill cover. Reddish with silver bars on back; may be
silvery with red blotches. To 30 cm (1 ft.).

Fig. 88

**Glasseye
Snapper**

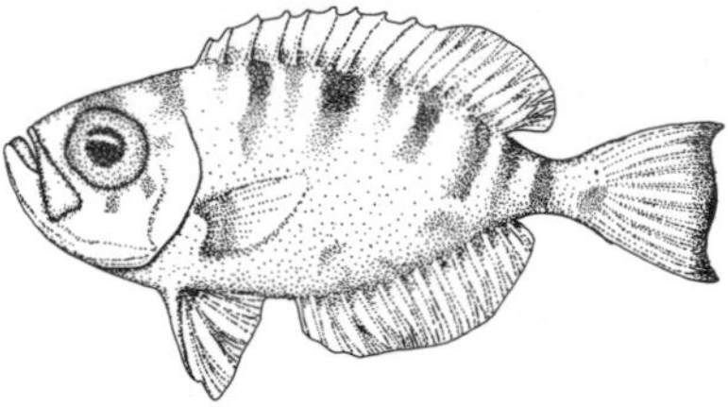

CARDINALFISHES Family Apogonidae
Small; red with black markings. 2 distinct dorsal fins. Nocturnal.
Freckled Cardinalfish, *Phaeoptyx conklini,* shown. Red with
black markings. Black stripes at base of dorsal fins. Tail edged with
black above and below. To 9 cm (3½ in.).

Fig. 89

**Freckled
Cardinalfish**

REMORAS Family Echeneidae
Thin, dark, elongate, with a corrugated sucker on top of head.
Attach to large fishes; eat ectoparasites and host's leftovers.
Sharksucker, *Echeneis naucrates,* shown. Tan, brown, or black,
with broad black horizontal stripes. Lower jaw protrudes. To 1.1 m
(3½ ft.).

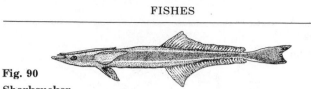

Fig. 90

Sharksucker

JACKS, POMPANOS, PERMITS, and PALOMETAS
Family Carangidae

Silvery. *Jacks:* blunt, pugnacious faces and deeply forked tails; many with bony scutes running along midline of body near tail. *Pompanos, permits, and palometas:* broad, disklike body. **Bar Jack,** *Caranx ruber,* shown. Dark bar covers lower lobe of tail and extends along back. Blue stripe under dark bar on back. Blue-gray above, silvery below. To 55 cm (22 in.).

Fig. 91

Bar Jack

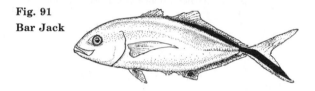

SNAPPERS Family Lutjanidae

Long sloping triangular head. Large mouth. Usually large canine teeth. Carnivorous. **Gray or Mangrove Snapper,** *Lutjanus griseus,* shown (see also Pl. 3). Gray with red tinges. Dark streak on dorsal fin and lower tail fin. Near mangroves. To 1 m (3¼ ft.).

Fig. 92

Gray or Mangrove Snapper

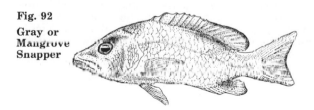

MOJARRAS Family Gerreidae

Broad, silvery, with deeply forked tails, puckered lips. In sandy areas, Turtle Grass beds. **Yellowfin Mojarra,** *Gerres cinereus,* shown. Indistinct black bars on silver-gray body; fins yellow. To 37 cm (15 in.).

Fig. 93
Yellowfin
Mojarra

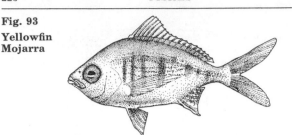

GRUNTS Family Pomadasyidae
Similar to snappers but tail more forked, head less sloping. Most
young have horizontal stripes. On reefs. **French Grunt,**
Haemulon flavolineatum, shown (see also Pls. 21 and 23). Yellow
stripes on silver, or bluish stripes on orange. Large schools near
coral. To 30 cm (1 ft.).

Fig. 94
French
Grunt

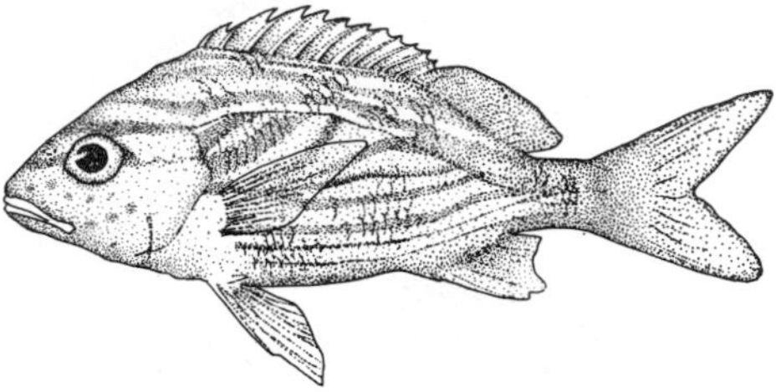

PORGIES Family Sparidae
Laterally flattened, broad-bodied. Head large, slopes sharply from
dorsal fin. Eyes high on head; mouth near bottom of head.
Saucereye Porgy, *Calamus calamus,* shown. Marbled, blotched,
silvery. Blue stripe below eye; bluish blotch at base of pectoral fin.
To 40 cm (16 in.).

Fig. 95
Saucereye
Porgy

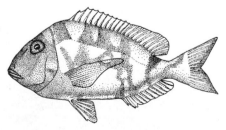

DRUMS Family Sciaenidae
2 distinct dorsal fins; first always larger, extended in most Caribbean species. Small downturned mouth. Many have high flaglike anterior dorsal fin, black stripes. **Sand Drum,** *Umbrina coroides,* shown. Drab, gray-lined, silvery. Barbel on chin. To 30 cm (1 ft.).

Fig. 96
Sand Drum

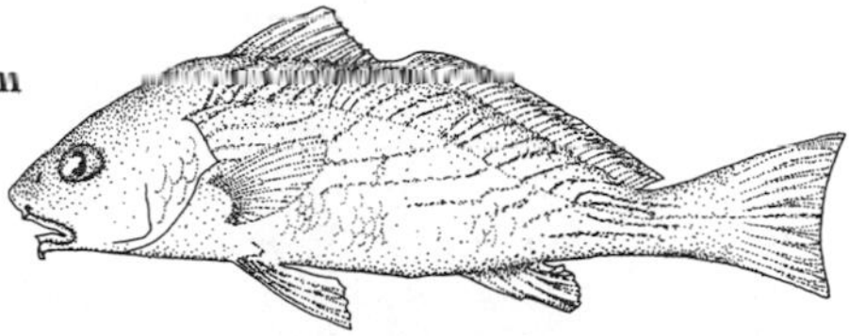

GOATFISHES Family Mullidae
Pair of long barbels on chin. Grubs in sand, usually in small schools. 2 species: Yellow and Spotted. **Spotted Goatfish,** *Pseudupeneus maculatus,* shown. Pale tan with 3 square black spots. When excited, suffused with red. To 25 cm (10 in.).

Fig. 97
Spotted
Goatfish

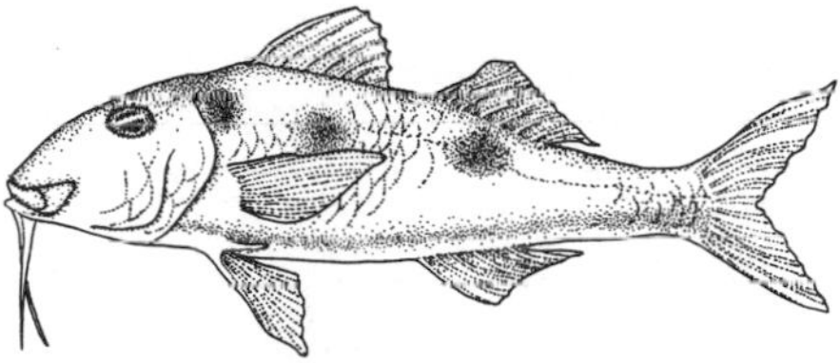

SEA CHUBS Family Kyphosidae
Flattened, oval, schooling. Small head; comblike teeth in mouth. **Bermuda Chub,** *Kyphosus sectatrix,* shown. Steel gray with yellow stripes. Yellow spot behind eye. Herbivorous. To 45 cm (1¼ ft.).

Fig. 98
Bermuda Chub

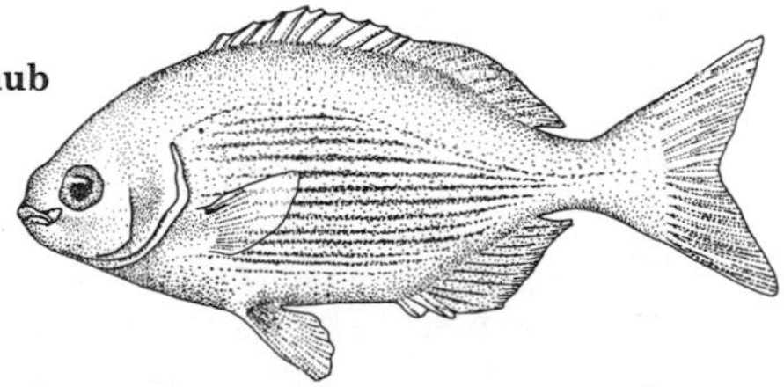

SPADEFISHES Family Ephippidae
Deep-bodied, flattened. 2 well-separated dorsal fins. **Atlantic Spadefish,** *Chaetodipterus faber,* shown. Black bars on gray background. Juveniles black; mature adults lose stripes. To 1 m (3¼ ft.).

Fig. 99

Atlantic
Spadefish

BUTTERFLYFISHES and ANGELFISHES
Family Chaetodontidae
Thin discus-shaped bodies. *Butterflyfishes:* often long snout. *Angelfishes:* usually larger, with a spine at base of gill cover. **Spotfin Butterflyfish,** *Chaetodon ocellatus,* shown. Black stripe through eye. Distinct black spot on posterior top of dorsal fin. Vague larger spot at base of dorsal fin. To 20 cm (8 in.).

Fig. 100

Spotfin
Butterflyfish

DAMSELFISHES Family Pomacentridae
Oval, broad-bodied; resemble freshwater sunfishes. Territorial. *Chromis* species more elongate with deeply forked tails; midwater. **Yellowtail Damselfish,** *Microspathodon chrysurus,* shown. Body and fins black, tail yellow. Juveniles have bright blue spots. To 15 cm (6 in.).

Fig. 101
Yellowtail
Damselfish

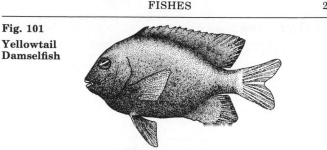

MULLETS Family Mugilidae
Elongate, thick-bodied. Large scales. Pectoral fin high, near top of
gill. 2 separate dorsal fins; forked tail. Large schools inshore. Herbivorous. **White Mullet,** *Mugil curema,* shown. Olive above, silvery below. Dark blotch at base of pectoral fin. To 1 m (3¼ ft.).

Fig. 102
White
Mullet

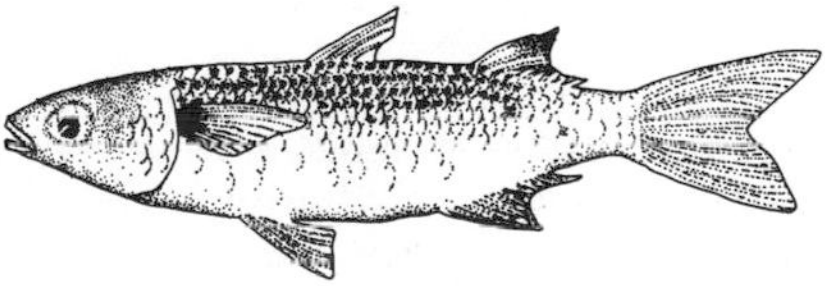

BARRACUDAS Family Sphyraenidae
Elongate pikelike body; large mouth and teeth. **Great Barracuda,** *Sphyraena barracuda,* shown. Young in Turtle Grass bed
are olive banded. Mature fish green to gray above, silvery on sides.
Black blotches on flanks. To 1.5 m (5 ft.).

Fig. 103
Great
Barracuda

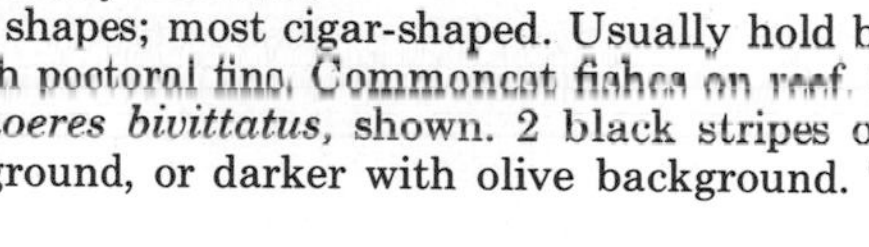

WRASSES Family Labridae
Various body shapes; most cigar-shaped. Usually hold body rigid
and swim with pectoral fins. Commonest fishes on reef. **Slippery**
Dick, *Halichoeres bivittatus,* shown. 2 black stripes on cream-
colored background, or darker with olive background. To 23 cm
(9 in.).

Fig. 104
Slippery
Dick

PARROTFISHES Family Scaridae

Large heavy scales in rows. Beaklike jaws. Thick heavy body. Tail never forked but may be crescent-shaped. Large and colorful. On reefs. **Queen Parrotfish,** *Scarus vetula,* shown. Male has crescent tail with orange longitudinal stripes on fins. Background color blue, with orange overtones. Wavy blue and orange stripes around mouth. Female gray with a broad horizontal white band from gill to tail. To 60 cm (2 ft.).

Fig. 105

Queen Parrotfish

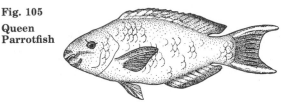

JAWFISHES Family Opisthognathidae

Small, blennylike, with huge mouth. Jaws extend beyond eye. Head bulbous. Long dorsal fin. In burrows. **Yellowhead Jawfish,** *Opisthognathus aurifrons,* shown. Pale yellow or grayish blue; no dark marks. To 9 cm (3½ in.).

Fig. 106

Yellowhead Jawfish

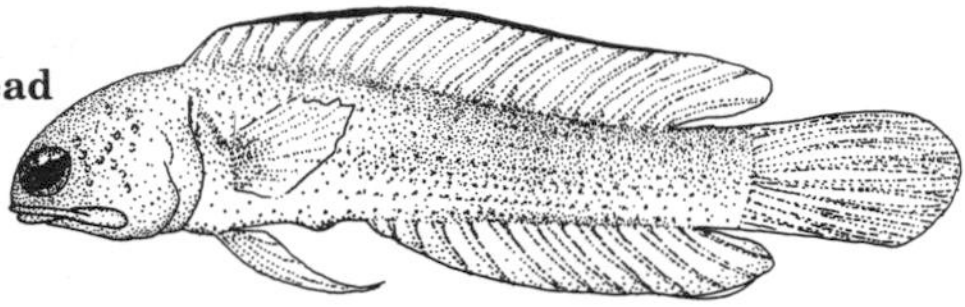

COMBTOOTH BLENNIES Family Blennidae

Small, scaleless. Teeth in comblike pattern. Single dorsal fin. Usually camouflaged; some species visible squatting on coral head. **Redlip Blenny,** *Ophioblennius atlanticus,* shown. Velvety black; with lips and edges of fins red. Squats on pectoral fins. To 11 cm (4½ in.).

Fig. 107

Redlip Blenny

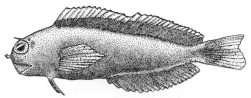

GOBIES Family Gobiidae
Small, with 2 dorsal fins; otherwise similar to clinid and comb-tooth blennies. Most have ventral fins united to form sucking disks. In tide pools, sponges. **Goldspot Goby,** *Gnatholepis thompsoni,* shown. Gold spot surrounded by black half-ring on shoulder. Brown bar under eye. To 6.3 cm (2½ in.).

Fig. 108
Goldspot
Goby

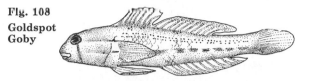

CLINID BLENNIES Family Clinidae
Small conical teeth. Some eel-like. Usually a long dorsal fin extending from head to tail. Most have fleshy hornlike cirri projecting above eyes. **Marbled Blenny,** *Paraclinus marmoratus,* shown. 5 vertical dark bands; 3 black spots. To 10 cm (4 in.).

Fig. 109
Marbled
Blenny

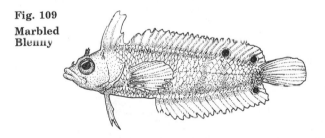

THREEFIN BLENNIES Family Tripterygiidae
Small. Dorsal fin in 3 distinct segments. Dark, with 5 brown-black bars on sides. On reefs. **Redeye Triplefin,** *Enneanectes pectoralis,* shown. 5 vertical brown bars on tan background; last bar darkest. To 3.8 cm (1½ in.).

Fig. 110
Redeye
Triplefin

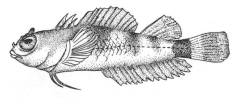

SURGEONFISHES Family Acanthuridae

Circular, laterally flattened. A thin white streak just before tail holds lancetlike spine. Commonest herbivores on reef. **Doctorfish,** *Acanthurus chirurgus,* shown. 10–12 dark vertical bars on brownish background. To 30 cm (1 ft.).

Fig. 111

Doctorfish

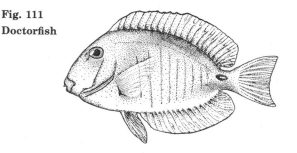

SOAPFISHES Family Grammistidae

Similar to basses. Large mouth, lobed fins. May produce sudslike froth of mucus if thrashing in water. **Soapfish,** *Rypticus saponaceus,* shown. Pale blotches on brown or gray background. To 34 cm (13½ in.).

Fig. 112

Soapfish

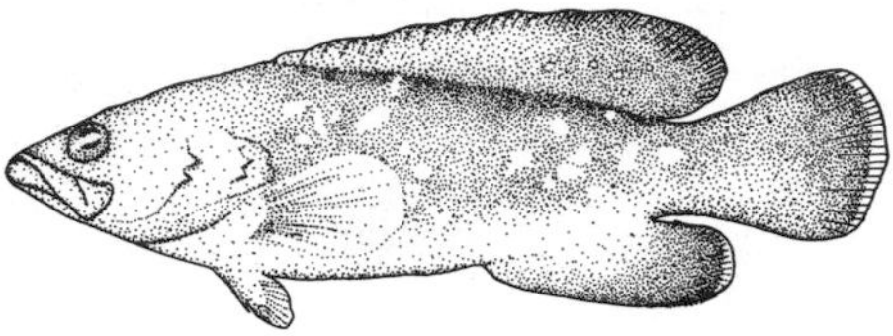

BASSLETS Family Grammidae

Small, colorful. Large eyes. Flaring dorsal fin; large anal fin. **Fairy Basslet,** *Gramma loreto,* shown (see also Pl. 24). Anterior purple (looks blue in deep water), posterior yellow. Large spot on dorsal fin. Under ledges. Common. To 7.5 cm (3 in.).

Fig. 113

Fairy
Basslet

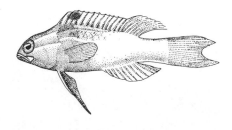

THREADFINS Family Polynemidae

Silvery. Half of pectoral fin normal-looking, half divided into fila-mentous rays. Face anchovylike, with snout protruding over mouth. **Smallscale Threadfin,** *Polydactylus oligodon,* shown. Silvery, almost invisible in surf. 2 dorsal fins; deeply forked tail. To 43 cm (17 in.).

Fig 114

Smallscale Threadfin

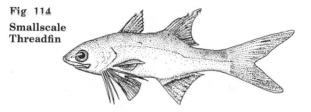

TILEFISHES Family Branchiostegidae

Elongate, with simple elongate dorsal and anal fins along most of body. Tail fin halfmoon-shaped. **Sand Tilefish,** *Malacanthus plumieri,* shown. Pale, sometimes greenish. In burrows at edge of Turtle Grass bed. To 60 cm (2 ft.).

Fig. 115

Sand Tilefish

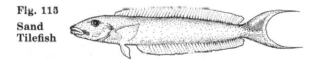

SWEEPERS Family Pempheridae

Small, compressed, deep-bodied. Long anal fin. Big eyes. In schools in caves. **Glassy Sweeper,** *Pempheris schomburgki,* shown. Beautiful coppery fish in glowing schools in caves. Red or dark stripe along anal fin. Nocturnal. To 15 cm (6 in.).

Fig. 116

Glassy Sweeper

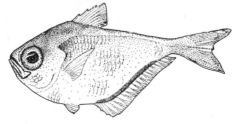

Order Pleuronectiformes

LEFTEYE FLOUNDERS Family Bothidae
Dorsoventrally flattened; one dark surface, one light. Both eyes on left side. **Peacock Flounder,** *Bothus lunatus,* shown. Tan or brown upper surface with blue rings. To 45 cm (1½ ft.).

Fig. 117
Peacock
Flounder

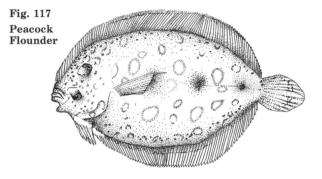

Order Tetradontiformes

TRIGGERFISHES and FILEFISHES Family Balistidae
Heavy, broad-bodied, compressed; 2 dorsal fins, the anterior one usually pointed and bony. *Triggerfishes:* dorsal spines can be locked in place by a "trigger"; swim by flapping soft dorsal fin. *Filefishes:* large vertical flap can be distended. **Ocean Triggerfish,** *Canthidermis sufflamen,* shown. Brownish or grayish without markings. To 60 cm (2 ft.).

Fig. 118
Ocean
Triggerfish

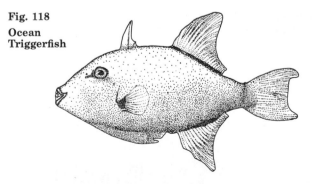

TRUNKFISHES Family Ostraciidae
Body enclosed within bony boxlike frame. Swim by lashing fins,
not tail. Usually a spotted or mosaic pattern. **Scrawled Cowfish,**
Acanthostracion quadricornis, shown. Black or blue pattern over
pale gray or green. Distinct horns. To 47 cm (19 in.).

**Fig. 119
Scrawled
Cowfish**

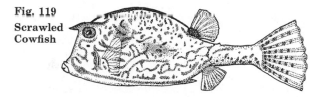

PUFFERS Family Tetraodontidae
Inflatable body covered with tiny spines. Large incisors; small
puckered mouth. Dorsal and anal fins far back, flapped for propulsion. **Bandtail Puffer,** *Sphoeroides spengleri,* shown. Row of
black spots. Back greenish, bottom whitish. To 18 cm (7 in.).

**Fig. 120
Bandtail
Puffer**

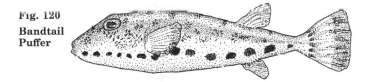

PORCUPINEFISHES Family Diodontidae
Inflatable, covered with long spines. **Porcupinefish,** *Diodon
hystrix,* shown (see also Pl. 26). Forehead spines smaller than those
just behind pectoral fins. Green back, pale brown sides; dark ring
around belly. To 1 m (3¼ ft.).

**Fig. 121
Porcupinefish**

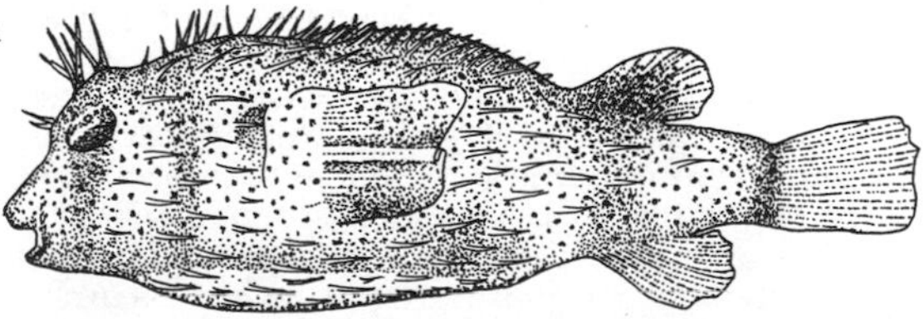

Sharks

William G. Bird

The word *shark* evokes dread in most people, even though they have never been face to face with one and are not likely to be. What mysterious influence do these oceanic carnivores have? We have invaded their domain, a kingdom unchallenged since the Devonian period some 350 million years ago. Now we are challenging the sharks for supremacy of the seas. Occasionally we lose when a shark attacks, but more often we destroy an animal about which we understand little. This destruction through fear and ignorance could very well upset the ocean's delicate ecological balance by removing an important link in a complex food web. There is still much to be learned about the role of sharks in marine ecosystems.

There are approximately 250 known species of living sharks. Most are small and probably harmless. One such example is *Squaliolus laticaudus,* which measures about 15 cm (6 in.) at maturity. Because it is rarely seen, it has not even been given a common name. The largest sharks — in fact, the largest of all fishes — the Basking Shark and the Whale Shark, are not carnivorous. They cruise the oceans, straining plankton through massive gill rakers, much like the giant baleen whales.

Only about 2 dozen of all species of sharks have actually been implicated in attacks on man. All sharks, however, should be treated with respect, since most are capable of inflicting bodily injury when provoked.

Sharks are classified with all other fishes in Superclass Pisces, but beyond this point they diverge. Together with skates, rays, and ratfishes, sharks belong to Class Chondrichthyes. They have been further classified in Subclass Elasmobranchii and Order Selachii. The shark is a member of the vertebrate subphylum but does not have a bone in its body. Instead it has a cartilaginous skeleton covered by a thin, nonbony, calcified layer. Unlike other fishes, which have 1 gill slit on either side of the body covered by a doorlike operculum, sharks have 5–7 gill slits with no covering. The fins of sharks are rigid, not hinged and depressible as in the bony fishes. The skin, although smooth in appearance, is covered by a mosaic of scales. These dermal denticles or placoid scales are different from the scales of other fishes, as they are made of the same material as the teeth. Pointing upward, these scales make the skin so coarse that it has been used as a type of sandpaper called shagreen. In many attacks serious wounds have been inflicted by the skin or fins of a shark. Sharks have no air bladder and therefore cannot change their buoyancy as do many bony fishes. As a consequence a shark will sink if it stops swimming. However, it can call on a number of compensatory mechanisms to slow its descent. For example, many sharks store a large supply of oil in the liver to afford a degree of positive buoyancy. Some scientists also believe that extra ballast in the form of inedible material in the cardiac stomach provides a modicum of negative buoyancy.

Sharks are amazingly well adapted to their role as carnivores in the vast reaches of the oceans. Their sense of hearing, which operates better at lower frequencies, can detect abnormal or struggling movements from a great distance. They are known to have been attracted from a distance of several kilometers to the scene of a disturbance, such as an underwater explosion. They can perceive sound as humans do, using their labyrinth and semicircular canals, but they also use 2 auxiliary systems: the lateral line system, found in all fishes, and the ampullae of Lorenzini, found only in sharks. The lateral line system is a thin line extending from the snout down the side of the body to the tail. The ampullae of Lorenzini are small pits under the snout anterior to the mouth. In both systems tiny hairs, located in canals under the skin, vibrate with the impact of sound waves, sending messages to the brain.

The shark's sense of smell is remarkably acute. It is a primary factor in the search for food. A tiny bleeding wound is often enough to invite an attack. It has been estimated that a shark's nares (nostrils) can detect blood when it is as dilute as 1 part per 100 million parts water. Substances other than blood, such as meat and fish juices, also stimulate sharks. Some substances are said to repel them, although the results of most experiments in this area are inconclusive. The shark's sense of taste, distinct from its sense of smell, helps it to distinguish between edible and inedible objects.

The eyesight of sharks is not as poor as was once suspected. Sharks seem to respond to intensity or brightness of light but not to color. However, their ability to distinguish contrasting shades is thought to explain a number of attacks. Studies have shown multicolored bathing suits to be attractive to sharks, especially if one of the colors is international orange (renamed by the experimenters yum yum yellow). A contrast in skin color, as when one is tanned unevenly, may also act as an attractant to sharks. In many sharks a reflecting layer, the tapetum lucidum, situated behind the retina, allows light to pass the ganglion cells of the retina several times, permitting the fish to see in dark or turbid waters. Most sharks also have a translucent membrane called the nictitans, which can cover the eye to provide protection. This membrane is often visible during an attack, when the eye may appear to be an opaque white void. Vision seems to be most important at close range, the dominant sense during the final attack rush.

Sharks' teeth are awesome weapons. Razor sharp and in many cases serrated along the cutting edge, the teeth are arranged in one or more functioning layers around both upper and lower jaws. Since sharks have no bones, the teeth are embedded in the gums and are easily dislodged. This poses no problem for a shark, since beneath the functioning rows of teeth are several other rows ready to move into place. Teeth are replaced frequently throughout the life of a shark. Associated with the teeth are nerve fibers whose junction is in the base of each functioning tooth. Any pressure on the tooth causes a reflex response within these nerve fibers that stimulates the muscles that close the jaw. Many a curious person has lost a finger or hand to a "dead" shark as he groped around inside the mouth. The force of a shark bite has been measured to be over 3 metric tons/cm^2 ($8\frac{1}{4}$ tons/in.^{2}) in a 2.4 m (8 ft.) shark.

Shark reproduction, like much of their behavior, has not been clearly described in many cases. It is known that fertilization is internal, with the male inserting one or both penislike organs, claspers, into the female genital opening. The sperms are then forced along a groove in the clasper. Most sharks are ovoviviparous — that is, the eggs hatch and develop within the female. The young are born alive. Newly born sharks are miniatures of their parents, ready, willing, and able to carry out their life's work.

In recent years the danger of sharks has been overdramatized. This has prompted the American Institute of Biological Science to compile a file of known shark attacks. According to a 1975 report there had been only 55 known shark attacks in all of the West Indies since records started being kept, and 105 attacks in Florida's waters. Nevertheless, caution is the better part of valor. Swimmers should pay heed to the following rules:

1. Never swim or dive alone; there is always a measure of safety in numbers.

2. Never remain in an area where blood or tissue juices are in the water. Spearfishermen should not keep their catch with them underwater on a stringer.

3. If dangerous sharks are known to be present, stay out of the water.

4. Avoid areas of turbid or dirty water where visibility is poor.

5. If a shark appears, move steadily but cautiously to safety. Avoid jerky, splashing movements.

6. Never provoke a shark, no matter how small or seemingly harmless.

7. Some sharks move inshore at night. Be particularly cautious when on night dives.

Common Species

Sharks are difficult to identify underwater. The accounts below will be most useful in identifying dead specimens. Whenever possible, sharks should be identified on the basis of tooth shape, the only feature exclusive to a given species; it is best to see an entire jaw, or at least tooth samples from both jaws. **Caution:** Do not get close enough to a live shark to be able to see its teeth clearly, and do not touch the snout of a dead shark (see p. 238). If it is impossible to examine teeth, use as many other features as possible. Keep in mind that coloration varies greatly within species and thus is not particularly diagnostic.

Except for the Nurse Shark (Family Orectolobidae), Shortfin Mako (Family Lamnidae), and hammerhead sharks (Family Sphyrnidae), the species listed below belong to Family Carcharhinidae.

Fig. 122

Shark

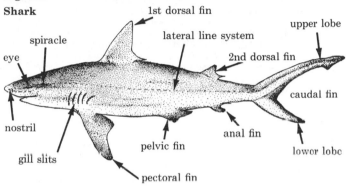

1st dorsal fin

upper lobe

spiracle

lateral line system

eye

2nd dorsal fin

caudal fin

nostril

anal fin

pelvic fin

lower lobe

gill slits

pectoral fin

SPINNER or LARGE BLACKTIP SHARK
Carcharhinus brevipinna
Very similar to Blacktip Shark (below), but *eyes smaller* (horizontal diameter $\frac{1}{4}$ the length of 1st gill slit, rather than $\frac{1}{3}$), *1st dorsal fin begins behind* (not over) *pectoral fins,* and *teeth in lower jaw unserrated.* Also similar to Reef Shark (see below). To 2.4 m (8 ft.)

BULL SHARK *Carcharhinus leucas*
Heavy-bodied. Gray above, fading to white below. *Snout blunt, rounded.* No spiracles or middorsal ridge. Teeth in upper jaw broadly triangular, coarsely serrated; ones in lower jaw narrower, finely serrated. To 3.6 m (12 ft.).

BLACKTIP SHARK *Carcharhinus limbatus*
Gray to blue-gray above, white below; *fins* usually conspicuously *black-tipped* (may be faded in older specimens); *wedge-shaped dark band from pectoral fins to pelvic fins.* Snout narrow, looks pointed from above. No spiracles or middorsal ridge. Teeth narrowly triangular, finely serrated. Similar to Spinner Shark (see above) and Reef Shark (see below). To 2.4 m (8 ft.).

REEF SHARK *Carcharhinus perezi*
Grayish above, fading to white below; fins of young may be dark. Similar to Blacktip Shark (above) and Spinner Shark (above), especially when young, but *gill slits* usually *shorter* and *1st dorsal fin more rounded.* Teeth triangular, serrated. To 2.7 m (9 ft.).

TIGER SHARK *Galeocerdo cuvieri*
Gray to grayish brown above, fading to white below; *dark vertical bars or blotches* along sides (pronounced in young, fade with age). *Snout very blunt, looks almost square from above.* Small inconspicuous spiracle behind each eye. Middorsal ridge between dorsal fins. Well-developed lateral keel on each side of caudal peduncle. *Teeth large, coarsely serrated* along full length, with *deep notch* at rear. To 9 m (30 ft.).

NURSE SHARK *Ginglymostoma cirratum*   **Fig. 123**
Yellowish to grayish brown above, fading to paler shade of similar color below; young may have dark spots. *2 barbels; one on each nostril.* Spiracle behind each eye. *No nictitans.* Dorsal fins large, well behind pectoral fins. *Lower lobe of caudal fin almost absent.* Teeth small, flattened, with inward-facing central cusp; designed for crushing prey. To 4.2 m (14 ft.).

Fig. 123

Nurse Shark

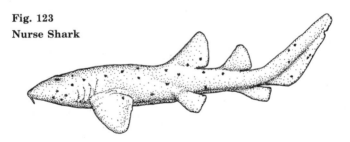

SHORTFIN MAKO *Isuris oxyrinchus*
In water, looks cobalt-blue above (deep blue-gray when freshly caught); pure white below. Snout sharply pointed. Caudal peduncle flattened laterally. *Caudal fin nearly symmetrical. Teeth very long, backward-curving,* unserrated, with no secondary cusps; become progressively more triangular toward back of jaw. To 3.6 m (12 ft.).

LEMON SHARK *Negaprion brevirostris*   **Fig. 124**
Yellowish brown above, fading to yellowish or whitish below. Snout blunt, looks rounded from above. No spiracles. Dorsal fins triangular; 2nd almost as large as 1st. *Teeth erect, unserrated, narrowly triangular.* To 3.3 m (11 ft.).

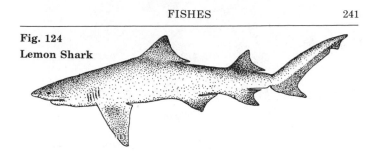

Fig. 124
Lemon Shark

HAMMERHEAD SHARKS *Sphyrna* species
Head hammer-shaped. At least 6 species, distinguishable from one
another by head characteristics. Potential size makes (1) Scalloped
Hammerhead, *S. lewini* — to 4 m (13 ft.) — (2) Great Hammerhead, *S. mokarran* — to 4.5 m (15 ft.) — and (3) Smooth Hammerhead, *S. zygaena* — to 4.2 m (14 ft.) — the most dangerous. These
3 species are gray or brownish to olive above, paler shade of same
color or white below. No spiracles. 1st dorsal fin very high and
erect; narrow in Great Hammerhead, broader in the others. Teeth
triangular, angled toward rear of jaw. In Scalloped Hammerhead,
teeth unserrated; in Great Hammerhead, finely serrated; in
Smooth Hammerhead, unserrated in young, may be finely serrated
in older specimens.

13

Intimate Relationships on the Reef

Paul Billeter

The coral reef, bathed in the radiation of the sun and presenting maximum stress to its inhabitants, stimulates change. The variability exhibited by the inhabitants is extraordinary. Every possible survival technique has been tried. If successful, the species lives on. On the reef, visible as nowhere else, are organisms that have taken the boldest of evolutionary steps: the development of interdependent relationships between separate species. Two organisms, sometimes quite diverse, forsaking independent lives, throw in their lot with each other in a more or less obligatory relationship.

The general term encompassing such relationships between species is symbiosis. There are 3 kinds of symbiosis: (1) parasitism, in which one organism benefits and the other is harmed; (2) commensalism, in which one organism benefits and the other is neutral (that is, neither harmed nor benefited); and (3) mutualism, in which both organisms benefit. A fourth kind of relationship is inquilism. An inquiline lives in the burrow, nest, or territory of its host in a more or less permanent arrangement.

These relationships are not simply isolated biological curiosities but often represent widespread and integral parts of the reef ecosystem. If you look for them diligently, examples of these relationships will be clearly visible as you float over the reef. Occasionally, as with the Long-spined Black Urchin and the Urchin Crab, the relationship is ephemeral. The crab usually lives within the protective perimeter of an urchin's spines, but it moves freely from urchin to urchin and can leave its cover at any time. More lasting is the relationship between the Red Snapping Shrimp and the Ringed Anemone. Mated pairs of these shrimp are found exclusively under the canopy of stinging tentacles of the anemone, but mates do not stay together for much longer than a month before one moves to a different anemone (and a different mate). Both the Urchin Crab and the Red Snapping Shrimp receive protection from their hosts. The Urchin Crab does not contribute to the relationship; thus it is commensal. The shrimp defends the anemone from fireworms and other predators, so this relationship is one of mutualism.

At the other, more permanent end of this spectrum of relationships lies the interaction between the coral animal itself and the one-celled plants living within its tissues. It is likely that without the presence of these mutualistic algae, the coral would not be capable of the high rate of metabolism that enables it to build reefs, and the whole coral reef ecosystem would not exist.

The degree of integration between symbiotic partners ranges from casual and part-time relationships to highly integrated partnerships with quite specific biochemical, physiological, morphological, and behavioral adaptations. It is difficult to categorize the thousands of symbiotic relationships because the nature of the relationships sometimes changes with time or other factors. Every reader of this book undoubtedly harbors in his body many potentially pathogenic bacteria or viruses without exhibiting any symptoms of disease or other harmful effects. These would have to be considered commensals. Go outdoors in cold weather, play a game of touch football, and then come indoors, tired and perspiring. The next day your commensals may have reacted to your altered physiological state by becoming disease-causing parasites.

Many symbiotic relationships have been reported from around coral reefs. This chapter will examine a few outstanding examples from the Florida-Caribbean region.

Endozoic Algae. Almost every invertebrate phylum has some members that harbor mutualistic one-celled plants called endozoic algae. They may be either green algae called zoochlorellae, dinoflagellates called zooxanthellae, or blue-green algae called zoocyanellae. In the marine environment zooxanthellae are the commonest. Presumably the majority of these relationships arose as autotroph-heterotroph symbioses (that is, a close relationship between producer and consumer). These relationships are probably of ancient origin. The coevolution of the partners has in some cases resulted in benefits that go beyond the usual animal-plant interactions. The coral's increased ability to produce its skeleton because of its zooxanthellae is an example (see p. 108).

The zooxanthellae of certain soft corals produce organic substances, including terpenes and related chemicals. (Terpenes are lipids — fats. Vitamin A, chlorophyll, shark liver oil, and natural rubber all contain terpenes.) Several terpenes are highly toxic to fishes, invertebrates, and bacteria. Thus the products of the zooxanthellae may be a defense against predation; they may prevent fouling by invertebrate larva, and they may kill harmful bacteria.

A fascinating relationship of the autotroph-heterotroph sort is chloroplast symbiosis. Certain sea slugs harbor not a crop of endozoic algae but simply the chloroplasts (photosynthetic organelles) obtained from the algae on which the sea slugs feed. These sea slugs pierce the algae cells and suck out the contents, including chloroplasts. Instead of being digested these stolen chloroplasts are maintained in the tissues of the slug, still carrying on photosynthesis. The preferred food of the slugs is often a group of green algae lacking internal cell walls. This makes it easier for the slugs to remove the chloroplasts. The common Lettuce Sea Slug, a chloroplast host, probably gets its chloroplasts from Grape Alga, an abundant species in the Caribbean.

Chloroplasts are especially abundant in a slug's areas of high metabolic activity, such as nerve centers, kidney, heart, and the mucous gland of the foot, which produces the carpet of slime on which the slug moves. In fact, it has been proven that carbon processed by the chloroplasts becomes part of the slime.

One researcher has found evidence that, while still inside the Hawaiian Sea Slug, the chloroplasts may be able to synthesize chlorophyll. Such evidence suggests that the slug possesses genes for regulating chlorophyll synthesis and perhaps even reproduction of the chloroplasts. This would indicate a highly integrated physiological relationship between slug and chloroplasts.

Chloroplast symbiosis is a particularly interesting relationship because it is not really a symbiosis in the pure sense. The relationship of the sea slug to the alga is one of predation. The relationship of the sea slug to the chloroplasts is more like a theft of services. The sea slug is often an adept and versatile biological burglar. For example, several sea slug species incorporate pigments from ingested food into their body tissues. This affords them camouflage. The feathered nudibranch *Fiona pinnata* becomes purplish when feeding on the By-the-wind Sailor, a jellyfish. The purplish hue is obtained from the prey and disappears if the nudibranch is fed colorless food, such as fish flesh.

Nematocysts and Symbiosis. Possibly the most accomplished of the nudibranch thieves are certain species that feed on cnidarians and obtain unfired nematocysts with their meal. These are deposited in specialized structures at the tips of the cerata (see p. 266). Here, exposed to the exterior, they serve a protective function for the animal. The Blue Glaucus, a pelagic nudibranch, obtains nematocysts by feeding on the tentacles of the Portuguese Man-of-war.

In the Caribbean and other warm seas the 7.5 cm (3 in.) Man-of-war Fish is found swimming among the tentacles of the Portuguese Man-of-war. Other members of the butterfish family, especially juveniles, seek shelter amid the stinging tentacles of that jellyfish and other pelagic cnidarians. The Caribbean Butterfish is commonly found associated with the Jellyball or Cannonball Jellyfish. The Man-of-war Fish is considered safe only as long as it avoids its host's tentacles. But the butterfish family may be more resistant to stings than other fishes. In fact, the Harvestfish feeds on the Sea Nettle, another stinging jellyfish. As with the Clownfish of the Pacific, it is speculated that the Man-of-war Fish and its relatives may lure other fishes into the deadly tangles of their host's tentacles. The jellyfish has no metabolic dependence on its fish associates and survives quite well without the Man-of-war Fish. This relationship seems to be a facultative mutualism — that is, a relationship not indispensable for the survival of either partner.

An example of facultative commensalism may be seen in the relationship between the Long-spined Black Urchin and the schools of larval fishes that swim among the urchin's spines. Just as the Man-of-war Fish seeks safety among the tentacles of its jellyfish partner, the larval fishes find a haven among the sharp spines of the urchin, where predators cannot penetrate. The herbivorous urchins receive no benefit from the relationship — only the fishes do.

To judge by the number and variety of associations between cnidarians and other organisms, the protection afforded by nematocysts is a commodity in great demand. Certain hermit crabs, such as the Star-eyed Hermit, are almost invariably found in association with sea anemones. The Tricolor Anemone is almost always attached to the snail shell in which the crab lives. The presence of the anemone on the shell is no accident, as both partners exhibit specific behavioral responses that facilitate their union. The crab can initiate the association by gently tapping the anemone, upon which the anemone relaxes, releasing its hold on the substratum. The crab then lifts the anemone and places it on its shell. The anemone can also initiate the association. When the hermit crab comes near, the tentacles of the anemone reach out and cling to the crab's shell. The response of an anemone to the tapping of its host and its hopping aboard a passing crab are both advanced behavior for a creature with such a primitive nervous system.

That either partner can initiate the establishment of this symbiosis suggests a benefit to both. The advantage of the relationship to the crab has been dramatically illustrated in experiments on the reaction of the Common Atlantic Octopus to the Star-eyed Hermit Crab. The octopus is one of the major enemies of the large hermit crab. It was shown that crabs without anemones are attacked faster and that the attacks are more frequent, last longer, and always result in death to the crabs. Crabs with anemone partners always survive.

The advantage of the relationship to the anemone is less well understood. It is speculated that by hitching a ride on the back of the scavenging crab the anemone is transported to food sources and environments not otherwise available to it.

The anemone has also been found attached to the shell of several species of spider crabs. The crabs are protected not only by camouflage (they attach pieces of sea grass, alga, sponge, and so forth to their carapaces) but also by procuring defensive weaponry (the anemone).

The Star-eyed Hermit Crab also associates with anemones other than the Tricolor Anemone. It collects small anemones, such as *Sagartiomorphe gutatta,* and places them along the inner lip of its shell.

Another example of a protective mutualism is the relationship between certain colonial anemones (Order Zoanthidea) of the genera *Parazoanthus* and *Epizoanthus* and their sponge hosts. These zoanthid anemones can be found on the surface of several species of sponges, including the Tub Sponge and the Common Loggerhead Sponge. The yellow or orange colors of the anemones are in marked contrast to the drab colors of their hosts. Experiments have shown that extracts of the anemone are toxic to certain fishes and that the Rock Beauty, a sponge-eating butterflyfish, will not eat sponges with anemones growing on them. This suggests that the contrasting colors of the anemone may serve as a warning to fishes and thus protect the sponge from predation. The sponge, used as a substratum, benefits the anemone by creating food-carrying currents in which the anemone is constantly bathed (see p. 72).

Cleaning Symbiosis. Cleaning symbiosis is an association in which certain shrimps or small fishes, called cleaners, feed on the ectoparasites or damaged tissues of the skin and oral cavity of host fishes. In this form of mutualism the cleaner receives food, and the host is rid of irritating parasites. Table 4 lists some of the Caribbean organisms reported to be cleaners. The list of species that avail themselves of the cleaners' services is too long to present here. It probably includes the majority of inshore fishes and many larger species that come from deeper waters to be cleaned.

Cleaning activity is often carried on at "cleaning stations." Look for a heterogeneous crowd of fishes, some lining up awaiting their turn. You may be lucky enough to see them standing on their heads, "yawning," or taking other uncharacteristic poses. As you swim closer, the fishes will reluctantly retreat.

Examine the site where you last saw the fishes. You may be greeted by a cleaner — a Sharknose Goby or a Neon Goby scooting over a boulder of brain coral, for instance, or a purple Pederson's Cleaning Shrimp undulating its long white antennae from a crevice in a coral rock. The shrimp often shares its crevice with a large anemone, such as the Ringed Anemone or the Giant Caribbean Anemone. (The relationship between the shrimp and the anemone is probably a protective symbiosis in its own right.) If you place a finger near the shrimp, it may inspect your finger with its antennae and may even climb aboard your hand. Then it will search for parasites, tugging at the small hairs of your hand. The gobies will not be so cooperative in exhibiting their cleaning behavior but will be quite bold and curious. They will not often take flight unless you make a threatening gesture or get too close. When you locate a cleaning station, approach it slowly and stop about 3 m (10 ft.) away. Position yourself on the bottom. (Snorkelers can simply float quietly at the surface and watch the activities below.)

The unusual movements of both the cleaner and host are a form of body language. Experimenters have described the ritual behavior engaged in by certain cleaning fishes and cleaning shrimps. The

Table 4. Cleaning Symbionts

Fishes

Sharknose Goby (goby)
Spanish Hogfish (wrasse)
Spotfin Hogfish (wrasse)
Slippery Dick (wrasse)
Bluehead (juveniles only; wrasse)

Yellowtail Damselfish (damselfish)
Porkfish (grunt)
Fairy Basslet (sea bass)
Bar Jack (juveniles only; jack)

Shrimps

Spotted Cleaning Shrimp
Pederson's Cleaning Shrimp
Banded Coral or Barber Pole Shrimp
Golden Coral Shrimp

Red-backed Cleaning Shrimp or Scarlet Lady
Peppermint or Veined Shrimp
St. Vincent Cleaning Shrimp
Two-clawed Shrimp

host fish approaches the cleaning station and "poses" (yawns, flares fins and/or gills, and so forth). This evokes responses from the cleaner, such as a "cleaner dance" (for the cleaning shrimp this is a rocking of the body and whipping of the antennae from side to side and back and forth). Next the cleaner inspects the host and removes the parasites. These ritual movements initiate and maintain the cleaning interaction. Other ritual movements signal the termination of cleaning.

Communication between different species of cleaners and hosts can be well developed. Some cleaning species rely entirely on cleaning for their food supply (obligate cleaners); others are only part-time cleaners (facultative cleaners). The most well-developed communication is found in obligate cleaners. The evolution of communication usually results in a ritualization of the communication patterns. This constancy makes the communication more efficient by reducing ambiguity. Certain host species exhibit a high degree of ritualization. In such cases the cleaner-host relationship is highly evolved. For example, a species of parrotfish performs tail stands 89% of the time it approaches cleaning stations; a species of surgeonfish poses in a head-up diagonal attitude 91% of the time. These poses clearly mean "clean me" and are correlated with a significant increase in cleaner activity. The highly adapted cleaners are almost never eaten by other species. Their distinct coloration and behavior are recognized as a sort of guild sign. In cases where the cleaners do not depend entirely on cleaning for food, communication is more ambiguous; sometimes these facultative cleaners are eaten by their hosts.

Most cleaning fishes are small and brightly colored species from such families as the wrasses, butterflyfishes, and gobies, which typically feed by nipping and browsing on surface growths among the cracks and crevices of the reef surface. Cleaning symbiosis probably evolved when certain species enlarged their feeding range by venturing onto the surfaces of members of their own or other species (probably herbivores or nonthreatening carnivores). This mutually beneficial relationship became more specialized. Other cleaners and hosts were added, and the result was the contemporary spectrum of cleaning associations.

Studies on the role of cleaning in reef ecology have produced varied results. In one experiment, after all cleaners were removed from a small reef, most other species left the reef. The territorial species that remained exhibited an increase in ectoparasites, invasion by microorganisms, and frayed and ragged fins. A similar experiment on a small Pacific reef did not result in increased symptoms of parasitism. Cleaning therefore seems to be a vital service in some places and less crucial in others. As symbiosis, it seems to range from obligate mutualism to facultative commensalism.

Parasitism. The ecological phenomenon of parasitism is similar to predation in that one of the interacting species feeds on the other. The parasite-host relationship differs from the predator-prey relationship in that parasites are usually smaller and more numerous than their hosts, live in prolonged or continuous association with them, and do not devour them.

Virtually every animal phylum includes some members that are parasites. Probably every animal you see on the reef (or anywhere else) has one or more parasites living on or in its body. The most conspicuous group of parasites of Caribbean fishes is probably the ectoparasitic isopods.

Isopods are crustacean arthropods. Both parasitic and free-living species are common in the marine environment. In addition, several commensal species may be found in the galleries of sponges or sharing burrows with other crustaceans.

The species that parasitize fishes (see Pls. 23, 26) are mostly members of Cymothoidae and related families. These are large isopods, often pigmented and in some instances facultative parasites. They attach almost anywhere on their hosts, especially on skin, fins, gills, and oral cavity. *Anilocra* is often seen attached to the head or gill covers of various snappers, grunts, and butterflyfishes.

The cymothoid isopods start life as males and become females later. This reproductive strategy ensures that the largest (that is, the oldest) individuals are females, which can produce and brood eggs. Isopods brood their eggs in a ventral chamber called the marsupium. Specimens seen attached to fishes are often gravid females, carrying large numbers of developing eggs on their undersurface. The presence of a mature female on a fish inhibits the development of males, preventing them from changing to females, ensuring the presence of a useful mate nearby. Thus the timing of the sex change is not strictly innate but is affected by the proximity and sex ratio of the population. Some immature individuals can pass through the male stage very rapidly without developing functional male organs and can thus also respond to population demands if females are in short supply.

Isopod parasites are often modified for their parasitic way of life. Their mouthparts are piercing and are used to penetrate the host so that they can feed on blood and tissue fluids. They also possess stout claws for attachment. Lesions caused by the claws and necrosis (tissue destruction) of the gills are often evident when an isopod is removed from a captured host. Many isopods are blind. The genus *Cymothoa* has several representatives that illustrate various stages in the degeneration of the eyes (sometimes a characteristic of parasitic animals). *C. exigua* has well-developed eyes; *C. caraibica* has small eyes; *C. excisa*, a common parasite of the mouth region of porgies, snappers, and chubs, has eyes in its male stage but loses them when it becomes a female; *C. ostreum* is totally blind. These modifications and reductions are minor compared to those of many of the parasitic copepods and barnacles, and even to isopods that parasitize crabs. These parasites are so highly modified that in their adult form they are unrecognizable as crustaceans.

Other Symbioses. The Elkhorn Coral or Gall Crab is a common commensal on Elkhorn Coral (and sometimes on Staghorn Coral). Look for a small crater with a raised white rim, about the size of a dime, on the branches of Elkhorn Coral. This is the home of the crab. As with most true crabs, the eggs hatch into a microscopic, planktonic zoea larva that grows and metamorphoses into a juvenile resembling a tiny lobster. This larva settles onto the surface of the coral. The coral's skeleton grows around the crab, forming a gall. The crab is quite mobile and is not restricted to its gall. If a crab is removed from its gall, its former home is readily reoccupied by another. Unlike most crabs, the Elkhorn Coral or Gall Crab is a filter-feeder, but it has been observed eating organic detritus and occasionally coral mucous accretions.

The Queen Conch is host to a symbiotic cardinalfish, the Conchfish. It is often found in the bottom of native boats in which these large snails are being collected. The relationship between the conch and the small fish is not well understood. The Conchfish is commonest in conchs from quiet water and seems to be nocturnal, inhabiting the snail's shell during the day and leaving at night to feed on small crustaceans. The conch apparently is a hideaway for the fish. Whether the fish returns to the same conch each night is unknown.

The Pearlfish inhabits the rectum of the Five-toothed Sea Cucumber (see p. 196). It enters the cucumber by backing in and occasionally has to force its way into its unwilling host. The fish has no scales; thus entry is easier. Its anus is near its gills, so it need not come far out of its host to excrete wastes. Like the Conchfish, the Pearlfish is nocturnal. The association is highly evolved; a Pearlfish can be attracted to a model of the cucumber, but only if the water emitted from the anus of the model contains cucumber mucus.

Look for red, brown, or yellow patches on the dead bases of corals, especially Staghorn Coral. The deeper you go, the more common sponge parasitism will be on the coral (see p. 124). Some species of sponges are exclusively parasitic; others serve as hosts to innumerable organisms, exhibiting every type of symbiotic relationship from parasitism to commensalism. The sponges *Cliona* and *Siphonodictyon* bore into corals and cover them with thin crusts, eventually killing the whole colony.

Swim close to a large sponge. You will hear a cacophony of pops and clicks as hundreds of tiny pistol and snapping shrimps inside the sponge go about their daily activities, popping their claws to stun prey organisms or to drive away potential enemies.

Sponges are apartment houses for symbionts of every description. Small gobies spend their lives in the galleries of massive sponges, never venturing outside (see p. 125). Worms of Family Syllidae can be found by the thousands inside sponges, their color indicating that they feed on the sponge's tissues. (The worms are transparent; so their color is determined by the food inside their digestive tracts.)

The coral snails live on corals, extracting food and zooxanthellae from the digestive tracts or simply browsing on the polyps themselves (see p. 115). The beautiful Flamingo Tongue spends its life on sea fans and other soft corals, browsing on the polyps. In a truly symbiotic relationship the snails normally do not damage the coral faster than it can recover.

A well-developed relationship exists between gobies and several species of pistol shrimps. A goby squats on its pectoral fins at the mouth of a shrimp's burrow. It ventures forth on short food-getting excursions but always returns to the burrow. When danger approaches, the nearly blind shrimp backs into the protective depths when it sees the goby dart headfirst into the same hole. This clear-cut inquilism can be seen on soft bottoms near the reef, usually in water about 2 m ($6\frac{1}{2}$ ft.) deep (see p. 215).

14

Dangerous Marine Animals

Ray Granade

Millions of years before man developed chemical warfare on land, marine creatures were using an array of effective chemical weapons in their fight for survival in the sea. Some, such as the sea anemones, jellyfish, and venomous cone snails, have used these weapons offensively, to capture prey, and defensively, to avoid being preyed upon. On the other hand, the tubules of Cuvier in sea cucumbers (see p. 194) appear to have evolved for strictly defensive purposes. And evolution has also provided some fishes, such as the scorpionfishes, with venomous spines as a means of defense. The spines themselves have developed from what were once fins, whereas the venom glands are apparently evolutionary modifications of mucous glands.

Most scientists who work with animal poisons agree that, although some of them may be simply incidental or "biochemical byproducts," many or most have evolved for a particular purpose. Like camouflage and symbiosis, they help the species endure in an often hostile, competitive environment.

Even a poison that is not actively employed as a weapon but simply produced in the body of an animal may serve a purpose. For instance, the Cabezon, a small fish of the Pacific coast, lays eggs that are poisonous. It has been observed that these are avoided by other animals that would normally feed on fish roe. Thus this species is aided in its survival by producing eggs that other animals have learned to avoid.

Throughout recorded history marine poisons have been a source of both fascination and concern to man. Despite centuries of interest and many years of active research, little is known about them. Not many of the thousands of poisonous substances in sea creatures have been isolated in pure form, and the chemical structure has been determined for only a few of these.

Marine poisons often have a very specific, selective action on one or more physiological processes in the human body. They may alter or inhibit the transmission of nerve messages, or they may have some direct effect on the heart.

Research on marine poisons may lead to the development of useful new drugs. Drugs that relieve pain, correct heart ailments, and relax tense muscles prior to surgery are but a few examples among many. Some marine substances appear able to fight certain forms of cancer; others are potent antibiotics.

Poison may be defined in various ways but is used here to mean any substance (whether a single chemical compound or a mixture of compounds) that has a harmful effect on a living organism. Marine poisons are usually divided into 2 basic types. Toxins are those that cause illness when taken into the body, as when a poisonous fish is eaten. Venoms, on the other hand, are delivered by a specialized apparatus, such as a hollow spine or fangs. A toxin is often dispersed through part or all of the body of a poisonous animal; a venom is usually produced by a gland near the base of a fang or spine, which delivers it into the victim.

The most deadly forms of sea life do not occur in Florida and Caribbean waters. In the tropical Pacific, on the other hand, stings of the Pacific Sea Wasp (a jellyfish) and stonefishes cause excruciating pain and may bring death within minutes. In the same region a carelessly handled Geography Cone Snail may inflict a sting that looks like nothing more than a tiny pinprick, but the venom can kill within minutes. And certain species of pufferfishes of Hawaii are so poisonous they bear the common name maki-maki, which means deadly death.

All of the above-mentioned animals have close relatives in our area that, though not as lethal, are still hazardous and must be treated with caution.

Venomous Marine Animals

Marine animals have developed chemical weapons to aid in their survival struggle against one another, and many can use these weapons quite effectively against humans as well. Most of these animals are classified as venomous. They introduce a venom into their victim by means of an apparatus ranging in size from the microscopic nematocyst of a jellyfish to the tail spine of a stingray, which is sometimes over 30 cm (1 ft.) long.

You will probably have little or no trouble with stinging sea animals when you explore the shore and reef as long as you exercise reasonable caution. But it is a good idea to be prepared by taking along a simple first-aid kit, which might include the following:

rubbing alcohol   meat tenderizer
antibiotic salve   adhesive tape
ammonia water (dilute)   gauze bandages
aspirin (or other pain reliever)   vinegar
tweezers

Most injuries inflicted by marine organisms, even those that are not serious, can become infected. Such wounds must be properly cared for to prevent this (see, for example, the treatment for coral cuts on p. 254). Infection is indicated by redness, swelling, tenderness, and pain around the wound. If swelling and pain become severe or if a fever develops, see a doctor.

Most venomous animals discussed in this chapter are described elsewhere in the book. We are concerned here primarily with the types of injury they can cause and how each type should be treated. Although knowledge of proper first-aid procedures is important, the timeworn adage "An ounce of prevention is worth a pound of cure" holds as true here as anywhere. One simple way to prevent many kinds of injury is to wear gloves when in the water. If you are a newcomer to the tropical marine environment, the most important preventive measure you can take is to learn to recognize as soon as possible the marine fauna for which you must be on the lookout. Until you are able to, if in doubt, *don't touch!*

Sponges. Two species of stinging sponges are worthy of note: the Fire Sponge and the Touch-me-not Sponge. Good advice, as anyone who has handled it with bare hands can tell you.

When handled, many sponges can cause skin irritation because of the abrasiveness of their spicules. However, the 2 species above seem to contain poisonous substances that are apparently delivered through breaks in the skin made by the spicules. The results are burning, itching, redness, and swelling. Some people are more sensitive than others; indeed, the symptoms may be due, at least in part, to an allergic reaction.

Not much can be done for sponge stings except to wash the affected area and apply alcohol to soothe the pain and itching, which will normally subside within a fairly short time anyway.

Cnidarians. This phylum contains perhaps the best-known sea stingers. Numerous venomous species occur in all 3 classes of Cnidaria.

In Class Hydrozoa the fire corals and the Portuguese Man-of-war are most significant. Flat-topped Fire Coral and Crenelated Fire Coral are abundant in most reef areas. Their sting is painful. You may be deceived by Crenelated Fire Coral, as it often forms a thin coat on dead gorgonians, true corals, and others, and it may be nearly the same color as the organisms it coats. It is important to be able to spot fire coral in all its many guises. A single brush against it will probably convince you of this. Ask someone knowledgeable about the reef to point out several examples of it, and carefully study Pls. 11 and 17.

The Portuguese Man-of-war, a colonial hydrozoan, has a potent sting. Large numbers are sometimes washed up on beaches after a storm. The tentacles, which may be broken up on the sand, can sting for some time after the animals are dead.

Class Scyphozoa (true jellyfish) contains many venomous species. A number of them cause stings so mild that they can hardly be felt, but some can cause serious and even fatal injuries. The most wicked stings are delivered by sea wasps (Order Cubomedusae). These are represented in Florida and Caribbean waters by the genera *Carybdea* and *Chiropsalmus* (see p. 66). The stings of other jellyfish are generally less serious.

In Class Anthozoa the Stinging Anemone (p. 75) seems to be the only stinger of significance in our area.

The results of cnidarian stings range from mild discomfort to great agony. However, fatalities in this part of the world are rare. Most cases are mild, the only symptom being a stinging sensation at the site of contact. More severe cases produce throbbing or shooting pains, with swelling and blistering of the affected area. Some stinging, such as that caused by cubomedusans and the Portugese Man-of-war, results in more serious symptoms, including violent pains, muscle cramps, nausea, difficulty in breathing, shock, paralysis, and convulsions.

The first step in the treatment of cnidarian stings is important. The tentacles often cling to the skin, continuously injecting venom. Immediately examine the wounded area for pieces of tentacle and remove them. Rubbing the area with sand is often recommended, but this will only break up the tentacles, allowing them to discharge more nematocysts. Instead, pick off the tentacles carefully, using gloves, a piece of cloth, seaweed, or a towel. Or sprinkle on powder or dry sand and scrape it off gently.

Apply alcohol as soon as possible. Dilute ammonia water (about 10 parts water to 1 part household ammonia) might also help. Meat tenderizer, though it might seem a rather unlikely remedy, is also sometimes effective and should have a place in your first-aid kit. One component of cnidarian venom is a protein, and proteins are broken down by an enzyme in the meat tenderizer. Wet the wounded area and apply the meat tenderizer liberally. Leave it on for at least 5–10 minutes.

If you are stung while swimming or diving, leave the water as soon as possible unless the sting is a mild one. The pain (and other symptoms) may rapidly grow worse and could impair your swimming ability. If pain is very severe or if you experience any of the more serious symptoms listed above, a prompt visit to a doctor may be in order.

Stony corals, such as Elkhorn, are sometimes reported to cause a sting. More important, though, even a gentle brush against one of these corals may result in a nasty cut or scrape that will heal slowly and will be prone to infection.

To treat a coral injury, wash it as soon as possible with soap and fresh water. Check carefully for coral fragments in the wound. Then apply an antiseptic (better yet, a triple-antibiotic salve, available in most pharmacies). If wounds are extensive, you might cover them loosely with a gauze bandage. Watch for signs of infection.

Mollusks. In this phylum 2 classes, Gastropoda and Cephalopoda, have venomous members. Venomous gastropods are represented by the cone snails, *Conus*. Of all the animals in the sea that make their living as professional poisoners, cone snails surely have the most interesting venom apparatus. Their venom-filled radular teeth are delivered, like tiny harpoons, by a thrust of the proboscis.

Some Pacific *Conus* species are deadly to man, but *Conus* stings are rare in our region. The Atlantic Alphabet Cone has been known to sting occasionally. Its sting was said to be no worse than a severe bee sting, and recovery was rapid. Nevertheless, all cone shells should be handled cautiously. Pick them up by the posterior (the large end) or with tongs. A *Conus* sting should be treated like a fish sting (see p. 257).

Among the cephalopods, octopods may be considered venomous and of potential hazard to man. The Common Atlantic Octopus, for example, can inflict a deep bite with its powerful beak, and a venomous substance may be introduced into the wound. This results in a burning or tingling sensation and then radiating pain, swelling, and profuse bleeding (the venom often has an anticoagulant action). Octopus bites should be given the same treatment as fish stings (p. 257).

Despite the sinister reputation of octopods, they are of little hazard to the wader or diver. They are shy and retiring animals. When handling an octopus, wear cloth gloves (to avoid letting it get a firm hold with its suction disks) and keep your hands away from its mouth.

Echinoderms. In Florida and Caribbean waters sea urchins are the only echinoderms that might be considered venomous. Although not actually dangerous, they probably share with the fire corals the dubious distinction of being the most noxious nuisance on the reef.

With their fearful spines sea urchins, such as the Long-spined Black Urchin, are well equipped to cause trouble. The spines are very sharp and readily penetrate the skin but do not come out easily. A look at a spine under a magnifying glass will show why: it bears countless tiny barbs pointed toward the tip, like porcupine quills. Remember that the spines of this sea urchin can penetrate a shoe sole, gloves, a wet suit, or practically any other type of clothing. Watch for Long-spined Black Urchins when you dive or wade at night. An area where none are visible in the daytime may be teeming with them after dark. And give sea urchins — all stinging animals for that matter — an extra-wide berth when there is a surge or strong current that might sweep you over them.

Treatment of sea urchin injuries consists of alleviating pain and removing any spines that have broken off in the flesh. Soaking the injury in hot water reduces the pain in many cases, but removing the spines is not so easy. Sometimes they can be pulled out with tweezers, but this usually just breaks them up. The traditional West Indian method of treatment concentrates on removing the spines by dissolving them in a weak acid. First some lime juice (citric acid) is rubbed over the area where the grayish spines are visible through the skin. Then warm vinegar (acetic acid) is applied. After about 10 minutes, more vinegar is dabbed on and a candle flame is held about 1 cm ($\frac{1}{2}$ in.) from the skin to keep the vinegar hot. The spines can be seen to be dissolving. After another 10 minutes of this treatment, the affected part is dried and melted candle wax is dripped on. After it cools and hardens, it is peeled off, taking with it the remnants of the spines. This technique cures the patient either by the validity of its chemistry or by the mystique of the hot vinegar and candles.

The latest method uses a beer bottle and meat tenderizer. Roll the bottle over the spines to crush them so that they will dissolve more easily. Then smear on meat tenderizer, which contains enzymes to digest proteins. This is supposed to destroy the proteinaceous toxins on the spines. Normally the spines are absorbed by the body within a couple of days. There may be a purple discoloration around the wound, which is simply pigment diffusing away from the spines; don't let it worry you.

Some sea urchins, such as the Sea Egg, have spines that, though relatively blunt and less likely to penetrate than those of the Long-spined Black Urchin, are less likely to dissolve once in the flesh. If they are still present after a few days, they may need to be removed by a physician.

Worms. Two polychaetes, the Fireworm and the Red-tipped Fireworm, can make things unpleasant for anyone who touches them. Their setae (bristlelike structures; see p. 135) are long and brittle, possibly carrying a venom. On the slightest contact with the skin the setae penetrate and break off, causing inflammation, itching, and numbness. When you handle fireworms, wear rubber gloves. The bristles will penetrate cotton gloves. Do not put the worms into a collecting bag; the bristles will become embedded in it and are sure to find their way into your hands later.

If you do come in contact with a fireworm, do not rub the injured area. Remove the bristles carefully with the sticky side of a piece of adhesive tape. Then apply alcohol or dilute ammonia water (about 10 parts water to 1 part household ammonia).

Fishes. In the area covered by this book most venomous fishes belong to 2 groups: stingrays and scorpionfishes of the genus *Scorpaena.*

In the Florida, Bahamas, and Caribbean area, perhaps the most dangerous rays are the stingrays (Family Dasyatidae). With the venomous, serrated spine on their whiplike tail they can cause an extremely painful and often serious injury. Their habit of lying partially buried in sandy bottoms makes them hard to spot, especially at night. When stepped on, a stingray can whip its tail upward, driving the spine into its victim. The spine itself often causes a deep cut or puncture. But it is the spine's venom that is responsible for agonizing pain and other effects. Stingrays (unless caught by hand or speared) will not attack a swimmer or diver. In fact, they cannot use their tail weapon effectively unless they are at least partially immobilized.

Two scorpionfishes are of concern in our area. The Spotted Scorpionfish is usually found on rocky or coral bottoms in shallow water. The Grass Scorpionfish is common on shallow grass beds. Other species occur but are smaller, less common, and less dangerous. Scorpionfishes are remarkably well camouflaged. Usually lying motionless, they blend into their background so well that they may be invisible. Their main venomous armament consists of a row of dorsal spines, each with a venom-producing gland.

Various symptoms may accompany injuries inflicted by venomous fishes. But severe pain is almost always the first one. Pain is usually the only symptom caused by Caribbean scorpionfishes. But stingray injuries may also cause faintness, rapid and irregular heartbeat, sweating, and muscular cramps. Death rarely follows such injuries.

Treatment of fish stings should begin as soon as possible. Stingrays often inflict open wounds, which should be washed thoroughly with seawater. It may be possible to wash out some of the venom. Examine the wound for pieces of the spine (or the sheath tissue that surrounds it) that may have broken off. Scorpionfish wounds are punctures, so removing the venom will usually not be possible. As in the case of jellyfish stings, a person who is stung by a fish should get out of the water as soon as possible. The victim should be kept warm and quiet.

There is some disagreement among physicians and researchers about exactly how to treat a fish sting. Most recommend that the injured area be soaked in hot water for at least 30 minutes. Application of a tourniquet is sometimes recommended, but a tourniquet or any other device that restricts blood flow is dangerous (it could cause the loss of a limb) and should be used only by a physician or other person trained in its proper use and aware of its hazards.

After a period of soaking, the pain of scorpionfish stings usually subsides without further treatment. In the case of stingray injuries, though, a physician should be consulted. This is especially true if the wound is deep or extensive, if pain is very severe or long-lasting, or if infection develops. A tetanus shot is recommended.

Stingrays usually strike their victims on a limb, but if the sting is in an area such as the chest or neck (as when the victim falls on a stingray in the water), it may be more serious. Medical help should be sought immediately.

Toxic Marine Animals

One authority on marine toxicology estimates that worldwide about 30,000 people are poisoned each year by eating toxic sea life. Undoubtedly this number will rise as man turns increasingly to the sea as a source of food.

Clupeoid poison is a powerful toxin found in certain members of the herring family that are eaten. This poison is rare, but unfortunately it is lethal. It has been said that if you start eating at the head of the fish, you will be dead before you come to the tail. Perhaps the most bizarre form of fish poisoning is given the impressive name ichthyoallyeinotoxism, though it is more commonly called hallucinatory fish poisoning. Occurring primarily in the Pacific, it results occasionally from eating fishes of the mullet and goatfish families. The victim first notices dizziness and loss of coordination; he may suffer profound mental depression and hallucinations; and if he tries to sleep, he usually has terrifying nightmares. Although not very ill physically, he often has a strong feeling that he is about to die. Almost nothing is known about this odd type of poisoning. Luckily for its victims, it is apparently never fatal, and its symptoms usually disappear in 24 hours.

Ciguatera. On July 7, 1972, the Brazilian cargo ship *Sao Marcos* arrived at the busy seaport of Mobile, Alabama, with a captain and crew so deathly ill that the vessel had been steered to the port by automatic pilot. All but 1 of the 25 men on board were nearly helpless, suffering from terrible pains in the muscles and joints, dizziness, violent nausea, and weakness so severe that they could not stand up. Some were even temporarily blind. Nearly all had to be hospitalized immediately, and recovery was very slow.

What malady had turned 2 dozen rugged sailors into feeble invalids? Two days earlier, while in the Florida Straits near Key West, some of the crew had caught a large barracuda. The fish looked like a good addition to the ship's food supplies and was served in a soup for lunch the next day. It was enjoyed by everyone on board except the steward, whose duties busied him until all the soup was gone. The steward was lucky. The fish soup, though delicious, was poisonous.

The barracuda is one of about 300 species of fishes that can cause ciguatera fish poisoning, a serious medical and public health problem in many tropical and subtropical areas of the world, especially around small islands and coral reefs. A person who eats an affected fish usually does not know that anything is wrong for a few hours. Then abdominal pains and nausea begin, as well as numbness and tingling in the mouth, which spread over the face and to the fingers and toes. These symptoms may be followed by others, including those experienced by the crew of the *Sao Marcos*. Some victims also encounter a strange symptom called paradoxical sensory disturbance, which is a reversal of temperature sensations: hot objects feel cold, and cold objects feel hot. Death rarely occurs, but complete recovery may take weeks, months, or even years.

Ciguatera is a mysterious poison. Scientists have shown that the fish itself does not produce it. They have also determined that pollution is not involved; indeed, ciguatera was known centuries before man began to pollute the sea. Nor is it caused by spoilage, since a fish may be toxic when eaten immediately after being caught.

Many natives of the tropics believe that fishes become toxic by feeding on poisonous "sea moss." A number of researchers have held a similar opinion. They have hypothesized that small herbivorous fishes feed on some species of filamentous algae, perhaps a blue-green algae, and store a toxin or toxins present in it. Larger carnivores, such as the barracuda, feed on these herbivores, thereby acquiring all the poison the latter stored during their lifetimes. (Fishes themselves do not seem to be harmed by the poison.) However, there is now evidence that one or more of the toxins may come from microscopic organisms, such as bacteria or dinoflagellates, ingested somehow by the herbivores. So the source of ciguatera poison remains an enigma, although a group of Japanese researchers seems to have definitively incriminated a species of dinoflagellate.

Another peculiar aspect of ciguatera, disconcerting to the scientist who studies it as well as to the fisherman who tries to avoid it, is its unpredictable occurrence. It is possible to catch 2 fish of the same species on the same reef at the same time and find that one is safe and the other is deadly; the 2 specimens would look and taste the same. Furthermore, a reef area where all the fishes are safe to eat might be just a few kilometers from a place where many fishes are poisonous. And an area where ciguatera has never been known to occur may suddenly begin producing poisonous fishes without warning.

One can see how a fisherman in the tropics might have a hard time feeding himself, his family, and his customers without poisoning everyone. Of course, most fishermen know the dangerous areas and avoid them. Yet even experienced fishermen sometimes catch toxic fishes, and they have devised some interesting methods of testing a suspect fish. Some believe that if a silver coin is cooked with a fish, the coin will turn black if the fish is poisonous. Others will taste the raw liver of a fish while cleaning it, believing that the liver of a toxic fish has a bitter or peppery taste. Many claim to be able to identify a poisonous fish by some unusual coloration, such as a greenish tint in the raw flesh, or black teeth. Still others place a small piece of the fish on an ant bed, with the conviction that the ants will not eat or even climb onto it if it is toxic. These practices have caught the interest of some researchers, but there is no evidence that they actually work.

No cure for ciguatera has yet been discovered. Medical treatment is desirable and sometimes imperative, but this usually consists only of alleviating the unpleasant symptoms and preventing complications. Many treatments for ciguatera have been used; like methods of testing a suspicious fish, they are unproven but interesting. For example, a British navy physician, writing in the early nineteenth century, recommended a treatment in which the victim was to "take freely of brandy or other ardent spirit. . ." This may have made his patient less unhappy about the situation, but it is not a cure. Even today native groups in a number of areas of the world use various herbal remedies for ciguatera. Two examples from the Caribbean are the "Bissie" tree, used in Jamaica, and the Buttonwood tree, used in the Virgin Islands. In each case the appropriate plant part (the seeds of Bissie and the leaves of Buttonwood) is boiled in water. The concoction is then strained and taken orally. Such medications are being studied in a number of laboratories to determine if they contain an antidote to ciguatera.

Getting down to practical matters: If you want to catch or spear your own fish dinner, how do you avoid getting ciguatera? Even in a relatively hot area the actual percentage of toxic fish is usually small, so your chances of being poisoned are rather slim. To make that risk even smaller:

1. Avoid those fishes that are most often toxic. Barracudas are the worst offenders in many areas. Although the meat and liver of some tropical sharks and moray eels are often used as food, they sometimes contain potent toxins similar or identical to those of ciguatera. Other fishes to be shunned are the Dog Snapper, the Greater Amberjack, large jacks, *Caranx* species, and large groupers, *Mycteroperca* species.

2. Ask local people for advice on the fishes likely to be dangerous. Keep in mind, though, that common names often differ from one locality to another.

3. Small specimens of a species are usually less likely to be toxic than large ones. And fishes caught well offshore (by trolling, for example) are usually safer than those caught near a reef or shore. However, neither of these rules is without exception.

4. The poison is usually concentrated in the head and viscera, so a fish should always be cleaned thoroughly before it is cooked. In particular, *never eat the liver of any tropical fish.*

5. The poison is not destroyed by freezing or drying, nor does cooking affect it. If you are tempted to depend on the testing methods described above, remember that many of the most avid proponents of these techniques are the people who have been poisoned most often.

Puffer Poisoning. Probably the most violent form of fish poisoning is caused by pufferfishes (Family Tetraodontidae) and porcupinefishes (Family Diodontidae); see p. 235. Some species are always deadly; others are never toxic.

Many puffers are more poisonous at one time of the year than at others, and the poison is usually present in only certain parts of the fish, such as the skin and some internal organs. Puffer poison has been chemically isolated and named tetrodotoxin. It acts by disrupting the flow of nerve impulses to and from the brain. An almost microscopic dose of pure tetrodotoxin can kill a person.

The symptoms of puffer poisoning usually develop within half an hour after the fish is eaten. Dizziness and uncoordination often begin the ordeal and are followed by numbness of the hands and feet. The victim soon has difficulty breathing and may be nauseated. Paralysis begins in the throat, arms, and legs, so he cannot talk, swallow, or move. No antidote is known, and little can be done except to induce vomiting (to empty the stomach) and, if necessary, apply artificial respiration. Death occurs in about 60% of all cases, usually because breathing muscles are paralyzed.

Pufferfishes have the distinction of being considered among the most useless, bothersome trash fish by some societies, and among the most desirable, sought-after treats by others. In Japan the puffer not only is eaten but is an expensive delicacy. Called fugu, it is served exclusively in certain licensed restaurants and is prepared only by specially trained chefs. The fugu cook is a highly respected individual who combines the culinary zeal of a French chef with the nimble-fingered deftness of a surgeon. He must be able to separate thoroughly the portions of the fish that contain tetrodotoxin from those that do not. He often cuts the edible portion (usually the flesh, fins, and testes) into intricate shapes and arranges these with vegetables on a platter, sometimes in the form of a bird or flower.

Pufferfishes are used in other dishes that you probably won't find on the menu at your neighborhood diner. One of these is *sake* (rice wine) mixed with strained puffer testes. "There is no more delicious Sake than this," declares a handbook of fugu cookery. Some recipes even call for poisonous parts of the fish. For example, the ovaries (usually very toxic) are eaten as pickled puffer roe. After being salted and preserved for 3–4 years, they lose enough of their toxicity to become a relatively safe food.

Avoid eating puffers and porcupine fishes. One commonly eaten species is the Northern Puffer or Blowfish, marketed under the name sea squab along the Atlantic Coast of the United States. Only the skinned back and caudal muscles should be eaten; the liver is quite toxic.

Glossary

Aboral: Opposite or away from the mouth, especially in radially symmetrical animals. In sea stars and jellyfish, the aboral surface is the uppermost surface; in polyps, the lower surface.

Ambulacra: In echinoderms, grooves on the underside of the rays from which the tube feet (podia) protrude.

Amebocyte: An amebalike cell that carries food and other substances through the body of sponges and other invertebrates.

Anoxic: Having an oxygen level too low to support most life.

Aperture: An opening. In gastropods, the hole in the shell from which the body extends when alive.

Apical: Near or at the tip of a projection.

Arm plates: In brittle stars, the calcareous plates on the arms. *Aboral arm plates* form the upper arm surface; *oral arm plates* form the lower arm surface; *lateral arm plates* bear the arm spines between the oral and aboral arm plates.

Arm spines: In brittle stars, the spines on the lateral arm plates.

Atoll. An incomplete ring of islands derived from coral reefs surrounding a submerged volcano.

Bank/barrier reef: A Caribbean offshore coral reef growing on a wave-cut platform.

Barren zone: The region of a coral reef seaward of the lower *palmata* zone and just landward of the buttress or mixed zone.

Barrier reef: An offshore coral reef running parallel to the shore; separated from the shore by a lagoon or channel.

Benthic: Bottom-dwelling; living on or under sediment, pilings, and so forth.

Bloom: A sudden abundance of a species due primarily to rapid development of eggs and larvae.

Branchiae: Gills; in annelids, fanlike structures used to filter food from water and for respiration.

Bursal slits: See **genital slits.**

Buttress zone: The region of a coral reef dominated by huge mounds of boulder coral; seaward of the lower *palmata* zone.

Calcareous: Containing calcium carbonate, a chalklike substance.

Calyx: In crinoids, the globular body.

Carapace: In Crustacea, region of exoskeleton composed of fused head and thorax. In crabs, whole exoskeleton seen from above; in shrimps, lobsters, region anterior to abdomen.

Caudal peduncle: In fishes, the narrow isthmus between the rear of the anal fin and the beginning of the tail.

Cephalopod: A squid or octopus.

Cephalothorax: In arthropods, the fused head and thorax.

Cerata: In nudibranchs, the fingerlike projections on the back.

Chela: In many crustaceans, a claw.

Cheliped: In decapod crustaceans, a claw-bearing leg.

Choanocyte: In sponges, an internal cell with a collarlike structure and a flagellum.

Chromatophore: In octopods, fishes, and other marine animals, a pigment-bearing cell used in camouflage.

Cilia: The microscopic hairs on the surface of corals, crinoids, and other animals; used for propulsion, for moving food particles, and for removing sediment and debris.

Cirri: In comatulid crinoids, the jointed appendages clustered around the aboral pole; look like and function as legs.

Climax community: A stable, balanced community — the end result of succession.

Cnidoblast: In cnidarians, a cell containing a nematocyst.

Coenosarc: In cnidarians, the living tissue of the polyp.

Columella: A central, stalklike structure. In corals, supports the polyp. In snails, the central core around which the shell develops; also, the inner margin of the shell aperture.

Comb teeth: In crinoids, the blade- or paddle-shaped projections on the oral pinnules.

Commensalism: A relationship between 2 organisms of different species in which one benefits and the other is neither benefited nor harmed.

Consumer: An animal that eats plants (see **primary consumer**) or other animals (see **secondary consumer, tertiary consumer**).

Conule: In sponges, a cone-shaped wart.

Corallite: A coral cup.

Corallum: A complete coral colony (coral head).

Cryptic: Hidden; living in holes, caves, burrows.

Cuvier's organs: See **tubules of Cuvier.**

Deep fore reef: The deepest part of a coral reef; a vertical cliff beginning at a depth of about 60 m (197 ft.).

Deposit-feeder: A sediment-eating animal.

Detritus: Material that is disintegrating or rotting — usually leaves, dead organisms, and so forth.

Disk: In brittle stars, the round, pentagonal, or lobed body that contains the internal organs and to which the arms and mouth frame are attached.

Diurnal tides: Tides that occur once a day — 1 high tide and 1 low tide during 24 hours.

Endozoic: Living inside an animal.

Epibiont: A plant or animal that lives on the outside of another plant or animal.

Epiphyte: A plant that grows nonparasitically on the surface of another plant.

Epizoite: An animal that lives on the surface of another organism.

Errantia: Polychaetous annelids that move about and do not live in burrows or tubes.

Feeding polyp: In cnidarians, a polyp specialized to obtain food. Also called a gastrozooid.

Filter-feeder: An organism that filters food, usually plankton or bacteria, from the water. Also called a suspension-feeder.

Foraminiferan: An ameba that produces a microscopic test resembling a snail shell.

Fore-reef escarpment: A slope or cliff seaward of the fore-reef terrace, at a depth of about 25–30 m (83–100 ft.).

Fore-reef slope: A sand-covered, gradual or sharply descending slope; the next-to-deepest part of the fore reef.

Fore-reef terrace: The uppermost portion of the fore-reef; a flat plain beginning at the base of the buttress or mixed zone, at a depth of about 20 m (66 ft.).

Fringing reef: A coral reef contiguous with the shore; lacks a lagoon.

Gastrodermis: In cnidarians, the "inner skin" (internal layer of cells) lining the gastrovascular cavity.

Gastropod: A snail, limpet, nudibranch, or sea slug.

Gastrovascular cavity: In cnidarians, an internal chamber in which food is digested and from which nutrients are transported throughout the body of the polyp or medusa.

Generalist species: A widely adaptable species, usually with a short life span and high biotic potential.

Genital slits: In brittle stars, the narrow openings on the oral surface of the disk on each side of the arm bases. Also called bursal slits.

Gorgonian: A soft coral of Order Gorgonacea, which includes sea fans, whips, branching soft corals.

Inferomarginal plate: In sea stars, a plate along the oral margin of a ray.

Inquiline: An animal living in the burrow, nest, or territory of another species.

Interbrachium: In brittle stars, the disk area between any 2 arms.

Lagoon: A body of water separated from the sea by a bank or coral reef. The region between a shore and a barrier reef or inside the ring of islands composing an atoll.

Lateral keel: In fishes, a ridge that usually extends horizontally from the side or from the caudal peduncle.

Lobate: Arranged in large lobes.

Lower *palmata* zone: The part of a reef crest that is seaward of the *palmata* zone; consists primarily of huge forests of Elkhorn Coral at a depth of about 3–6 m (10–20 ft.).

Lunule: In sea urchins, an oval perforation in the test; one edge may be open along the margin (marginal lunule), or several closed lunules may form a radiating pattern.

Madreporite: In sea stars, the opening of the water-vascular system; perforated with minute holes to permit water to pass into and out of the system; often looks like a large bright dot near the center of the aboral disk.

Marginal plate: In sea stars, one of the uniform nodules along ray margins.

Medusa: A jellyfish; has a bell-shaped body and downward-facing mouth.

Mesenterial filament: In cnidarian polyps, a threadlike extension of a mesentery; contains nematocysts and produces digestive enzymes.

Mesentery: In a coral polyp or anemone, a vertical, curtainlike partition of tissue inside the body; corresponds to the stony septum in corals.

Mesoglea: In jellyfish, the acellular, jellylike material composing much of the body.

Mixed zone: The highly populated region of most bank/barrier reefs seaward of the lower *palmata* zone. Begins at a depth of 6–8 m (20–27 ft.).

Mutualism: A relationship between 2 organisms of different species in which both benefit.

Neap tide: A period of minimal tidal movement, occurring for a few days twice a month; low tides are not very low, and high tides are not very high.

Nematocyst: In cnidarians, a microscopic structure that is sticky, poisonous, or otherwise entrapping; used to capture plankton and for defense.

Nictitans: In sharks, a membrane that can be extended over the eyeball; when extended, gives the impression of a featureless, white eye.

Oolitic limestone: Rock composed primarily of petrified corals or the skeletons of other calcareous organisms.

Operculum: Any door- or lidlike structure closing off a shell or tube. In polychaetes, the structure that plugs the tube when the worm retracts. In snails, the "door" used to close the shell aperture.

Opportunistic species: A species with a rapid reproduction rate not adapted precisely to any habitat but able to adapt to a wide range of habitats; usually the first to dominate a new environment.

Oral: Pertaining to the mouth or the area around the mouth. In sea anemones, the oral disk is the flattened part of the tentacle-fringed upper portion of the body; in sea urchins, the "bottom" (region applied to the substratum).

Oscule (osculum): In sponges, a large excurrent hole through which water leaves. In cylindrical sponges, the hole at the top; in massive and encrusting sponges, one of the holes that are often scattered over the surface or on raised chimneylike projections.

Ostium: In sponges, a hole or pore that allows water to enter.

Palmata **zone:** The region of the reef crest of a bank/barrier reef that is closest to the water surface; composed almost exclusively of Elkhorn Coral.

Palps: In polychaetes, the paired projections growing from the front of the head.

Papillae: In brittle stars, calcareous structures. *Dental* (*tooth*) *papillae* are small plates at the apex of the jaw below the teeth and above the oral papillae; *oral papillae* are projections of various shapes around the perimeter of the lower surface of the jaw.

Parapodia: In polychaetes and other animals, soft paired appendages or folds running the length of the body.

Parasitism: A relationship between 2 organisms of different species in which one benefits and the other is harmed.

Patch reef: A coral boulder or a clump of corals unattached to a major reef structure.

Pedicellariae: In sea stars and sea urchins, tiny jawlike modified spines scattered over an animal, which clean and protect its surface.

Pelagic: Swimming or floating above the bottom; living in the open water.

Periostracum: In seashells, the hairy or horny outer layer.

Periproct: In sea urchins, the anus.

Periproctal plates: In sea urchins, the small oval plates at the apex of the aboral surface; surround the anus, surrounded by the genital plates.

Peristomium: In polychaetes, the first body segment behind the prostomium. In sea urchins, the mouth.

Petals: In sea urchins, the ambulacra in the aboral or dorsal surface that often look like a 5-petaled flower.

Pharynx: In polychaetes, the anterior part of the digestive tract; modified for feeding purposes, often eversible, and armed with teeth. In other animals, the throat region.

Photic zone: The region of ocean that light can penetrate — approximately the upper 50 m (165 ft.), but deeper in tropical seas.

Pinnate: Resembling a feather; having projections opposite each other on a central stalk.

Pinnule: In crinoids, a lateral appendage of an arm. *Oral pinnules* are those closest to the disk.

Plankton: Organisms that cannot swim against wind-driven ocean currents; drifters. Range from tiny larvae and eggs to huge jellyfish.

Planula: In cnidarians, the ciliated oval larva.

Pneumatophore: An air-containing organ. In the Portuguese Man-of-war, an air-filled bladder.

Podia: In echinoderms, tube feet or homologous structures.

Podial scales: In brittle stars, the 1 or 2 scales at the base of each podium.

Polychaete: A class of worms with distinct parapodia and setae on most body segments.

Polyp: An attached animal with a columnar body topped by a ring of tentacles — for example, a coral or sea anemone.

Primary consumer: A plant-eater.

Producer: A green plant that produces food through photosynthesis.

Prostomium: In polychaetes, the head; often bears eyes and antennae.

Radially symmetrical: Symmetrical around a central axis, so that cutting along any plane through that axis produces mirror-image halves. A radially symmetrical animal is round and lacks a distinct head.

Radial shields: In brittle stars, the 5 pairs of calcareous plates on the aboral surface of the disk near the arm bases.

Radula: The filelike "tongue" of a snail.

Rays: In sea stars, the arms.

Rear zone: The region on the lagoon side of a reef crest.

Reef crest: The shallow portion of a bank/barrier reef that is seaward of the lagoon; consists of a rear zone, reef flat, *palmata* zone, and mixed or buttress zone.

Reproductive polyp: A polyp specialized for reproduction; a gonozooid.

Rhinophores: The paired tentaclelike olfactory (smelling) organs on the head of a nudibranch or sea slug.

Rostrum: The knifelike, often serrated structure projecting like a horn from the head of a shrimp or crab.

Rubble zone: The shallowest part of a reef crest, landward of the *palmata* zone; consists of broken pieces of Elkhorn Coral washed back by storms. Also called the *Zoanthus* zone.

Scutes: In fishes, bony plates.

Secondary consumer: A carnivorous animal that eats herbivorous animals (primary consumers).

Sedentaria: Polychaetous annelids that live in tubes and burrows.

Semi-diurnal tides: Tides that recur twice a day — 2 high tides and 2 low tides every 24 hours.

Septum: The vertical calcareous partition inside the column (body) of a coral polyp or cup.

Sessile: Attached to the bottom or to rocks, pilings, and so on.

Setae: The bristles extending from the parapodia of polychaetes or from the appendages of many tiny arthropods.

Sole: In sea cucumbers, the flat ventral surface.

Specialist species: An organism that is precisely adapted to a specific habitat. Compare with **generalist species.**

Spicules: Tiny calcareous or siliceous slivers. In worms, refers to setae; in corals and sponges, they form a meshwork skeleton.

Spiracles: In sharks and rays, a pair of holes above and behind the eyes. In sharks, act as accessory nostrils; in rays, as openings for water entering the gill chambers.

Spring tide: Period of greatest tidal range occurring twice each month, with highest high tides and lowest low tides.

Stolon: In cnidarians, a horizontal rootlike structure connecting polyps.

Substratum: The bottom — for example, muddy, rocky, or sandy substratum.

Succession: The evolutionary sequence whereby plant and animal communities replace one another until they reach a stable climax community.

Superomarginal plates: In sea stars, the plates along the aboral margins of the rays.

Suspension-feeder: See **filter-feeder.**

Suture: In snails, the thin groove at the junction of each 2 whorls.

Symbiosis: Any relatively long-term interdependence between 2 species. Parasitism, commensalism, and mutualism are subsumed under this term. A **symbiont** is either of the 2 participants in symbiosis.

Teeth: In brittle stars, the broad calcareous plates that form the column in the jaw cavity at the jaw apex.

Tentacles: In sea cucumbers, a ring of sensory and food-getting projections with extensions that make them look branched; may be (1) dendritic — greatly branched to form fuzzy masses; (2) digitate or simple — relatively thick and unbranched; (3) peltate — having a long stem that branches to form a disk-like distal end; (4) pinnate (featherlike) or palmate (palmlike) — having a broad stem and short fingerlike digits; or (5) plumate — having a long stem with broad leaflike extensions projecting at right angles.

Tertiary consumer: A carnivore that eats secondary and primary consumers.

Test: In aquatic animals, the outer, shell-like, capsular, or rubbery covering, made of nonliving substance. In sea urchins, the hard, outer calcareous covering to which the spines are attached; when dried and bleached, with spines removed, often mistaken for a seashell; not always an exoskeleton, because all echinoderms have a thin epidermis (layer of skin) outside the test, thus it is an endoskeleton (internal skeleton).

Trade winds: Relatively constant winds originating at the equator; blow from the east in the tropical northern hemisphere.

Trophic pyramid: An ecological model describing the distribution of energy in an ecosystem. Plants (producers) form the base, and energy in the upper levels is reduced as the pyramid narrows toward its apex.

Tubules of Cuvier (Cuvier's organs): In sea cucumbers, the sticky, white or pink tubules ejected from the anus as a defense mechanism.

Umbilicus: In snails, the hole at the base of the columella at the bottom of the shell.

Umbo: The pointed portion of a bivalve shell.

***Zoanthus* zone:** See **rubble zone.**

Zooplankton: Drifting or floating aquatic animals — fish eggs, larvae, jellyfish, and so forth.

Zooxanthellae: Dinoflagellate photosynthetic algae (protists) living in the tissues of corals and other organisms.

Field Library

The publications listed below can be taken with the serious naturalist and used as supplements to this *Field Guide*. An asterisk means that the book is an inexpensive paperback. A square means that the book is suitable for laymen.

■ *Cairns, S., and G. Voss. 1977. *A Guide to the Commoner Shallowwater Gorgonians of Florida, the Gulf of Mexico, and the Caribbean Region*. Sea Grant Public Education and Information Services, University of Miami, Coral Gables, Fla.
■ *Chaplin, C.G., and P. Scott. 1972. *Fishwatcher's Guide*. Valley Forge, Pa.: Harrowwood Books. (Printed on plastic; can be taken underwater.)
■ Colin, P. 1978. *Caribbean Reef Invertebrates and Plants*. Neptune City, N.J.: T.F.H. Publishing Co.
■ *Gosner, K. 1978. *A Field Guide to the Atlantic Seashore*. Boston: Houghton Mifflin. (Covers more northern waters but refers to Florida species.)
■ *Greenberg, I., and J. Greenberg. 1977. *Waterproof Guide to Corals and Fishes*. Miami: Seahawk Press. (Printed on plastic; can be taken underwater.)
■ *Hanlon, R., and G. Voss. 1975. *Guide to Seagrasses of Florida, the Gulf of Mexico, and the Caribbean Region*. Sea Grant Public Education and Information Services, University of Miami, Coral Gables, Fla.
■ Humfrey, M. 1975. *Seashells of the West Indies*. New York: Taplinger.
■ *Morris, P. 1973. *A Field Guide to Shells of the Atlantic and Gulf Coasts and the West Indies*. Boston: Houghton Mifflin.
■ *Opresko, L., D. Opresko, R. Thomas, and G. Voss. 1978. *Guide to the Lobsters and Lobster-like Animals of Florida, the Gulf of Mexico, and the Caribbean Region*. Sea Grant Public Education and Information Services, University of Miami, Coral Gables, Fla.
■ *Opresko, L., R. Thomas, F.M. Bayer, and G. Voss. 1976. *A Guide to the Larger Marine Gastropods of Florida, the Gulf of Mexico, and the Caribbean Region*. Sea Grant Public Education and Information Services, University of Miami, Coral Gables, Fla.
■ Randall, J. 1968. *Caribbean Reef Fishes*. Neptune City, N.J.: T.F.H. Publishing Co.

- Roessler, C. 1979. *The Underwater Wilderness.* New York: E.P. Dutton.
- Smith, F.G.W. 1971. *A Handbook of the Common Atlantic Reef Corals.* Austin: University of Texas Press.

  Taylor, W.R. 1972. *Marine Algae of the Eastern Tropical and Subtropical Coasts of the Americas.* Ann Arbor: University of Michigan Press.
- *Viertel, J. 1978. *Underwater Holidays.* New York: Grosset and Dunlap.
- Voss, G. 1976. *Seashore Life of Florida and the Caribbean.* Miami: E.A. Seemann Publishing Co.
- *Voss, G., L. Opresko, and R. Thomas. 1973. *The Potentially Commercial Species of Octopus and Squid in Florida, the Gulf of Mexico, and the Caribbean Area.* Sea Grant Public Education and Information Services, University of Miami, Coral Gables, Fla.
- *Warmke, G., and R.T. Abbot. 1975. *Caribbean Seashells.* New York: Dover.
- *Welkerling, W.J. 1976. *South Florida Benthic Marine Algae.* Comparative Sedimentology Laboratory, Rosenstiel School of Marine and Atmospheric Science, University of Miami, Miami, Fla.

  Wiedenmayer, F. 1977. *Shallow Water Sponges of the Western Bahamas.* Experientia Supplement 28. Basel, Switzerland: Birkhauser Verlag. (Huge and expensive.)
- Zeiller, W. 1974. *Tropical Marine Invertebrates of Southern Florida and the Bahama Islands.* New York: John Wiley.

Index

This index lists the scientific and common names of all the species discussed in this *Field Guide*. Numbers in **boldface** refer to plates on which species are illustrated and to pages where the most detailed descriptions (accounts) of species (or in some cases, families) can be found. Numbers in *italic* refer to additional illustrations (line drawings and photographs) in the text. Scientific names (in *italics*) are keyed to the pages on which the text appears, not to the illustrations; for illustrations of a particular species, see entries after its common name. Obsolete and alternate names for species are also given; an equals sign (=) after a scientific name directs the reader to the current or preferred scientific name. Although it is impossible to list all the alternate common names for a species, which may vary quite a bit locally, *see* cross references are given for the most "popular" alternate names. For more details about how to use this book, see "About This Book," p. 1.

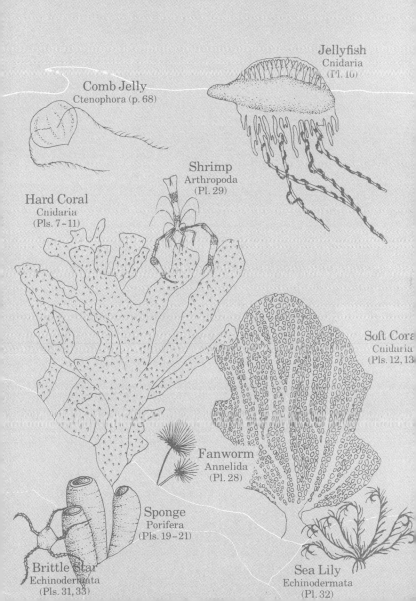

Jellyfish
Cnidaria
(Pl. 10)

Comb Jelly
Ctenophora (p. 68)

Shrimp
Arthropoda
(Pl. 29)

Hard Coral
Cnidaria
(Pls. 7–11)

Soft Coral
Cnidaria
(Pls. 12, 13)

Fanworm
Annelida
(Pl. 28)

Sponge
Porifera
(Pls. 19–21)

Brittle Star
Echinodermata
(Pls. 31, 33)

Sea Lily
Echinodermata
(Pl. 32)